Status of Social Science Research in India

Critical Engagements and Future Directions

Status of Social Science Research in India

Critical Engagements and Future Directions

Editor
Gautam Gawali

MANAK
PUBLICATIONS PVT. LTD

Published by

MANAK

PUBLICATIONS PVT. LTD

B-7, Saraswati Complex, Subhash Chowk,
Laxmi Nagar, New Delhi 110092 (India)
Phone: 91-11-22453894, 22042529
E-mail : manak.publications@gmail.com
Website: manakpublication.com

Subsidiary Office in USA
MANAK PUBLICATION, INC
8145 KOLB AVE, ALLEN PARK, M.I. 48101 (USA)
E-mail: manakpublication.USA@gmail.com

First Edition 2018

ISBN 978-93-7831-423-2

Laser Typeset by: Tabrez Ali, Aadil Printographics, Delhi
Printed in India by: Nice Printing Press, New Delhi (India)

Contents

Foreword ix
Acknowledgements xi
About Contributors xiii
Introduction xxv

PART I
THEORY AND RESEARCH

1. Introduction 3
   — *Gautam Gawali, Mrudul Nile & M.R. Prabhu*
2. Inter-Disciplinarity in Social Science Research: Shifting Goals and Missing Paths 58
   —*R.S. Deshpande*
3. Doctoral Social Work Research: Emerging Themes 76
   — *Surinder Jaswal & Melody Kshetrimayum*
4. Social Work Research in Western India and its Contemporary Relevance: A Critique 100
   —*Chandrakant Puri*
5. Trends in Methodology of Doctoral Research in Social Science 110
   — *Anil S. Sutar*
6. Research in Education: Retrospect and Prospects 121
   — *Shefali Pandya*

7. Goa University Pioneering Social Science Research in Goa 136
— *Remy Dias*
8. Understanding History as Concrete Science 173
— *Marzbaan Jaal*
9. Issues of Theorisation and Data Validation: Need for New Paradigms in Research in Political Science 184
— *Mrudul Nile*
10. Current Research Trends in Anthropology in Western India 203
— *Anjali Kurane*

PART II

Themes and Issues of Enquiry in Social Sciences

11. Trends in Women's Studies in Western India 217
—*Vibhuti Patel*
12. Critical Engagements with Research in Psychology in Western India 243
— *Gautam Gawali*
13. Changing Perspectives of Disabilities: Trends in Research 271
— *Varsha Gathoo, Kasturi Kulkarni & Jignya Shah*
14. Dalits and Sociology in India: Resisting the Cognitive Blackout and Beyond 289
— *Ramesh Kamble*
15. (Up)Rooted Through Routes: Understanding the Impact of Diaspora on Gender 307
— *Preeti Shirodkar*
16. Dalit Studies in Maharashtra: Priorities and Concerns 317
— *Pralhad G. Jogdand*
17. Gujarat Over Time: Progress Towards Growth, Development and Inclusiveness 329
— *Niti Mehta*

18. Intersectoral Migration of Weaker Section Labourers in the Field of Sugarcane in Maharashtra 356
    — *Balaji Kendre*
19. Poverty, Malnutrition and Health Status of Tribal Population in Nort-Western Part of Maharashtra 368
    —*K.C. Ramotra*
20. Agricultural Priorities for Food Security in Western India 392
    — *Vijay Laxmi Pandey & Niharika Venkatesh*
21. Social Exclusion Research 408
    — *Ramesh Dandge*

Index 419

Foreword

I am indeed pleased for the initiative undertaken by the Western Regional Centre of the Indian Council of Social Science, Mumbai, Maharashtra to organise a conference on the current status of social science research in Western India, and subsequently published the papers in the form of book. This is probably the first books of its kind which present the status of social science research in Western India. Therefore Professor Gautam Gawali, former Director of the Western Regional Centre, Mumbai deserves the appreciation of us all, but particularly of the ICSSR, Delhi.

The books brings out the present problems confronting the social science research in the country. Therefore, the book has a value from the point of view of policy for the social science research in. Western Region. I would like to use this opportunity which Professor Gawali has offered me by asking me to write a foreword. There are number of challenges that we face today on the form of social science research. At a general level we find a regular tendency at policy level to accord low priority to investment in the social science research compared with the sciences.

We failed to recognised that the knowledge that is generated through social science research is as useful as the knowledge generated by sciences. It should be recognised that both generate knowledge and results in technologies which bring positive changes. The only difference is that, due to the the complex nature of human relations. It is here the difference in the outcome and certainty of scientific technology and social technology emerged. Since the social sciences deals with aspects of human behaviour, complex human behaviour, and it takes time and efforts to get hold of human processes.

The social science research has a vital role in enriching society's understanding. It indeed play an emancipatory role, no public policy can be developed, and no market interaction can occur without the social science knowledge. In this sense the social science become an emancipator project, with engagement with various questions affecting the society and country. In this context, therefore, the neglect of social science research is bad policy which need to be reversed. In India we have few challenges on our had as far as social science is concern. These challenges include: adequate funding for social science research, more funding o increase research output, comparable to China, Brazil and other counties at our level of development, attention to many issues which are neglected in teh socials science research, which the book also mentioned, enhance the research facility in the universities with social science department, and research institutes, particular attention to ICSSR institutes, and government institutes, International Collaboration in social science research as it promotes the quality of social science research, improve the quality of research make social science more policy oriented, and improve the research capabilities of researchers engaged in social science research in universities and collages. We need to pay attention to these issues to enable the social science research to perform its role and also enable it to help in improving the teaching in universities and colleges by creating new knowledge for the students. This book will bring the awareness among the policy makers and the government to pay attention to social science research in Western Regions.

Professor Sukhadeo Thorat
Professor Emeritus, Jawaharlal Nehru University, Delhi, and
Chairman, ICSSR, Delhi

Acknowledgements

In writing and editing this book I have been aware of the enormous debt I owe to many people who have contributed to this book. For their intellectual support and challenge around research matters I would like to thank all the contributors of this book. I would like to express a huge thanks to Indian Council of Social Science Research (ICSSR), New Delhi for constantly encouraging and providing all kind of support to carry out interdisciplinary research in Social Sciences through their Regional Centers. I would also like to thank my advisory committee members and the Chairman of Western Regional Centre, Mumbai, and express my appreciation for the support and encouragement offered by Dr. M.R. Prabhu, Consultant of Western Regional Centre, my personal secretary and office supervisor Mrs. Sangita Shirgaonkar, Mr. Ravi and Mr. Sanjay Karnik for providing administrative support. I would also like to thank Dr. Wilbur Gonsalves and other faculty members, non teaching staff and research students of Department of Applied Psychology and Counseling Center for their support. I would also like to express my gratitude to Dr. Dolly Sunny, present Hon. Director ICSSR:WRC.

Dr. Mrudul Nile, Dr. Chandrakant Puri, Dr. Shefali Pandya, Dr. Ramesh Kamble, Dr. Surendra Jondhale and Dr. Avadhoot Nadkarni deserve a particular mention for their assistance and academic contribution in so many different ways. Their efficiency and availability have enabled this process to run smoothly and enjoyable. I would also like to express a huge thanks to Manak Publications Pvt. Ltd., New Delhi for their never ending encouragement and assistance particularly in the face of my constantly changing deadlines.

Last but by no means least, I would like to thank my wife Pushpa, my daughter Poonam and son Puneet who saw me through this effort and provided all the support, time and opportunity to focus on something like this.

Gautam Gawali

About the Contributors

1. **R.S. Deshpande:** Professor R.S. Deshpande is currently Advisor and Director, Centre for Development Studies, PES University, Bangalore, where he started courses on MSc in Applied Economics and MSc in Development Studies. He is also Honorary Visiting Professor, Institute for Social and Economic Change (ISEC), Bangalore. He was formerly Rajiv Gandhi National Fellow, Indian Council of Social Science Research (ICSSR), and before that Director of ISEC. Dr. Deshpande steered the mega study on "Farmer at the Millennium" and completed many research studies. He has authored 17 books and more that 140 research papers published in national and international journals. Professor Deshpande was invited as visiting Professor to the University of Ottawa, Canada; Saskatchewan Institute of Policy Planning, Regina, University of Paris, France, Lund University, Sweden. He worked as a consultant to the World Bank, Asian Development Bank, Land Equity Australia etc. He is recipient of many awards and Gold medals. He received a Lifetime Achievement Award from Dr Babasaheb Ambedkar Marathwada University, where he was educated. He was the President of the Indian Society of Agricultural Economics, Platinum Jubilee Conference, held at Punjab Agricultural University, Ludhiana in

November, 2015. He is member of many Boards of Studies, Governing Boards of Institutions/ Universities and prestigious Government Committees.

2. **Surinder Jaswal** and **Dr. Melody Kshetrimayum**: Prof. Surinder Jaswal is a Professor and Deputy Director (Research), Mumbai Campus. She is also the Dean for the School of Research Methodology Centre for Health and Mental Health, School of Social Work - Mumbai Campus. She has done her M.A. from TISS and Ph.D. from London.
   Melody Kshetrimayum is an Assistant Professor for Research and Development, Mumbai campus. She has completed her M.Phil and Ph.D. from TISS, Mumbai.
3. **Chandrakant Puri:** Chandrakant Puri is a Chair Professor, Rajiv Gandhi Centre for Contemporary Studies, University of Mumbai. After completing his MSW (TISS) he started working with primitive tribal communities in Maharashtra in the year 1992 where he implemented various developmental projects including the Self-Help Housing project which was nominated for the World Habitat Award in 1995. Puri coordinated the Baseline Socio-Economic Survey & Plain Table survey of 8000 project affected families under the Mumbai Urban Transport Project II, which became the basis for the Resettlement & Rehabilitation Policy for Urban Poor of Government of Maharashtra, this study was sponsored by the World Bank (1995-1997). He was an as Assistant Director of Social Sciences at SNDT University. He became Director of the Centre for Distance Education in 2006. His interest of working with socially excluded communities lead him establish the Centre for Study of Social Exclusion & Inclusive Policy at SNDT Women's University where he worked as its Founder Professor cum Director (2009 to 2013). Dr. Puri is author of 2 books and has published over 50 research articles. He has successfully guided 04 M. Phil scholars and 12 Ph.D. students are working under his guidance in the subject of Social Work, Social Exclusion and Inclusion,

Contemporary Studies etc.

4. **Anil S. Sutar:** Anil S. Sutar has graduated in B.A. with Economics, Applied Statistics and Sociology as the core subjects from the Karnatak University, Dharwad in the year 1994 and later on he obtained Masters degree in Sociology from the same university. Dr. Sutar was awarded Junior Research Fellowship (JRF) by the University Grants Commission (UGC) New Delhi to pursue research in 1998. Sutar with research fellowship obtained M. Phil and Ph. D. degrees in Sociology from the Karnatak University, Dharwad. He has started his academic career as an Assistant Professor in the Tata Institute of Social Sciences (TISS) in 2001 in the Department of Research Methodology. Dr.Sutar is currently Professor and Associate Dean, School of Research Methodology at TISS Mumbai. Dr. Sutar has 16 years of experience in teaching the research methodology at master and at doctoral level programmes. Dr. Sutar has been involved in training and dissemination activities related to research methods and analysis. He has been involved with training activities for the Saci WATERs, UNICEF's District Facilitators (Dfs). Dr. Sutar has been invited as resource person for the research related national and international workshops. Dr. Sutar has been guiding M.A. and Ph. D. students for their research on diverse social, political and educational themes. His core areas of research interest include- qualitative and quantitative research methods, education, participatory governance and leadership. He has published a number of papers on themes of research methodology and democratic decentralization in national and international journals.
5. **Shefali Pandya** – Shefali Pandya is currently a Professor and Former Head at the Department of Education, University of Mumbai. She has a teaching experience at the post-graduate level of about 27 years. She has written 13 books and successfully guided 34 Ph.D. and 11 M. Phil students. She has also taught at SNDT Women's University and University of Mumbai. She has been a

member of several statutory bodies of University of Mumbai. She was also a Board of Studies Member at M.S. University of Baroda, Pune University and D.Y. Patil Deemed University. She has also been a member of Research & Recognition Committee of Dr. Babasaheb Ambedkar Marathwada University and Pune University. She has been associated with quality assessment work carried out by national agencies.

6. **Remy Dias** – Remy Dias is currently functioning as Deputy Director of Higher Education – Govt. of Goa and is Head of the History Research Centre for Doctoral Studies, Govt. College of Arts, Science & Commerce, Quepem-Goa (Affiliated to Goa University, Goa). He is a recipient of the prestigious Fundação Oriente Long Term Scholarship for doctoral studies in Portugal in 2002. He has edited two books, participated in a number of International, National and State Level Seminars, Conferences & Workshops and has about 20-24 research papers published in International and National Books & Journals. He has also been invited as resource person and subject expert at various National and State Level academic and research events. Special areas of research include: Agrarian History of Portuguese Goa; Cultural history of indigenous people; and Consumption history.
7. **Murzban Jal** – Murzban Jal is Professor and Director at the Centre for Educational Studies, Indian Institute of Education, Pune and the author of The Seductions of Karl Marx, (ed) Zoroastrianism: from Antiquity to the Modern Period, The New Militants,Why We Are Not Hindus and (ed.) Challenges for the Indian Left. Jal is a Freudo-Marxist who basis his research on Marx and Freud's theories of alienation in late capitalist society. He combines Marx's theory of the reification of consciousness and Freud's theory of neurosis and psychosis. His recent claim is that the old stages theory of psychoanalysis where neurosis and psychosis are divided into two distinct stages of mental illness is now redundant. Instead he claims that both neurosis and psychosis are integrated

as "neurosis-psychosis". Combining the understanding of neurosis-psychosis as the new disorder of contemporary society, he argues for a model of psychotherapy in the form of understanding the process of humanization, where knowledge is articulated as the cultivation of the human mind. This process of the cultivation of the human mind and the process of humanization, Jal claims, are constituted in the parallel process of de-alienating humanity. This de-alienating humanity is central to his philosophical and scientific repertoire.

8. **Mrudul Nile** – Mrudul Nile is Associate Professor in the Department of Civics and Politics, University of Mumbai. He started his academic career as Assistant Professor in Ramnarain Ruia College, Mumbai (2001-2013). He was former Director, Department of Students' Welfare, University of Mumbai from 2008-2014. He has authored a book on Right to Information which was published in the year 2014. During the 16th Lok Sabha Elections, he has also studied the impact of NOTA (None of the Above) option available to the citizens in all six constituencies of Mumbai. This minor research was sponsored by the ICSSR-WR. He has participated in the India-China Think Tank forums both in India and China in the year 2015-16. He has presented papers on Indian Political Process in leading think tanks in China in 2017. Mrudul Nile was selected for a Program sponsored by the U.S. Department of State in the year 2011, under the Fulbright-Hays Act of 1961 at the United States Institute on U.S. National Security Policy Making during January 2, 2011 to February 13, 2011. He was also selected by the ICSSR for the "International Seminar on Economic Development for Young Scholars" at the Graduate School of Chinese Academy of Social Sciences (GSCASS), Beijing, People's Republic of China, held during August 20, 2012 to September 18, 2012. He is due to submit a report on a Major Research Project sponsored by Indian Council of Social Science Research (ICSSR), New Delhi on

"Governance and Democratisation of Health and Issues of Inclusion" Interests of Dr. Mrudul Nile includes, Indian Governmental Process and Public Administration.

9. **Anjali Kurane** – Prof. (Dr.) Anjali Kurane, Professor & Head in the Department of Anthropology, & Director, Interdisciplinary School (IDS), Humanities and Social Sciences Co-ordinator, Centre for Social Sciences and Humanities (CSSH), Savitribai Phule Pune University, Pune. She is Socio-Cultural Anthropologist, has done specialization in Urban & Development Anthropology. Since last more than twenty six years, she is teaching in the Savitribai Phule Pune University, and actively engaged in research. Her areas of special interest in teaching and research include Urban, Rural, Tribal and Women's Development, Indian – Urban, Tribal & Rural society, Weaker Sections of Indian Society that includes Caste, Tribe & Women Issues, Gender Studies, Anthropological theories, Ethnicity, Ethnic Identity, Ethnic Diversity, Ethnic Conflict, Social mobility, Social-cultural Change, Social Exclusion, Urbanization and Migration. She has published Five Books and Several Articles in International & National journals. At present she is a member of editorial and advisory board of Six International journals.
10. **Vibhuti Patel**–Vibhuti Patel is Professor and Head of Economics Department of SNDT Women's University. Her areas of specialisation have been Gender Economics, Women's Studies, Human Rights, Social movements and Gender Budgeting. She had authored Women's Challenges of the New Millennium (2002), co—authored Reaching for Half the Sky (1985), Indian Women Change and Challenge (1985) and Status Report for ICSSR- Critical Evaluation of Women's Studies Researches during 1947-1988 (1989). She is co-editor of series of 15 volumes—Empowering Women Worldwide. She has been a member of Expert Committee for IGNOU, M of S & T and NCERT (Delhi) during 2005-2012. Currently she is President of Women Power Connect, Vice President of

Indo- Global Social Service Society and Board Member of Indian Council of Basic Education and Maniben Nanavati College for Women, Anusandhan Trust, VACHA, Women's Research and Action Group in Mumbai, and ICSSR-sponsored Centre for Social Studies (Surat). She is also Advisory Board Member of Institute of Indian Culture (Mumbai).

11. **Gautam Gawali** – Gautam Gawali is a Professor and Head of Department of Applied Psychology & Counseling Centre, University of Mumbai and Ex.Hon. Director, Indian Council of Social Science Research (ICSSR), Western Regional Center, Mumbai. He has presented research paper and chaired the session in British Psychological Society's Silver Jubilee Conference at London, UK in 2001. He also presented research paper in the centenary Conference of National Career Development Association (NCDA), Boston, USA in 2013. He was also invited to deliver a talk on "Caste Mind" by University College London (UCL), UK in 2015. He has several research papers /publications and 4 edited books in his credit. He was a member of Eleventh Five Year Plan Working Group on Empowering the Disabled, Reforming the Social Deviants, Care of Elderly and Caring the other Disadvantaged of Planning Commission, Government of India. He was on the Governing Body of Tata Institute of Social Science (TISS) up to 2014.
12. **Varsha Gathoo**–Varsha Gathoo is the HOD Education at the Ali Yavar Jung National Institute for the Speech & Hearing Disability under the Department of Empowerment of Persons with Disabilities (Divyangjan), Ministry of Social Justice & Empowerment Government of India. She is a Fulbright Senior Research Fellow and a LEND fellow of University of Connecticut USA & has published articles and chapters in national and international journals and books such as Status of Disability in India. She has also contributed for the development of manuals for special & inclusive education for various National & International Organizations & Universities such as RCI,

NCERT, IGNOU, YCMOU, Tamil Nadu Open University, World Bank & Mauritius Institute of Education, besides being the All-India President of NCED-India, Chairperson Adhoc BOS -Special Education & various committees of RCI & Universities Co-Authors: Ms Jignya Shah & Ms Kasturi Kulkarni PhD Scholars AYJNISHD(D)

13. **Ramesh Kamble**–Ramesh Kamble teaches Sociology in the University of Mumbai since last three decades. The areas of his research engagements and interests are: critical caste studies, critical cultural studies and critical discourse studies. He has worked on complexities of marginalisation, conceptual practices of power, humiliation.
14. **Preeti Shirodkar** – Ph.D. in English Language and Literature, Preeti Shirodkar, with 25 years of experience in teaching English Language and Literature, occupies herself with creative and critical writing and editing. She has successfully undertaken varied research projects, presented 44 papers, nationally and internationally and published 22 research papers, 16 articles and 4 books on Communication and Soft Skills, bearing the titles Knowing Your Words' Worth, Unscrambling Emails, Professional Skills' Development and Fundamental Skills for Budding Professionals. She has taught at various levels, in India and abroad, conducted training programmes and delivered talks, for the academia and industry, and shouldered diverse responsibilities in her career. Currently, she is serving as an Associate Professor, Communication and Soft Skills, at the Mumbai Educational Trust. She is a recipient of the Indira Gandhi Women Achiever's Award, among others.
15. **Prof. P.G. Jogdand** – Prof. P.G. Jogdand was the Former Professor and Head of Sociology Department at the University of Mumbai. He was also the Former Dean of the Faculty of Arts University of Mumbai. He has 6 Books and 21 Articles to his credit. He has guided 16 Ph.D. and 3 M Phil students. He has visited Russia (twice) France, Germany, UK, USA, South Africa, Netherlands and

Bangkok. He worked as a member of various committees - UGC, ICSSR, Planning Commission, Ministry of Social Justice and Empowerment, Govt. of India.

16. **Niti Mehta** – Niti Mehta is Professor and officiating Director at the Sardar Patel Institute of Economic and Social Research (SPIESR), Ahmedabad Prior to this she was associated with the Agro-Climatic Regional Planning Project of the Planning Commission wherein she was involved in formulating resource based decentralized agro-climatic plans for the country. Her research interests are agriculture development, employment, agrarian growth and rural transformation, urbanisation and related areas. Dr. Mehta has authored and co-authored several research papers in journals and books. Her books relate to hired labour in agriculture, sources of agricultural growth and total factor productivity, and human development at the district level.
17. **Balaji Kendre**–Balaji Kendre, Associate Professor, Department of Sociology, University of Mumbai, Santacruz (E) Kalina, Mumbai. M.A., (2001) University of Pune, Pune, Ph.D. (2009) S.R.T.M. University Nanded under the supervision of Dr B.C. Barik, former vice-Chancellor of Sambalpur University, Odisha, he has served as Assistant Professor at the Department of Sociology, Shivaji University Kolhapur (2003-2013). His areas of Specialisation are Sociology of Development, Sociology of Migration, Sociology of Communication, Sociology of Education, Sociology of Law and Sociology of Marginalised Groups in India. He has published two books and several research articles in refereed journals. He had organised two National Seminars and participated in several national and International conferences and seminar across the country. He has been academically associated with many agencies/departments of the Government of India and Government of Maharashtra. He intends to work in the area of Tribal Studies and Human Rights in India in near future.
18. **Krishan Chand Ramotra** – Krishan Chand Ramotra was

the Professor & Head, Department of Geography, Shivaji University, Kolhapur. He was UGC Junior Research Fellowship and Senior Research Fellowship holder. He has published 67 research papers and has 1 book published. He has successfully guided 16 Ph.D. students. He was also a BOS member and member of various academic bodies at State and National Level.

19. **Vijay Laxmi Pandey** –Vijay Laxmi Pandey is Professor at Indira Gandhi Institute of Development Research (IGIDR), Mumbai, India. IGIDR, is an advanced research institute established and fully funded by the Reserve Bank of India for carrying out research on development issues from a multi-disciplinary point of view. She obtained her Ph.D. in the area of 'Agricultural Economics' from G. B. Pant University of Agriculture and Technology, Pant Nagar, Uddhamsingh Nagar, India. She was recipient of Senior Research Fellowship of Indian Council of Agricultural Research. Dr. Pandey's areas of interest are agricultural economics, environmental economics, rural studies and gender issues. She has vast experience of conducting household level survey. She has successfully completed many national and international research and consultancy projects including UNDP, FAO, CIMMYT, the World Bank, Bill and Melinda Gates Foundation etc. She has a large number of research publications, which include research papers in peer reviewed journals, books, magazine articles, and policy reports. Presently, she is involved in Bill and Melinda Gates initiative on "System of Promoting Appropriate National Dynamism for Agriculture and Nutrition (SPANDAN)".

20. **Ramesh Dandge** – Ramesh Dandge is a Retired Professor of the Department of Economics, Shivaji University Kolhapur. He has 30 years of teaching and research experience and has guided 15 Ph.D. students and 21 M. Phil students. His areas of specialization are Agricultural Economics, Socio-economic Issues of marginalized communities. He has completed six research projects and presented 32 research papers in seminars/workshops.

He has also organized around 30 seminars/workshops and participated in 64 seminars/workshops. He has published 30 research papers and 8 books/ booklet/ working papers. He has worked as the Director of Centre for the Study of Social Exclusion and Inclusive Policy and coordinator of Rajmata Ahilyadevi Holkar Study Centre. Moreover, he has administrative experience as Head, acting Registrar, member of SENATE, BOS, API committee, Advisory committee.

21. **M.R. Prabhu** – M.R. Prabhu has been the former Consultant and former Director of Western Regional Centre, ICSSR. He has published several papers and one book in his credit. Dr. Prabhu during his tenure as Director of Western Regional Centre has conducted and monitored number of research methodology workshops in western region of India. He himself also has conducted research and contributed significantly in the field of social sciences.

PART I

Theory and Research

1

Introduction

Gautam Gawali, Mrudul Nile and M.R. Prabhu

Social science research in India has had an eventful past moving in various directions in the history of this country. India boasts a number of 777 universities with 356 State universities, 122 Deemed to be universities, 47 Central universities and 252 private iniversities within which there are more than 500 departments of Social Sciences. While universities are the locus of academic research, there are more than 200 government research institutes and autonomous research organizations which undertake social science research as well. Some NGOs and policy research initiatives such as 'Think Tanks' have also produced specific development focused on research products but generally do not have longer term interest in research and the quality of their research is not yet established.

The social complexities we are facing and the direction of social change we are undergoing as a whole is comprehended by social scientist to produce knowledge in its simplest form and be available for reviews. The social scientists consider it part of their ethical and moral function to reflect the conditions of free and democratic society based on social justice because this in itself is a precondition for the freedom of research and autonomous learning. This concern becomes even more urgent due to a challenging political system that seeks to control the production of socially relevant knowledge. For instance, the impediment of politicizing research and (mis)using this knowledge as an instrument to introduce hidden political agenda and ideologies which may not be acceptable to all.

In such circumstances social scientists are expected to maintain a safe distance from such designs and should take care to protect their autonomy as producers of critical social knowledge. Thus social scientists, who have participated in the process of social change through their rigorous writing and research in various disciplines like economics, political science, psychology, history, sociology and so on, cannot be party to promote their own interest and personal agenda in any way or form. This could range from their political ideology to their economic policy or their economic interest in any particular section. On the contrary they should analyze and address social problems independent of any ideological stance. The social scientists ought to be rooted in their theoretical and methodological perspectives that have evolved through their disciplinary engagements.

It would be a resolute departure from academic practice if a social scientist, even in a renowned academic institute, is seen joining hands with political parties openly on public forum in order to receive personal gains. It is precisely this practice that renders them socially irrelevant. In order to make this work, the social scientists first of all, must perform analytical function with regards to structural inequalities and power structures. To increase their social relevance they must engage in the critical analysis of society and seek not only to draw attention to current problem areas but also to find alternative ways to address them within the society itself. For example; they could study the different forms of discrimination & exclusion and make suggestions for social and political reforms in order to achieve democratic objectives and nurture hopefulness within the society.

The concern to produce socially relevant knowledge

hence demands identifying with certain knowledge practices and orientations. Some of which could be articulated as follows:

A. Identifying General Relationships

Significant social phenomena may be significant because they are common or general and they affect many people either directly or indirectly. One of the major goals of social research is to identify general patterns and relationships. In a way this objective is considered the primary goal because social research that is directed towards this end resembles research in hard sciences, this resemblance gives social research more legitimacy, making it seem more like social physics and less like social philosophy or a mere political ideology.

We have to accept that social science research has tried to follow the direction of the pure sciences in the development of its research methodology; this orientation was considered most valuable especially when one is searching for general patterns. For example, if we know that the general cause of caste aggression might be the concentration of members of a deprived caste in lower social classes, all sensible social scientists can work together to eliminate these conditions from Indian society or at least neutralize their impact and perhaps purge ourselves of serious caste antagonism.

Prejudices surrounding caste and gender are widespread in India and cannot be chased away unless they are confronted head-on. Integrative approaches of interdisciplinary research in social sciences can provide useful means of dealing with such complex and morally erroneous problems. Interrelationship among various social researches can offer generalizable social scientific knowledge.

As more and more is learned about general patterns, the general stock of social scientific knowledge increases and it becomes for social scientists to systematize knowledge and make connections that might otherwise not be made; because of the general underdeveloped state of social scientific knowledge we are not sure about the situations which are typical and which are not. So knowledge of general patterns is best achieved through examination of many comparable situations or cases, the more the better.

B. Testing and Refining Theories

Primary goal of social science research is to improve and expand the pool of ideas known as theories by testing their implications and to redefine their power to explain; testing is carried by deriving hypotheses from theories and implications of these theories are tested with data that bear directly on the hypotheses, and hypotheses that fail to receive support lose their appeal.

Theories are the core and underlying strength of the social sciences discipline. They guide researchers in their respective discipline. Theories guide practitioners in their intervention strategies to solve social quests. They also provide researchers with a basic understanding of how to see the larger psychosocial picture in their own personal and professional life. Theory is a set of interrelated concepts used to describe, explain, and predict how society and its parts are related to each other. These aspects help a social scientist to work on concepts and make them accessible and applicable to the society he or she lives in.

C. Making Predictions

Social researchers use theories to derive predications as what they expect to find in a set of data and accumulated social scientific knowledge is also used predictions about the future. Two kinds of knowledge help us make predictions, knowledge of history and knowledge of general patterns; as knowledge of history helps us to avoid repeating mistakes and knowledge of general patterns is useful for making projections about likely future events. One of the important goals in social science is to make predictions but it's not always the case that prediction and understanding go hand in hand. Sometimes our predictions are accurate but our understanding of the actual underlying processes that produce outcomes is incomplete o erroneous.

Social sciences have been commonly perceived as less beneficial to society as compared to the natural sciences like engineering and medicine. But the effects of social sciences cannot be gauged by just looking at number of published works, papers and projects, therefore, the direct benefits to the society cannot be demonstrated. However, research in social sciences and humanities are very relevant in transition process of a country.

It can help identify the need for social reform in a developing country. It can also help address challenges and identify possible solutions in areas essential to a country's political stability and socio-economic development, such as inter-community relations, protection of minorities, nation building, and good governance. The social scientists are also supposed to predict the future complications particularly in economics, social and political arenas in the country. "Why did nobody see this coming?" asked the British Queen during a visit to the London School of Economics in November 2008, referring to the global financial crisis.

D. Interpreting Culturally or Historically Significant Phenomena

Knowledge of general patterns is not the only kind of valuable knowledge especially when it comes to understanding social life. In the social sciences, knowledge of specific situations and events, even if they are uncharacteristic, can be highly valued. The significance of most historical phenomena is derived from their atypical nature; the fact that they were dramatically non-routine formed an impact on who we are today.

That is the reason why many social researchers address important historical events like social movements, freedom movements and socio-economic reforms in their research. We are concerned with these events and their interpretations because of its relevance when it comes to understanding the current psychosocial complexity of our society.

Since we assume that the knowledge we attempt to produce is aimed at social change, commitment to certain key social concerns is paramount. Some issues in this regards could be as follows:

(i) Social Justice

Social justice is a central theme for many studies conducted so far. Post liberalization period we are experiencing that the idea and research on issues of social justice is not appreciated and encouraged amongst the research scholars. When the idea of affirmative action took center stage of the public discourse on equality and justice some time back, we often come across researches digressing on the issue. Some of the major themes under social justice that have assumed more and more space is migration, forced migration, issues of refugees, marginalization, displacement etc.

A closer look at these newly emergent areas of studies comes from an economic perspective. These researches aim to study the economic inequalities more than the problem of social inequalities. They unfortunately put the social cause of these inequalities on the back burner and therefore the root cause of these inequalities is often searched in the 'temporary' economic states which have little hope to change due to the changing economic policies, these studies do not actually answer the core areas which fall under the social realm.

The Constitution of India begins with its first article by saying "India that is Bharat" this statement is more social as the term connotes a social relationship between its people and that whatever this constitution promises is for the welfare of the people of India. Therefore the social aspect of India has to be a base of any study and the superstructure of economic, political and cultural can be studied as super structure, at the core of this base lies the hard reality of practiced untouchability, exclusion and stratification.

Social Justice Enquiry essentially means studying imbalance in both equity and equality, the barriers it has and access which is granted. It also includes critical stance towards social orders, structures and processes that are detrimental to the social good.

According to Kathy Charmaz, qualitative research can

use grounded theory methods to advance social justice enquiry. These methods begin with inductive logic, use emergent strategies, rely on comparative enquiry and are explicitly analytical. This approach is most needed in the emerging studies of social justice. The frontiers of study in social justice are changing many folds with a lot of intervention of liberal economy and the mainstream Hinduised society. Grounded theories can help detect these interventions and locate the issues of social justice from this perspective.

(ii) Exploring and Commitment to Diversity and Multiculturalism

The Fourth Review Committee of the Indian Council for Social Science Research (ICSSR 2007) reports that social science research is driven by two factors: an interest in the functioning of society in its diverse social, cultural, political and economic aspects and in understanding the variables that influence them, and the practical needs of the policy-makers and managers in government, civil society and the private sector for reliable data and professional analysis

Caste has always been a central category in social science discourse in India and there is a significant and growing body of work on its economic, political and social implications. The issue of reservation for disadvantaged caste groups in higher educational institutions and government jobs at the central and state levels has led to major upheavals and unrest between the pro and anti-reservation movements over the last decade. With the emergence of cultural studies, a specifically Indian school, known as Subaltern Studies has been developed. Represented by post-colonial and social historians, subaltern studies have contested the strong elitist bias that characterized the writing of modern Indian history, and has provided an alternative framework.

(iii) Giving Voice to the Voiceless

Social science researchers are expected to challenge the faulty assumptions about certain communities that have been targeted. It brings forth through proper channels of social inquiry what was previously unknown and make it accessible to initiate change.

A new concern with knowledge, a desire for evidence-based action, and a greater recognition of the relevance of social science are all part of the challenges facing social researchers in the 21st century. The demand for social science work is outstripping supply, the demand from central government, local government, non-governmental organizations and the private sector is greater than the current set of social scientists that can deliver on demand. To meet the complex and heterogeneous challenges of the 21st century, enterprise of knowledge building in social science in the coming future needs combined efforts at robust theory and praxis; also including a strong grounding in IT based research methodology to manage cross-cultural, metacentric, macro level, inter-disciplinary and trans-disciplinary research projects.

With this perspective in mind, ICSSR-WRC had organized, a three day Conference on the following themes:

1. Status of Social Science Researches in the Western India: Area studies, Sectoral analysis, state profiles during last 25 years
2. Critical engagement in researches in mainstream disciplines such as sociology, anthropology, ethnography, political science, psychology, economics, education, management, social work, geography, history and philosophy.
3. Evaluation of researches in inter-disciplinary subjects such as women's studies, Dalit studies, environmental studies, health studies, disability studies, Tribal studies and studies of social exclusion and inclusive policy in Maharashtra, Gujarat, Goa, and Daman.
4. Priorities in Social Science Researches: Theoretical and Practical Concerns

According to the report of the Fourth Review Committee of the Indian Council of Social Science Research (ICSSR), 'social science research is chiefly driven by two forces: (a) interest in knowledge about the functioning of society in its diverse social, cultural, political and economic aspects, and in understanding the factors that shape them; and (b) the practical needs of policy makers and managers in government, civil society and the private sector for reliable information and professional analysis'(2007:5). (Ref: Indian Council of Social Science Research, 2007. Restructuring the Indian Council of Social Science Research. New Delhi: ICSSR.)

(Brief description of the key areas covered in the chapters included).

The book is divided into two parts namely the emerging theoretical considerations and research prospect in the current socio economic scenario of the country.

In the following part of the introduction, a brief summary of the papers is drawn for the benefit of the readers of this volume.

Professor R.S. Deshpande, in this article has outlined the need of interdisciplinary research. The article throws light on the need of the indiciplinarity in the social science and its interdependence on various branches and sub-branches of social sciences. Inter-disciplinarily in social sciences has been a topic of discussion for quite some time but precious little has been done to foster the interest in the across institutions in India. The history of education in this country as well as elsewhere in the world has reinforced the idea of compartmentalized education and fragmenting the domain of monolithic knowledge. The boundaries in the dissemination and spread of knowledge have been strengthened in the delivery system of the knowledge. Researchers also confine themselves inside these artificial boundaries; we have a large demand for social sciences and especially the interdisciplinary understanding of social sciences in the policy framework of this country. The World Social Science Report concludes that "Many of the challenges that the social sciences are asked to address required knowledge beyond the confines of single disciplines, and at times encompass the domains of natural sciences and humanities so it is important to encourage interdisciplinary research and to institutionalize it. India is an institutional economy and an interdependent society but Indian students over generations learned the knowledge as they understood from the masters trained in the Western world, least realizing that many of the theorems and theories do not apply to Indian context, we really failed to understand many of the intricacies in this country. Thanks to some academicians who understood the country as well as its people in finest detail could analyze the situation properly. I must mention at this point that Dr. Babasaheb Ambedkar was one of those ardent researchers who understood the Indian society threadbare and he was a true inter-disciplinarian. He was an ardent student of social anthropology, an excellent economist, a public finance expert, a barrister of law, and constitutional expert. He had understood the society bottom up and therefore he could analyze the question of caste from various dimensions. Inter-disciplinarity relates to two distinct strands one relating to the core of the discipline and the other interaction with tenets of the other discipline, if one thinks of a design of interdisciplinarity, it begins with the concepts and hypotheses in the core discipline of the researcher. When a researcher feels inadequacy or demand for explanation and support from the other disciplines, the researcher enlists the matching concepts and paradigms from another discipline. Social Science Research in India has been undergoing a critical phase with the drop in quality on one hand and increasing the quantity on the other, today we lack in vibrancy of topics, evaluation and accountability of the research conducted by a researcher. Our teaching in social sciences and the dogmatic syllabus-based knowledge delivery system has bounded the students in a particular discipline without any exposure to the other social sciences, but then filed of social sciences experienced phases of development; compartmentalization of knowledge began and it was strengthened. Today, Social Sciences are on the cross roads. One effect of the disciplinary boundaries was the multiplication of sub-disciplines and no symbiotic relation in the knowledge generation. We need to take steps to merge these crevices with the new instruments available. Today we are able to collaborate across globe with the touch of finger tips, access any knowledge field at our desk and consult specialists all over the world and now it has become essential to expose the young talented students to cross-discipline knowledge store houses.

Dr. Surinder Jaswal and Melody Kshetrimayum has taken a stock of the emerging areas in the social work research. The paper is essentially a pointer towards the untapped areas of research in social work. Research in social work, advances the development of knowledge by investigating problems, needs, events, developments and change in individuals and in their social context, Social work as an important applied social science discipline, has sought to understand and reflect upon situations with the help of its social science knowledge base and methodology. Currently, doctoral research has become an important component of social work education and practice to integrate scientific methods; Research in social work has focused research methods, paradigms and methodology. The paper was about to locate and analyze the emerging themes in social work research and also to project the over view of research in social work in TISS which is complex and multi-dimensional and it includes planning, services, programme, management, perceptions, support systems, politics, development and experiences, investigated in different settings that range from rural and urban settings to medical and correctional settings and from voluntary and government settings to educational and custodial settings. The broad spectrum in social work research can be linked to India's ancient and modern aspects of socio-cultural ethos and political history, with the change in India's social, economic, political, cultural conditions and other developments, the nature of the themes also changed accordingly. From the period 2004-2014 the School of Social Work was awarded twenty nine theses across fifteen themes and the methodology adopted to study the emerging themes in doctoral research was primarily Qualitative and Mixed Methods Approach, thus also pointing to the fact that the methodology in social work does not limit itself to either Quantitative or Qualitative methodology but it is represented by both paradigms. The paper highlighted there are different types of studies to research in social work like studies with Formative Research, studies with Impact Assessment Research, studies with Social Movement Research, studies with Historical Research. The review of the emerging themes of social work research, the methodology adopted indicates that social work research is rooted in the socio-cultural realities of the context in which it operates. The different themes of research in social work during the early years of 1960s-70s were broadly in needs and services and in social welfare administration. However, the current review reveals that over the last decade doctoral research has focused on studying context-specific reality. This changing trend in doctoral research gives prospect for social work education and practice to grow and develop in the country.

Dr. Chandrakant Puri, in his paper entitled Social Work Research in Western India and its Contemporary Relevance: A Critique, Professor Chandrakant Puri has reviewed the social work research in western India and its contemporary relevance based on the empirical data collected from several social work institutions and has observed key areas of concern giving several recommendations to strengthen the social work research in western India. Using the definition of Lal Das (2000) as a basis of analysis, which says that the Social Work Research as "systematic investigation into the problems in the field of social work. The study of concept, principles, theories underlying social work methods and skills are the major areas of social work research. It involves the study of relationship of social workers with their clients, individual groups or communities on various levels of interaction or therapy as well as their natural relationship and functioning within organizational structure of social agencies", However, Dr. Puri argues that very few contemporary social work research fulfill this criteria.

A review of social work research identifies that the contemporary social work research lacks in evidence based practice. There is a huge gap between the teachers who do research but do not practice in the field and the practitioners, who practice in the field are not able to use scientific research results in their practice. Another key observation is that the social work research is more of a 'social science research' than 'social work research'. This is more so when one analyses the recent studies undertaken in the subject of social work at the universities / colleges by the students/ research scholars. A trend worldwide suggests that the academic research largely remains un-utilized as it does not get communicated to the practitioners or the policy makers or to the NGOs involved in advocacy. There are several practitioners who are involved into action research but lack in scientific methodological rigors as there are no formal training programmes for the capability building of practitioners in India.

In view of the above, a study was undertaken by the author wherein, a questionnaire was sent to the colleges from Maharashtra, Gujarat and Goa to study the practice of research at post graduate, M. Phil and Ph.D. level. Along with other information, the lists of dissertation completed at the respective academic institution in the last two years were asked for, which were analyzed in order to understand its contemporary relevance.

The study reveals that the majority of the social work research lacks in 'action' which distinguishes social work research from social science research. As defined above, social work research hardly informs professional practice. Most of the studies are undertaken in two areas of the definition, assessment of needs and understanding impact of legislation etc. It is hardly seen contributing in other two important areas, demonstrating relative costs and benefits of social work services and advance professional education in the light of the changing contexts of practice. There is a huge gap between the 'researcher 'and practitioners'. Research result largely remains un-utilized as it does not get communicated to the practitioners / policy makers / NGO / in advocacy.

The author has given several recommendations at the end in order to strengthen the social work research in the western India.

Dr. Anil Sutar essentially talks of the qualitative research in social sciences. He lays emphasis on research methodology that is most conducive to the social science research. Research methodology has been regarded as a crucial requirement for the social science research, Social scientists in India as elsewhere in the world have been emulating the methods of natural sciences with an understanding that their research would be considered more scientific, it is being observed that experts of quantitative methods advice the feminist researchers and also researchers who adopt qualitative methods to use numbers and statistics. In one sense, following methods of natural sciences has emerged as *'methodological sanskritization'* where social science researchers by using statistics and computer softwares try to achieve up-ward mobility – towards more scientific status from that of anecdotal status. Thus, there are concerns that in most of the cases; the emulation of methods of natural sciences just ends up as ritual without contributing to the advancement of theorization and conceptualization in social sciences. Over a period of time efforts have been made to broad base social science research methodology and to encourage use of 'other' methods in research, The India Council of Social Science Research (ICSSR), through its various policy guidelines, workshops and other knowledge dissemination activities took lead in encouraging methodological pluralism in social science research in India. It is quite evident that qualitative methods are accorded equal weightage in the ICSSR sponsored workshops on research methodology. This paper makes an attempt to explore the shifts that have taken place in the research methodology of social sciences by analyzing the methodology components of the doctoral theses awarded in social sciences by a social science institute. The study is based on the content analysis of 105 Ph.D. theses awarded in inter-disciplinary areas of social science by a reputed social science institute based in Mumbai, based on the primary objective chapter in theses was identified and data was analyzed on these themes across different time periods to understand the trends. The study found that quantitative methodology was dominant during 1970s, 1980s and 1990s as methodology of social science theses, however doctoral theses were increasingly adopting non-quantitative methodologies from the year 2000 onwards; thus, one could not also jump to the conclusion that quantitative methods have been sidelined in favor of qualitative methods in the social science research but social sciences have become more eclectic. Towards diversity of research designs, it is not only pluralism in terms of qualitative methodology gaining importance on par with quantitative one but it is also diversity of research designs/ methods within the framework of qualitative methodology that has further enriched the element of methodological pluralism in social science theses. Several changes have been found in the methodological aspects of social science doctoral theses across different time periods, thus research methodology is moving from methodological monism towards methodological pluralism. Compared with the theses of 1970s, 1980s and 1990s, the doctoral theses of 2000s and onwards engage with methodological issues in more critical and nuanced manner. The relation of theory and data, ontology, epistemology, logic and methods are dealt in more critical manner in theses of present days than that of 1990s and before. However, research ethics which forms the core of methodology has not yet received considerable attention of the doctoral theses in social science.

Dr. Shefali Pandya in her paper examines the trends in the research in education. A lot of socio-psychological problems in the research are being dealt in her paper. Educational research has attempted to discover laws underlying human behaviour so that a science of educational practice can be developed, This general model has been taken from the natural sciences in which the experiment was assumed to be the sine qua non for testing the validity of a theory and its application based on correlational studies providing the initial, preliminary information, a large majority of correlational and experimental studies produce trivial results and do not account for more than 10 % of variance in the outcome variables; research usually takes into account one or two variables at a time and thus, dictum of "whole is bigger than the parts" is lost sight of. There is little effort to study the context of education as a dynamic part of the culture.

The present trends in educational research do not take into account the meaning of an experience for the participants of a study. This leaves out understanding how and why a person behaves in a particular manner, a large part of current research focuses attention on identifying gender or school type differences without trying to understand why these differences arise or how to deal with the consequences of such differences. But it is also seen that volume of empirical research has increased but equally important is the shift from empirical to action research which has become a hot favourite especially among school teachers. Now a days there is a change in the terminology too, the term research study is becoming old fashioned, now it is called 'research report'; this shift in terminology has important bearing on our thinking. The primary role of the researcher becomes not 'studying', but 'reporting'. This reporting is to the society and to the funding agency. In this paper it was highlighted that there is corruption at Masters' degree level research as it is restricted to surveys, single group experimental research. Moreover, after the implementation of the sixth pay commission, there is a tremendous jump in the number of publications on account of API and the requirement of at least two publications by each PhD student. Many of these lack rigour and are paid publications in substandard journals. Little research is found to be conducted in university departments or in colleges of education in the field of comparative education, politics of education or economics of education. Most of the research studies in economics of education are conducted by agencies like NUEPA etc. There is very little attempt to study multilevel data. Besides, studies focus organisational effectiveness but not on organisational improvement. Thus, the findings of research on organisational effectiveness are largely academic and of no practical significance. A review was done in two prominent areas by the author they are, educational technology and sociology of education to know the prospects. There is a strong need for capacity building and strengthening research skills and abilities in both the research guides and students, and it has become necessary to enhance the relevance and quality of educational research, Future research needs to review various conceptualization, models and reforms agenda in education with reference to its adaptability in diverse socio-economic and cultural contexts, because technology and teaching trends have evolved and changed very speedily in the last few decades. However, education methodology and associated research methodology have not yet evolved at the same rate as information technology. Every university needs to develop and implement R & D policy with reference to educational research and research in higher education is also the need of the hour.

Dr. Remy Dias has attempted to look at the development of social sciences in Goa. As there is only one state university in the state, uses a vast canvas to measure the activity of research in Goa. Knowledge has been a key factor in economic development and aiding incrementally better insights of societal functioning from twentieth century, with subsequent rapidity of change due to impact of globalization, role of higher education institutions in furthering research and scholarship is becoming vital in 'liquid modernity', but has societal understanding and research kept pace with fast evolving socio-economic dynamics. Indian Council for Social Science Research, besides furthering research, has also been attempting to survey research activity and estimate its quality in various fields of social sciences carried out in India. Organization of National Seminar by ICSSR (WRC-Mumbai) on 'Status of Social Science Research in Western India: Critical Engagements and Future Direction' held at Mumbai University from 14-16 November, 2014, under stellar leadership of its Hon. Director, Prof. Gautam Gawali, is to estimate progress of social science research in Western India and the effort is indeed commendable. This paper made an attempt to gauge advances in social science research for Goa region and identify expansive gaps for further exploration. There is now increasing realization that social sciences have potential of offering scope and down to earth latitude to educational considerations and as such need to be carefully listened to. In university system social sciences are newest part which has gained prevalence over humanities through claim to be only voice that is trying to gain a broad picture of social reality and thus make predictions for future. Social scientists are viewed as participants in socio-historical development of human action and understanding. Social science research has developed by leaps and bounds in Goa erstwhile Portuguese colony now, research is in the form of PhD theses, Masters level dissertations besides a huge mass of project-reports by UG student. It is only recent years that Goa University has stipulated that PhD researchers must have at least one each international and national level peer-reviewed publication prior to award of degree. With a young 'A' Grade NAAC accredited Goa University (established in June 1985) and a host of other institutions like Xavier Centre of Historical Research, Historical Archives of Goa, Goa Konkani Akademi, Gomantak Marathi Academy, etc. there has been a steady output in terms of research in post-liberation period. Paradoxically, however, it is a fact that there is a dip in quality and quantity of knowledge production as compared to colonial times. Attempts are now made to analyze development in social science research in Goa and situate same within perspective of 'liquid modernity'. Higher education in Goa as elsewhere in India and throughout the world is facing times of significant change, as a result of historical factors, such as globalization, massification of higher learning, specialization and fragmentation of disciplines and commodification of knowledge, with implication for social science studies and research. Goa University established in June 1985 by an Act of Goa government today has 55 colleges and other higher education institutions affiliated to it, 30 in general education and 25 in professional education with total enrolment of about 28,000. Having oriented itself towards imparting advanced knowledge and to develop human resource, Goa University, with one of best teacher-student ratio, has attained an important place in realm of higher learning. Within a short span of last two and half decades of its existence, University has shown distinct visibility and a promise of growth in teaching and empowering young men and women of region. With its well-designed curriculum, Goa University currently offers, under CBCS, 32 PG programmes on campus, which provide ample opportunity to students to pursue their diverse academic interests. It was observed that award of doctoral theses in Goa University was mostly in 1990s and then after award of PhDs declined especially in social science. The paper made an attempt to give a cursory view of social sciences researches in Goa across a few disciplines and the observations were that the present status of social science research in Goa indicates that there is a need to address issues of methodological sophistication, adequate content coverage with focus on social relevance and above all researchers should strive to effectively communicate their research findings to intellectual community through peer-reviewed publication. A major lacuna of studies in social sciences in Goa is that display of lack of clarity about concepts and ideas is quite evident.

Dr. Mazbaan Jaal, has very well attempted to philosophise history from the point of concrete science. It is without doubts that though there is an abundance of excellent social scientific research being carried out in India, there is in the last resort some sort of what the author would like to call an: "unhappy crisis" within the social sciences. The idea of "unhappy crisis" the author derived from the Hegel's idea of the "unhappy consciousness" that he conceptualized in his *Phenomenology of Mind*, coupled with the theory of crisis in the sciences that Georg Lukács in *History and Class Consciousness* and Edmund Husserl talked of in his *The Crisis of the European Sciences*. In this sense we are in opposition to Althusser's position to the idea of the crisis of the sciences. The author attempts to discuss the problems of the crisis of the sciences. Science cannot be taken in an uncritical way that Althusser certainly suggested, a science that is somehow beyond critique, keeping in mind the problems raised by Husserl followed by the formulation of the Frankfurt School, it is Luckas' critique that remains the basis of author's paper and how this helped in the development of social sciences in India; there are multiple understandings of the social sciences. One form follows the Weberian logic where science is understood as vocation. Neo-liberalism however has transformed this understanding of science as vocation into the understanding off science as business. But there is a third perspective that lies rather buried and this is the theme of science as a revolutionary endeavor. This paper is based on the third perspective of social sciences especially in Western India and considering that there has been a shift to the right in Indian politics where serious sciences are now being confused with fascist mythopoetics; the very idea of science is now being devalued. The third idea of science is basically a Marxist idea; this idea was also a part of foundation of education in India. However with the triumph of the fascist forces in the 2014 elections, followed by the victory in the state elections in Maharashtra and Haryana, and also with the now fascistization of education by the RSS, the role of the social sciences has totally changed. Science as vocation and business will now be subservient to the fascist forces. Unfortunately studies in fascism in India in particular and Asia in general have not taken centre stage of academic imagination. One could point to Jairus Banaji's works on fascism that have raised the issue of fascism. However the finer details in the Asiatic mode of production and the role of caste hegemony have not been brought out in his works. Reading Critical Theory, especially Adorno a theme continuously recurs to haunt the reader, the theme of calculation and control. The modern sciences thus have at its underlying epistemic base, the theme of calculation and control. Science thus no longer wants to know nature—it wants to *control* it. The modern sciences are thus constituted within this peculiar fusion of technology and domination, rationality and oppression. There are two important and intertwined questions with respect to the social sciences in India. The first deals with the question of Marxism as a rigorous social science, especially in its applicability in India in particular and other South Bloc nations in the periphery of global capital accumulation; but there is another question that emerges. If an alternative form of Marxism is possible which keeps the caste system as the central part of its discourse, then where would one put the works of Phule and Ambedkar.

Dr. Mrudul Nile has attempted to understand the problem of theorisatiion and appeals for data validation in social scence research so as to draw some generalizations from the research. This he opines would standardize the process of theory building. The growth of political science, its concepts and the ideas have always been a part of the social constructions; Political science thrived upon these social constructions which have relied for its development of the political events, thus political variables are always influenced by social developments. Concepts and themes like sovereignty once constituted the basic foundation and the fundamental ideas around which the discipline of political science revolved. Many studies have been conducted on ideologies, and probably this is the only subject which is very well grounded with the theoretical aspects of the cultural, economic and political construction of the social order. These theories are still serving as the common platform to understand the social relations and economic priorities in any nation state. The ideas of identity and nationalism have grown in this background. The fact remains that the people across the continents have not thought of theories of political science as theories of politics alone but understood them from the point of view of social discourse. The initial studies were more normative and concerned with issues like how the state ought to be and the like. Most of these studies were influenced by religion and moral philosophy, by the end of the 19th century; we experienced the wave of social movements not only in the sphere of state but also in the realm of economy, society and culture too. Very broadly, these movements may be put under the title of renaissance and reformation. Parallel to this newer thought processes formed the basis for contemporary political theory. These theories have grown due to the socio- economic cultural and political developments in the society and the need for the newer thoughts. Another finding put forward by the author was on interdependence of research methodologies in the political science. Since early 1930 one may trace major changes in the study of political science. The emergence of political sociology and political economy embarks upon the new techniques of the study of political science where there were studies, methodologies and theories borrowed directly for the discipline of sociology, anthropology, psychology, mathematics, statistics and other natural sciences Political science initially was developed on the basis of observations which lead to the theory building. After the First World War, a need was felt to understand the social and political shifts among various states and communities. Then the Behavioral School of Thought attempted to understand the processes based on the empirical studies conducted with the help of psychology, mathematics and statistic. The reason why the studies got highly interdisciplinary is because it started asking questions of human existence and survival. These questions never fell into the core subject matters of either political science, sociology, economics or psychology. Hence not only there was a growth of the parameters of the study but also the techniques and models adopted by each other to understand the phenomenon in their own core subject areas. Political theory is engaged with current political issues and is self-reflective about political life. It has a strong ethical component and develops alternative conceptualizations of how we might organize social and political relations. Theory thus is understood, as an aspect of the whole discipline, interwoven with each concentration, recently, in the more globalized world, which is entrenched with the notion of competition, meanings of sovereignty and democracy has changed the structure of the world order. There are claims of strong nationalism and democracy but still more than half of the world is suffering from poverty, hunger and violence. On the other hand the largest democracies like India and the United States of America have fallen prey to the antagonistic politics and the politics of 'Selective Nationalism'. The research inadequacies in political theory have brought the world to the brink of a doomsday. The problems of terrorism, nuclear war, communal conflicts and freedom movements are unavoidable. Post-World War II, the world saw some peace and development for some time, it was essentially because the nations which were at wars did not have enough resources to fight more wars. Hence, the economy of abundance certainly makes the world more and more unsafe. It is essential that we work towards making political science adaptive to the development of the subject in the other parts of the world like United States of America and Europe. Of course, it will take some time for culture of political science to attain those heights in India. But an initiation towards following the trend can bring some important changes in the way we approach political science in our country and more specifically, in the western India. Methodology and Perspectives of political science studies in India should aim to attain similar stature as that of the universities in the United States of America. The author also used models for data which is helpful in generating testable predictions which can subsequently serve as hypothesis in the data analysis.

Dr. Anjali Kurane argues for a shift in research in Anthropology. She opines that research should not only study the origin of the mainstream communities and social institutions but should focus on the marginalized social entities. Anthropology traces its roots to ancient Greek historical and philosophical writings around 400BC about human nature and the organization of human society. Toward the end of the 19th century anthropologists began to take academic positions in colleges and universities, American anthropologists of the 20th century went on to establish anthropology departments at universities throughout the country. Anthropology was principally concerned with the non-western isolated cultures, later on as simpler societies started getting increasingly involved into urban societies; Anthropologists shifted their attention from simpler cultures to more complex cultures. In the 1970s many anthropologists, motivated towards looking the meanings of particular important cultural symbols and rituals within cultures themselves to demonstrate how this one symbol or ritual shapes or reflects an entire culture and to understood the culture of the people by examining important rituals. In India, Anthropology developed in the late 1940s and in India, Anthropological research endeavor had its beginning from the western colonial encounter. The twentieth century is the era of the development in the Indian Anthropology the predominant trends are marked by a shift of focus from tribes to castes and more than fifteen years long engagement with village studies; During the period, late 1940s and 1950s, Anthropologists devoted to Indian research were focused on village and institutional studies. One of the dominant trend emerged during that period was holistic sense in combining both physical and cultural anthropology. The paper concern was the development over the last twenty five years with several broad recent trends *in Anthropology and more specifically in Socio cultural Anthropological research and studies in Western India.* All over India so as in Western India Anthropological researches whether at individual level, department level and institutional level focused 'tribe' as their core area for study to understand Indian society and culture and developed monographs on various tribes. It was a general view that Anthropologists study only ethnic groups and tribes. Ethnicity and ethnic conflict have been key concepts in Anthropology to understand intercultural interaction within a plural society and became central focus for research in 1990s in Western India. The current researches areas focus on ethnic identity and social mobility, ethnicity and urbanization, ethnic conflict, ethnic movements, ethnic politics, ethnic separatism, situational ethnicity, resources competition and so on. The current dominant research trend in development anthropology directly related to development issues and problems of tribes, Dalits, Dalit women, women, trafficking children, livelihood, health, malnutrition, education, gender discrimination, social exclusion and poverty, casteism and role of governments, NGOs, international development organizations in the process of Development, *anthropology and policy, process of policy development, modernization and so on. In* Western India current thrust areas and trends of researches are in urban anthropology, development anthropology, cultural anthropology, symbolic anthropology, medical anthropology, growth and Nutrition and emerging trend in molecular anthropology, as the study of the communities is the basic theme of the Anthropology, we should look how

Anthropologists can make positive contribution to multiple socio-cultural problems that communities face in the process of development. Contemporary anthropology should focus on restoring social health of the communities and planning for welfare of the people.

Dr. Vibhuti Patel, examines the trends in women studies with reference to the shift from women studies to gender studies. She argues about the dynamics of power relations in her paper. The need to study women's issues in academic institutions and to conduct research based on experiential material and affirmative action had begun to be discussed among Indian women's studies scholars by the early eighties, the dialectical relationship between 'pedagogy' and 'praxis', vis-à-vis the 'women's question', has been a matter of great concern for pioneers of Women's Studies (WS) in Western India and the author in this paper tries to examine the issues like the genesis of interaction between WS and WM in India, the contribution of WS to mainstream academia, ; the analytical tools and the theoretical insights provided by WS and the WM in the Western India; the research methodology and agenda of the WS, ongoing debates on the scope and limitations of WS within institutionalised structures, the shift of focus from WS to gender studies; the economics and politics of funding, consultancy and priorities in research. Women's studies start with the premise that women have subordinate status in our society so the knowledge-based created by WS should be used for empowerment of women. Thus WS has a transformative potential in terms of changing the gender based power relations. WS in India evolved as a result of state patronage after the declaration of the United Nations International Women's Year (UN-IWY). Publication by the Government of India in 1975, of the Report of the Status of Women Committee, TOWARDS EQUALITY, reopened the debate on the women's question. The Report revealed the deteriorating conditions of women. The birth of the women's liberation movement in Western India was a result of the radicalisation of Indian politics in the late 1960s and the early 1970s. In the late 1960s there was an upsurge internationally of the black movement, the women's movement, the anti-war movement and the working class movement. These were independent, self-determining and democratic movements, which questioned all hierarchical structures, the UN Declaration of 1975 as an International Women's Year coincided with the Emergency Rule in India. By the time the Emergency was lifted in 1977, several women's groups had developed around democratic rights issues in Pune, Mumbai, Panjim, Vadodara. The press swung into "action" after the imposed silence of nearly two years. Atrocities committed against women during the Emergency were openly documented and reported in the press. When analysing the origin, development and direction of women's studies (WS) in India; it is important to understand its relationship with the Indian women's movement (WM). It was in the early 1980s that women's studies' centres, functioning autonomously or within the university system, started accepting empirical and experimental evidence from the women's movement. It was a time when participatory research, action research and subaltern studies were gaining ground in the field of social sciences. This process indirectly facilitated the interaction of WS and the WM. In the last 35 years, the principal body of higher education, the University Grants Commission (UGC), has given primary attention to WS. SNDT Women's University in Bombay was the first to establish a WS unit, in 1974. Now it has a fully established Research Centre for Women's Studies (RCWS) and the UGC has accorded it the status of a Centre for Advanced Research in Women's Studies. The response of academics to WS in mainstream academia is mixed; now there is a search for new paradigm in WS, the first step in this direction was to make women visible in various disciplines, highlighting their role and contribution and capturing their experience. WS Sociologists in Western India made pioneering contribution by challenging structural functional analysis that predominated researches on women. They also enriched debate on caste question by bringing intersectionality of caste, class and gender with perspective of stand-point theory in their researches. A new move now from WS to Gender studies is on the demand from academia, while WS focuses on patriarchal control over women's sexuality, fertility and labour, gender studies focuses on power relations that are socially constructed and result into subordination-domination relationship between men and women in a multi-layered manner resulting from class, caste, location, race, ethnicity and religion; with Gender Studies and Women Studies there is a one more study i.e. the Feminist Studies, The difference between Women's Studies and Feminist Studies lies in the ideological framework. Women's studies are about women, may or may not have a feminist perspective, The strength of feminist studies lies in its challenge to androcentric frameworks and generalizations in scholarship and women-centered inquiry remains critical to analytic vision. Women's Studies, by design, are about transformation, the state of art profile of researches in WS in the Western India at the end of this exercise is not neat and clear, as women's life is also not simple. It is full of contradictions. We need more systematic work to challenge the mainstream academic disciplines, build new paradigms and provide significant theoretical understanding.

Professor Gautam Gawali critically evaluates the research work carried out in the field of psychology particularly in western part of India. In western India, the focus of psychological research was more on experimental psychology. When researchers realized that the application of experimental psychology in actual practice and particularly in industry as a source of employment is very limited; they started working on other areas of psychology specially applied psychology. In his paper, he further highlights the major problems faced by the departments of psychology in India like lack of infrastructure, lack of full time teachers and lack of internship / field work facilities.

He also discusses the psychosocial complexities in the Indian society particularly contemporary research issues such as caste based discrimination, women's issues and gender discrimination, discrimination faced by the marginalized groups / socially disadvantaged groups and persons with disabilities, positive youth development and unemployment and its consequences, social justice. Caste system in Hindu social order is still an important determinant of people's economic choices. Casteism serves simultaneously both to rationalize the hierarchical domination of one group over other group(s), and maintain psychological, social and material advantages for the dominant group. Both active casteism and passive acceptance of caste-based privilege disrupt the mental health and psychological functioning of both victims and perpetrators of caste injustice. Hence it opines that where the scope is ever widening for specializations like the industrial and clinical psychology, the opportunities for the social psychologist are broader and deeper and can offer endless opportunities. Quite significant numbers of teachers and researchers in the field of psychology and particularly those who have access to public funding have not dwelled very effectively and scientifically into the social multicultural ethos of India. Some of them are continuously trying to create Indian psychology as their base which is mostly religious. There is an attempt to treat Indian psychology (IP) as Positive Psychology (PP). Indian psychology (IP), unlike PP, is not of a recent origin. To increase the acceptance for Indian psychology they need to systematically study the social structure of caste and gender discrimination and differentiate between structural disadvantages, which imply large, pervasive and systemic effects, and incidental disadvantages, which imply suddenly, imposed conditions requiring adaptation to a novel situation. Positive psychology was recently established as a new perspective specifically addressing the study of well-being, quality of life, strengths and resources. Researchers in the field of positive psychology have started providing a comprehensive reference that focuses specifically on how a culturally-informed approach to positive psychology can help capitalize on the strengths of racial minority groups and have a greater potential to positively impact their psychological well-being.

Women in India also are victims of social order like other marginalized groups. A full participation in social and economic life is central to women's freedom and sense of self realization. Thus fulltime employment/work of women should be considered as an opportunity for them for the expression of their self and also their social and emotional liberation. Therefore researchers need to focus on career opportunities of women in contemporary society. It is the burgeoning field of women studies that has pointed to the need for considering gender as an analytical category in research. The concept of gender has been recognized as cultural and distinct from sex which is merely biological.

Community Need Based Research—Needs is the gap between what is and what ought to be, it can be felt by an individual, a group, or an entire community. It is a need of an hour that social scientists should involve themselves in community-based research in communities and institutions of higher learning around the country. In Indian community the humanistic approach of study encourages a proactive stand of activism, advocacy, and social justice that promotes awareness, wisdom, purpose, respect, interdependence, and peace.

In the last decade, both rural and urban areas, the percentage of disabled persons has increased. About 5-6% of the Indian population has some kind of disabilities. Psycho-socio and vocational rehabilitation is the most challenging task before the rehabilitation professionals. Therefore, researchers in the field of rehabilitation of people with disability need to sensitize society in general towards special population.

Dr. Varsha Gathoo, Kasturi Kulkarni & Jignya Shah in their papers argue, disability estimates varies across the different countries as nations diverge in defining and recognizing various categories listed in the legal frameworks. On an average the World Health Organization estimates that 10% of any population is disabled. In addition, approximately 85% of the world's children with disabilities under 15 live in developing countries. Disability was referred to as 'infirmity' in India till 1993, the infirmities included insanity, deaf-muteness, blindness and leprosy. It was only in 2001 that Independent India began a comprehensive Census enumeration of people with disability. Census 2001 revealed over 21 million people in India to be suffering from one or the other kind of disability. This was equivalent to 2.1 per cent of the total population. Other demographic details documents note that 75 per cent of persons with disabilities live in rural areas. Among the five types of disabilities on which data was collected, visual disability emerged as the top category at 48.5 per cent. Others in sequence were: Disability in movement (27.9%), mental (10.3%), in speech (7.5%), and in hearing (5.8%). The disabled by sex followed a similar pattern except that the proportion of disabled females was higher in the category of visual and hearing disability. The Census (2011) is seen to have extended data on eight types of disabilities namely, disability 'In Seeing', 'In Hearing', 'In Speech', 'In Movement', 'Mental Retardation', 'Mental Illness', 'Any Other' and 'Multiple Disability' and there seems to be just the marginal increase from 2.13 per cent in 2001 to 2.21 per cent in 2011. Factors which contributed to the changing demography of persons with disabilities in India are political will, technological advancements and support, human resource development, advocacy for disability. There has been a paradigm shift in policy towards Persons with Disabilities since the Ninth Five Year Plan, The Draft Rights of persons with disabilities Bill, 2014 being ratified is based on guidelines of UNCRPD and hence envisages fostering a Social model of disability. A survey was conducted and followed medical model the inference of the finding was that in spite of the change in the overall perspective of disability the research undertaken is not in congruence with the trend. A newer trend of mixed model researches has also been emerging in the present investigation including issues of disability in denotified tribes, unemployment, livelihood, job opportunities, job satisfaction, marital expectations so also transgender issues, homeless Children, feminism etc. Out of the total of 202 abstracts investigated 14 were pertaining could be categorized under this trend.

Dr. Ramesh Kamble argues about the functional paradigms in Dalit studies. The year 2016 marks a centenary of Dr. Ambedkar's essay titled *Castes in India: Their Mechanism, Genesis and Development*, this important essay which was presented in May 1916 at the 21 Golden Weiser's Seminar in University of Columbia, was the first serious attempt by an Indian social scientist to grapple with the question of caste, which Dr. Ambedkar saw as intersecting with women's subjugation. A cursory glance at glance at the history of the development of sociology in India, especially at the Bombay school, suggests institutionalized closure towards the Dalit social experience, quest and movement for equal humanity and justice and as well as silencing of contribution made by Dr. B.R. Ambedkar. The author in this paper attempts to investigate as to how and why the leading scholars of Bombay School of sociology, through organized, institutionalized knowledge-practice, practiced such a closure and Foucault's articulation of knowledge/power was drawn to analyze this closure witnessed in the Bombay school knowledge engagement. The author mentioned about some aspects of Foucault's theory of subject and alluded to his analysis of the discursive construct of 'man' for a number of reasons, first it help the author to look critically at the practice of sociology at Bombay School critically, second it helped to investigate as to how the margins in general and Dalits in particular figured in this practice and also to analyze the sociological practices that exhibits both construction of Dalit knowledge-subject by that practice, as well as Dalit knowledge-subject critically becoming aware of the knowledge/power operating at the institutional settings of making of sociology, third Foucauldian perspective helped to understand the various attempts on the part of Dalit knowledge-subjects in recuperating the primacy and autonomy of themselves as thinking beings and thereby intervening into and attempting to reconstitute that practice. In the era of colonial modernity, in the edited volume on Doing Sociology in India, Patel draws attention to the link between colonialism, anthropology and sociology in India. Looking at the close links with nationalism and sociological tradition in India, Patel asserts that sociologists in India as that which analyses one's own society in one's own terms without colonial and neo-colonial tutelage. The post-colonial development of sociology witnessed shift from the 'book-view' to the 'field-view' and fostered participant observation as an insider's perspective' of doing sociology, review of development of sociology in India and in Bombay raised fundamental question, such as while sociologists were committed to the cause of nationalism but did they criticize the nature of this nationalist fervor as Ambedkar did? Critically investigating into the birth of sociology in Bombay, Manorama Savur has pointed out that Ghurye's training in Sanskrit and Indology led to articulation of appropriate approach to sociology in India, she quotes Ghurye to show that for him, "anthropological approach to sociology is the most appropriate" and that his stress on anthropology as guiding development of sociology led to perpetuation of 'anthropolised' sociology in Bombay and Savur also pointed out Ghurye despite being father of Indian Sociology practiced and propagated Hinduised Sociology. Patel's critical appraisal of M. N. Srinivas' Anthropology/ sociology, reviewing Srinivas' work, especially his understanding of 'Varna' and 'Jati', 'social change' and 'social mobility', and the methodological shift his work, and the functionalist paradigm as an appropriate approach to the study of Indian society which become prominent through prominence of Srinivas in academia, resulted in institutionalization of the *Savarna* vision of India. The practice of sociology and anthropology in India thus presents *colonization* of these disciplines by the upper castes in the post-colonial times by constituting upper castes' perspectives translating into authoritative account of knowledge of Indian society. Thus doing sociology in India was to remain committed to and to reproduce the upper caste perspectives on Indian society. Moreover, under these pursuits of knowledge, though 'caste', 'community' 'religion', 'culture' and 'nation' were important categories and context of knowledge formation, those who suffered denial and violence on account of caste system and religion, or those who were denied the membership of human community through practice of untouchability, or those did not count in articulation of nation were neither objects of this knowledge, nor their perspectives on caste, community or nation had any place in knowledge production. An important aspect and consequence of the recent Dalit scholarship has been the visibility of the category 'Dalit' in sociological pedagogical practice. Though the struggle to make visible the category 'Dalit' as an autonomous analytical category to analyze social processes and to assert the importance of Ambedkar's contribution to the making of the discipline of sociology has been challenging, today it is certain that the sociological knowledge and pedagogy is incomplete and even irrelevant without referring to the category 'Dalit' and Ambedkar. This paper was one such modest attempt to highlight and herald the Dalit arrival in sociology.

Dr. Preeti Shirodkar, examines about the intersectionality of diaspora and gender. The well crafted paper opens up new vista of enquiry of diaspora enquiry. Considering the length of time that 'diaspora' as a lived reality has been in existence, the constitutive identity has been further problematized by the overlapping, yet exclusive, issues that are brought into focus by the dynamics of gender and its contribution to diasporic identity; terming this 'intersectionality', Avtar Brah – a prominent thinker in the diasporic space, asserts the need to provide due consideration to this unique identity. Explaining 'intersectionality' as the interlinking/crossing of the diasporic space, with that of gender, she argues that the dilemmas arising from this have not been given the consideration that is due to them, which may result in subsuming a doubly marginalised identity, that of women diasporics in the larger diasporic identity, which in turn may result in homogenising it, at the cost of burying its unique subalternity. Diaspora by its very nature, as a scattering, involves a 'movement', which brings along with it a spacio-temporal distancing from the homeland that may be at times out of choice or at other times enforced by the emerging realities of the socio-political milieu, this results in issues that are diverse and multiple, which according to Jha, arise because Indian diasporic women are caught between the two extremes of nativity and naivety, tradition and modernity, and the past and the present. As regards women, in the early stages of diaspora, one of the chief reasons that they migrate is for marriage and settling, something, that they have more often than not, not envisaged and which is sprung upon them in the context of an arranged marriage, as can be seen through the experience of Ji Bai from Vassanji's *The Gunny Sack*, making it a reality that is doubly traumatising –that of accepting their changed status, from being a girl to becoming a woman, while simultaneously having to adjust to the new weather and environment, the latter, which is in a context that is both physical and cultural. Additionally, women, who by their very nature are receptacles of memories and are expected to be repositories of culture, face greater emotional upheaval, both in trying to maintain cultural and religious purity, while attempting to blend in with the demands of the new place, whether in their own context or that of their family, especially the younger generations, which often being born and largely brought up in the land of settlement, have divided/changed loyalties, resulting in inter-generational conflict. Another challenge, which though basic is much deeper, is that of language. Constituting expression and the power that comes with it, it is also emblematic of the paradox that underlines women, who are largely not given a voice or whose voice is often written off and yet the language of expression is known as the mother tongue, since the child first acquires it from his/her mother and then often turns it against her. Constituting a dilemma for the diasporic women is learning another tongue that of the place they have moved to, as it will be a source of their assimilation or even power in the new home, as witnessed and expressed by Meena Alexander, as also how to continue instilling the mother tongue in succeeding generations, as the language can evoke with it an entire universe and culture.

Ironically though, diaspora studies is still considered an upcoming field that is becoming increasingly interdisciplinary; and one would not be wrong in asserting the importance of keeping one's focus on the place and value of women's voice in it, as an expression of a subalternity that is defined by both place and gender and, in that, is one that constitutes the voice of the doubly marginalised that may get subsumed in the glitz, glamour and clamour of creating and noting history, resulting in mistakes, which, if repeated, would become difficult to control, as regards both the depth and spread of their effects, and, while some women in diaspora themselves would not like to be confined by or would even like to outright reject the label, with others trying to stretch its margins to find refuge within its parameters; as also while acknowledging that like all other experiences, the intersectional spaces occupied by diasporic women would themselves be open to varied sub categories and groups and homogenising them would dilute their diversity as those of their experiences, what needs to be noted is that this intersectional space occupied by women, who have been (up)rooted, through routes, is one that needs to be carefully considered, researched and documented, for what it has to offer. What is important is to account for the effect of intersectionality on the diasporic space, at a time when neither the (up)rooting nor the routes can be denied, so that it becomes an experience that is recounted with a sigh of relief and not of pain, in a world in which it has become an undeniable marker of identity – whether that of the individual or the nation state.

Dr. Pralhad Jogdand, takes a stock of work in Dalit studies. He also subtly draws linkages between work carried out and the inconsistencies of research in the current scenario. In this paper the author makes an attempt to review studies carried out in the area of sociology of Dalit studies/weaker sections in Maharashtra state to unfold the major issues addressed by the researchers in their respective research works addressing themes like social mobility, protective discrimination policy, conversion to Buddhism, Dalit literature, community studies, Dalit movements, Dalit entrepreneurship, Dalit women, new economic policy and Dalits, educational enrollment of the Dalit students, Dalit identity etc. The research carried out in the last 20-25 years in Maharashtra provides some valuable insights and also show emerging trends in this area and as per the author some themes have not been probed yet and therefore he intends to identity the unexplored areas for further studies to be undertaken and reviews the studies carried out in the area of sociology of Dalit studies or underprivileged in Maharashtra State in order to identify the gaps in research and indicate new areas which may be examined by the scholars in future. Sociology of weaker sections or Dalit studies emerged as an area of specialization in the eighties. A large number of studies were undertaken and a few studies have been published in the last two decades in the country. Maharashtra is not exception to the studies under reference. Sociology of weaker sections or sociology of Dalit studies is now a common course taught in almost all the Universities in the state of Maharashtra and other parts of the country, Dalit studies is not just a new body of knowledge about Dalits and that. It is a new perspective to study Indian society and to redefine the existing disciplines. After Independence, an illusion was created and hope generated that the path of development pursued by the leaders and policy planners of India will take off the country from a backward to a prosperous and egalitarian society eliminating all sorts of inequalities. After 60 years of our planning and all that what has been the trend of our development, the contradictions of socio-economic order remain almost the same. Half a century is a considerable time in the history of a society to correct its mistakes and imbalances but even at the twenty first century neither the society nor the state has been able to resolve its contradictions; the Dalits have yet to experience the so-called fruits of development. It is in the light of these assertions among the Dalits at the grassroots level, it is the proper time to take a critical review of the studies undertaken by the scholars (Dalits and others) in Maharashtra. The Dalits are not happy with their wretched (ascribed) status; hence they are trying to go for new kind of status. With a view to change the degraded status, the Dalits have used a Sanskritisation formula. Sunanda Patwardhan has made an interesting study of the process of sanskritisation at work among the several scheduled castes groups in Maharashtra such as Ex-Mahars, Mangs, Chambhars, Dhors and Holars; Patwardhan looks at the concept of identity from many angles she also brought out the fact that the conversion to Buddhism did not alter the condition of the Mahars materially as the stigma of untouchability still lingered. Y.B. Damle has done a micro study in the light of this process at Pune, "Reference Group Theory with regard to Mobility in the caste system in India" (1968), he exhibits as to how the Dalit students changed their surnames after Brahmins. According Damle this was an attempt to imitate the way of life of the Brahmins with a view to change their status. Over a period of time the Dalits realized the limitations of this process and started searching for other avenues. S.M. Dahiwale discusses "Occupational mobility among the persons from the Ex-untouchable castes in Kolhapur city", Dalit movements and social change is yet another important theme on which considerable research has been done, and the following studies examined the genesis, development and consequences of Dalit movements on the people at large. Gail Omvedt's study "Dalit and the Democratic Revolution: Dr. Ambedkar and the Dalit Movement in Colonial India" (1994), provides details as to how Dalit Movements arose in A.P., Karnataka and Maharashtra in Colonial period. Recently, B.V. Bhosale has done a study on "Sociological Study of Charmakar Community in Maharashtra" wherein he focused on the traditional occupation (leather), social status and role of Charmakars in politics and Dalit movements. There have been attempts to analyze the consequences of conversion to Buddhism; the tendency of revolt finds expression in creating writings of Dalit writers. It is through Dalit literature, the Dalits exhibited their suffering and dissatisfaction. Its language was new reflecting a new revolutionary consciousness and an ideological awakening, Dalit literature movements has been studied by scholars like Vidyadhar Pundlik and Kulkarni, D.S. Manwar, S.P. Punalekar they tried to unfold the social, cultural and political facets of Dalits. Moreover, they underlined the relationship between self-narratives and sociology. Dr. Ambedkar's contribution for the upliftment of the Dalits is amazing. He made the Dalits a political factor to reckonwith. The use of the political means to change the condition of status of the Dalits was first made by him. Very recently a few studies have been undertaken on the plight of Dalit women. N.D. Jatratakar's study on "Devdasi in Belgaum District: A sociological study", deals with the Devdasi custom which literally means "female slaves of the deity" or girls dedicated to Yellamma goddess. The Researcher highlighted the sexual exploitation of the Dalit women in the name of custom i.e. Devdasi, Sharmila Rege made a significant contribution for the theme under discussion. "Writing caste/writing Gender: Narrating Dalit Women's Testimonios" is a testimony of her contribution for constructing Dalit feminism. In this study Sharmila talks about the specific problems – caste, class and sexual exploitation – of the Dalit women; of late a few studies carried out mapping the impact of globalization/new economic policy on Dalits. The different facets of the Dalits have been unfolded by the scholars/writers. Most of the studies are empirical which analysed different processes and currents at work at the grassroots level. A few studies have attracted the attention of the policy planners and the leaders who have been trying to enlighten the people. The author in his paper brought to our notice the areas which are left untouched they are violation of the human rights of the dalits, internal tensions between the four major Dalit Caste groups, no major breakthrough in the formulation of theory, role of educated elites and their role in social transformation. Such a study may bring out how the role of the caste organizations may have changed in recent decades; conducting interdisciplinary research in this area is the need of the hour.

Dr. Niti Mehta attempts to draw relations between growth, development and inclusiveness in Gujarat. She critically examines the increasing disparity in the process of development. Gujarat has been a frontline state since the accelerated reforms began in 1992-93. The state enjoys an entrepreneurial culture and people's participation in the development process. Gujarat has a developed industrial economy and commercial nature of agriculture. The state is urbanizing at a rapid pace, its urban population increased to nearly 43 % in 2011, being considerably more urbanized than the rest of the nation. Development in Gujarat is aided by natural advantages that the state possesses, such as its location and presence of a long coastline. However, the economy also faces severe constraints, notably its location in the semi-arid region of the country, the relative deficiency and uneven distribution of natural resources. The state is also highly vulnerable to climatic variations. Agriculture is affected by erratic and uneven rainfall that often leads to scarcity conditions, the state has limited mineral base. The state faces severe environmental degradation in several regions, in the nature of declining vegetation, soil erosion, deforestation, water logging, increased salinity of land and water arising from over use of canal water and over drawl of ground water. Up to the beginning of the last decade Gujarat was beset by large spatial imbalances in the levels of development. Development was biased in favor of areas having proximity to the urban corridors. The remote hilly areas in the east and to the south witnessed little growth of per capita income or employment. As a result, regional imbalances were glaring; education and health care facilities faced problems of delivery and access. The selective path of development posed major impediments to distributive justice. The state witnessed considerable growth acceleration, beginning early 2000s, fuelled by unprecedented agricultural and industrial growth. Under the circumstances, the optimal use of resources for realizing full potential of the economy requires a careful re-appraisal to ascertain whether growth acceleration ushered in equitable and inclusive development outcomes or not. Gujarat's economic development has been often acclaimed as a highly effective growth and private sector driven model, in fact, the average growth rate of GDP in Gujarat over the last two decades has been higher than the national average. The author divided the paper into five sections; first two sections traced the economic growth experience of Gujarat in the decade of 2000s. The third section deals with "business as usual" approach, the fourth section highlights aspects that have faced neglect due to growth oriented approach and stresses the need for a more inclusive vision for the future development path. The last section concludes with a brief discussion on how to operationalize an alternate vision. Gujarat has in recent years earned the tag of "most favored state" with investors;

Liberalization process had considerable impact on the state's economy. It resulted in growth acceleration especially in the secondary sector to around 7 per cent, of which manufacturing grew at nearly 6%, tertiary sector witnessed a faster growth pattern 9 per cent p.a. It was seen relative sectoral product per worker in primary sector in 1983-84 was 0.61 and since then there is a rapid decline. In 2011-12, the RSPW has again taken a severe beating, declining to 0.30, this being the lowest ever. Despite decline in the share of output from the primary sector, it is noteworthy that people employed in the sector have recorded an increase over 2004-05. Declining RSPW obviously implies rapid fall in the relative labor productivity in the primary sector and a sharpening of rural-urban inequalities. This is likely to have negative implications for the cause of equity and inclusiveness. Other forms of inequalities are manifest in the state. The development path followed by the state so far has led to a reversal of the equalization process. The neo-classical economic growth accounting models do not lay adequate stress on aspects such as inter-regional inequalities and unequal distribution of gains or the crucial sustainability issues. On the other hand, it is becoming clear that human development efforts of the government have increasing returns while efforts on development of physical capital have started yielding diminishing returns in terms of basic welfare objectives of the government. The "business as usual" economic growth paths aiming at more returns and capital investments often lead to wasteful practices and negative externalities. Gujarat being a front runner in economic growth in recent times and "Gujarat model" of development attracting attention necessitates careful monitoring, especially in areas where markets impose heavy social costs. Hence implications of high growth on poverty, bypassed regions (tribal and coastal areas), weaker sections (SC/ST, women) deserve serious attention. Policy interventions are also important so that unleashing of market forces does not destroy common property resources. A vision for inclusive agricultural development is also required. Gujarat had fared poorly in terms of social and human development indicators in the past. Quite evidently the state has shown noteworthy improvements on some of these counts. There is a wide rural-urban disparity in the access to safe drinking water. The same is true with reference to education. State's education system, including tertiary education requires considerable upgrading. Domestic supply of technical/ professional personnel is inadequate compared to the likely demand. Also, literacy gap over space (rural, urban) and gender for both rural and urban areas persists and is quite high, the other important characteristic of imbalances in growth in the state is the spatial distribution of poverty. There exists a wide variation in poverty levels within the state; it is apparent that the real challenge that Gujarat faces is to remain on a high growth trajectory and also usher in a people centered and inclusive development process that also envelopes equity and sustainability concerns. Despite high growth of the economy and rapid decline in poverty, Gujarat shows mounting pressure on natural resources, land and water, widening rural-urban and regional disparities. Certain sections of the population (weaker sections, asset less, women, poor) are being largely bypassed by the development process. Inter-sectoral growth disparities prevail. Falling relative share of the primary sector bodes ill for the largest share of the state's workers and the dependent population. Gujarat has been a significant beneficiary of the liberalization process and it has been one of the fastest growing states despite considerable shocks experienced in the form of natural and other calamities. But the development paradigm needs rethinking so that the benefits of growth reach out to the largest sections of its residents and sustainability aspects remain in place. The vision drivers in a people's centered approach of growth would be poverty alleviation, equity, empowerment of communities together with agricultural and industrial development. A vision has to have at its core a "non-poor" state, elimination of ignorance, illiteracy, disease and inequalities of opportunities. The human resource base of a state is its greatest wealth.

Dr. Balaji Kendre, in his paper examines the plight of marginalized cane cutters. The paper concentrates on the social stability and social mobility are essential features of all human societies in the world, migration of human population is age old phenomena and various reasons are responsible to happen it. Migration is also viewed as form of social and economic mobility in modern day's societies; the nature and extent of migration has undergone rapid changes in last three centuries when model of capitalist development forced on all societies to adopt its agenda by so called developed nations (capitalist) but unfortunately the exploitative aspects of migration process are rarely studied and highlighted in academic circle. The reason is most vulnerable sections such as Schedule Castes, Scheduled Tribes, Denotified and nomadic tribes, special backward classes and women from these groups are most vulnerable of Indian society are the victims of this kind of capitalist model of development. T.K. Oommen (2001) a visionary sociologist from India articulates Indian society in different way according to him, 'like all societies Indian society too is *stratified* based on age, gender, rural-urban differences and class but unlike many of them Indian society is marked by considerable *cultural heterogeneity* too, particularly because of a large number of speech communities counting more than one thousand five hundred including some six hundred tribal communities. But India's *religious plurality* complicated by the uneasy co-existence of religions of Indic and non-Indic origin is a rare phenomenon in most contemporary societies. However, what is unique to India is the all-pervasive *caste hierarchy* legitimized through the Hindu doctrine of 'Karma and Reincarnation' which is rare and unique characteristic of Indian society. Social stratification or division of labor is ubiquitous and natural phenomena in its origin which help to sustain and function society. The bases of social stratification in other than Indian society are liberal and dynamic in nature where as in India caste is considered as one of the important base of division of labor but according to Dr. B.R. Ambedkar, it is not division of labor but it is division of laborers. Seasonal migration of wage laborers in the field of sugarcane harvesting areas of Western Maharashtra is not age old phenomena but it has come into existence with the changes in agrarian policies of the government forced by capitalist agenda. Laborers come from backward areas of Marathwada and Vidharbha region as well as from western Maharashtra region but most of them come from Beed district of Marathwad which is also popularly known in Maharashtra as the district of sugarcane cutters. The constitution of India has provision to ensure and reduce social and economic disparity among the groups and regions but fortunately people in power have no regret in continuing disparities in the state. The efforts of the state governments are not sufficient to ensure social and economic disparities are reduced; there was desperate need to investigate this type of movement facilitated by the agenda of capitalist mode of development. The beginning of commercial sugar industry in western Maharashtra is very recent phenomena and it is mostly run on cooperative basis. Sugar industry in Maharashtra is one of the organized industries in rural area of Maharashtra. Some scholars believes that the sugar sector has changed the agricultural life styles and outlook of agricultural development, the data with regard to the socio-economic background and working conditions at destination of migrant sugarcane cutters was collected by author for his doctoral work in 2009 clearly highlight that the rights of labor class are openly violated in all aspects. Minimum facilities like food, shelter and security of children and women from harassment by others are everyday phenomena which are unrecorded. Atrocities by local people and by middleman are their part of life. The caste system is responsible for all this because they cannot get united at destination because of caste background; caste hierarchy found in Maharashtra is still operating through its own way of superior and inferior status in social life. This kind of experience is found at place where workers settlements are made. Workers from Scheduled Castes were kept at outside of main settlements at factory site. This paper highlighted how regional disparity and intersectoral migration of weaker section people is neglected phenomena by civil society members. Laborers are the backbone of any kind of economic development and if we neglect the interest of theses section development cannot be sustainable.

Dr. K.C. Ramotra, argues for the the development of Tribals in North-Western part of Maharashtra. The problem if poverty malnutrituin and the issues of health so far after the formation of the new state in 1960 has not been resolved yet. In India the Scheduled Castes and the Scheduled Tribes are such communities, which are deemed as downtrodden communities; they are not only economically but also socially occupy the bottom position. The tribals are generally stricken with absolute poverty, not only in the economically backward state of Bihar, Orissa or Madhya Pradesh but also in an advance state like Maharashtra, which is one of the most industrialized and urbanized states in the country, the main focus of discourse is on tribal poverty, malnutrition and health that are very much interrelated and inter dependent. In tribal societies the relations of production are still homogenous barring a few those who have commenced sedentary agriculture or have migrated to urban area for earning their livelihood. It is easy to understand that tribal societies are un-stratified, their economy is underdeveloped, and specialization is absent wherein producers themselves are consumers. Nutrition is defined as the science of food and its relationship to health, malnutrition has been defined by the World health organization (WHO) as "a pathological state resulting from a relative or absolute deficiency or excess of one or more essential nutrients. Poverty can be defined as social phenomena in which a section of the society is unable to fulfill its basic necessities of life. This paper study intends to measure poverty, malnutrition and body mass index (BMI) of the Scheduled Tribes to comprehend their overall health status in north western part of Maharashtra state. The area undertaken for the present study was north-western part of Maharashtra comprising four district viz. Nandurbar, Dhule, Nashik and Thane and 40 tahsils, the primary data was collected by intensive fieldwork in the year 2006-2009 to bring out the hidden grass-root reality which made us to comprehend the living conditions and their surrounding environment where they reside; what kind of food they consume for computing the caloric intake, for adult tribals the average calorie requirement for moderate work with body weight about 60 kg considered 2875 kilocalories and for children up to the 6 age group was on an average 1465 kilocalories; the work which tribals pursue is mostly moderate to heavy, hence the average requirement of calories is considered for a moderate work. Body mass index (BMI) is one of the important indices to determine the health on the basis of weight and height, attempts to measure the poverty in India dates back to pre-independence but since 1950s onwards a systematic effort has been made to define poverty line; the D. T. Lakadawala committee in 1991 the planning commission appointed for calculating poverty line and submitted its report in 1993 on the advice of nutrition experts in 1993 adopted 2400 calories per day for rural person and 2100 calories per heal for urban person. Finally in 2009 the planning commission set up the expert committee under the chairmanship of Suresh D. Tendulkar who used the National Sample Survey organization for the year 2004-05 for computing the poverty. The Tendulkar committee originally calculated on the basis of a basket of food providing normative calories enabled the person or household to purchase that basket, the change in food consumption and calories was a matter of consumer choice that must be respected therefore, in this connection for the purpose of computing poverty among the tribals as per the Tahsildar office Nashik in 2008-09 any family with an average of four members with annual income (for all sources) below Rs 20,000 or below Rs 5000 per member of the family is deemed to be below poverty line (BPL) and those who were having income above Rs 20,000 were considered as above poverty line (APL). The problem of malnutrition in India as a which a serious one since every third adult and 2/5ths of children are underweight due to malnutrition and more than 50 per cent of them die because of this problem. The state of health of children, no doubt is serious one in Madhya Pradesh, Bihar, Uttar Pradesh, Orissa, etc. but it is astonishing to notice in Maharashtra, which is one of the advanced states in India in terms of industrialization, urbanization and per capita income, more than 43.09 per cent of the total tribal population in the state is concentrated having very serious problem of malnutrition and under-weight of children below the age of 0-6. As per the survey conducted in 2006-09 it is found that on average 56.03 per cent tribal children in this part suffer from insufficient calorie intake. They are so malnourished and under-weight that their poor health condition itself reflects from them. This insufficient intake of calorie problem is very much related to their extremely poverty stricken condition. It was also found that the overall calorie intake for the whole tribal population in the area under study was such that near about 56 per cent of the tribal population was having food much less than what it was required daily (2875 calories) for an adult man moderately active and 11 villages were above average condition of malnutrition. Body Mass Index (BMI) is a simple index of weight-for-height which is commonly used by doctors to comprehend the health of an individual whether he/she is underweight, overweight; it was out found that more than one-third of the tribal population was underweight with much below the BMI value of 18.5 in the north-western part of Maharashtra. The main health problem of tribals in this part is that where they are highly concentrated they are mostly poverty stricken and not capable to buy the food grains supplied by the government under Public Distribution System for them. It was astonishing to note that almost all 10 villages like Umbaripada, Dhaner, Amli, Navagaon, Raikot, Bardipada, Boratipada, Kondaibari, Torankudi and Lagdwal in Sakri tahsil of Dhule district are such villages, which are mostly economically well off as nowhere, the proportion of tribals below poverty exceeds 10 per cent except Kondaibari (15.90%) and Lagdwal (11.26%). Within this, Dhaner, Amli and Boratipada have been identified with all households were above poverty line (APL). One-third of the tribal households in the study area were having per capita income below Rs 2500, considered extremely poor and 17.35 per cent moderately stricken with poverty as their per capita income was between Rs 2500 and Rs 5000. In all more than 50 per cent tribal population was below poverty line. There is a strong correlation between poverty and malnutrition and significant at 1 per cent level. That means poverty leads to malnutrition and finally it affects the health of the tribals in general and their children more seriously in particular, Provision of food grains on *Rashan* Depots in accordance with Public Distribution System; it requires proper implementation so that needy people can get food grains as per the quantity per person is prescribed by the government. Medical facility is an immediate requirement and should be provided with top priority to bring down the death rates in general and of tribal children due to malnutrition and other problems in particular. It is also suggested that development of infrastructure in tribal areas should not lead their further exploitation. Their development is an uphill task but if it is being done honestly and sincerely and with political will, it will certainly bring development in tribal areas.

Vijay Laxmi Pandey & Niharika Venkatesh discuss about food secutity in Western India. The Western region comprising of Gujarat, Maharashtra, Goa and Daman, together constituting approximately fifteen per cent of India's population and land area, contributes around 25 per cent of the country's total GDP, in the western region, Maharashtra and Gujarat together account for about ninety nine per cent of the population and 99.5 per cent of gross cropped area. In Maharashtra the share of agricultural sector has reduced from 24.7 per cent in 1980-1981 to 10.3 per cent in 2008-2009, while in Gujarat it has reduced from 37.2 per cent to 18.4 per cent. However, the number of people employed in agriculture has continuously increased, thus, agriculture is the major source of livelihood for more than fifty per cent of the population in the western region and more so in the rural areas, where incidence of poverty along with under-nutrition are high. Intuitively one may expect that the higher economic growth would lead to better nutrition outcomes through increased income and food expenditures. On the contrary, the high economic growth in this region is not matched by the progress in human development and nutrition status, as per the IFPRI India State Hunger Index compiled for seventeen states, Gujarat and Maharashtra are at the bottom of the Hunger

Index ranking, occupying thirteenth and tenth position respectively. These two states fall into the 'alarming' category, or second highest severity level in terms of hunger; Maharashtra and Gujarat are also among the ten states having highest percentage of stunting in children below the age of five (46.3 per cent and 51.7 per cent respectively). Improvement in the prevalence of stunting over the period 1992-93 to 2005-06 has been lowest in these two states. The intra-regional and intra-state disparity and contradictions are quite pronounced in this region, in Maharashtra, the suicide prone districts-Amravati, Yavatmal, Buldhana, Akola, Washim and Wardha have higher size of landholding as compared to state and national average, it is important to note that in spite of this, crop cultivation is not economical in these areas. This is something that needs to be looked at more closely. However, efforts are underway to address this issue in the research and policy arena. There is in general lack of emphasis on producing food for providing balanced food through agricultural research and interventions. Attention is needed to increase availability of nutritious food that caters to both macro and micro nutrient requirements and initiatives are taken in this area to improve the situation, it is required to have a concrete plan for improving the food security of the people in this region. The large intra-regional and intra-state disparities require a standard "nutrition-considerate farming system model", which can be modified to cater location-specific need. The Farming System for Nutrition (FSN) model suggested by Das, Bhavani & Swaminathan (2014), could be one possible option. This model has been developed to identify location specific inclusive models to address the nutritional need of farm and non-farm families based on their resource endowments and surrounding environment. Western India has witnessed very high economic growth, and agriculture continues to play an important role here. Ironically, undernourishment cases also continue to be very high. If the agricultural priorities are set right and food security given its due in the policy area, agriculture sector has the potential to tackle under-nutrition through its direct and indirect linkages. Therefore, policies that seek to tackle food security through agriculture are the need of the hour.

Dr. Arjun B. Patel in his paper examines the negation of Phule and Ambedkarite thought in Gujarat. The paper is based on the governance processes in last two decades in Gujarat. The paper discusses the ideological propaganda as a state agenda. An ideology is usually defined as a set of conscious and/or unconscious ideas which constitute one's goals, expectations, and actions, German philosophers Karl Marx and Friedrich Engels defined the term Ideology as the ideas of the ruling class are in every epoch the ruling ideas. The class which has the means of material production at its disposal, has control at the same time over the means of mental production, the function of ideology would be the continual reproduction of the means of production and thereby to ensure the continuous dominance of the ruling class; i.e. Brahmins in Indian cases. Italian Marxist philosopher Antonio Gramsci has introduced the concept of hegemony by which he means that ideology's power derives primarily from consent as opposed to the use of force. Secondly, Gramsci argued to expand ideology from a set or formal ideas to include "common sense." By the latter he means habitual attitudes which have been assimilated from ruling class ideas, i.e. they appear completely natural or commonsensical and according to the French critic Louis Althusser mainly two types of "apparatuses" used for maintaining dominance; "repressive state apparatuses" RSAs i.e. the army, police, etc. which have explicit agendas to exert control and "Ideological State Apparatuses" ISAs i.e. the media, education, the family which often function semi-independently and without explicit intent to exert control. In Indian situation consciously or unconsciously the Brahminical ruling class promotes or subverts dominant ideology through its intellectual class. Marxist critics sometimes contend that the social sciences are enmeshed in a bourgeois worldview that makes objectivity impossible. Such thinking has given a jolt to the establishment; Post-modernist writers seem to disdain the ideas of truth and objectivity in the social sciences altogether, preferring instead the slippery notions of multiple discourses and knowledge/

power. Thus, objectivity in social science is very much related with the class interests. If one compare the objectivity in India, the intellectuals of Brahminical ruling class, who dominates this field always talked loudly for maintaining the `objectivity' in Social Science but they themselves have not come out fully beyond the narrow caste interests. It gets reflected in their all the decisions taken right from choosing the topic, its approach, interpretation, analyses, description, up to drawing inferences, etc. Ambedkar said that India has not produce Voltaire; the Christian clergy who fought against his own fraternity who were responsible for keeping the general masses under subjugate position; Ambedkar also goes on saying that if one (addressing the backwards) fight against the Brahminical system, the Brahmins will make all efforts to distract you from your task'. Thus, ideology, hegemony and objectivity is very well inter-related with each other. Seeing the spread of Brahminical forces, Brahminical rightist forces of Gujarat are powerful in all walks of life, since last two decades or so and has consolidated their position in such a way that they are not going to become redundant in the near future, unless something miracle happens. Unfortunately, there is dearth of studies that explains why and how the Sangh Parivar and its associated branches have successfully inroads their ideology in the minds of the people at the grass root level and extending its influence from urban to rural and tribal areas. After firm footing in Gujarat's power position, the rightist party tried hard spreading its net at the all India level by projecting the developmental level in Gujarat, and it worked in 2014 elections and BJP came into power. One will hardly find a single intellectual in Gujarat from the upper castes devoted his/her career on Phule-Ambedkarties ideology. Skillfully the upper caste intellectuals, particularly Brahmin, Baniya and Patidar have never brought Brahminical system in the analysis by-passing the above mentioned perspective; prior to fall of Marxism in Soviet Russia, many Brahminical intellectuals often boasted as the champions of the up-liftment of weaker sections. Of course, it is a matter of inquiry to what extent such studies have helped in ameliorating the condition of the downtrodden people, as they have not touched upon the very basis of system which generates such social problems. But it is sure that it has kept many scholars ignorant about the working of the Brahminical social system. In one of the book written by well-known political sociologist on social movements in India was suppose to cover major social movements concerning the Brahminical social system but instead the concept of Movement was defined in such a way that it has encompasses all the non-social movements which has no direct relevance with the subject under scrutiny, like-wise even in works related to Indian social aspects, the Brahminical intellectuals have not given due space to the Phule-Ambedkariate thoughts which address the Brahminical social system. The author tried to analyze the reservation issue in the context of Hindu (Brahminical) unequal social system and exposed its limitation and hypocrisy of the Brahminical scientists and experts and noticed that the ultimate outcome of the argument of the Brahmin- Baniyas scholars irrespective of the differences in their ideology they derived the inferences that the reservation should not be given in the present form. The OBC lots who form about half of the total population of the country were remained deprived of their social justice and their constitutional rights even after 65 years of independence in which the Brahmin intellectuals have played their ugly role in it. Phule-Ambedkarites ideology the left ideology was also not able to make its presence in Gujarat academic filed. Particularly after the collapse of Soviet Russia it has got synchronized further almost at the level of non-existence. The Brahmins and Baniyas have not only controlled the hardware part of academic world but also software part of it. They have not only established their hold over deciding the academic and non-academic matters like recruitment, promotion, etc; but they set the curriculum what to teach and what not to teach; which topic to take up/ or not take up for research; which theoretical perspective/approaches/framework can be used/ not to be used in the analysis. As of now, no one in Gujarat has studied Varna Vyavastha, no Brahminical intellectual thought out to reproduce the works of Phule and

Ambedkar which are so important in present day situation. In Indian situation the aspects such as caste, class, dominance, hegemony, power, politics, status–quo, social system, socialization, etc, are very much interwoven with each other so intensively; The `state' though its ought to behave in `neutral' and `value free' manner in reality found tilting towards the interests of the dominate classes belong to upper castes.

Dr. Ramesh Dandge, traces the problem of social exclusion. He examines the structural discrimination and routinisation of exclusion in his study. Social exclusion is a multi-dimensional concept hence it needs to understand through various perspectives; social exclusion is the denial of equal opportunities imposed by certain groups of society on the others, which ultimately lead to the inability of an individual to participate in the basic social, political, economic functioning of society. The process of social exclusion and discrimination results in economic deprivation of the marginalized communities in term of high magnitude of poverty, unemployment, low standard of living and social deprivation in term of low educational status, lack of access of housing, medical facilities and other social amenities. In India, social exclusion revolves around the social inter-relation and institutions that exclude, discriminate, isolate and deprive some groups on the basis of group identities like caste, race, gender etc. Historically in India the caste system has regulated the social and economic life of people which is based on the division of people into social groups or castes, in which the civil, culture and economic life of people are predetermined or ascribed by birth and made hereditary which in turn, put restriction on change and mobility. Among marginalized communities' dalits are most disadvantaged groups because due to notion of untouchability and low social strata. The practice of social exclusion and discrimination operates in economic, social, religious, political spheres etc. dalits are also suffer from discrimination in the land lease market. They don't get land for cultivation on lease even if they are ready to pay higher rent. Moreover they are discriminated in sale and purchase of land both for agricultural use and residential purpose. Dalits workers having equal capability, efficiency and skilled are excluded from labor market and those who are engaged in labor markets are subjected to the practice of discrimination either in term of promotion, wage payment and working condition. Thus employment opportunities are denied in labor market particularly in unorganized and private sectors on the ground of the caste and notion of untouchability even though they are found to be equally competence and efficient. Even in the product market Dalit entrepreneurs have to face discrimination in selling their products, even they keep good quality of products for marketing, due to notion of untouchability. Generally higher castes consumers don't purchase goods from Dalit sellers which ultimately adversely affect growth prospect of business of such Dalit entrepreneurs. Therefore their participation in industrial sector as self-employed/entrepreneurs is found to low. In social sphere also Dalits face social exclusion and discrimination in access for social infrastructure like, education, housing, health etc. provided by government public institutions or private institutions. In civil and culture spheres social exclusion is occurred in the public services like entry into temple, public distribution scheme and common property resources. In the political sphere, dalits/tribes faces discrimination in the use political rights and in participation in the decision making process. The cumulative impact of such social exclusion and discrimination has been resulted to socio-economic deprivations of Dalits and created significant inequality between Dalits and non-dalits. Against background of social exclusion and discrimination Centre for the Study of Social Exclusion and inclusive Policy (CSSEIP)), Shivaji University, Kolhapur has organized eighteen seminars, workshops, and also conducted fifteen research projects it was observed from seminars/workshops and research projects that process of racial/caste/gender based discrimination and social exclusion have been active in the society. Due to prevalence of caste system dalits, women, DT/NT minority communities have been suffering at varying magnitudes with respect to social discrimination and exclusion.. Among these groups dalits are most sufferers due to notion of untouchability, women have been victimized due to caste and gender, therefore their participation in panchayat raj institution was quite low. There has been caste based distribution of land among the various castes, land which is major source of income in rural areas has been controlled by mostly upper caste communities and marginalized communities particularly Dalits have been deprived from possessing such productive resources, moreover labor market discrimination in unorganized sector is serious issue.. Hence it is required to implement an inclusive policies at wider scale for reducing the level of social exclusion and thereby improving the socio-economic condition of these communities. Reservation policy in employment market for these communities and groups that have suffered social, educational, and economic exclusion associated with caste, ethnicity, gender, and religious identities has been implemented. However it has benefitted to the small section of the marginalized communities hence the policy of social and economic empowerment is essentially directed towards improving ownership of capital assets such as agricultural land and business along with the educational levels and skills of discriminated groups is required to implement at wider scale. As it has been reality that economic deprivation through economic exclusion has been mainly concentrated in landless laborers, small farmers and workers in unorganized sector hence broad based socio-economic inclusive policies are required for their sustainable and overall development. Against this background, there is a need to rethink about reorganization of existing agrarian structure in which reallocation of land resources be made on the basis of the relative share of social groups (SC, ST etc.) in total population and the relative socio-economic backwardness of the each caste because in rural areas land is major source of income, this strategy would be useful in breaking up monopoly of higher castes over the ownership of land resources.

References

Charmaz, K. (2005), Grounded theory in the 21st Century: A Qualitative Method for Advancing Social Justice Research. In N. Denzin & Y. Lincoln (Eds.), *Handbook of Qualitattve Research* (3rd ed., pp. 507-535). Thousand Oaks, CA: Sage.

Indian Council of Social Science Research (2007), *Restructuring the Indian Council of Social Science Research*. New Delhi: ICSSR.

Social Science Research in India (2011), *A Mapping Report DFID South Asia Research Hub.*

2

Inter-Disciplinarity in Social Science Research

Shifting Goals and Missing Paths

R S Deshpande

Introduction

Inter-disciplinarity in social sciences has been a topic of discussion for quite some time but precious little has been done to foster the interest in the across institutions in India. Almost every research area in social sciences require knowledge and methodology of the other disciplines, other than the discipline where the problem has originated. The history of education in this country as well as elsewhere in the world has reinforced the idea of compartmentalised education and fragmenting the domain of monolithic knowledge. Today in every discipline of social sciences it is the syllabus that guides the entire learning process. The boundaries in the dissemination and spread of knowledge have been strengthened in the delivery system of the knowledge. Researchers also confine themselves inside these artificial boundaries (Blackmore et. Al 1998, dealt with the boundaries confining knowledge).The iron grip of syllabus does not allow students as well as researchers to go out of the apparent discipline and learn from another stream of knowledge. We have a large demand for social sciences and especially the interdisciplinary understanding of social sciences in the policy framework of this country. The World Social Science Report concludes that "Many of the challenges that the social sciences are asked to address required knowledge beyond the confines of single disciplines, and at times income pass the domains of natural sciences and humanities. It is important to encourage interdisciplinary research and to institutionalise it. It has been suggested that interdisciplinary research centre should be created to improve our understanding of social aspects of major global challenges such as environmental changes"(UNESCO, 2010, p. 356). The domain of social sciences has been changing in the world very fast and the need for inter-disciplinarity is felt very strongly. The World to Social Science Report has been subtitled very appropriately as "knowledge divides", indicating that in order to understand the problems of the society, economy and polity we have divided the field of knowledge into small fragments. As a result we fail to understand the reality of the situation to the fullest extent.

India is an institutional economy and an interdependent society. The development of social sciences in India has been designed on the western lines by those who got trained in the Western world initially. Mindlessly, (if I can allocate to use that word), these stalwarts implemented the same process of knowledge in the portals of Indian universities. Indian students over generations learned the knowledge as they understood from the masters trained in the Western world, least realising that many of the theorems and theories do not apply to Indian context. The feeble voices raised by the knowledge oriented teachers as well as intellectuals were suppressed under the pressure of purity of the elitist knowledge. The process continued for over generations for getting that the country like India where interdependence is predominate every social action as well as the development of the society. As a result, we really fail to understand many of the intricacies in this country. Thanks to some academicians who understood the country as well as its people in finest detail could analyse the situation properly. I must mention at this point that Dr Babasaheb Ambedkar was one of those ardent researchers who understood the Indian society threadbare and he was a true inter-disciplinarian. He was an ardent student of social anthropology, an excellent economist, a public finance expert, a barrister of law, and constitutional expert. He had understood the society bottom up and therefore he could analyse the question of caste from its various dimensions. Those interested may read his essay written in 1916 on caste in India or the famous book *"Annihilation of Caste"*. Similarly, in the recent past Mark Granovetter and his colleagues underscored the use of Sociology in understanding economic life, a very simple but rarely visited hypothesis (Granoveter, 1992). There are innumerable examples available in the literature.

The demand for inter-disciplinarity in knowledge assimilation as also knowledge delivery in this country is very large. Blindly following the Western models we have compartmentalised the social science disciplines into small cubicles for getting the large overlapping area and the necessity of understanding those nuances. None of the universities and not many research institutions foster inter-disciplinarity in their research and in fact I found that even in the School of Social Sciences in a most prominent university of this country, there is hardly any dialogue between different disciplines (I was a member of the NAAC team for accreditation). It is strange that the exhibition is belonging to very close social science disciplines never interact with each other nor they would like to exchange ideas with other colleagues. The emerging themes in social sciences research in India essentially require an interdisciplinary frame. I had been involved in evaluation of many of the ICSSR research projects and themes. Not many themes required knowledge of a single discipline and most of the themes were essentially interdisciplinary in nature. Most of the researchers however, lacked training in the other discipline and therefore, the projects may not get full justification. For example, a theme of Impact of Watershed Development is not essentially in agricultural economics theme but involves hydrogeology, sociology, policy analysis, forestry, agronomy, soil sciences and many other branches of knowledge. Similar examples can be had from the Development of Tribal Areas in Madhya Pradesh which needs the knowledge of anthropology, economics, sociology, history and many other branches. All this indicates that the demand for learning inter-disciplinarity and understanding the knowledge from the sister disciplines or bordering disciplines becomes an essential component in the toolbox.

In this paper we intend to analyse the need for inter-disciplinarity in social science research especially from the point of view of planning and policy. Initially we would be getting into understanding the concept of inter-disciplinarity as different from multi-disciplinarity. We also briefly deal with the ARC model of knowledge seeking and then more further to the role of Western Regional Centre of ICSSR. We try to discuss the connection between partners and major trends in the WRC catchment areas. There is a question that crops up in our mind namely "Do we really meet the needs of the region?" And after analysing the needs we turn towards the themes and issues that the Western regional Centre should focus upon.

Understanding Inter-disciplinarity

Inter-disciplinarity relates to two distinct strands one relating to the core of the discipline and the other interaction with tenets of the other discipline. Among the important aspects of Social Sciences: (i) development or most desirable changes in the production scenario, with quantitative shifts at different stages, (ii) emerging institutions and organisations managing development, and (iii) the interaction between institutions and the processes of development; are critical ones. The concept of development began with a pure theory of growth, debated various models of development reaching finally to human development index and manifested itself into freedom as development. The transition had the spirit of inter-disciplinarity as its driving point. However, many researchers are not clear about the difference between inter-disciplinarity and multi-disciplinarity. This is a general problem and could be often confronted in literature (Piaget et al 1970). The former is polymeric structure whereas, the latter is a mixture.

If one thinks of a design of interdisciplinarity, it begins with the concepts and hypotheses in the core discipline of the researcher. When a researcher feels inadequacy or demand for explanation and support from the other disciplines, the researcher enlists the matching concepts and paradigms from another discipline. It is difficult to borrow the concepts directly from their mother discipline and hence need modifications. These need to be discussed and clarified from the researchers of the other disciplines and then applied with modifications to create an acceptable and new inter-disciplinary framework. It is only possible to clarify this with a live example. I along with a student of mine from Public Administration were confronted with a problem. Dr Anitha, a student of Public Administration chose to work on efficiency of Bureaucracy. There are a number of theories available in Public Administration that have efficiency as the core concept. Montgomery Van Wart (*Public-Sector Leadership Theory: An Assessment in Public Administration Review*, Vol. 63, No. 2 (March-April, 2003), pp. 214-228) provides a good overview of the theories of leadership. But after the research the author concludes "Indeed, no matter where you look in or for this subfield, the needs are great and the research opportunities are manifold". That gave us an idea of confronting Psychologists with the theories of efficiency and leadership. After consulting the Social Psychologists and Clinical Psychologists (that was a very difficult period), we came to a point where we decided to administer a Psychological tests to the sample bureaucrats. MBTI test was administered and we got exemplary results to classify the bureaucrats into three homogenous groups. The mission was accomplished combining Public Administration with Social Psychology and Clinical Psychology.

The concept therefore, transcends from, a mere tool of

facilitating the work, to a methodology generating collaboration between specialists in different branches of knowledge. (Above diagram was initially experimented in Deshpande and Raghvendra, 199). The central theme of inter-disciplinary research, therefore, is to reshape or recognize the field of knowledge by means of dialogues across disciplines. That must be dominated by exchanges which are not temporary constructs but enhance the depth of analysis. Such compositions emerge more out of the specific problem of the researcher than a simple tool across shelf. A new extension of the field of core discipline emerges especially from the union of neighbouring subjects of the intended study.

Three Pursuits of Knowledge

There are three important pursuits of knowledge that provide path in any research design. It is emphasized by many authors that information is a power and that can be enhanced with borrowing across the disciplines (Randall et al, 1974). These could be learnt simply from the basic curiosity of a human being. In any research pursuit the first concern of any social scientist is to "attribute" certain measurement to the phenomenon being observed and researched.The measurement depends on the researcher's requirements of *'attribution'* in clarifying meaning and quantification of the social phenomenon.Issues arising out of liberalization and the market behavior require the understanding of economics as also the social structure. Similarly, any of the consumer behaviour studies require basic tenets of consumer psychology. Even the political phenomenon of voting behavior or the identification of dominant caste and the caste discrimination need attribution of some characteristics to the phenomenon.

Quantification leads us to the second important line of pursuit in any interdisciplinary research. This involves locating the determinants of the phenomenon and trace its genesis. *'Relating'* a particular social phenomenon with the other variables defined under the system is the second important pursuit of knowledge. Researcher tries to track the path of the behavior of the social phenomenon with respect to other events in a historical sense. Economists call it regression or correlation analysis but it actually amounts to understand the behavior of the phenomenon in question. One must keep in mind to clearly demarcate the boundaries in the given system. In social sciences, most of the social phenomena are virtually so inter-connected that each of these has some influence on the other variables. In that case it becomes necessary to prioritize the variables, so as to make hierarchy based on the intensity of the influences (for example, the wastages in primary school education can be explained in terms of the availability of infrastructure, the distance of schools, the student-teacher ratio, etc.).

Third, any analysis basically deals with the 'classification' based on homogeneityof the variablesdictating any social phenomena. Classification becomes necessary to identify the homogeneity of the group, but it also helps to map the inter-group differences and attain a control over on intra-group determinants of the phenomenon. There are a large number of factors on which one can rest the classification of groups but such exercise will always be guided by the immediate concerns of the researcher. These three pursuits of knowledge viz., the attributional relational and classificational help us to clearly understand the behaviour of any social phenomenon and such pursuits do not form water tight compartments. In other words, any social problem can have more than one pursuit at a time. It is only through this process that we tend to understand the social realities.

It is here that the interdisciplinarity originates. It has become essential in understanding any and many social phenomenon. Amartya Sen argued expanding the horizons of a discipline in order to enhance the understanding of a social phenomenon. He puts economics in the question box. He states: "The variety of social, political, and ethical influences that the economic approach to human behaviour, as it is rather misleadingly called, leaves out and makes that approach inappropriate for use not only in the related disciplines but also in economics itself. What is problematic in this attempt at extending the so called `economic approach' to other disciplines is not so much the differences between the nature of economics and these other disciplines, but the limitations of the `economic approach' applied to economics itself". He further stated that "It is in fact, plausible to argue that while the gap between economics and related disciplines should clearly be reduced and while the programme of `expanding the domain' of economics is not in itself objectionable, the expansion has to take a broader view of the respective disciplines themselves" (Sen, 1991: pp. 25-26).

Social science research in India has been undergoing a critical phase with the drop in quality on one hand and increasing the quantity on the other. Naturally a large amount of research with substandard quality has been dished out in the portals of knowledge. The challenges in the interdisciplinary research in social sciences are many and one of the most important challenge in this context is enhancing the quality of social science research. Today, we lack in vibrancy of topics, evaluation and accountability of the research conducted by a researcher. Once the searches conducted and published in either a good or an obscure journal the author prefers to stay away from it. Only a few countable researchers continue to revisit the issues that they began with. New journals, new research institutions and private consultancy bodies have been essentially dabbling with low quality research. A few decades back research was a voluntary activity involved with the hobby of the researcher and hence it had essentially inbuilt mechanism to check the quality. The new forces and social sciences and the new disciplines as also the increased availability of the data has increased the depth of the research. On one side the researchers are confronted with intricately involved issues in social sciences and therefore research has become a little difficult than it was a few decades back. On the other side the availability of large computing facilities and software programs have made things easy and save time significantly. However, that has not added to any improvement in the quality of research. Among the emerging challenges to this is to understand the basic tenets of other disciplines and design as well as execute a well thought to interdisciplinary research. Most of the researchers are designed from the precincts of one discipline and travel into the domain of other disciplines. Our teaching in social sciences and the dogmatic syllabus-based knowledge delivery system hasboundedthe students in a particular discipline without any exposure to the other social sciences. An economist is trained only in the economic analysis without understanding any part of the sociological or political science theories. This puts strong constraints on the understanding of a social phenomenon. Added to this the domain of research has been changing very fast. Put a large amount of research is done for the purpose of evaluating government programms, understanding and intervention and its impact, interest areas of the funding agency. The funded research has really taken the entire research field in the direction in which the funds are flowing. Therefore, project oriented research and quick consultancy based researches have taken front seat in the entire social science research portfolio. No theoretical research or long-term research agenda is ever thought of. Researchers are compelled to hop a jump around the research projects and research interventions based on the funding agencies whims and fancies. In this context the state sponsored research is also receding and largely the government supports only monitoring and evaluation research that supports implementation of their programmes. With an increased competition for the research fund as well as racing with others in influencing the state policies the researchers do not prefer any inter-institutional or interdisciplinary collaborations. This is extremely detrimental to the growth and depth of social science research. Unfortunately, total neglect of interdisciplinarity and multidisciplinary has led to myopic understanding of the social issues (Thomas, Alan 1998). This is strengthened by the teaching in universities on the basis of syllabus drawn a just before based on the Western teaching methodologies. The damage is quite significant and we do not have original and incremental knowledge based research.

Connecting Partners: Challenges for Western Regional Centre (ICSSR)

Western Regional Centre of ICSSR has a larger responsibility to connect the partners situated in the western India to effectively implement interdisciplinary research. Given the markets of research and the competition for funding as well as publishing, it is not an easy task. There are four dimensions of this connectivity across institutions falling in the western India or for that matter in any of the regional centres of Social Science Research under ICSSR. First comes the research environment and culture that is developing in the region. We do not have strong connectivity between the State government and the researchers in western India. It is quite unfortunate that the government does not take research seriously in many fields and that happens mainly due to the quality of the research dished out by the researchers in the region as well as the apathy of the government to show any inquisitiveness to learn. Developing research markets is another dimension of the connectivity. In the region research markets have not been developed well especially in social sciences for an obvious reason that funds have not been flowing either from private sector or from the government sector for the purpose of social science research. If this has to be enhanced, social scientist may how to step out of their barriers and take up research that touches the very umbilical cord of the society. Researchers today shy of getting into the problems that would attract larger attention in terms of agitations or revolts. Third, the current trends in social science research are largely dominated by impact and evaluation studies dished out by the government departments or some funding agencies. These do not provide any fascinating research attraction. Lastly, research has now reached to a place where it is totally guided either by the funding agency or by the current trends in the market. Larger researchers either in the form of books or research papers could be categorised as moulded research. The mould for such researches are readily available and it requires the researchers only to board the new data, new region and a bit of new hypothesis to churn out a new research.

There is hardly any attempt to reach out of the boundaries set in the discipline as also set by the research culture in the universities are institutions. It is only this kind of new research culture that could unshackle the researchers from the iron moulds that have been set in the universities and research institutions.

Western Regional Centre of the ICSSR is situated at Mumbai and in the campus of Mumbai University. Traditionally it has been closely associated with the Department of Economics of Mumbai University and therefore has close association with the discipline of economics. That explains the domination of the researchers in economics and it is in the centre past that other social sciences disciplines are also participating in the research programmes of WRC. The Western Regional Centre has a comfortable guesthouse converted from the erstwhile hostel and this is available for researchers as well as research students from the region. WRC is also equipped with good infrastructure and funds to manage research in the region. One of the major challenges however, has been its location in Mumbai and historically its distance from the far-flung universities in the state of Maharashtra, Madhya Pradesh, Gujarat and Rajasthan. This has reflected upon the spread of coordinated research in the region and therefore one of the major challenges in front of the WRC is to encourage the coordinated research in the western region. Researchers from the rest of the region are historically known for their work in sociology, economics, political science, psychology and anthropology. There are quite a few research institutions and consultancy centres in the catchment area of WRC. It will not be exaggeration if one states that the Western regional researchers have been leaders in many of the social science research themes. But most of them have been working either independently with the research centres, universities or research institutions. Reading institutional collaboration between many of the sporadic centres is one of the major challenges in front of the WRC. The solution of this challenge will automatically meet the requirement of interdisciplinarity in research in the Western Regional Centre. One however needs to ask some embarrassing questions at this juncture. The researcher must try to find if the research conducted by the researcher has any direct relevance to the current social problems or provides some solution to the existing issues in the society, economy and political field. The researcher also must concern with the areas of research that help in enhancing the quality of life and causing an incremental welfare for the people. One must reflect on these questions and the very process of seeking answers to these questions shall lead the researchers to get into close interdisciplinarity and compel them to understand the nuances of other disciplines in social sciences.

Major Trends in Social Science Researches in Western Region

History of research in western India is replete with many fundamental initiatives. The Department of Economics of Mumbai University has made its name prominent in the entire world with contributions by many stalwarts. A large body of seminal research had come out of the department of economics in the field of public finance, agricultural economics, macroeconomics, econometrics and political economy. The fundamental research on caste and tribes was conducted in Mumbai as well as Pune. One cannot forget the contributions made by Gokhale Institute of Politics and Economics as well as the Indian Institute of Education situated at Pune. The contributions of the Tata Institute of Social Sciences are unique in many ways and especially when it comes to field research and activism. The tradition and culture of research that sprouted and expanded in the western region is unparalleled in any regional history of India. Among the positive trends we can easily make out the remarkable growth in the number of institutions faculties and research output in the western region. It is however necessary that WRC should get connected with all these nooks and corners in the western region and incorporate them in a coordinated fashion to produce exemplary output. The sophistication in research and technology generated research is also an important component that the western region can boast upon. Another positive trend which has its own negative externality is the increasing specialisation is in the Western regional social sciences disciplines. The micro specialisations and splitting up the departments had taken place in the western region only. That has positive as well as negative externalities in the process of knowledge generation. Among the negative trends observed in the western region is the distance of social science researchers from the policy frame. There are only a few research is that reach the policy doors and actually it is the government which keeps researchers at a distance from advising them properly. We cannot of course compare the phenomenal growth in natural and physical sciences in the western region with the social sciences, but that has an important lesson to learn. It is in the very same region that natural and physical sciences have achieved tremendous growth as compared to social sciences. That is a point to worry. Today there is a lot of social science research output that comes out of the western region which has hardly any use for policy or can be called as adding an incremental knowledge in the very discipline in which it is located. The reason probably is the absence of understanding the nuances from other disciplines and also constructing walls on the borders of the discipline so that no influences be allowed from other disciplines. That has largely detrimental effect on the growth of the social sciences in the region.

When we analyse the growth of researches in social sciences it is necessary to consider the forces of demand and availability of supply. In Western region there are number of social science researchers who can meet the demand for social science research in the region. A large number of them are located in the universities and therefore engaged in full-time teaching. With the growth in the syllabus and the methods of teaching it has become difficult for the teachers to spare time for personal research and therefore the output from the universities has not been comparable to the output from research institutions. Even under the pressure the research carried out in the western region on the issues like poverty, inequality, growth, econometric modelling, caste and tribes, social discrimination, political and agglomerations, history and historical social sciences; have been noted as excellent researches internationally. There is large focus on Empiricism Interpretivism and the methodological traits like dognitivism, behaviourism and positivism dominate the research philosophy across disciplines in the region. The only problem that crops up in fine tuning the research is the absence of collaboration and interdisciplinarity. This is the point at which the Western Regional Centre must intervene and produce researchers that span across the disciplines.

Emerging Themes and Issues

Indian social sciences today are at crossroads with multiple currents going past every discipline. The new forces of liberalisation and globalisation have opened up various issues including the marketization of research. The commercial traits entering into the domain of research have influenced the researchers in two possible ways. First one is to run along with the western culture of research with larger empiricism and second to meet the demands of the funding agencies. Largely, the research and social sciences are guided by the demands of the funding agencies and very small part of it emerges out of the researcher's long term personal thinking process. Researchers are also guided by the current teams more frequently discussed in the international and national debates and discussions. Therefore, it is not surprising that teams like social conflicts, climatic change, social adjustments of the diaspora, gender discrimination, discrimination in the castes, increasing fundamentalism, globalisation, trade and SEZ, violence and intra-household violence, urbanisation and natural resource depletion; are some of the examples that have dominated the research arena. Over the last six indicates we have different phases in research in social sciences. The first phase was more or less a descriptive research which brought forth the nuances at the micro level and inherent contradictions in the social process. Theoretical research was predominant and during the second phase the place was taken by empiricism. Large number of surveys and village studies were carried out to understand the economy and society of the villages. The issues pertaining to poverty and uneven development dominated the third phase. During this time a lot of technical mathematical and statistical work took place across the disciplines and in fact mathematics and statistics came to dominate the research in economics. In the process of the purse. Mathematics a good number of scholars have only attempted to mathematicise this simple economic behaviour. This was the fourth phase in the development of research in social sciences in India. The last phase and the current phase of research is largely based on the experience that the country gets in various fields due to the changing economic policies and globalisation.

There are quite a few issues that emerge here. The foremost being a falling quality of original research and researcher's preference to easy methods of research. Therefore, a large number of researchers prefer a ready-made 'mould' of research in which they would just pour the data and bring out the new issue in the new region or new timeframe. Umpteen number of mould based researches have been carried out and are being generated in the social science research area. We cannot stop this onslaught because that happens to be an easy method of getting through a degree or a funding agency. The funding agencies are also happy if the researchers tow their line of thinking and provide them good glossy paper printed research with exactly the idea that they wanted to get out of field. Today almost every research in social sciences requires strong interdisciplinarity as the life has become truly complex and every social phenomena is impacted by economic policies, social structure, political behaviour, social psychology, anthropological traits and many things. However, a large number of researchers in any of these fees are not trained in the discipline other than their own. That brings the biggest difficulty in understanding the core issue in researchers.

Disciplinary regimentation and cordoning by researchers is equally responsible for the lack of interdisciplinarity. We are shy of asking for additional knowledge to other disciplines. Like in Polymer chemistry a Monomer amalgamates to a Polymer and the process has a lot to understand our gathering of a mass movement in a mob sociology. WE do not ask an electrical engineer the T & D losses and that explains the flow of funds from the State to the local institutions. The trickledown theory and its failure in the Indian context has a lot to get explanation from a semi-permeable membrane used in chemistry. Researchers and knowledge seekers (If we call them so), have become knowledge proof and would not like to venture out of their set paths and strictly regimented learning. It is not preferred to expose our ignorance and hence we carry it along with us as an uneasy accompanying luggage.

Road Ahead

The field of social sciences experienced three broad phases of development. Initially it was largely confined to understand the new phenomena and propose new hypotheses on the basis of observations. Interpretivists dominated the scene of research in social sciences. Most of the works were explorative in nature and the debates were quite strong. Ideologies dominated the stream of thinking and the intermixing of flows was considered as detrimental. As a result strong disciplinary boundaries were created even in closely connected disciplines and neither the faculty not the books were shared. Compartmentalisation of knowledge began and was strengthened. Even disciplines like sociology, social anthropology or anthropology separated and so also other subjects. The World Social Science Report identifies these as eight divides: (i) Geographic Divide; (ii) Capacity Divide; (iii) Internationalisation of knowledge production divide; (iv) Discipline Divide; (v) Divide between Mainstream and Alternative Approaches; (vi) Managerial Practice Divide; (vii) Academics and Policy Makers Divide; viii. Society and Academics Divide (UNESCO, 2010, p. 349). The second phase began with the strong influence of developments in Social Sciences in the Western World. The strong (wealthy) academicians who could afford western education went ahead for training in the universities abroad. They came back as 'twice born' and dictated the path of understanding Indian Social structures and Indian economy. The hierarchy of the fields of knowledge got introduced as sciences taking the upper crust and the descriptive social sciences at the bottom. Voices that depicted the indigenous knowledge (M G Ranade, D G Karve, Iravati Karve, from Western India) were side-lined and the western theories and research themes dominated. There are differences between the national traditions of knowledge and the international flows. That strengthened the existing compartmentalisation. The empirical research across social sciences disciplines emerged during the third phase of developments. Statistics, field surveys and models based on the themes dished out in the western journals took the front line. As a result quantitative and qualitative analytics entered in every social science department. No doubt these have extended the horizons of knowledge but distanced the researchers from the deep thinking and logical positivism.

Today, social sciences are on the cross roads. One effect of the disciplinary boundaries was the multiplication of sub-disciplines and no symbiotic relation in the knowledge generation. We need to take steps to merge these crevices with the new instruments available. Today we are able to collaborate across globe with the touch of finger tips, access any knowledge field at our desk and consult specialists all over the world. The boundaries created hitherto are getting shattered or at least we have the opportunity to do so. It is essential to expose the young talented students to cross-discipline knowledge storehouses. This must begin at the formation level and impress up on them that there exists no 'caste like' hierarchy in the fields of knowledge. Monism of knowledge should be impressed and the hybridisation of concepts helps to clarify technically difficult issues. Institutional boundaries should also be crossed to generate new collaborations and listening to the ne flow of knowledge should be inculcated at the young age. Tomorrow is brighter only if we derecognise the artificial boundaries created in the field of knowledge.

References

Blackmore, Chris and Ison Ray (1998), "Boundaries for Thinking and Action" in Thomas, Alan et. al. (1998).

Deshpande, R.S. and Raghvendra, P.S. (1999), *Inter-Disciplinarity in Educational Research: A View of Process, in Felicitation Volume of Prof P.R. Panchamukhi,* Himalaya Publications, Mumbai.

Granovetter, Mark and Richard Swedberg (Ed.) (1992), *The Sociology of Economic Life,* Westview Press, Boulder.

Piaget, Jean (1970), "General Problems of Inter-disciplinary Research and Common Mechanisms", in UNESCO (1970) *loc cit.*

Randall, Allan (1974), "Information, Power and Academic Responsibility", *American Journal of Agricultural Economics,* Vol. 56, No. 2.

Sen, Amartya (1991), "Economic Methodology, Heterogeneity and Relevance", Deepak Banerjee (Ed.), *Essays in Economic Analysis and Policy: A Tribute to Bhabatosh Datta,* Oxford University Press, New Delhi.

Thomas, Alan, Joana Chataway and Marc Wuyts (1998), *Finding Out Fost : Investigative Skills for Policy and Development,* Vistaar, New Delhi.

United Nations Education Scientific and Cultural Organisation (1970), *Main Trends of Research in the Social and Human Sciences,* Mountan Press, The Hague.

United Nations Education Scientific and Cultural Organisation (2010), *World Social Science Report: Knowledge Divides,* International Social Science Council, Paris.

3

Doctoral Social Work Research

Emerging Themes

Surinder Jaswal and *Melody Kshetrimayum*

Introduction

Research in social work, advances the development of knowledge by investigating problems, needs, events, developments and change in individuals and in their social context. Further, research in social work continues to evolve as a mechanism that gathers data that can be used toward enhancing well-being and socially just outcomes (Wronka 2008). Research enables the students to be equipped with skills for systematic assessment, intervention and evaluation of human problems. The assessment, evaluation and findings of research help students to suggest solutions and promote development of individuals, groups, community and the nation at large.

Social work as an important applied social science discipline, has sought to understand and reflect upon situations with the help of its social science knowledge base and methodology (Sheppard 1995). This understanding and reflection is achieved by conducting research. Traditionally social research was used for making a community aware of its needs, problems and material resources, mobilizing a critical protest against the existing social situation and utilizing evidence as the basis for social policies and programmes (Kulkarni 1964).

Currently, doctoral research has become an important component of social work education and practice to integrate scientific methods with the art of practice to help understand the causes of human problems and suggest solutions (Zimbalist 1977). Doctoral research also offers a means to innovate and make professionals become creators and critical users of knowledge to bring about change and make positive impact on professional practice (Costley and Stephenson 2009). Contribution of doctoral research to knowledge development may enhance social work literature, methodology or theory. Research in social work has focussed on research methods (Philips et al. 2012), paradigms and methodology (Lyons 2002; Nash 2011) as well as epistemological positions (Dellgran and Hojer 2003). Studies have also provided insights on narrative as an important method of social work research, use of qualitative method, debates on use of methodology and predominance of qualitative methods being used in doctoral research in social work. Emerging themes in doctoral research is another important aspect which remains to be studied to locate the trends in social work research. An understanding of the emerging themes will reveal the current interest of social work education and provide a direction for practitioners and future researchers.

Methodology

The paper attempts to locate and analyse the emerging themes in social work research. For identifying the emerging themes, all the doctoral theses awarded by the School of Social Work, at the Tata Institute of Social Sciences (TISS), Mumbai in the last ten years (2004-2014) were selected. During this period, the School of Social Work awarded twenty nine thesis that covered fifteen different themes. The themes of the earlier thesis and themes of thesis awarded in the last ten years were compared. The themes that have been studied earlier were removed from the list. The remaining themes which have not been studied earlier, were labelled as 'emerging themes'. These themes were then analyzed by exploring how these themes were studied, the approach to the subject under study by identifying the `type' of research undertaken, the research design used to study the theme, methodology adopted to study the subject and their contribution to knowledge building and focus of social work implications.

Overview of Social Work Research

Social work research at TISS is a complex and multi-dimensional phenomenon where knowledge, perspectives and practices are often interlinked and compared. The themes of doctoral theses in TISS included planning, services, programme, management, perceptions, support systems, politics, development and experiences, investigated in different settings that range from rural and urban settings to medical and correctional settings and from voluntary and government settings to educational and custodial settings. A review of the doctoral work in the past ten years indicated an enormous increase in the number of thesis awarded by the School of Social Work that encompasses broad spectrum and types of research. The broad spectrum in social work research can be linked to India's ancient and modern aspects of socio-cultural ethos and political history such as caste-based social hierarchy, experience of colonisation, independence movement, the birth of a new nation, its cultural and linguistic diversity and presence of voluntary social work since ancient times (Kuruvilla 2005). The selection of themes by the researchers is influenced by this complexity and diversity in socio-cultural ethos and political history. With the change in India's social, economic, political, cultural conditions and other developments, the nature of the themes also changed accordingly. Besides, significant developments that took place in TISS also contributed to the changing nature of the themes of doctoral work.

Table 1 provides an overview of social work research

undertaken from 1964* to 2003. Thirty nine thesis spanning twenty nine different themes were covered in this period. It is seen that the themes of social work research have been rapidly changing since 1964 with only a few themes like health, mental health, women's studies, criminology and community development being consistently researched.

TABLE 1
Themes of Doctoral Research in Social Work (1964-2003)

Sl. No.	*Themes*	*Year of Award 1964*-2003*
1.	Mental Health	1975
2.	Social Welfare	1978
3.	Management	1978
4.	Social Work Education	1979
5.	Mental Health	1979
6.	Health	1979
7.	Health	1979
8.	Women's Studies	1981
9.	Management	1984
10.	Rural/Community Development	1984
11.	Women's Studies	1984
12.	Disability Studies	1985
13.	Management	1985
14.	Mental Health	1985
15.	Criminology	1988
16.	Health	1989
17.	Management	1989
18.	Medical Social Work	1989
19.	Criminology	1990
20.	Social Legislation	1990
21.	Resource Mobilization	1990
22.	Mental Health	1992
23.	Child Care	1992
24.	Rural/Community Development	1992
25.	Health	1992
26.	Social Work Practice/Social Responsibility	1993
27.	Mental Health	1993

28.	Social Policy	1993
29.	Substance Use/Addiction	1994
30.	Mental Health	1995
31.	Urbanisation	1995
32.	Health	1996
33.	Ecology and Environment	1996
34.	Substance Use/Addiction	1997
35.	Adoption	1997
36.	Resettlement and Rehabilitation	1999
37.	Management	2000
38.	Aging	2002
39.	Substance Use/Addiction	2003

* 1964 -beginning of doctoral research program at TISS

It is seen that during the first phase of doctoral research between 1964 and 2003, themes such as mental health, management and health were the most frequent, followed by substance use/addiction. Themes such as Women's Studies, Rural/Community Development and Criminology were studied more than once. Other themes, namely Social Work Education, Social Welfare, Disability Studies, Medical social work, social legislation, Resource Mobilisation, Child Care, Social Work Practice/ Social Responsibility, Social Policy, Urbanisation, Ecology and Environment, Adoption, Resettlement and Rehabilitation and Aging were studied the least.

The changing nature of the focus of research was also observed. The focus of the studies changed from institution-based or service-based problems and needs to studies that focused on improvement and development of the condition of individuals who are the 'subject' of their studies. Thus, over a period of four decades the focus of social work doctoral research expanded it's vision from the limited objective of studying institution-based or service based issues to encompassing different themes with different focus such as development and improvement of individuals, community, and material resources.

Emerging Themes in Social Work Research

In the period between 2004 and 2014, the School of Social Work awarded twenty nine theses across fifteen themes. Table 2 illustrates all the social work theses submitted during the last decade. With mental health and health themes still dominating in the last ten years, themes of criminology, women's studies, disability studies, power relations, Criminology and social work education were also studied by social work doctoral scholars. However, these themes have also been studied repeatedly in the past.

From the above table it is seen that while eight themes had been investigated earlier, seven new themes were researched during this phase. The new themes are social movements, disasters, voluntary organisations, administration, agriculture, corporate social responsibility and Social Entrepreneurship. Table 3 presents the emerging themes and frequency of investigation. It is seen that Disasters and Social Movement were the most frequently studied themes in the last ten years - post the restructuring phase of the school of social work and institute.

TABLE 3
Emerging Themes of Social Work Research

Emerging Themes	*Frequency*
Disasters	2
Social Movements	2
Agriculture	1
Corporate Social Responsibility	1
Social Entrepreneurship	1
Administration	1
Voluntary Organisations	1

Methodology of Social Work Research

The methodology adopted to study the emerging themes in the doctoral research was primarily qualitative and mixed methods approach (combination of qualitative and quantitative approach). However, qualitative methodology was seen to dominate over mixed methodology to capture the multiple realities that are socially constructed by individuals from within their own contextual interpretation (see Table 4).

Studies with Qualitative Methodology: The emerging themes of disaster, social movement, agriculture, corporate social responsibility, social entrepreneurship and Administration adopted the qualitative methodology to study the emerging themes. Most of the studies focused on small-scale research where personal experiences of small number of participants were analysed. The motive to use qualitative methodology may be that it allows social work to describe itself in rich detail, give meaning to multi-faceted problems and begin a process of giving a voice to the recipients of social work services (Gibbs 2001). The focus of the doctoral research on context-specific realities also provides the justification for adoption of qualitative methodology. Thus, over the last decade the non-positivist epistemology that could capture the reality that is attributed to human mind and actions has been the dominant epistemological foundation of social work research. A more detailed discussion of the methodology adopted by the doctoral studies over the last decade is presented below.

The study on 'living with floods' assumed that people who experience floods and reside in flood-prone areas since generations have lived with floods much before the modern state machinery came into existence and thus, they are most aware of the benefits accruing from periodic inundations, as also its hazards. Their indigenous knowledge, settlement pattern and architecture in the floodplains reveal unique modes of adaptation. To capture these voices, the study adopted ethnomethodology that focus on the methods by which observable social activities are produced and accomplished by members of society. Rooted in social constructivist approach, the study relied on co-construction of data by the researcher and the researched. Ethnography and case study method were used to investigate the phenomenon of flood in its real-life context. Narrative analysis was carried out to analyse the data with constant iteration.

Studies on social entrepreneurship, social movement, agriculture, corporate social responsibility and administration reflected social entrepreneurship, social movement, organic farming and land acquisition respectively as context-based phenomena. Within the constructivist paradigm, these studies assumed that reality is subjective and multiple and is also constructed socially by the participants and the researcher. Constructivism aimed toward interpretive understanding of subjects' meaning. It assumes the relativism of multiple social realities, recognizes the mutual creation of knowledge by the viewer and the viewed, and aims toward interpretive understanding of subjects' meanings (Charmaz 2000). With this assumption as the base, the studies adopted qualitative methodology in which ideology, practice and meaning attributed by people to the social phenomena of social entrepreneurship, social movement, organic farming and land acquisition were studied in their natural setting. By adopting qualitative methodology, the studies insisted on the importance of meaning as it is embedded in people's lives and experiences.

Theoretical, purposive and snowball sampling methods were dominantly used by the researchers to identify research participants upon saturation. The very nature of theoretical, purposive and snowball sampling methods to remain context-specific and the strength to ensure that the concepts discovered completely represent the context of the phenomenon studied (Mahtani 2004) provided the rationale for using them to identify participants. Underpinned by the methodology used, the doctoral research showed distinct use of multiple methods across all themes. Unstructured interviews and observation were the main methods adopted to inquire about the phenomenon of context-specific realities. Other methods used were focus group discussion (FGD), group interviews, oral history and structured interviews. Use of multiple methods not only enabled the researchers to capture multiple perspectives but also established validity of the studies. Since analysis of non-standardised, open ended data calls for procedures which are in accordance with the assumptions and characteristics of qualitative methodology and which permits exploration of meaning in their context (ibid), the data analysis of the doctoral research was dominated by thematic analysis. However, researchers also used diverse methods of data analysis namely content, comparative, and descriptive analysis.

Qualitative methodology facilitates the exploration of complex phenomenon in a manner that is holistic and context-specific, and is conducive to the development of complex constructs so that they closely correspond to the field situation (Mahtani 2004). These features of qualitative methodology gives it the potential to be utilized as the most suitable methodology in social work research. Dellgran and Hojer (2003) also report that Swedish doctoral researchers in social work also used qualitative methods a great deal more than quantitative methods to capture the experiences and meanings from various groups of clients/ practitioners.

Studies with Mixed Methodology: The emerging themes which were studied by adopting mixed methodology were Disasters and Voluntary Organisations. The study on 'household disaster recovery' in the context of hazards such as floods entailed obtaining multiple kinds of information regarding people's assumptions of the risks, their evaluation of risks in the context of their household assets and vulnerability (*etic*) and their lived experiences and their personal interpretation of facing it (*emic*). The author found the pragmatism paradigm (which allowed and guided mixed methods researchers to use variety of approaches to answer research questions) suitable to address this requirement of exploring these dual perspectives. The assumption that constructions can change and are tested and modified in relationships, formed an important foundation of the study. The researcher also recognized that although concepts and ideas might be constructed, they conform to relevant aspects of phenomena that exist outside social processes. Therefore, the mixed methodology was adopted since the focus was on generalizing the theoretical insights gained from the findings of the study area while highlighting the various experiences and perspectives of the respondents.

The study on Voluntary Organisations used multiple unit case study design to explore various nuances of the problem under consideration. Based on the meta-theoretical framework of logical positivism which proposes that social science research is based on collection and analysis of empirical data and findings and conclusions are then derived from this data (Yin 1993), the study used multiple unit case study design that combines both qualitative and quantitative data.

Thus, the need of tackling the research problem from various perspectives supported the use of mixed methodology in these studies. For identifying participants, the studies used theoretical, simple random and selective (purposive) sampling methods. The studies used both probability and non-probability sampling methods to include data that are both rich and in-depth as well as descriptive. While the study on Disasters used multiple methods, namely the in-depth interviews, observation, group interviews and survey to collect data, the study on voluntary organizations used only structured and unstructured interviews. The studies carried out cross-organisational, thematic and descriptive data analysis to analyse the data. Sampling methods, methods of data collection and types of data analysis were constructed/ adopted using both quantitative and qualitative assumptions. Thus, methodology in social work research does not limit itself to either qualitative or quantitative methodology but is represented both by qualitative and quantitative paradigms. Researchers (Maynard et al. 2014) have reported the predominant use of quantitative methods but Gibbs (2001) observed that both qualitative and quantitative elements are present in doctoral dissertations.

Types of Social Work Research

Research in social work was carried out with specific purposes such as assessment of needs, monitoring and evaluation, collection of information to plan programmes and initiatives, and for assessment of activities for social change. Table 5 shows the types of research that the doctoral researchers adopted to achieve their research objectives.

TABLE 2

Themes of Doctoral Research in Social Work (2004-2014)

Sl. No.	*Themes*	*Description of the Studies*	*Year of Award*
—	—	No social work theses submitted	2004-2005
1.	Disability Studies	Study on parental efforts in the developmental tasks of their adolescents with Hearing Impairment.	2006
2.	Mental Health	Caregivers of Dementia Patients: With Reference to Stress, Coping, Social Support and Caregiver Activities.	2006
3.	Voluntary Organisation	Study of volunteerism in Indic faith-based voluntary organisations.	2007
4.	Power Relations	Study on the relations of power in the agrarian sites of village in a historical perspective.	2008
5.	Mental Health	Study on promoting Child Mental Health with families in Jamaica.	2008
6.	Mental Health	Study on Family Response to Women living with Schizophrenia.	2008
7.	Social Movement	Study on Self-Determination movement in Manipur.	2010
8.	Criminology	Study on youth arrested in Extortion Cases in Mumbai city.	2010
9.	Mental Health	Study on stigma, discrimination and rights among persons living with Mental Illness.	2011

10.	Health	Study on the Psychological Experiences of Survivors with Breast Cancer.	2011
11.	Health	Study on Sexual and Reproductive Health Practices.	2012
12.	Health	Study on utilization patterns of Health Services by widows living with HIV/AIDS.	2012
13.	Disaster	Study on the disaster recovery of households in the context of vulnerability to floods in Karnataka.	2012
14.	Women's Studies	Study on migrant single women working in ITES (information technology enabled sectors) in the context of hybrid culture.	2012
15.	Mental Health	Study on participation in the community and the quality of life of people Living with Schizophrenia.	2013
16.	Health	Study on Self-Concept of children with HIV and receiving Antiretroviral Therapy (ART).	2013
17.	Health	Study on Utilization of Healthcare Services in a conflict situation.	2013
18.	Administration	Study on the politics of land acquisition for development projects under the neoliberal regime in the country.	2013
19.	Community Development	Study on stakeholder's perspectives of the Community Health Worker (the Accredited Social Health Activist, ASHA).	2013
20.	Social Work Education	Paradigms of Social Work Praxis with reference to street children.	2013

21.	Social Work Education	Study on Institutions of Social Work Education and the role of social work educators in developing indigenous knowledge.	2014
22.	Agriculture	Study on Karnataka Organic Farming Policy.	2014
23.	Corporate Social Responsibility	Study on role of Corporate Social Responsibility in Sustainable Development with reference to a Social Project on Solid Waste Management.	2014
24.	Social Entrepreneurship	Study on the process of Social Value Creation in the context of social entrepreneurship.	2014
25.	Disability Studies	Study on perceived benefits of school recreation of the development of students with Hearing Impairment.	2014
26.	Women's Studies	Study on informal credit Institutions and the empowerment of women.	2014
27.	Social Movement	Study on Zeliangrong movement in North East India.	2014
28.	Disaster	Study on living with (the politics of) Floods.	2014
29.	Criminology	A Study of Juvenile in Conflict with Law and Rehabilitation	2014

Studies with Formative Research: Formative research was the dominant research type adopted by the researchers. It collects information and data needed to plan programmes, describes the needs of the community or population, the factors that puts people at risk, the context in which the programme will operate as well as the resources available and what interventions are currently being implemented and by whom (UN Womenn.d). The study on disasters in Assam used formative research to examine the political context where governmental policies vis-à-vis floods are implemented as well as people/ community affected by floods. The study identified the most vulnerable groups (Mishing and Hajong people who suffer from the consequences of flood and erosion) to socio-economic gradient of floods. It showed the need to include micro level realities (people's knowledge) in a definite manner for understanding the macro realities. to be holistic. The absolute neglect of people's knowledge has had severe impacts for the communities and the State. The study also found out that the uniform policy with interventions such as embankments has spelt doom in the long run and that suitable interventions to deal with local problems of flood and erosion is needed.

Another study on disaster recovery examined the nature of household and community level assets in order to analyse the structures and processes that influence disaster recovery. It observed that the social vulnerability seen in the post- flood situation was mirroring the social structures in the pre-flood phase where one's caste, gender and landholding determined access to resources through access to power structures in the village. The pre-existing vulnerability continued even after disaster took place. There were several macro-level factors related to floods that were beyond the control of even the social support systems and networks within each village. It was observed that disaster politics was one such factor that had an influence on disaster recovery. Due to difference in political interest, the entire region of a district was excluded from the benefits of rehabilitation. The author suggests that identifying the power relations between the key stakeholders

TABLE 4

Methodology adopted to study Emerging Themes in Doctoral Research

Themes	*Approach*	*Sampling*	*Methods*	*Analysis*
Disaster	a) Qualitative b) Mixed	— Theoretical	Ethnography, case study. In-depth interviews, observation, group interviews, survey	Narrative Thematic and Descriptive
Social Movement	a) Qualitative b) Qualitative	Purposive, Snowball —	In-depth interviews, oral history, observation, Focus group discussion, Case Studies	Thematic and Content Historiography
Agriculture	Qualitative	Snowball, Purposive	In-depth interviews, observation	—
Corporate Social Responsibility	Qualitative as dominant approach	Purposive	In-depth interviews, Focus group discussions, observation, structured interviews	Thematic and descriptive
Social Entrepre-neurship	Qualitative	Theoretical	In-depth interviews, observation	Comparative
Administration	Qualitative	Theoretical, Snowball	In-depth interviews, Focus group discussions	Thematic
Voluntary Organisation	Mixed	Simple random, Selective	Interviews (structured and unstructured)	Cross-organisational

and factoring in the power dynamics of the disaster context will help to plan for interventions for effective disaster recovery of households.

Both the disaster studies examined the characteristics of the target populations and the factors that put them at risk or in vulnerable situations. They also identified gaps in the implementation of interventions so that suitable interventions could be implemented.

The study on social entrepreneurship explored the interplay of opportunity recognition, resourcefulness and capabilities of social entrepreneur/s to create social value by adopting formative research design. The study identified the capabilities of all the social entrepreneurs required for social value creation as well as entrepreneurial capabilities. The capabilities identified included social values, desire to work for a social mission, commitment and passion, self-confidence, confidence on their deeply believed ideas, perseverance and extreme hard work. Entrepreneurial capabilities consisted of knowledge and skills acquired through formal education, working experiences and past life experiences, readiness to fail, willingness to learn, networking and persuasion, innovation and creativity, rebellious nature, love for challenges, risk taking ability, ability to understand changing situations, decision-making and leadership. The study observed that the social entrepreneurs recognized social problems as their 'opportunities' for solving the identified social problems and for creating social values; but they identified opportunities because of their capabilities. After identifying opportunities, they mobilized resources to solve social problems and create social value, but they mobilised resources using their capabilities only. These capabilities were found to influence the entrepreneurs in taking decisions and action to create social value in order to bring about desired social change or creating social impact by solving social problems/issues. The author suggests that the findings may provide guidance regarding areas of emphasis in the courses on social entrepreneurship, thereby helping to design the curricula for educating students of social entrepreneurship.

The study identifies the capabilities of the entrepreneurs as the most important dimension in the process of social value creation that can be used to improve existing social entrepreneurship education.

Similarly, the study on administration used formative research to examine the political context of land acquisition for development projects under the neo-liberal regime in the country, especially the acquisition of agricultural wet land areas. It examined the politics of rehabilitation and resettlement that still depend on the bargaining and political power in the hands of the communities being displaced and which continues to affect the marginalized sections, especially *dalits* and *adivasis*. Policy modifications were inadequate and lacked an integrated vision in terms of social and ecological realities. The author argues that policies were formulated within the neoliberal development framework delimiting social and environmental justice. The research studied the context within which the policies of rehabilitation and resettlement were implemented as well as the nature of conflicts and struggles in association with land acquisition and conversion.

The study on voluntary organizations also adopted formative research to explore the implications of volunteer involvement for volunteers, organisations and society at large. The implications explored for volunteers included personal gains, self-growth and actualization through volunteer involvement; volunteer involvement as enabling the exploration of self-identity and meaning; satisfaction gain through involvement, strengthening the base of one's faith in the community and a source of activity engagement. Implications for organizations included service contribution, spreading organizational message, contribution to organizational development, enhancing organizational image and contribution to organizational effectiveness. Lastly, implications for society included spreading organizational message, contribution to society, social welfare and development, instrumental connection between self-identity definition through the organization, collaboration in organizational mission and in effect contributing to society. The study explored that in volunteerism, dimensions of spirituality and organizational ideology, were being viewed as a moral duty arising out of faith, a sense of satisfaction and community and social network developed there from.

Studies with Impact assessment research: Impact assessment research was used by two studies with themes on Agriculture and Corporate Social Responsibility. The study on Agriculture examined the implementation of Karnataka Organic Farming Project in one of the project villages and farmer's perspectives on farming in this context. The study observed the impacts of the project on farming through farmer's perspectives. The impact of the project on the existing informal network between the farmers was also examined. The farmers pointed out that there was increased farm labour in organic farming. Transition to organic farming was difficult for them without adequate and timely financial support. After the conversion stage, organic agriculture produced higher yields with low external inputs. In addition, the project helped in strengthening of the already existing informal network between the farmers.

The study on Corporate Social Responsibility (CSR) studied the impact of a social project at the micro and macro level, the various challenges faced in achieving sustainability with the help of Corporate Social Responsibility. The study reflects how the CSR project has created micro and macro level impacts such as protection of the environment, community mobilization towards cooperation in maintaining clean surroundings, solution to Municipal Corporation on waste management, employment generation for youth and solution to global waste problem. The major challenges faced by the project were in terms of community mobilization, marketing of the organic compost produced and managing the waste workers.

The above studies adopted impact assessment research to identify the impacts of farming and social projects on farming and sustainable development respectively. While the studies had other related research objectives, the main aim was to study the impacts of the projects. Both the studies examined the implementation of the projects and observed the impacts in their respective fields.

Studies with Social Movement Research: The study on Zeliangrong movement in Manipur examined the identity discourses, perspectives of people on the movement and present dynamics of the movement. The evolution and the changes brought by the social movement were examined by using social movement research. The Zeliangrong movement emphasized identity and the main goals of the research were integration and self-determination of the Nagas. But this goal changed to homeland as other Nagas under the stewardship of Naga National Council were found to be favouring the teachings and practices of Christianity apart from harboring antagonism for traditional belief system. The study attempted to understand different perspectives among Zeliangrong on the movement as it evolved over the years and presents the dynamics of the Zeliangrong movement. The study emphasis was thus on examining the evolution of the movement and how people perceived the change.

Studies with Historical Research: The study on self-determination movement in Manipur documented and assessed the activities by individuals, groups and institutions in the past that contributed to the present form of the self-determination movement. It attempted to capture social change through social movement by using historical research. In addition to documentation of the pre-colonial history of Manipur, it critically investigated events and experiences of the series of armed struggle by the people of Manipur post the forceful merger of the state with the Indian Union. It examined the factors contributing to the self-determination movement and the nature of the movement in Manipur by using historiography.

Types of Social Work Research and Knowledge Building: Studies on Disasters, by using formative research contributed to literature, theory-generation (individual characteristics of members of households and structural determinants were identified as key factors of the household vulnerability), policy planning (the findings of the study could be useful in policy planning of flood management in Assam and in understanding floods as a governance issue with ramifications on ecology as well as the socio-economic and political aspects of the state), disaster management (identification of the power relations between the key stakeholders and factoring in the power dynamics of the disaster context) and social work intervention (engaging and influencing the larger structures and processes will help to affect the household and community vulnerability and aid community recovery).

By using formative research, study on social entrepreneurship contributed to theory building (that social entrepreneurs mobilized resources only after identifying opportunities which contradicts the effectuation theory), social entrepreneurship education (provide guidance regarding areas of emphasis in the courses on social entrepreneurship, thereby helping to design the curricula for educating students of social entrepreneurship) and social work education (findings may guide social work educators about the entrepreneurial and management skills and abilities to be developed among social work students in order to make them competent and capable to deal with social challenges in a more effective and innovative way). The study on administration also contributed to theory-generation (discourse contributes to the accumulation of resources by dispossessing the people directly dependent on them for land and livelihood). The study on Voluntary Organisations contributed towards social work implications (within the broad post 'modernity' frame of taking cognizance of faith as an institution exercising influence at multiple levels, the findings urge the incorporation of faith oriented discussion in the larger development discourse of social work).

The study on agriculture used impact assessment research to bring out the impacts of Karnataka Organic Farming Policy on farming and informal networks of the farmers. It also suggested to include the farmer's perspectives and their way of farming in the policy planning of organic farming policies. The study on corporate social responsibility also used impact

TABLE 5
Types of Social Work Research

Sl. No.	*Themes*	*Types of Research*
1.	Disaster	a) Formative research b) Formative research
2.	Social Movement	a) Social Movement research b) Historical research
3.	Agriculture	Impact assessment research
4.	Corporate Social Responsibility	Impact assessment research
5.	Social Entrepreneurship	Formative research
6.	Administration	Formative research
7.	Voluntary Organisation	Formative research

assessment research to examine micro and macro level impacts created by the corporate social responsibility project. It also contributed to policy planning by exploring how social projects are made financially, institutionally and operationally sustainable and suggested designs for sustainability.

The social movement study on Zeliangrong movement, contributed to the existing literature on change in the course of movement and reflected on different perspectives on Zeliangrong movement based on oral traditions, myths and literature. The study on self-determination movement documented the movements and explored the nature of the movements by using historical research. It also identified the factors that contributed to the self-determination movement in Manipur and established the causes behind persistent movements in Manipur in spite of various attempts by the government to suppress it.

Social work researchers used different types of research to contribute to existing literature, theory-generation, education, policy planning, management and interventions. The studies with emerging themes contributed to knowledge building by identifying the context of disasters, land acquisition for development projects, process of social value creation, implications of volunteer involvement, the impact of the social project at various levels and social change created by social movements.

Conclusion

The review of the emerging themes of social work research, the methodology adopted indicates that social work research is rooted in the socio-cultural realities of the context in which it operates (Vijayalakshmi 2004). The reviewed studies attempted to be responsive to the social needs by engaging in knowledge building, theory-generation, policy planning, management and interventions.

The trends of social work research show that it is evolving into context-specific research which is based on non-positivist epistemology. The review of emerging themes in social work research thus allows us to infer that social work research at the Tata Institute of Social Sciences is evolving with the changing contextual conditions in India and more importantly becoming context-specific. The different themes of research in social work during the early years (1960s-70s) were broadly in needs and services, in social welfare administration, evaluative studies or in the outcome of services (Herlekar 1964). Bodhi (2011) opined that professional social work practice in India is suffering from a theoretical naivety that is devoid of any organic linkage to its own social reality. However, the current review reveals that over the last decade doctoral research has focussed on studying context-specific reality. This changing trend in doctoral research gives prospect for social work education and practice to grow and develop in the country.

References

Biocon (2009), *Flood Relief in Bagalkot District of North Karnataka*. Biocon Foundation: http//www.bioconfoundation.org/bfound-partners-flood.asp.

Bodhi, S.R. (2011), 'Professional Social Work Education in India,' *The Indian Journal of Social Work*, 72 (2). pp: 289-299.

Charmaz, Kathy, (2000), Grounded Theory: Objectivist and Constructivist Methods. In Norman K. Denzin and Yvonna S. Lincoln (Eds), *Handbook of Qualitative Research*. California: Sage Publications.

Costley, Carol and Stephenson, John, (2009), "Building doctorates around individual candidates' professional experience" in David Boud and Alison Lee (Eds): *Changing Practices of Doctoral Education*, Oxon: Routledge.

Davison, Judy, (2004), "Dilemmas in Research: Issues of Vulnerability and Disempowerment for the Social Worker/ Researcher," *Journal of Social Work Practice*, Vol. 18 (3). Pp: 379-393.

Dellgran, Peter and Hojer, Staffan, (2003), Topics and Epistemological Positions in Swedish Social Work Research, *Social Work Education*, 22(6), pp. 565-575.

Desai, Murli, (2004), Needs for Social Work Knowledge Development in India, *"The Indian Journal of Social Work*, 65 (1). pp: 8-31.

Desai, Murli. Jaswal, Surinder and Ganapathi, Sudha, (2004) "Issues and Directions for Promoting Relevant Social Work Knowledge," *The Indian Journal of Social Work*, 65 (1), pp: 151-170.

Gallaher, Carolyn, (2009), *Researching Repellent Groups: Some Methodological Considerations on How to Represent Militants, Radicals, and Other Belligerents.*

Gibbs, Anita, (2001), "The Changing Nature and Context of Social Work Research," *British Journal of Social Work*. 31. pp: 687-704.

Herlekar, Anita, (1964), "Research in Social Work," *The Indian Journal of Social Work*, 25(2), pp. 117-123.

Kulkarni, P.D. (1964), "Social Research and Social Planning," *The Indian Journal of Social Work*. 25(3), pp. 193-199.

Kuruvilla, Susan, (2005), "Social work and social development in India in Iain Fergusan," Michael Lavallette and Elizabeth Whitmore (eds.): *Globalisation, Global Justice and Social Work.* Oxfordshire: Routledge (Taylor and Francis Group), pp. 41-54.

Lyons, Karen, (2002), "Researching Social Work: doctoral work in the UK," *Social Work Education*. 21(3), pp. 337-346.

Mahtani, R.P. (2004), "Application of Qualitative Research Methodology for Developing Social Work Practice Models," *The Indian Journal of Social Work*, 65 (1). pp. 49-72.

Mair, J. and Marti, I. (2006), "Social entrepreneurship research: A source of explanation, prediction and delight," *Journal of World Business*. 41. pp. 36-44.

Maynard, Brandy R. et al. (2014), "The Empirical Status of Social Work Dissertation Research: Characteristics, Trends and Implications for the Field," *British Journal of Social Work*. 44. pp. 267-289.

Murickan, Jose, George, M.K. Emmanuel, K.A. Boban, Jose and Pillai R, Prakash, (2003), *Development Induced Displacement: Case of Kerala*. New Delhi: Rawat Publications.

Nash, Mary, (2011), "Self-Reflexive Student Research and its implications for Social Work Education," *Social Work Education*, 30 (3). pp. 331-344.

Philips et al., (2012), "Encouraging Research in Social Work: Narrative as the Thread Integrating Education and Research in Social Work," *Social Work Education*. 31 (6). pp. 785-793.

Roberts, D and Diederichs, N. (April 2002), "Durban's Local Agenda 21 Programme: Tackling Sustainable Development in a post-apartheid city". *Environment & Urbanization*.14 (1). pp. 189-201.

Sen, S., (1998), "Religion, Relief, Rehabilitation: Landmarks in the Development of Voluntary Organisations in India," *Humanscape*. 5(5). pp. 27-30.

Sheppard, Michael, (1995), "Social Work, Social Science and Practice Wisdom," *British Journal of Social Work*. 25. pp. 265-293.

UN Women n.d. Situation analyses/ Needs assessments (Formative Research) http://www.endvawnow.org/en/articles/334-situation-analyses-needs-assessments-formative-research-.html. (Accessed on 5-1-2015).

Vijayalakshmi, B., (2004), "Building Social Work Knowledge: Some Issues," *The Indian Journal of Social Work*. 65 (1). pp. 73- 86.

Wronka, J., (2008), *Human Rights and Social Justice: Social Action and Service for the Helping and Health Professions*. Thousand Oaks, CA: SAGE.

Yin, R.K., (1993), *Applications of Case Study Design*. London: Sage Publications.

Zimbalist, S.E., (1977), *Historic Themes and Landmarks in Social Welfare Research*. New York: Harper and Row.

4

Social Work Research in Western India and Contemporary Relevance

A Critique

Chandrakant Puri

Introduction

Social work research may be defined as systematic investigation in to the problems in the field of social work. The study of concepts, principles, theories underlying social work methods and skills are the major areas of social work research. It involves the study of the relationship of social workers with their clients, individual groups or communities on various levels of interaction or therapy as well as their natural relationship and functioning within the organizational structure of social agencies (Lal D.K. Das, 2000)

A review of social work research by the Institute of Research and Innovation and Social Work Services identifies that contemporary social work research is weak as it lacks in research in social work practice and wherever evidence based practice exists, it is not accessible to practitioners. There is huge gap between teachers who do research but do not practice in the field and the practitioners, who practice in the field largely but are not able to use research results in field. One more observation about social work research is that they are more like 'social science research' than 'social work research'. This is more so when one looks at the recent studies undertaken in the subject of social work at the universities by the students/research scholars. A trend worldwide suggests that academicians who do research not necessarily use its result into the field or it remains un-utilized as it does not get communicated to the practitioners or the policy makers or to the NGOs involved in advocacy and grassroots work. There are several practitioners who are involved in to action research but they lack in methodology as there are no formal training programs for the capability building of practitioners in India.

In view of the above, a study was undertaken by the author wherein, a questionnaire was sent to the colleges from Maharashtra, Gujarat and Goa to study the practice of research at post graduate, M. Phil and Ph.D. level. Along with other information, the list of research dissertation completed at the respective academic institution in the last two years was asked for, which was categorized and analyzed in order to understand its contemporary relevance. Further, a case study was done of a Premier Social Work Institute to understand academic research at all levels.

Definition of Social Work

The following definition was approved by the IFSW (International Federation of Social Work) General Meeting and the IASSW General Assembly in July 2014:

> "Social work is a practice-based profession and an academic discipline that promotes social change and development, social cohesion, and the empowerment and liberation of people. Principles of social justice, human rights, collective responsibility and respect for diversities are central to social work. Underpinned by theories of social work, social sciences, humanities and indigenous knowledge- social work engages people and structures to address life challenges and enhance well being".

Social Work Research

Scientific inquiry commonly refers to the process of gathering fact-based information in a systematic way. In social work, it refers to the process by which social workers ask questions, develops and carry out investigations, make hypotheses or corroborate evidence (Gibbs & Gambrill, 1998). An essential component of scientific inquiry is critical thinking, which is the intellectual discipline process of actively and skilfully conceptualizing, applying, analyzing, synthesizing, and/or evaluating experience, reflection, reasoning, or communication, as a guide to belief and action' (Fisher & Scriven, 1997)

Functions of Science and Research

Reid (1997) articulated three major functions for social work practice. First, scientific perspectives and methods can provide a framework for practice activities and help obtain the best results possible. It is a way of thinking that offers strategies for action. Second, research is an essential tool towards building knowledge that can be used for practice. Research can serve as a generative tool to develop and refine theories for practice and can be used to evaluate practice effectiveness. When knowledge is empirically grounded, it strengthens practice decisions. Third, research serves a practical function for social workers in the field, to evaluate their own practice with individuals, agencies, or communities. It is common for social workers to conduct needs assessment, quality assurance, programme and practice evaluation, productivity studies, and program evaluation. Data gathered for specific practice situations can be used to make practice decisions and actions.

Need of Social Work Research

As stated by Ilango Ponnuswami & Francis (2012), through social work research, the profession can assess the needs and resources of people, evaluate the effectiveness of social work services, demonstrate costs and benefits of social work services, advance professional education and understand the impact of legislation and social policy on the clients and communities they serve.

It is very obvious that in social work research the study of a problem is from the point of view of social work and that of professional social work. The designing of research, problems, data collection and its interpretation will have to be attempted in a manner as would be useful to professional social work which would add new knowledge to social work theory and practice and improve the efficiency of professional social workers (IGNOU, 2010). A substantive part of social work practice is concerned with micro-level practice, such as working with individuals, groups, or a community.

History & Significance of Social Work Research

Social work has reached a significant developmental milestone in its professional identity as it collectively celebrates over a century of professional practice that targets individual and societal transformation (People & Leighninger, 2007). Historically, social workers have used a combination of research and practice strategies to advocate for improved social conditions for underserved populations, (Day, 2008: Maschi, Bradley, & Ward, 2009). In fact, social workers' striving for "new possibilities" for humankind parallels the global social movement for human rights (United Nations, 1994), particularly with an emphasis on the "intrinsic" value of every person, and the use of individual and group action to promote social justice as a form of equitable social structures that provide people security and development while upholding their dignity".

Since the beginning of the profession, research in the form of a scientific method has been used to understand individual and social problems and to guide, assess, and intervene with underserved populations, especially the poor (Zimbalist, 1977). The United Nations (1994) has made a distinct reference to social work as a human rights profession because of its long-standing commitment to well-being and justice.

Research Review in Social Work in India

A review of the studies by student social workers and sponsored study by the Central Social Welfare Board in India shows that most of the researches employed survey research designs and were concerned with description of different social problems using basic statistical methods. Only a few of these researches used research designs for causal and diagnostic analyses. As the Committee on Social Science Research observed, "Much of the research in social work cannot meet the standards of rigorous social work research and there is s conspicuous absence of competent criticism which would ensure minimum standard of quality. A number of studies have been done on the same problem, these are invariably non-comparable because the methodological tools differ, the basic concepts vary and findings is divergent.

Research curriculum in social work education has traditionally been modelled on social science research. This is most probably the reason why research in social work in India is in no way different from the social science researches. As such, social work researcher largely, view the culmination of research as the drawing of conclusions from the research findings through the process of deductive reasoning. These conclusions, obviously, contribute neither to knowledge base of social work nor to the social work practice. Seldom do they try to test the interventions or evaluate the outcome of their interventions. The research findings have hardly any relevance to social work practice. As a consequence, social work researchers and social work practitioners as well fail to see the link between social work research and social work practice. Most of them develop a notion that they have nothing to do with research. My recent engagement with several State Universities, Central Universities and Deemed Universities as expert evaluator of the research dissertations at Master and Doctoral level confirm these views in totality.

Social work research needs change in its focus, research design, measurement, and sampling so that the research findings become relevant and useful for social work profession and thereby demonstrate the accountability of social work interventions.

In most of the doctoral research dissertations in social work, research scholars have used survey research designs. Further, a good number of these researches were confirmatory researches. It is imperative for social work researchers, to realize that social work research is a problem solving method and it seeks to accomplish the same humanistic goals as does social work practice. For this, social work researchers have to use appropriate social work research designs to study specific topics from field work experiences related to social work.

Ideally, the social work research is supposed to provide:

- Scientific perspectives and methods to provide a framework for practice and help obtain the best results possible
- Offers strategies for action
- Evaluate practice effectiveness
- Helps evaluate their own practice

Methodology Adopted for the Present Study

- A questionnaire was sent to 127 Universities/Colleges from Maharashtra, Gujarat and Goa out of which only 09 Institutions responded;
- 1362 Research Titles / abstracts of MSW dissertations were reviewed;
- A case study of a Premier Social Work Institution was developed to understand the research activities from Masters to Doctoral level.
- 39 Ph.D. dissertations were studied.
- Discussions were held with several academician / researchers involved in social work research.

A. Major Findings

The above graph shows that only 1.70 per cent research fall under the category of 'social work research' as only 4 out 234 fulfil the criteria of a social work research.

B. Target Group of Study

The researchers have undertaken research on various groups. The top three groups were women, dalit and tribals. The lowest preference was given to old age, disability and child related issues.

C. Issues Studied

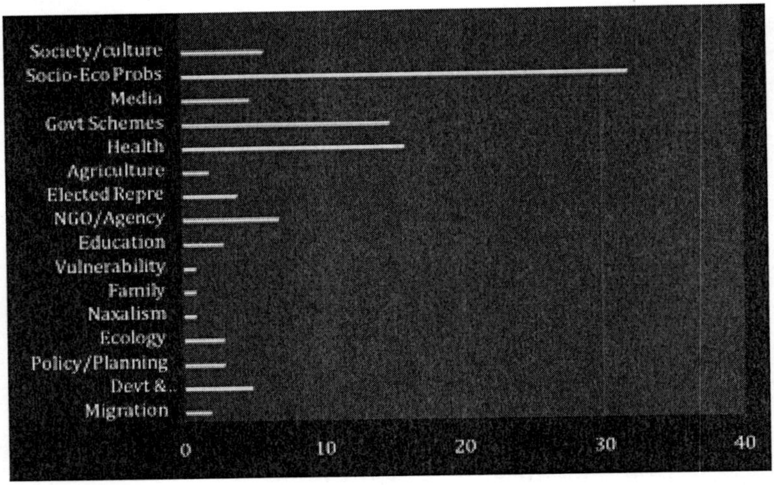

The majority of the studies were carried out in the area of finding the socio-economic problems followed by health and Government schemes. The lowest priority was seen in the areas of vulnerability, family and Naxalism related issues.

In order to understand the research culture in social work, a case study of a premier institute of social work in western India was conducted wherein the content analysis of research titles was done. 39 PhD thesis were analysed (in the year 1964 to 2003) and 55 dissertations were analysed for the year 2013. Following are some of the findings:

PhD theses fall broadly on the following thematic areas:

Sr. No.	*Thematic areas*	*Number*
A	Medical Social Work	17
B	Education	04
C	Management	05
D	Development	05
E	Administration	03
F	Ecology and Environment	01
G	Adoption	01
H	Women Studies	02
I	Disability Studies	01
	TOTAL	39

The MSW theses fall broadly on the following thematic areas:

Sr. No.	*Thematic areas*	*Number*
A	Social Groups such as SC/ST/DNT	12
B	Democracy, Politics	03
C	Right to Education	05
D	Disability	17
E	Children	02
F	Youth	03
G	Labour	02
H	Displacement	02
I	Surrogacy	01
J	Disaster	02
K	Human Trafficking	01
L	Programmes	01
M	Naxalism	01
N	Miscellaneous	03
	TOTAL	55

The content analysis shows that a variety of topics have been covered by the research scholars. The topics are of contemporary relevance. However, the analysis of the methodology shows that a majority of the studies lack 'action', which should be an integral part of social work research.

Overall Observations

- Most of the studies undertaken as social work research do not qualify to be social work research. They are more like 'social science research' as they lack 'action'.
- Contemporary social work research is weak in Social Work practice;
- As defined in the social work definition, social work research hardly informs professional practice. Most of the studies are undertaken in two areas of the definition viz assessment of needs and understanding impact of legislation etc. It is hardly seen contributing in other two important areas viz demonstrating relative costs and benefits of social work services and advance professional education in the light of the changing contexts of practice.
- There is a huge gap between the 'researcher 'and practitioners'
- Research result largely remains un-utilized as it does not get communicated to the practitioners / policy makers / NGO / in advocacy.

Recommentations

1. The Social Work research methodology should be promoted in all schools of social work. Wherever possible, the methodology should be taught in the workshop mode with the aim of developing research skills among the student social workers.
2. Social work research must be conducted using social work research methodology where action is an integral part. This must be made compulsory to be made eligible for the degree in social work.
3. Social work research must also be conducted on neglected aspects such as cost benefit analysis of the service system and advanced professional education.
4. Social Work Colleges / Institutes must prepare documents on 'research needs' based on the local conditions and efforts should be made to follow the

same so that the local issues can be studied scientifically.

5. A wide gap is seen among social work research teachers and practitioners. This should be narrowed down. The institutes must organise interface programme with the local agencies and conduct capacity building program for the practitioners in research methodology.
6. Social work educators and researchers must conduct joint research which will be useful for social work practitioners.
7. In order to utilise social work research results, dissemination workshops should be organised and publications should be planned so that the same can be utilised for social action, social policy making and advocacy.

References

Ghosh, Lal Das, Bhaskaran (2008), *Research Methods for Social Work Hardcover*, SAGE Publications, New Delhi.

http://ifsw.org/policies/definition-of-social-work/

http://www.socialworkpolicy.org/research

https://catalogue.pearsoned.co.uk/assets/hip/gb/hipgbpearsonhighered/samplechapter/0205594948.pdf

http://docplayer.net/520003-Social-work-research-and-evaluation-foundations-in-human-rights-and-social-justice.html

http://www.criticalthinking.org/pages/critical-thinking-where-to-begin/796

http://www.academia.edu/3395378/Social_Work_-_Research_Perspectives

Mathew Grace, 2010, *Social Work Research*, IGNOU, New Delhi.

Ponnuswami, I. & Francis A., (2012), "Professional Social Work Research Perspective", Delhi, Authorpress.

The Institution for Research and Innovation Social Work Services: Practitioners Research in Social Services Literate review. http://docplayer.net/520003-Social-work-research-and-evaluation-foundations-in-human-rights-and-social-justice.html

5

Trends in Methodology of Doctoral Research in Social Science

Anil S. Sutar

Introduction

Research methodology has been regarded as a crucial requirement for the social science research. However, what is understood as research methodology is a quite problematic. Most of the disciplines in social science have directly or indirectly been influenced by the methods of natural sciences. It has been argued that there could be possibility of unified methodology leading to social scientists emulating the methods of natural sciences. The philosophical assumption that methods of natural sciences can also be used to explain social reality has led to methodological monism in social science. This has led to the dominance of positivist approach to research in social sciences. The human beings have been assumed to be capable of being studied like objects. This approach has given larger scope for statistical tools and methods in social science research. The importance of quantitative/statistical aspects in social science research have been exaggerated to such an extent that any research without statistical treatments is looked down and not considered as scientific. In this context, Burgess (1981) mention the reports of Clapham (1946) and Heyworth (1965) committees which dealt with the requirements of social research. He reveals that both these reports emphasizes on statistical and mathematical skills as crucial for social science research. This has led to methodological monism where methodology basically focused on sampling, data processing and computer programming and statistical analysis. This in turn has promoted quantitative research methods especially surveys as dominant research design in social sciences. The issues of looking at social reality from different perspectives, empathetic understanding of the researched, the field work could not gain any importance in the methodological deliberations of social sciences. Burgess (1981) reveals that the reports of Clapham (1946) and Heyworth (1965) did not mention anything related to research design. Nor is there any mention of sociologists employing a range of methods or requiring competence in fieldwork techniques such as participant observation and unstructured interviewing, in acquiring the ability to handle personal documents,oral history data, and historical materials. In the context of India, the importance of statistics and computer application have been overemphasized in social science research. To cite an example, the UGC (minimum standards and procedure for awards of M.Phil/Ph.D. Degree) Regulation, 2009 only mention about quantitative methods and computer applications as necessary components of course on research methodology for the M. Phil and Ph.D programmes. Hence, in the history of growth of social science research, the quantitative methodology was the dominant way of doing research and an ability to use statistical techniques was of paramount importance.

Social scientists in India as elsewhere in the world have been emulating the methods of natural sciences with an understanding that their research would be considered more scientific. It has been observed that the experts of quantitative methods advise the feminist researchers and those researchers who adopt qualitative methods to use numbers(sample) and statistics so that their studies could also claim the status of scientific. In one sense, following methods of natural sciences has emerged as *'methodological sanskritization'* where social science researchers by using statistics and computer softwares try to achieve up-ward mobility – towards more scientific status from that of anecdotal status. Thus, there are concerns that in most of the cases, the emulation of methods of natural sciences just ends up as ritual without contributing to the advancement of theorization and conceptualization in social sciences.

Over a period of time efforts have been made to broad base social science research methodology and to encourage use of 'other' methods in research. Sil (2000) argues that it seems worthwhile to set aside the quest for uniform methodological tenets in favour of greater methodological pluralism, shifting the focus from common rules or standards to a common appreciation of the trade-offs involved in pursuing different methods and research products. The Indian Council of Social Science Research (ICSSR), through its various policy guidelines, workshops and other knowledge dissemination activities took lead in encouraging methodological pluralism in social science research in India. It is quite evident that qualitative methods are accorded equal weightage in the ICSSR sponsored workshops on research methodology. Along with moving towards methodological pluralism, the research methodology need to be understood in a broader sense where it help the researchers to address the philosophical, logical and moral questions that confronts them during the research. Burgess(1981) contends that research methodology could help students to consider the links between problem and method and between theory and data. It is understood that now a days most of the universities impart research methodology teaching in more holistic manner. The paper explores the shifts that have taken place in the research methodology of social sciences by analyzing the methodology components of the doctoral theses awarded in social sciences by a social science institute.

Methodology

The study is based on the content analysis of 105 Ph.D theses awarded in inter-disciplinary areas of social science by a reputed social science institute based in Mumbai. The analsysis includes the first very thesis in social science awarded in 1971 and the theses awarded thereafter till 2014. The time period of 1970 to 2014 is also sufficient enough to reflect on the possible trends across different periods. All theses are available to public access through the website of the institute. These theses pertain to disciplines such as management, sociology,education, psychology, anthropology, health studies. Since, the thrust of the institute is on inter-disciplinary and multi-disciplinary research, the Ph.D have been awarded in the broader umbrella of social science. Based on the primary objective of the study i.e., to understand the changes taking place in the methodological components of doctoral theses, several parameters such as type of methodology, type of research design/method, discussion of different aspects of methodology, nomenclature of methodology chapter in theses have been identified and data are analyzed on these themes across different time periods to understand the trends.

Analysis and Discussion

Towards methodological pluralism: The study found that quantitative methodology was dominant during 1970s, 1980s and 1990s as methodology of social science theses. However, doctoral theses are increasingly adopting non – quantitative methodologies from the year 2000 onwards. The qualitative methodology has become quite popular among doctoral scholars during 2000s, 2010s and afterwards. It can be noticed that the mixed methods also started gaining importance along with qualitative methods (see Table 1.1). This is paradigmatic shift as there was a time where no one thought of social science research without having numbers. Moreover, the trends shows that the phenomenon of reconciliation between quantitative and qualitative methods is quite active now a days which is reflected in the fact that scholars adopting mixed methods is quite significant during 2000s and 2010s. Thus, one could not jump to the conclusion that quantitative methods of have been sidelined in favour of qualitative methods in the social science research but social sciences have become more eclectic.

TABLE 1.1
Methodology adopted in Doctoral theses across different time periods

Period	*Type of Methodology*			*Total*
	Quantitative	*Qualitative*	*Mixed Methods*	
1970-79	7	—	—	7
1980-89	10	—	—	10
1990-99	19	1	1	21
2000-2009	13	15	5	33
2010-2014	6	19	9	34
Total	55	35	15	105

Towards diversity of research designs: It is not only pluralism in terms of qualitative methodology gaining importance on par with quantitative one but it is also diversity of research designs/methods within the framework of qualitative methodology that has further enriched the element of methodological pluralism in social science theses. It can be noticed that during 1990s qualitative research confined only to ethnography as method of study. However, it adopted various other designs such as case studies, participatory action research and ethnographic studies from 2000 onwards (see Table 1.2). The overall trend shows that doctoral theses in the social sciences are moving towards methodological plurism from that of methodological monism.

Towards dealing with methodological issues in more nuanced/sophisticated way: It is found that doctoral theses in social science during 2000s and onwards have given fair treatment to methodological issues than those theses of 1970s and 1980s. Several parameters such as whether the research methodology was treated in a separate chapter in the theses,

TABLE 1.2
Research designs/methods adopted in the theses

Period	*Research designs/methods*						*Total*
	Survey	*Comparative Study*	*Case Studies*	*Ethnography*	*Participatory Action research/ Intervention studies*	*Mixed Methods*	
1970-79	7		—	—	—	—	7
1980-89	10	—	—	—	—	—	10
1990-99	16	3	—	1	—	1	21
2000-2009	13	—	11	4	—	5	33
2010-2014	5	1	13	3	3	9	34
Total	51	4	24	8	3	15	105

whether there was clarity in writing the title of the methodology chapter and the complexity of methodological issues discussed in the methodology chapter have been analyzed to demonstrate the degree of sophistication of dealing with methodological issues across the time periods. As far as, writing research methodology as a separate chapter is concerned, there is no such significant difference across different time periods. It is found that research methodology has been treated fairly well by way of allocating a full-fledged chapter for it in almost all the time periods (see Table 1.3).

TABLE 1.3
Location of Research Methodology in the structure of the theses

Period	*Location of Research Methodology*		*Total*
	As part of other chapter	*As a separate chapter*	
1970-79	3	4	7
1980-89	--	10	10
1990-99	2	19	21
2000-2009	2	31	33
2010-2014	6	28	34
Total	13	92	105

However, when it comes to the nomenclature of the research methodology chapter, it is found that there is significant difference across the time periods. It can be noticed that the period from 1970s till 1999 marked quite uncertainty in using the title for methodology chapters. This could be the reflection of the lack of clarity on what constitute research methodology. It could also because of the fact that during those days research methodology was understood in more narrower sense of treating it as design or plan of the study. That is why during this period research methodology was sometimes understood as research plan and design. There is considerable understanding about the nomenclature of research methodology chapters from 2000 onwards. During this period, it is found that narrower notion of methodology

TABLE 1.4
Nomenclature of Research methodology chapter in the theses

Period	*Nomenclature of Research methodology chapter*				*Total*
	Not applicable (as there is no separate chapter)	*Introduction/ Problem/Study*	*Research Design*	*Methods/Methodology/ Research Methodology*	
1970-79	3	—	4	—	7
1980-89	—	4	3	3	10
1990-99	2	—	2	17	21
2000-2009	2	3	2	26	33
2010-2014	6	—	—	28	34
Total	13	7	11	74	105

as research design is being replaced with a much broader notion of research methodology (see Table 1.4)

Similarly a distinct patterns across different time periods have been noticed in terms of the methodological issues discussed in the research methodology chapters. Most of the doctoral theses from the period 1970s till 1999 dealt basically with more technical aspects of data collection such as tools for data collection, sampling, variables, hypotheses and respondents. There was hardly any discussion about philosophical issues concerned about the nature of reality (Ontology), the best way to acquire the knowledge about the reality (epistemology) and discussion about logic. Whereas the doctoral theses from 2000s onwards have engaged with more critical issues of methodology. This critical element is found in all types of research – quantitative, qualitative and mixed methods of that period (see Table 1.5).

TABLE 1.5
Issues discussed under Research Methodology chapter in the theses

Period	*Issues disscussed*		*Total*
	Techniques and Methods	*Ontology; Epistemology; logic and methods and techniques*	
1970-79	7	—	7
1980-89	10	—	10
1990-99	15	6	21
2000-2009	8	25	33
2010-2014	6	28	34
Total	46	59	105

Research ethics at the periphery: It is quite evident that research ethics is an important pillar of research on par with ontology, epistemology, logic and methods. However, it is found that no serious treatment is given to research ethics in social science research. It can be seen that research ethics was not at all discussed in the theses of 1970s, 1980s and 1990s.

Some of the theses from the period 2000 to 2014 do mention ethics but they never deal with critical issues of research ethics. These theses basically confine research ethics to mention about informed consent and issues of confidentiality in few lines. It is also found that most of theses in social science across different periods discuss about limitations of the study such as researcher's inability to select large sample, the study not being able to make generalizations. But the issues of researcher's relation with researched, the rapport building, principles of maleficence, justice and ethical dilemmas have not been discussed. It is found that only few theses from the period 2010-14 could critically engage with research ethics (see Table 1.6).

TABLE 1.6
Discussion about ethical issues in the Methodology chapters of the theses

Period	*Discussion of research ethics*			*Total*
	No Discussion	*Discussed somewhat*	*Detailed Discussion*	
1970-79	7	—	—	7
1980-89	10	—	—	10
1990-99	21	—	—	21
2000-2009	28	5	—	33
2010-2014	18	8	8	34
Total	84	13	8	105

Conclusion: Several changes have been found in the methodological aspects of social science doctoral theses across different time periods. Quantitative methodology which was dominant form of doing research during earlier decades has given way to Qualitative and Mixed methods. Now a days, there is also diversity in terms of research designs/methods of the study within qualitative research. Thus research methodology is moving from methodological monism towards methodological pluralism. Compared with the theses of 1970s, 1980s and 1990s, the doctoral theses of 2000s and onwards engage with methodological issues in more critical and nuanced manner. The relation of theory and data, ontology, epistemology, logic and methods are dealt in more critical manner in theses of present days than that of 1990s and before. However, research ethics which forms the core of methodology has not yet received considerable attention of the doctoral theses in social science.

References

Burgess, G.R., (1981), Objectives in teaching and using Research Methodology. *Sociology*, Vol. 15, No. 4.

Rudra, Sil, (2000), The Division of Labour in Social Science Research; Unified Methodology or "Organic Solidarity"? *Polity*, Vol. 32, No. 4.

The UGC (minimum standards and procedure for awards of M.Phil/ Ph.D.Degree) Regulation, 2009 accessed from the UGC website http://www.ugc.ac.in/oldpdf/regulations/mphilphdclarification.pdf

6

Research in Education
Retrospect and Prospects

Shefali Pandya

Retrospect

Salient Features of the Trends in Educational Research

1. Most of the research is concerned with the process of education and/or teaching or the pedagogy rather than its consequences with an emphasis on the dependent-independent variables model (treatment and its effect). There is very little effort to understand how this effect takes place or the multiple effects of several variables on complex human behaviour.
2. A large majority of correlational and experimental studies produce trivial results and do not account for more than 10 % of variance in the outcome variables.
3. Research usually takes into account one or two variables at a time and thus, dictum of "whole is bigger than the parts" is lost sight of. There is little effort to study the context of education as a dynamic part of the culture.

4. The present trends in educational research do not take into account the meaning of an experience for the participants of a study. This leavesout understanding how and why a person behaves in a particular manner.
5. A large part of current research focuses attention on identifying gender or school type differences without trying to understand why these differences arise or how to deal with the consequences of such differences.
6. Many of the research are a-theoretical in nature.
7. There is a complete lack of R & D policy at the macro level as well as at the University level. Thus, research conducted by academicians has no link with national development and is unable to solve problems identified the larger system.
8. There is a complete lack of a review at the university level of the research conducted and its impact on educational policies and practices.
9. Increasingly, educators are looking to research about how students learn to influence teaching practices and tools. What seemed like on-the-fringe experiments, like game-based learning, have turned into real trends, and have gradually made their way into many (though certainly not most) classrooms. This includes in particular, research on (a) Brain-Based Teaching, (b) Game-Based Learning, (c) Power of Perseverance, (d) Questioning Homework and (e) Cultivating Creativity.
10. The trend of tool construction as a research study started in the 1970s and has continued till today. Strictly speaking, constructing a tool is not a research study in itself.
11. The volume of empirical research in education has increased considerably thanks to the necessity of API. However, the contribution of research in terms of improvements in the form of insights it provides into the empirical complexities, in empirical techniques, and its applications is not as high. Few significant

methodological improvements have taken place. After all, multiplication of number of blind applications of a technique to new and old sets of data does not form progress in applied research.

12. Equally important is a shift from empirical to action research. Action research hasbecome a hot favourite a few teachersespecially among school teachers. Except for a few action research programmes, many action research activities end up in a fiasco, essentially because action research cannot be an alternative to theoretical and empirical research.
13. Most of the action research jump into it without fulfilling the basic condition of a sound theoretical formulation of a viable development model and as a result they cannot but fail. They may be having genuine educational and social commitment. But this commitment is a necessary, but not a sufficient condition for the success of action research programmes. Neither action nor research could be found finally in such action research programmes as these do not bring about a long term and genuine change in the educational context, processes or outcomes.
14. In case of a few internationally funded projects, there is a tendency in the recent past towards a shift from data analysis to collection and compilation of data. The international funding agencies which do not know even the basic information about us or a given region, seem to be more interested in information rather than the analysis. Researchers play to the tune of those who pay for.
15. There is a change in the terminology too. The term'research study' is becomingold-fashioned. Now-a-days it is called 'research report' or simply and more commonly 'report'. This shift in terminology has important bearing on our thinking. The primary role of the researcher becomes not 'studying', but 'reporting'. This reporting is to the society and to the funding agency. Reporting on research theme,

issues etc. have become secondary in such cases.

16. There is also a shift seen in terms of research production to research management. The role of the researchers is not necessarily restricted to conducting research, but its co-ordination. Researchers become research managers whose focus is expected to be not knowledge production but utilisation of finances allotted to it and the associated bureaucratic procedures. The funding agencies do not make any distinction between research and any other area of physical output production on the one hand, and between research in education and any other area, serve as 'brokers' between financiers of research and researchers. Thus the shift takes place from conducting of research to co-ordination and management of research.
17. A large majority of the research studies are quantitative in nature. Even those studies which claim to have collected qualitative data are largely adopting the post-positivist paradigm. However, these assumptions and convictions are being increasingly questioned. There is a gradual but slow shift towards the adoption of the constructivist/interpretive paradigm. In the past four or five years, there is a very slow movement towards the adoption of the transformative and pragmatic paradigm of research with the use of mixed methods design.
18. There is a split between the functions of teaching and conducting research. An important reason forthis divide between teaching and research was theseparation of the personnel and location of the two activities. Till the middle of 1970's, most research in the field of education took place in the University Departments of Education. It wasundertaken by teachers and, therefore, could get incorporated directly and quickly, if notspontaneously, in teaching and reference material and class room instruction. A systemof encouraging research among teachers by

making 'contribution to knowledge' as animportant criterion in appointment predominantly at higherlevels, had beenin place in the Indian university system from as far back as 1920's (Shah, 2005).

19. An increase in teaching load,which was also prescribed as 'norms' by University Grants Commission around thattime, left very little time for research for teachers in most universitydepartments and affiliated colleges. Those with higher levels of motivation and able to put in extra effort also found itdifficult to carry out any additional projects due to rather rigid bureaucratic financial and administrative procedures in the universities. Universityresearch got mostly confined to masters and doctoral degree dissertations the quality of which alsodeteriorated due to lack of adequate rigorous supervision.
20. The masters' degree research can hardly be called knowledge in the true sense and is restricted to surveys, single group experimental research, identifying problems of students or teachers and identifying and analyzing types of errors made by students. Thus, any claims of research traditions in the field of education in the university departments being strong and vibrant is mostly confined to doctoral research and funded research.
21. There is corruption in research at the Master's degree level.
22. Moreover, after the implementation of the sixth pay commission, there is a tremendous jump in the number of publications on account of API and the requirement of at least two publications by each PhD student. Many of these lack rigour and are paid publications in substandard journals.
23. The importance of educational research for advancement of knowledge and for social policy formulation is widely recognised. Educational research based on empirical data and material yields results and implications that could be used for short

and medium term strategies, policies and programmes for not only educational development but also social, political and economic development. However, little research has been undertaken by individuals by in to evaluate the on-going policies and programmes and its findings were used to revise, modify and change them. Most of the research specifically aimed at evaluating policies has been conducted either by national institutions and that sponsored by government agencies with specific objectives of examining the performance of policies and programmes found use in decision making. A very large majority of educational research is termed by policy makers 'academic', implying that it is not of use for policy making. This is partially true as many researchers often do not consider it important to work on subjects or questions of direct bearing on policy and sometimes treat such research as of inferior variety. The importance of an anticipated and direct relationship between rationally comprehensive scientific research and coherent and sound policy formulation was often lost and a false dichotomy between 'academic' research and 'relevant' policy educational research developed. In fact, it has been observed that critical analytical research on various policy issues is gradually replaced by research on how to implement the government programmes and policies. On account of the emphasis on policy relevant research, as against 'abstract' or 'academic' research, researchers are required to highlight the policy relevance (use) of their research proposals and to highlight policy implications of their concluded studies. Thus prescriptive research is more valued than analytical research. The prescriptions, however, tend to be more generalised, non-controversial, than location/region specific. As the phenomenon of policy use dominates the whole research scene, it is not surprising to find condemnation of 'other' research as 'academic' research, or 'professional' research, if not as extraneous research.

24. In the same context, evaluative research, i.e., evaluation of the programmes (generally state supported or internationally supported) also takes a crucial place. Such policy relevant research — research on implementation and evaluation—also necessitates speedy results. As a result, preference for public support for research shifts from 2-5 years (or longer) duration research studies to 3-6 months (or shorter) duration, if not instantaneous research studies. The consequence of all this is the emergence of fast-buck, short-cut, quick-result oriented research culture. Research reports are 'manufactured' practically overnight. When research design, research methodologies, sample design, statistical techniques, etc., are common, the modern technology, particularly the computers and widespread availability of software packages also come very handy in manufacturing research reports in a short time even by the novice. The contribution of "professional (commercial)" consultants in this business is also noticeable. In fact, expected to enhance their bio-data. There is a distinct shift from conducting research to managing research in some cases. Often in the case of funded or sponsored research, Gresham's law holds good : "bad money drives out the good.'
25. There have been instances of research studies by all the students of the same guide on the same theme but involving different locations or different standards/classes/subjects without any variations and without significant knowledge generation.
26. Little research is found to n conducted in university departments or in colleges of education in the field of comparative education, politics of education or economics of education. Most of the research studies in economics of education are conducted by agencies like NUEPA etc.

27. There is very little attempt to study multilevel data. Besides, studies focus organisational effectiveness but not on organisational improvement. Thus, the findings of research on organisational effectiveness are largely academic and of no practical significance.

I would like to review research done in two prominent areas that are of importance to the society at large. These two areas are educational technology and sociology of education.

Educational Technology

Educational technology research has moved through several stages or"ages", which are as follows :

1. The age of instructional designwith a focus on content
2. The age of the message designwitha focus on format including the perception principles (organization, similarity, and proximity contiguity), the learning principles (limited capacity, similarity, and primacy-recency), the concept-formation principle (simultaneous display of examples).
3. The age of simulationwitha focus on interactions (Cognitive Constructivism)
4. "The new age" of research with a focus on learning environments (Social Constructivism – Collaborative Learning Environments) "situated" or "anchored" cognition points out that learning cannot be easily separated from the "act of knowing" and that "what is learned" is an integral part of "how it is learned and used". Situated approaches to cognition emphasize the need to construct learning environments that engage students in meaningful and purposeful activities. Thus, the content of cognition (what is known) and the process of cognition (how it is known) cannot be separated from the context and the act of knowing. Consequently, educational technology is seen as a major tool to create adequate learning environments where enhanced situated cognition takes place.

This implies that (a) trends in educational technology research synchronised with and depended on the evolution of learning theories from behaviourism to cognitivism and later on to constructivism, (b) trends in educational technology research also synchronised with and depended on the technological changes from learning machines to technologies of virtual reality, (c) a clear shift is visible from the design of instruction to thedesign of learning environments, (d) there is a positive effect of educational technology on learning, but the effect size varies considerably. This variance is due to factors of context, learner characteristics and the characteristics of technology. Thus any evaluation of the impact of a particular educational technology should investigate into the type of technology used in a specific context, its interactive effect with what characteristics of the learner on the outcomes of learning. Such an evaluation is inevitably local, because learning is a local, contextual, concrete phenomenon, not an abstract process. (e) computer technology has the prospects of being a strong and flexible tool in facilitating educational outcomes, (f) learning is much more dependent on the activity of the learner than on the quantity of information and processing opportunities provided by the environment. In other words, the key to efficacious application of media in learning is not so much how the "message" itself is presented, but the degree to which students are motivated to exploit the environment in order to achieve their personal learning goals, (g) the mere installing of hardware does not lead to anticipated results, (h) the advancement of educational technology use in learning was itself influenced by the dominant scientific paradigm and the use of the tools created and (i) a clear shift from the design of instruction to the design of learning environments is noticed. This shift from content-focused tolearner – focused instruction also implies that learning outcomes are owned by the learners and the technology should empower them to reach their idiosyncratic learning goals.

Sociology of Education

Four major areas may be identified by the various

components of this category, namely, (a) the scheduled tribes, (b) the scheduled castes, (c) other backward communities and economically backward individuals, (d) the physically handicapped and the mentally challenged. In each of these areas there are a number of sub-areas originating from the foci of the several contributions. In the field of the scheduled tribes, research themes include(i) the school in the tribal community including classroom environment, (ii) educational institutions such as ashram schools and other schools, (iii) intelligence, personality and the cognitive abilities of tribal students, social and scientific attitudes of tribal students and their adjustment, (iv) dropout, wastage and stagnation, (v) educational needs of tribals-achievement motivation, self-perception, aspirations and academic achievements, (vi) family structure, parental behaviour and conservation, (vii) effect of deprivation and cognitive and non-cognitive abilities of tribal students, (viii) education, social change and modernization case studies of ashram schools, reasons for dropouts in ashram schools, problems of teachers and students in ashram schools and experimental studies on ashram schools for personal effectiveness of students. With reference to the scheduled castes, research has focussed on (i) barriers to education, (ii) non-enrolment, non-attendance, wastage and stagnation, (iii) problems of scheduled caste students, (iv) utilisation of scholarships, (v) education and social status, (vi) opinions about reservation policy, (vii) personality patterns of scheduled caste students, achievement motivation, problems of values and level of frustration, (viii) life tendencies, meaning of success and self-concept among scheduled castes, (ix) academic achievementof SC/ST students and (x) attitudes of college teachers towards scheduled caste students. Bedsides, research on other disadvantaged sections include themes such as (i) education of minorities, (ii) education of urban slum dwellers, (iii) education of rural children, (iv) case studies of school dropouts, (iii) behavioural and personality concomitants of socio-economic deprivation, (iv) experimental studies of development of life skills in school dropouts (v) life-style of slum dwellers in relation to education, (vi) intellectual and non-intellectual factors in the academic achievement of disadvantaged students of professional colleges, (vii) changing social awareness of social realities, (viii) reading abilities of backward castes in the context of their intelligence, anxiety, need for achievement and other demographic variables, (ix) utilization of facilities for backward students, (x) parental life styles, intellectual achievement responsibilities, adjustment and cognitive performance of under-privileged children, (ix) effect of print size and print colour on reading efficiency of disadvantaged language development. Research also focussed on comparative studies of the scheduled caste, scheduled tribe or among the scheduled caste and caste Hindus or among the backward and the higher castes with the objective of providing a better view of existing social reality. However, very little of these findings have translated into policy formulation or modification. In fact, its use in classroom practices is also negligible.

Future Prospects

This section includes suggestions regarding new research themes, strategies and training needs.

1. There is a strong need for capacity building and strengthening research skills and abilities in both, the research guides and students. This is a trivet-like concern as follows (Obanya & Touré, 2003) :

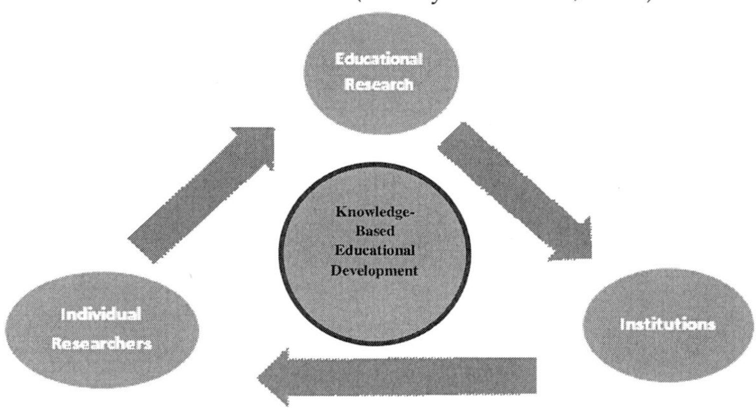

This in turn implies that apart from capacity building in individual researchers, there is also a need to develop institutions and bring about a positive mind set in the administrators for effective research endeavours.

2. It is equally necessary to enhance the relevance and quality of educational research. This involves (a) Providing training in research methodology on a continuous basis, (b) Providing training in research reporting and academic writing, (c) Writing research papers that meet the highest academic and technical standards and publishing them, (d) Developing creativity in the area of research communication, (e) Developing and maintaining strong involvement in policy-oriented research, (f) Involving policy-makers in research planning, (g) Sending research findings to policy-makers and (h) Developing and maintaining intra-national and international networking.

   This entire process is shown diagrammatically as follows:

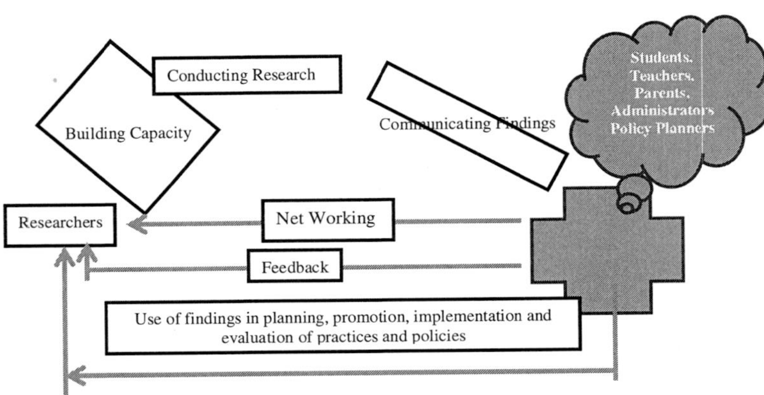

The formal institutions would require strengthening research through (a) formaltraining for their individual functionaries – guides and students, (b) in-service training through participation in development-oriented educational research, (c) retooling, particularly inthe domain of ICT and networking with other institutions, and (d) the development ofa research agenda that orients most research activities towards areas of direct application to on-going educational development projects.The less formal institutions include NGOs and interest group networks around specific areas of educational development. Interdisciplinary groups would be expected to ensure better research through the mutual enrichment from a variety of research paradigms and approaches. Such less formal structures would also require retooling, in much the sameway as the strictly formal institutions.

3. Future research needs to review various conceptualization, models and reforms agenda in education with reference to its adaptability in diverse socio-economic and cultural contexts, because technology and teaching trends have evolved and changed very speedily in the last few decades. However, education methodology and associated research methodology have not yet evolved at the same rate as information technology. There is a need to conceptualise and develop amodel which has the right unification of technology and tradition suitable to the Indian and regional contexts and requirements.
4. There is almost a complete lack of meta-analysis of findings in the Indian context. This needs to be paid attention to. This also needs creation of data banks which could be used for meta-analysis as well as secondary data analysis.
5. There is a need to train research guides in application ICT in educational research. One of the emerging areas that need attention is educational data mining which includes a set of computational and psychological methods and research approaches for understanding how students learn. New computer-supported interactive learning methods and tools such as intelligent tutoring systems, simulations, games have

provided openings for collecting and analysing student data, to discover patterns and trends in those data and to make new discoveries and test hypotheses about how students learn and build models. Educational data mining generally emphasises reducing learning into small components that can be analysed and then influenced by software that adapts to the student (Siemens & Baker, 2012).

6. There is also a need to train research guides in the use of ICT-based data collection tools for survey research such as mobile phones, personal digital assistants (PDA), web-based surveys, audio-computer assisted self interviewing and social media channels.
7. Training in the use of design-based research is essential as it is an emerging paradigm for the study of learning in context through the systematic design and study of instructional strategies and tools.
8. Evaluation research is the need of the hour especially covering government and UGC schemes and policies so as to make the endeavour of educational research fruitful, effective and efficient.
9. Every university needs to develop and implement R & D policy with reference to educational research.
10. Research on higher education is also the need of the hour.

References

Altbach, P. (2006), "The Dilemmas of Ranking", *International Higher Education*, 42, 2-3.

Braun, D. & Merrien, F.X. (1999), *Towards a New Model of Governance for Universities? A Comparative View*. (London, Jessica Kingsley).

Foray, D. (2004). *The Economics of Knowledge* (Cambridge, MA, MIT Press).

Geuna, A. and B. R. Martin (2003), "University research evaluation and funding: an international comparison", *Minerva*, 41, 277-304.

Hazelkorn, E. (2005), *University Research Management. Developing Research in New Institutions* (Paris, OECD Publishing)

Koç, M. & Ferneding, K.A. (2007). "The Consequences of Internet Café Use on Turkish College Students" *Social Capital*. 6(3), TOJET.

Kulik, C. & Kulik, J. A. (1991). "Effectiveness of computer-based instruction: An updated analysis." *Computers in Human Behavior*, 71, 75-94.

Kulik, J. A. (1994). "Meta-analytic studies of findings on computer-based instruction." In E.L. Baker, and H.F. O'Neil, Jr. (Eds.) *Technology Assessment in Education and Training*. Hillsdale, NJ: Lawrence Erlbaum.

OECD (2003a), "Changing patterns of governance in higher education", *Education Policy Analysis* (Paris, OECD Publishing).

Pai Obanya & Kathryn Touré (2003) Emerging Trends in Research on the Quality of Education A synthesis of educational research reviews from 1992-2002 in eleven countries of West and Central Africa http://www.rocare.org/ROCARE_SYNTHESIS_ADEA_Emerging.pdf accessed on 2nd November 2014.

Rogers, E.M., (1995). *Diffusion of Innovations* (4th ed.), New York: The Free Press.

Shah, A.M. (2005), "Higher Education and Research: Roots of Mediocrity", *Economic and Political Weekly*, May 28 – June 04.

Siemens, G., Baker, R.S.J.D. (2012), Learning Analytics and Educational Data Mining: Towards Communication and Collaboration. Proceedings of the 2nd International Conference on Learning Analytics and Knowledge.

Sivin-Kachala, J. (1998), *Report on the Effectiveness of Technology in Schools, 1990-1997*. Washington, DC: Software Publishers Association.

Thompson, A. D. (2005), "Scientifically Based Research: Establishing a Research Agenda For The Technology in Teacher Education Community." *Journal of Research on Technology in Education*. 37(4), 331-337.

Wishart, J., Ramsden, A. and McFarlane, A. (2007), "PDAs and Handhelds: ICT at your side and not in your face." *Technology, Pedagogy and Education*, Volume 16, Issue 1, 95-110.

7

Goa University Pioneering Social Science Research in Goa

Remy Dias

Introduction

Knowledge has been a key factor in economic development and aiding incrementally better insights of societal functioning from twentieth century. Colonization and decolonization have made this erstwhile subject region realize that by and large societies which are proficient to generate, decide on, get a feel for, and commercialize knowledge have better chance of achieving sustained growth and enhanced quality of life, for its constituents when service sector growth is outpacing industrial output and farm productivity.[1] With subsequent rapidity of change due to impact of globalization, role of higher education institutions in furthering research and scholarship is becoming vital in 'liquid modernity'. Has societal understanding and research kept pace with fast evolving socio-economic dynamics? Indian Council for Social Science Research, besides furthering research, has also been attempting to survey research activity and estimate its quality in various fields of social sciences carried out in India.[2]

Organization of National Seminar by ICSSR(WRC-Mumbai) on 'Status of Social Science Research in Western India: Critical Engagements and Future Direction' held at Mumbai University from 14-16 November, 2014, under stellar leadership of its Hon. Director, Prof. Gautam Gawali, is to estimate progress of social science research in Western India. Effort is indeed commendable.

This paper attempts to gauge advances in social science research for Goa region and identify expansive gaps for further exploration. Goa University professes that all its post-graduate programmes are designed keeping in mind 'industrial requirements and societal needs in perspective, and are intended to offer gainful employment opportunities'.[3] With 'skill enhancement' and 'employability' being focus of PG programmes under Choice Based Credit System (CBCS) at Goa University, learners in line with liquid modernity are in pursuit of temporary, tentative and unarranged bits of knowledge and helpful competences and hence implication for research and scholarship in social sciences requires deeper probing.

We know that 'research and scholarship' on whole refers to uncovering or producing new knowledge, or solving particular practical or theoretical problems for societal good.[4] While 'research' is seen as systematic and painstaking enquiry leading to research output, through 'scholarship' intellectuals and academics keep themselves abreast with advances in their disciplines so that they can communicate latest (intra) disciplinary advances in knowledge to students, fellow researchers and peers. There is increasing realization that social sciences have potential of offering scope and down to earth latitude to educational considerations and as such need to be carefully listened to. In university system social sciences are newest part which has gained prevalence over humanities through claim to be only voice that is trying to gain a broad picture of social reality and thus make predictions for future.[5] Social scientists are viewed as participants in socio-historical development of human action and understanding.[6] This accentuates value of critical research in social sciences for a multicultural country like India besotted with mass of societal problems.

Social science research has developed by leaps and bounds in Goa – erstwhile Portuguese colony – which research is in form of Ph.D theses, Masters level dissertations besides a huge mass of project-reports by UG students. Teachers at both university and colleges also undertake various research projects of funding agencies. Only a fraction of this research gets published through efforts of some teachers – API (academic performance index) and PBAS (performance bases assessment system) has started to play catalytic (sometimes cataclysmic) role for teachers – and research guides. Problem nonetheless is of identifying what constitutes good research in a scenario of little peer-reviewed publication output. It is only recent years that Goa University has stipulated that PhD researchers must have at least one each international and national level peer-reviewed publication prior to award of degree. MPhil programme is almost non-existent in social sciences at Goa University which fact coupled with reality that hardly anybody clears NET-JRF in social sciences from Goa should make educational planners introspect. Quality of research is not dependent on, whether it is masters, doctoral or post-doctoral level work, sponsored or otherwise. Often there are comments made on Ph.D research in popular press as well as journals and conferences. Lot of research and publication in social sciences happens outside bounds of formal structure as well.[7] For published research to be of value it must aid building up of theories and improving related practices. Short of this, erroneously conducted research is not only inferior to what might be an intelligent layman's common sense but may also be harmful.[8]

Historical legacy of Goa having first printing press in Indian sub-continent, vast and diverse 'print' literary output from 1830s, well-documented innumerable source material, relatively high literacy rate, qualified professional spread across vast colonial sea-borne empire for generations, etc., have made it easier for researchers to conceptualize research themes of their own interest and societal relevance. Although researchers in Goa have better English language skills, stifling impact which 450 years of Portuguese colonialism had on Goan mind is evident in research output both in quantitative but more in qualitative terms. Ethnic cultural cleansing by colonizers had a rather debilitating impact with result that there are hardly any studies of presenting 'perspective from below' or alternate viewpoints. Rather, dominant viewpoint gets recycled endlessly.

With a young 'A' Grade NAAC accredited Goa University (established in June 1985) and a host of other institutions like Xavier Centre of Historical Research, Historical Archives of Goa, Goa Konkani Akademi, Gomantak Marathi Academy, etc. there has been a steady output in terms of research in post-liberation period. Paradoxically, however, it is a fact that there is a dip in quality and quantity of knowledge production as compared to colonial times. Important research questions that shall be addressed are: What is varying canvas of PhDs produced in social sciences across various research institutes? Why number of Goan scholars undertaking minor and major research project is but insignificant? There was a period when Goans contributed to journals regularly, especially, during colonial times. Why has publishing languished in post-liberation period from a high position of being a publishing hub during colonial times? For instance, *Boletim do Instituto Vasco da Gama* was a Journal in social sciences that published quality research in pre-colonial times. Today, *Boletim* rechristened as '*Govapuri*' (Panaji: Institute Menezes Braganza) carries small literary pieces with quality papers being few and far between.[9] While Colleges across Goa have in-house research journals, Goa University has had none, neither in sciences nor social sciences. Publication of critical research papers in social science by faculty leaves much to be desired with impact factor of Journals in which they are published being generally low. Much publication is also in form of books rather than as research articles in peer-reviewed journals of repute.

Common thread which runs deep in social science research is that 450 years of colonial isolation has made people obsessed with land of their birth with most studies limited to territorial boundaries of nascent state, liberated from colonial yoke in 1961. This in a way also limits scope of the current paper, besides mandate of seminar organizers to 'write on advances in social science research and identify gaps for Goa region'. Thus, attempt is to make an analysis of recent trends in social science research within geographical space of Goa. It is interesting to note that 'Goa' is focus, object and subject of most researchers. Why do Goa scholars not research on other areas and reach out to fellow scholars? This perhaps is a colonial hangover as a result of artificial barrier that Portuguese masters erected between Goans and fellow Indians. It is also a fact that research in social science is more descriptive in nature. Another interesting fact is that inter-disciplinary and collaborative studies are few and far between.

Attempt is to analyze development in social science research in Goa and situate same within perspective of 'liquid modernity'. *Liquid Modernity* is based on predicament of constant change, on redefining social emancipation in terms of freedom and caravan living, on individuality framed within consumption of multiple identities, on time as trumping space, on work as occurring in labyrinth of dystopia and on communities presented as phenomena that are no longer rooted in culture and tradition but which swarm together momentarily around shared events.[10] This has had tremendous impact on higher education in general and research in social science in particular. Focus of paper is to (a) explore and anlayse concept of Liquid Modernity, (b) offer a critique of Liquid (Higher) Education which pursues temporary, tentative and unarranged bits of knowledge and focuses on helpful competencies, in relation to research in social science for Goa region and (c) understand implications for future research prospects.

Research in liquid modernity, theoretical framework

Higher education in Goa as elsewhere in India and throughout the world is facing times of significant change, as a result of historical factors, such as globalization, massification of higher learning, specialization and fragmentation of disciplines and commodification of knowledge, with implication for social science studies and research. Caste based politics and reservation, regional considerations and political affiliation or plain ability to satisfy rent seekers emerged as major considerations for academic appointments rather than competence and excellence, etc., add to complexity of issue though it is not subject matter of current paper.[11] Further, parental preference and consequent filtering which sets in motion with (sometimes prior to) declaration of Xth Standard results, lack of good educational counselors, etc., societal expectations, peer pressure, etc., leads often to intelligent students, opting for or pushed and pulled into science education to pursue lucrative careers in engineering, information technology and medicine. Few are those who exercise option to pursue higher education in social sciences and humanities by design and choice. Everybody though wants high marks and percentages, even in liberal arts. Excellent performance at examination, however, does not ensure 'life-long learning' and in absence of critical thinking, good path-breaking social science research is rare. Scenario becomes exciting, only with those who change bandwagon midway being unable to undergo rigours of science education and research or 'late bloomers' of social sciences and humanities who wake up or are (rather often) awakened (by circumstances and situations like refresher courses, research methodology workshops, subject related conferences/seminars, etc. or research-guides), to potentials of research-activity in social sciences.

Change that higher education is witnessing is also result of philosophical and sociological revolutions that have followed modernity. Although change and adaptation have been constant features in history of higher education world over,[12] current crisis appears particularly significant. Crisis of university system world over is being described as tremendous, massive, fast-moving,[13] radical, disruptive, breath-taking, structural, daily, rapid, uneven and immense.[14] Though not all would agree with these drastic proclamations, there is a shared consensus that university is facing unprecedented changes.[15]

Radical changes facing higher education in times of liquid modernity today are such that some critics question its relevance and others predict its complete demise. Although not all would agree with these drastic proclamations, there is a shared consensus that university is facing unprecedented 'Incredulity and doubt are widespread, encompassing a questioning of any foundation... (and) authority invested in certain groupings – universities, scientific communities, research councils, professional bodies, and government – is often treated with suspicion and skepticism'. Whether university is really in crisis or is simply finding its way forward in a sea of change, development need careful contemplation, for, university is ultimately society's best institution. Historically, university has provided social scientists and ideas contributing towards evolution of culture but has proven to have matchless potential in enhancing scientific progress, improving human life and acting 'as an affirming flame for cultural life of a society'.[16]

Liquidity refers to a reality that is in continual motion and change and in which transformation, continuous becoming, chaos and unending crafting of identity are key features. This type of reality is one where attitudes of epistemological perplexity and privatization of authority are declared as normal and normative and all values are exalted in an enriched framework of freedom. Newness of content is based on predicament of constant change, on redefining social emancipation in terms of freedom and caravan living, on redefining social emancipation in terms of freedom and caravan living, on individuality framed within consumption of multiple identities, on time as trumping space, on work as occurring in labyrinth of dystopia and on communities presented as phenomena that are no longer rooted in culture and tradition but that swarm together momentarily around shared events.[17] Liquid education is educational philosophy of liquid modernity that dismantles previous higher learning and pursues temporary, tentative and unarranged bits of knowledge and helpful competences. It is un-authoritative activity of learners that, lacking cultural purpose and rational framework, operates outside bounds of structure in service of market. Three key features can be seen in this definition, namely that liquid education dismantles previous higher learning, that it pursues temporary, tentative and unarranged bits of knowledge and that it focuses on helpful competences (often for professional self-development). Doctoral and post-doctoral research undertaken in social sciences need to be viewed within this perspective.

Social Science Research in Goa

Goa University, established in June 1985 by an Act of Goa Government, is located on a picturesque campus spread over 427.49 acres area on Taleigao plateau overlooking Zuari Estuary, within close vicinity of capital city of Panaji, in North Goa. Besides being most important location for post-graduate studies, it also serves as academic nerve-centre of higher education system in Goa. Today Goa University has 55 colleges and other higher education institutions affiliated to it distributed across Goa, 30 in general education and 25 in professional education, with total enrolment of about 28,000. Most of these are enrolled in undergraduate programmes and main campus which is primarily for post-graduate and doctoral students has an enrolment of about 2,000. Interestingly, vast majority of students enrolled in various programmes are women. Goa University has always been a favorite choice for academic pursuits of students aspiring higher education in State.

Many of post-graduate programmes at Goa University are designed keeping in mind industrial requirements and societal needs in perspective, and are intended to offer gainful employment opportunities. All PG programmes include Dissertation work to promote research temperament among students. Over years, Goa University has established good linkages in relevant areas of study with other institutions of higher learning and research organizations in country and outside. Memoranda of Understanding have been signed with several national and international Institutions. Recently, Visiting Research Professor Program (VRPP) has been initiated with respect to seven Chairs introduced by University with generous support from Goa Government in Liberal Arts, Social Interdisciplinary Studies, etc., and distinguished personalities from various disciplines have been nominated as visiting Professors.[18] It would be worthwhile if doctoral research activity of those pursuing PhD in social sciences is in some way vetted (informally or through some other mechanism) by Visiting Chair Professors in which manner researchers would have gained sharper and better perspective by drawing on latter's monumental research experience. Research and researchers shall undoubtedly gain immensely through this.

Having oriented itself towards imparting advanced knowledge and to develop human resource, Goa University, with one of best teacher-student ratio, has attained an important place in realm of higher learning. Within a short span of last two and half decades of its existence, University has shown distinct visibility and a promise of growth in teaching and empowering young men and women of region. With its well-designed curriculum, Goa University currently offers, under CBCS, 32 PG programmes on campus, which provide ample opportunity to students to pursue their diverse academic interests. Systematic multilevel process of revision of syllabus takes into confidence all its stake holders including alumni, parents, industry, students, teachers, external members and other experts. Employability is enabled through KSA (Knowledge, Skills and Abilities) development with help of a well designed curriculum. Quality as well as quantum of Research is ensured through closely monitored theses/ dissertations, project work, paper publications, seminars etc. Following table gives number of PhDs submitted in various Social Sciences and Humanities. It also includes list of PhDs completed in various Indian vernacular languages as the subject matter of research is seen to be largely of social relevance.

List of PhD Theses submitted to Goa University (1985-2010)[19]

Subject	*No. of PhDs*	*Subject*	*No. of PhDs*
Commerce	16[20]	Latin American Studies	01
Economics	13[21]	Management	13[22]
Education	10[23]	Marathi	11[24]
English	21[25]	Philosophy	9[26]
History	19[27]	Political Science	7[28]
Konkani	3[29]	Women' Studies	—
Sociology	18[30]	—	—

The subject matter of research has included areas as Economics and HR, women issues, reproductive health, feminist studies. In literature identity issues have been taken up along with comparative studies, language and regional identity, script muddle, environmental ethics and ecology (handled in passing), freedom struggle, social justice, post-liberation evolving political scenario, ethno-medicine and healing practices in Goa, schizophrenia, cultural location of alcoholic beverages in Goan society, in-migration, etc. An in-depth analysis of the research activity in social sciences is attempted herein. It is observed that award of doctoral thesis at Goa University is mostly in early 1990s. Thereafter, there is a decline in award of PhDs, especially in social science. This may be due the fact that following implementation of Vth Pay Commission recruitment was on hold throughout the country. And when accomplished faculty retired positions remained vacant for long. Knowledge production was thus adversely affected.

(i) Historical Studies

Goa University's History department has been most vibrant since inception with thrust areas being 'Indo-Portuguese History, Maritime Studies... with a special focus on the history of Goa (through) understanding historical developments at regional, national and international levels within an interdisciplinary analytical framework'. Under guidance and stellar leadership of first Vice-Chancellor of Goa University Prof. B. Sheik Ali, a reputed Historian the history department of Goa University has organised Golden Jubilee Year Session (1987) of Indian History Congress, hosted XI Annual Conference of Place Names Society of India (1990), an International Seminar on Maritime Activities in India with special reference to the Portuguese 1500-1800 (2001) and a National Seminar on History of Goa (2003). One of the best practices of the Department is that in collaboration with Directorate of Archives and Archaeology, Government of Goa, it organizes annual seminars on a specific theme of History of Goa from ancient to modern. This has resulted in several publications containing proceedings of research paper presented at these annual conclaves.

One of the must reads before initiating any research activity on Goa is an analytical book *Goa through the Ages: an Economic History* (1990).[31] The volume contains well researched papers on evolving contours of economic history of the region with contribution by noted national and international historians.[32] *Goa through the Ages: an Economic History* is part of five-volume series planned by Goa University as an endeavour to further cultural heritage of Goa and its people. The project was entrusted to historians with long experience of research in region's history and culture. Book brings together a sifted and synthesized picture of Goa's economic history. It has incorporated, information and insights with facts and figures galore, which have come in the recent past in sizable doses, largely as a result of the research promoted by International Seminars on Indo-Portuguese History since 1978 (ISIPH).[33] In the book some aspects have found less attention than other important areas of concern. One aspect which has received adequate attention is Trade – both international (more maritime) and hinterland (though not less in importance). This not only reflects its importance in Goa's economic history as a result of its littoral nature and strategic location but also may have to do with funding of research. However, contrary to the overstress that has been observed in the past histories on the overseas connection, the emphasis has been shifted to the coastal and hinter-land linkages of that trade. This approach has helped to question some stereotypes and past generalizations and is a collective effort of social scientists, including historians, anthropologists, demographers, and economists making the work more comprehensive than the traditional book written by historians alone handling economic and other related issues.

Another good publication is the proceeding volume of papers presented at the seminar organized by Dept. of History, Goa University in 1986: *Goan Society through the Ages*, (1987), which volume discusses caste (including Christianization of caste), religion, urbanization, etc. in Goa down the ages.[34] It also deliberates extensively on issues like Portuguese Common Civil Code, status of women, Christian folk songs, etc. A critical work for research students to situate Indo-Portuguese History is M.N. Pearson's *Cambridge History of India 1.1 The Portuguese in India* (1987). The seminal work assesses influence of and impact of Portuguese four and half centuries on India, 'which influence (is) varying very widely, ranging from massive to miniscule according to three criteria: time, place and category (for example, social, religious, economic, political). At a particular time, in a specified place, we find a substantial Portuguese impact on a particular category of Indian life; change on or more of these criteria (say a different time or place) and the influence may well decrease to a considerable extent'. The central finding of the book is that in many areas Portuguese influence was but minor, in a few areas it was substantial.[35]

Documentation (sources) for Indo-Portuguese history is vast and varied and its full potential may never be exploited for unraveling trials and turbulences of the past. M. N. Pearson writing on Historical Archives of Goa (HAG) and Indian History, states that:

> 'In 1972 I started the original version of the chapter by saying that: the Historical Archives of Goa are one of the most neglected archives on the subcontinent. So far as I know I am one of only five people affiliated with an American or European university (the other four being C. R. Boxer, J. B. Harrison, A.R.

> Disney and the late I. A. MacGregor) who have spent any extended period of time in these archives, and a few Indian scholars have followed up S.N. Sen's visit to Goa nearly fifty years after ago... The reason for this lack of interest are difficult to set out, but in the case of Indian historians the main problem has been an inability to read Portuguese, a result of the lack of instruction in this language in the subcontinent. Financial considerations have also militated against Indians spending much time in Goa, as also the fact that until 1961 Goa was foreign, and often hostile, territory.'[36]

A decade down the line M.N. Pearson changes tack and highlights that:

> 'It is a pleasure to be able now (1980) to note that much has changed; indeed Goan historiography seems to be on the verge of renaissance. Young Goans are beginning to engage in serious research into the history of their homeland. There are still problems of perspective evident: Goans today tend either to condemn or condone all the actions of the Portuguese in the past. But as Portuguese rule fades into a more distant memory this problem will solve itself. Perhaps even more important, at last some senior Indian historians, in Maharashtra, Gujarat and elsewhere are encouraging their students to learn Portuguese and do their research in Goa. This is most welcome development, and should contribute exciting new perspective to the study of the history of the Portuguese in India.'[37]

Modern day scholars like Teotonio R. de Souza,[38] K.S. Mathew, B.S. Shastry, P.P. Shirodkar, Mahmai Kamat, P.D. Xavier, Charles Borges, Celsa Pinto, Pratima Kamat, Pius Malekandathil, etc. have strived and endeavoured to contribute original works of importance to Indo-Portuguese history. Nevertheless, lull from late 1990s is both disheartening and inexplicable. Seminars are conducted and conferences held at regular interval and yet publications are few and far between. It is possible that faculty and students (potential researchers) are bogged down with academic work consequent upon introduction of semester system of examination from the early 1990s. Lack of liberal finances for research could also be a factor though organizations like Fundação Oriente – Panjim,[39] Fundação Calouste Gelbenkain – Lisbon, Instituto

Camões – Lisbon, have been liberally supporting Indian scholars undertaking studies in Indo-Portuguese history and culture.

Few of the PhD thesis which have contributed significantly to body of knowledge in historical studies for Goa region during Portuguese occupation are *'Socio- Economic History of Goa with Special Reference to Communidade System: 1750-1910'*, (Remy A.D. Dias, 2004); *'Reconstructing Urban Maritime History of Goa: A Study of Port-Capital of Chrandrapur, Gopakapattana and Ella'*, (Mary Alvita D'souza, 2008); *'A Socio-Cultural History of Goa from Bhojas to Vijayanagara'*, (V.R. Mitragotri, 1992); and *'Goa Struggle for Freedom, 1946-1961: Contribution of National Congress (Goa) and Azad Gomantak Dal'*, (S. S. Risbud, 2002), besides host of other theses.

Yet, much needs to be done if the ocean of sources on Indo-Portuguese at Historical Archives of Goa, Panjim and source material at Xavier Centre of Historical Research, Porvorim-Goa, are resourcefully tapped for reconstructing region's history. Goa University has stopped short of publishing Bibliographical works on *Pissurlencar's Collection* and *Nuno Gonçalves Collection*.[40] Digitization, transliteration, translation, commentaries, etc, on some of the important works in these and other *Gifted Collections* would go a long way in promoting critical research in Indo-Portuguese history. Besides acquiring Portuguese language skills, calligraphy, mastering Marathi in modi-script, etc, researchers also need a good grounding in modern and post-modern critical theories in order to present their works in perspective. Department of History, Goa University, was 'planning to offer M.Phil. programme from the academic year 2013-14' to do course correction. Yet academic year 2014-15 is nearing end and proverbial gap between cup and lip is wide and seems unbridgeable for aspiring students, a rather major spoke for research advancement despite state government directive to its fully funded state university.

A welcome change is the introduction of a Masters level course, *'Doing History': An Introduction to Historical Method* where students are introduced to how historians work, how to 'do' history, that is, to the methods of historical research. It is intended to introduce students to basics of doing research in discipline of history, process of writing history, including selection of topics, techniques of historical research, use of primary sources and secondary literature, historical criticism, analysis and synthesis. Course does focus on writing skills, organization of material into a clear and readable paper, creation of a thesis statement, development of one's writing and proper style for bibliography and footnotes. Overall objective of the course is, therefore, to provide student with information, skills, and tools needed to do research in discipline of history. This type of courses is actually a must for all disciplines given that generally researchers' methodology in social sciences is such that it leaves much to be desired.

(ii) Studies in Sociology and Education

Afonso M. Botelho examines contentious issue of mother tongue medium of instruction at primary level in *Language and Early Schooling in Goa* (2007), which led to denial of grants-in-aid to English medium primary schools in Goa from 1990s by PDF government and thereafter. Diocesan Society of Education (DSE) with largest number of primary schools changed medium of instructions to Konkani drastically reducing, for some time enrolment in English medium schools. Soon, however, English schools began multiplying and enrolment within them, increased phenomenally despite exorbitant fees. Intake of students in English medium schools, however, is largely confined to upper and middle classes as lower class parents find it financially constraining.[41] Remittances of those working abroad have found their way to coffers of English medium schools for last quarter of a century. There is need for a study to document how medium of instruction issue and subsequent development led to increase in iniquitous gap between 'haves' and 'have-nots'. It would be interesting to research how self-financing educational institutions help 'haves' dominate socio-economic scenario to the detriment of legitimate interests of 'have-nots' and marginalised section of society? Quite a number of migrants' children are also at receiving end too and this needs deeper probing.

Government policy of providing grants-in-aid to mother tongue medium of instruction led to an increase in number of students enrolled in the Konkani medium schools and arrested fast declining strength in Marathi enrolment at primary level. Mother tongue and regional language education were encouraged as government gave them necessary support, but it also led to English medium schools being more exclusive. Afonso M. Botelho also grapples with question whether mother tongue and regional language are equally efficacious in education of children granted that both mother tongue and the regional language were treated on par, and English medium schools not considered for grants. While linguists and educationists encourage education in mother tongue with many considering it best medium of education, regional language has never been recommended as appropriate medium of education though it has been forced upon linguistic minority communities by governments who pay lip service to narrow definition of mother tongue and direct their resources towards education in mother tongue qualifying according to broad' definition, i.e., regional languages.[42]

According to Afonso M. Botelho in Goa, 1990 education policy consolidated position of primary education in the regional language, Marathi. Botelho emphatically states that adoption of official language Konkani in Devanagari script as medium of education has not facilitated literacy acquisition and smooth development of child, for standardised Devanagari script is a dialect of just small dominant section of Goans. Adoption of Konkani in Devanagari script has meant that other dialects, especially Roman dialect, are grammatically incorrect, thereby creating amongst parents an inferiority complex, being speakers of the 'deficient' dialect.

He concludes his study by ardently stating that:

> Mother tongue education during early schooling cannot be considered to be a magic formula, a panacea for all societies,

> especially when secondary, higher education and employment opportunities require proficiency in English (which) requirement has resulted into a marked preference for English medium during early schooling, which, however, is not available to children of low income groups.This inaccessibility creates and sustains various forms of social inequality… (so) policy needs further consideration, especially since a majority of parents prefer English medium of instruction at early schooling. Though mother tongue education is ideally best for early schooling, complexity of socio-linguistic context in Goa needs to be taken into consideration. … (thus) education policies need to be formulated based on the linguistic situation prevailing in the field not on ideological discourses trying to conform reality to them, rather than they being based on reality.[43]

More research is required to unearth facts and policy analysis and responses in Goa region as to why socio-economic inequalities increase. Language is power and Joanna G. Pereira in her thesis *Language and the Public Sphere - a Sociological study of the Language Question in Goa since 1987*, (2010) has dealt with broad spectrum of language issue from sociological framework and within historical perspective for Goa region. After 'delineating a transition from functional to contested multilingualism in Goa' Joanna G. Pereira attempts 'codifying and interpreting perspectives on antiquity of Konkani, development of Konkani public sphere, and prevalence of multiple public spheres in Goa'. She summarizes that multilingualism that characterizes public sphere in Goa has followed a different trajectory from that which is found in other parts of subcontinent with Konkani public sphere overshadowed by twin hegemonic influences of Portuguese and Marathi. She emphatically delineates that 'Language has played a vital role in Goa's post liberation socio-political history. Parochialising trend in post-colonial Goa has taken a linguistic turn as it was generic of the process of State formation in India.' Thus, every major political transition that Goa has experienced has been cloaked, either overtly or covertly, in the garb of language.[44]

Sheila M. D'Souza has focused on women in mining and non-mining regions in her work *Reproductive Health and Quality of Live* (2008), within broad parameters of Sociology of Medicine. Positive impacts of living in mining region are virtually seen in rise of family socio-economic standards in general and also increased socio-economic standards among women. Observance of fasting, use of folk medicine, religious ways, health practices, social beliefs, and cultural norms are deeply rooted among rural women. Cultural norms, gendered roles and spouse's influence alter way women make choices and affect their reproductive well-being. Women's role in biological reproduction or procreation (childbearing / child-rearing), low participation in social and economic production signifies gender division of labour within household and in all spheres of life.[45]

Most important period in life span of women is reproductive period, which extends from menarche to menopause; intervening periods are marriage, pregnancy, childbirth and contraception. During pregnancy women face specific problems and are not able to recognise danger signals during pregnancy, though proportions of deliveries assisted by health care provider have increased. Sheila M. D'Souza writes that 'pregnancy is a special problem because of big change that takes place when a woman conceives and then bears children...she remains unwell for nine months' (emphasis mine). During pregnancy, childbirth, and post-partum period women's circumstances, diet, work load, rest and conditions at delivery have a strong influence on reproductive well-being. Women view marriage as a means of security in terms of positive aspects like improved standard of living, approval and respect from others, feeling of self confidence and overall happiness, though they expressed loss of freedom to do things they enjoy. Study indicates a strong emphasis on fertility and motherhood, as a woman's role in family is primarily child bearer, especially once she is married.[46]

Sheila M. D'Souza's work shows that women primarily bear brunt of reproductive labour and succumb to dependence on practices associated with poor lifestyle and low well-being (e.g. depression, worry, tension, and feeling low). Starting from most intimate social labour, i.e., reproductivity and child rearing, it is seen that women have low autonomy or control over her reproductive choices, sexuality, fertility as well as on major decisions regarding upbringing of her own children. Besides, women also experienced reproductive-health problems, vulnerability during childbearing years, spouse harassment and family problems. Culture, education, work, exposure to health services, access to mass media, women's pre-disposition, child bearing, decision making and amount of illness during reproductive age place undue stress on women. Low employment opportunities, educational attainment, access to land, credit, and income leads to low autonomy among women and lack of control over reproductive health choices. This study highlights important socio-cultural factors and behavioural practices that affect reproductive health and well-being among women. Study also establishes relative importance of social and health aspects of reproductive health and quality of life among women and potential impact of reproductive health on quality of life among women in Goa.[47]

While Sheila M. D'Souza's has compared women in mining and non-mining areas, Gregoria A. Ruiz in her thesis *'The Youth in Contemporary Goan Society –A study in Sociology of Youth'*, (2010) compares and contrasts the marked disparity between hinterland areas have less access to educational services and economic opportunities as compared to the youth in coastal belt and urban areas with Scheduled Tribes being in a more disadvantageous position. While ideation of youth regarding family relationships deviates from the traditional pattern in India they are none too happy about limited job opportunities in the region and 'migration is viewed as solution to this dilemma'.[48] Sizeable number of students pursue higher education only to migrate for greener pastures.

Educational standards in Goa leave much to be desired. It is a known fact and a common refrain that Goan students lag behind in any all-India completive exams. In education at all levels Principal is 'leader' who determines pace of corporate transformation and success. This involves creating a winning culture, or efficient work-process or any other number of ancillary attributes which are sine qua non for success. Russell

D'Souza in his PhD thesis '*Leadership Behaviour of Principals in High and Low Performing Secondary Schools of Goa in Relation to Certain Relevant Variables*', (2006), emphasizes on importance of importance of quality human resources for success of education system. Underscoring stellar role of leaders in education Russell states:

> School Principal as leader of group harnesses, searches and exploits untapped potentialities of group members for their own growth and for institutional growth. A vibrant, dedicated, self-driven and polished staff emerges as a result of experiencing effective leadership behavior of the school Principal, a favourable school organizational climate and availability of psychological, physiological and environmental circumstances that cause a person to say 'I am satisfied with the job'.[49]

Thus need of the hour is transformational principal leaders who through charismatic and inspirational role are able to motivate teachers to act not out of self interest but out of commitment to a higher ideal of transcendent goal.[50] Actually studies are required to investigate on issues like knowledge economy and income disparities, innovation and inequality, inclusion in education, etc. Studies are also required to investigate regarding (including social) relevance of education on whole. It would be in fitness of things if Goa had a dedicated research centre in education.

(iii) Research in Commerce and Economics

Goa faces peculiar economic problems which are unique to the region which has been taken up for research by scholars. For instance, Anna R. Ferrao e Fernandes, in her thesis *Marketing Practice and Problems of Pharmaceutical Companies Registered in Goa*', (2009), concludes that smaller pharmaceutical units are adversely affected by the competitive marketing that takes place leading to company-chemist-doctors nexus in rural areas where substitution of prescription at the chemist level takes place and the Drug Control Administration is inadequately staffed to effectively regulate and monitor the pharmaceutical industry in Goa. Manasvi M. Kamat, '*Goa's Iron Ore Exports:*

An Empirical Investigation into Growth, Contribution and Competitiveness', (2009) discusses growth trajectory of mining industry accounting for 25 per cent of country's production and 46 per cent of its exports earning substantial foreign exchange.[51] Manasvi M. Kamat concludes that sub-scale mining, lack of logistics infrastructure and regulatory hurdles and delays are major constraints for mining. Besides, few mines produced more than two million tonnes annually and threat of environmental degradation results in higher costs in mining and shipping, leading to low investments in the sector and in sterilisation of low grade resources.[52] Mining scam which Shah Commission had highlighted, loss to exchequer, and environmental and moral havoc that new rich of mining industry has created in Goa needs thorough critical evaluation by a team of qualified professional researchers. Besides, often common resources of tribal communities end up being exploited by the rich capitalist through lease of land for mining and other activities. This aspect needs further exploration in an unbiased manner to show how tribal community leaders, activists, and others are acquiesced, silenced or bought over by capitalist to further their insatiable greed.

Deepali P. Karmali, in her doctoral work *'Factors Determining International Trade in Services: An Econometric Analysis Using Country Level Panel Data'*, (2006), tried to determine whether trade in services depended on trade in goods along with other factors. Study states the obvious that trade in services would be engine of economic growth in developed as well as developing countries bridging the north south divide as labour rich developing countries would get maximum benefits from service trade growth. However, it is also a fact that trade is services is destabilizing traditional societies world over with people moving to newer and farther areas.[53] Is it not a fact that trade in services is a western requirement to capitalise on cheap labour of developing countries to further its dominance? This needs deeper probing. Further, Goan Diaspora spread world over is also good area of research which may need a band of dedicated interdisciplinary team to understand complex issue across time and space. Savio da Piedade Faleiro in well researched PhD thesis *'Economic implications of HIV/AIDS on individuals and households in Goa'*, (2011), concluding that hardships and adversities for household affected by HIV / AIDS are manifold with a very negative and depressing impact on employment and income of those affected. Economic dilemma of households gets compounded due to discrimination which households have to endure.[54] It should be also remembered that discrimination is at hands of a highly literate Goan society with constituents behaving irrationally and sometimes in a provocative manner towards affected people which needs thorough analysis through scientific inquiry. There is also a need for a study on social and political 'drivers' of HIV / AIDS in Goa.

Blanche R.C.S. Mascarenhas e Fernandes, in *'Trade Unions in Goa – a Comparative Study'*, (2009) discusses about issues affecting labour in industry in pre- and post-liberation Goa. Anilkumar G. Garag in his doctoral research work titled *'Valuation of Futures in Indian Stock Market – An Empirical Analysis'*, (2009) has brought out relationship between (i) cost of carry and risk free rate of return, (ii) cost of carry and change in risk free rate of return (iii) change in futures price and change in cost of carry and (iv) change in open interest and change in futures price. Garag concludes that change in futures prices cannot be explained by change in open interest and change in cost of carry. He has brought out the finding that investors do not consier that risk free rate of return is as the cost of carry and there is no relation between change in cost of carry and change in risk free rate of return.[55] Harip Khanapuri in PhD thesis *'Dynamics of Returns in Emerging Markets: Evidence from Asian and Indian Stock Markets'*, (2009), concludes that emerging markets in Asia provide good investment opportunities to international portfolio investors as they provided significant high average daily positive returns which higher than those in developed countries. The emerging markets in Asia were also volatile indicating that they are high risk investment avenues for portfolio investors.[56]

Suresh Shanbhogue has studied socio-economic impact

of public finances in Goa for his doctoral work. His study indicates that fundamentals of the state are quite stron in terms of production, consumption, exchange and distribution. The state also has high GDP and per capita income. Study also bring out the fact that increasing trend of non-development expenditure mainly on paying salaries, pension and interest payment on borrowings is cause of concern in long run. Study also brings out serious impact of cost and time overruns in implementation of projects. Indeed Goans must fight against their *susegad* nature as it is taking a heavy economic toll. Study highlights inadequate monitoring mechanism to oversee implementation of state policies leading to inordinate delays in achieving goals.[57]

(iv) Research in English and Indian Languages

Canvass of research undertaken at languages departments is wide, varied and quite interesting. Cidalia Bodade, in her research on *'Shashi Deshpande's Women Characters Are They Empowered Women or Do They Define a Mask of Tranquil Feminity? Or Creative Feminity.?'* (2006), highlights plight of Indian women who feel smothered and fettered in a tradition-boung, male-dominated society. Women are aware of their strengths and limitations but find themselves thwarted by a society conditioned overwhelmingly by a patriarchal mindset. Deshpande's women protagonists are victims of prevalent gross gender discrimination first as daughters and later as wives.[58] Maria Isabel Santa Rita Vas, in a well researched study *'Performing Change: A Study of Theatre in Context of Social Transformation in Three Asian Cultures in Twentieth Century'*, (2008), tells about the fact that societies in India,China and Sri Lanka in twentieth century struggling over colonial rule or political upheavals became sites for contestations. Hegemonic tussle, revolutionary language, new constructions of gender, ethnic or religious identity and space, took centre-stage and theatre of these countries presented a tussle between tradition and modernity with regard to these issues. Significantly, theatre space which had been rather a 'colonised space' through exclusion of subalterns like women and tribals had begun to be contested for the period under study.[59]

Prema Angela Rocha, '*Salman Rushdie: A Critical Study of His Novels*', (2008), attempts to show how history, politics and identity of Indian subcontinent viewed via consciousness of the migrant dominates narratives of Rushdie's novels. Prema Angela Rocha brings out how colonial and no-colonial power structures, notion of plural identity, migration, belonging, post-colonial social tabulations like corruption in public sphere, cultural polarization and fragmentation dominate Rushdie's writings.[60] It is generally written that India has always been a deep rooted value system, though day to day reality may indicate otherwise, Reshma Tabassum, in '*Gender, Female Sexuality Power and Family Relationships in Novel of Mulk Raj Anand, R. K. Narayan and Raja Rao: A Critical Study*', (2009), shows how 'exhibiting trends of true Indians, (they) affirm values of life and display supreme faith in moral order in their novels.[61]

The departments of Hindi, Marathi and Konkani have contributed substantially to research for the last quarter of a century since setting up of Goa University. However, due to want of time and space it is appropriate to discuss in brief contribution to research in Konkani only. Nayak, Jayanti, in her thesis 'Konkani *Lokvedantali Baylechi Pratima: Ek Samajik – Sanskrutik Abhyas*', (2004), discusses life and times of women in Konkani folklore and literature. The work shows the subservient nature of women in a patriarchal society as seen in Konkani folk-stories, proverbs, songs, etc. Prakash Narayan Naik in his doctoral thesis '*Kathakar Chandrakant Keni: Ek Mullyankan*', (2010), has extensively researched on significant contribution of Chandrakant Keni to enrichment of Konkani literature in post-liberation period. Chandrakant Keni was the editor of Marathi daily 'Rashtramath' and Konkani newspaper 'Sunaparant'. Keni won Sahitya Academy Award for his Konkani book *Ashad Pawal*. His role during Opinion Poll (1967), which was held to decide about Goa's political status with Indian Union, i.e., to merge with neighbouring Maharashtra or remain as a union territory, will forever remain etched in the annals of Goas history. Keni had played important role in language issue. Gunani Sadanand Desai, has worked on *'Shenoi Gonyababanlen Konkani Sahitya ani Samajik Chetna'*, (2008). Shenoi Gonyabab was a noted Konkani writer and activist who had started writing in Konkani at the time when he was in Bombay. He gave a series of lectures on *"Goenkaaranchi Goianbhaili Vosnook"* (Goan migrants outside Goa) at the Saraswat Brahman Samaj, Mumbai, in 1927. He also wrote a historical book on *'Albuquerquan Goen Koshem Jiklem'* (How Albuquerque Won Goa). Shenoi Gonyabab is also famous for his translation of the Bhagwad Gita into Konkani. Rajay R. Pawar has researched extensively on Konkani poetry which is apparent in his thesis *'Konkani Kavitentalen Goyache Samaj Darshan (1960 te 1990 meren ujavada aayillya devnagritlya Konkani kavitchya sandbhart)'*, (2011). Studies in Konkani are supported by Goa Konkani Akademy, Directorate of Art & Culture, Govt. of Goa, etc.

However, Konkani literature is vast and varied and in several scripts. Research carried out is just tip of the iceberg and much ground need to be covered. While lately there have been attempts to research on Konkani in Devnagari script there is enough scope for systematic research on Konkani in Roman (romi) script. Popular theatre like *'tiatr'*, *'khell-tiatr'*, *natak*, and Konkani songs, folk literature, customs and traditions, etc., need to be researched for better understanding of social dynamics. For instance, Reginald Fernandes, Caridade Damaciano Fernandes and Eliot Ely are some of the best selling novelist in Roman script Konkani whose works await exploration by researchers for understanding kaleidoscope of Goan society. There is much scope for studies on content analysis which is a versatile tool for social science and media research.[62] Scope and context of media effects research is also a virgin area which requires exploration by social scientists.

Church contribution to preservation and furthering of studies in Konkani also requires adequate research. There is scope to unravel reasons for Catholics in Goa being highly consumerist community. Concomitantly Goan Catholics pursuing higher education and research dwindling with every passing day. Instead call of sea attracts Goan Catholics.

Catholics of Goa over last four to five centuries have prefer to spread across the globe both in the Muslim and Christian world. So, Catholic Diaspora studies are also need of hour. Catholic culture is slowing being swamped in post-liberation period following out-migration of community in large numbers and in-migration of people from across the ghat region. Studies need to be conducted to know Goans and Catholic community cope with such issues. In fact it would be interesting for a team of social scientists from various disciples to band together to conduct a focussed study on intergroup relations between majority and minority community, for in recent years we have started to realise that so-called minority problems are rather majority problems.[63]

Conclusion

The paper has attempted to give a cursory view of social science research in Goa across a few disciplines. In a short paper like this it is not feasible to make a comprehensive study. However, a few observations which can be made is that the present status of social science research in Goa indicates that there is a need to address issues of methodological sophistication, adequate content coverage with focus on social relevance and above all researchers should strive to effectively communicate their research findings to intellectual community through peer-reviewed publication. A major lacuna of studies in social sciences in Goa is that display of lack of clarity about concepts and ideas is quite evident.

Besides, hardly anybody discusses how their research work has added to theory building. Indeed most of the thesis and other publications are descriptive in nature. It is observed that generally researchers in Goa opt either for quantitative or mixed methodology of research. Qualitative research is yet to pick up in social sciences. It is also time for researchers to take to new form of knowledge production which is context-driven, problem-focused and interdisciplinary. This is labelled as mode-2 knowledge production which involves multidisciplinary teams brought together for short periods of time to work on specific problems in real world. Social Science research in Goa across various fields is still traditional in that it is academic, investigator-initiated and discipline-based knowledge production.[64] However, organisation of 'Capacity Building Workshops' by ICSSR (WRC-Mumbai) in collaboration with Directorate of Higher Education in 2013 onwards is a step in right direction. It would be in fitness of things if ICSSR conducts short term courses for PhD guides and reviewers as systematic review would go a long way in ensuring quality of social science research.[65] Establishment of Centres for Research Methodology at all universities and select colleges is also a need of the hour. Course on research ethics is also a felt need. Researchers also require a good grounding in critical theories of society. Hopefully, in years to come this would bear good fruits in form of better environment for social science research in Goa region.

NOTES

1. Government of India (2013), *Economic Suryey: 2013-14 Services Sector*, pp. 173-191, http;//indiabudget.nic.in/es2013-14/echap-10.pdf, accessed on 28 December, 2014.
2. A. Chakrabarti, (2007), *Higher Education and Research in India: an Overview*, Helsinki: Sitra Reports, p. 18.
3. https://www.unigoa.ac.in/contentarticledisp.php?id=1 accessed on 10th November, 2014.
4. I.M. Minch, (2013), Higher education and research in India, *International Journal of Social Science & Interdisciplinary Research*, 2 (3), 106-9.
5. A. Bloom, (1987), *The Closing of the American Mind*, New York: Simon & Schuster, p. 353; Oxenham, M. (2013). *Higher Education in Liquid Modernity*, London: Routledge, pp. 5-6; Hackmann, H. & St. Clair, A. L. (2012), *Transformative Cornerstones of Social Science Research for Global Change*, Paris: Report of the International Social Science Council, p. 4.
6. D.E. Comstock, (1982), "A method for critical research," in Bredo, E. & Feinberg, W. (eds.), *Knowledge and Values in Social and Educational Research*, Philadelphia: Temple University Press, pp. 370-390.
7. Following sites gives publication in social sciences by Goa

based publishers: http://www.scribd.com/doc/76671049/Goa1556-Catalogue-Books-from-Goa#scribd; http://libcat.unigoa.ac.in/cgi-bin/koha/opac-search.pl?q=pb:Broadway%20Publishing%20House.

8. Often literature review is cursory, research methodology is suspect, and findings indicate hardly anything more than know knowledge.
9. H. Scholberg, (1982), *Bibliography of Goa and the Portuguese in India*, New Delhi: Promilla & Co. Pub. The book gives almost a complete picture of publishing activity in and on Goa during colonial and in immediate post liberation period. Read, Shastry, B.S. & Navelkar,V. R. (1989). *Bibliography of Dr. Pissurlencar's Collection*, Vol. I-III, Bambolim: Goa University Pub.; Navelkar, V.R. (1997). *Bibliography of Dr. Nuno Gonsalves Collection*, Taleigao Plateau: Goa University Publication.
10. M. Oxenham, *op. cit.*, pp. 1-51.
11. Narayan, J. (2005), *Reforming Higher Education in India*, http://www.loksatta.org/cms/documents/advocacy/highedu.pdf, accessed on 26 December, 2014; Altbach, Philip G., Reisberg, L. & Rumbley, Laura E. (2009). *Trends in Global Higher Education: Tracking an Academic Revolution*, http://www.uis.unesco.org/Library/Documents/trends-global-higher-education-2009-world-conference-en.pdf, accessed on 26 December, 2014.
12. A. Smith & Webster, F. (1997), 'Conclusion – an affirming flame', in Smith, A. & Webster, F. (eds.), *The Postmodern University?* Buckingham: Open Uni. Press, pp. 99-113.
13. R. Kumar & Hill, D. (2009), *Global Neoliberalism and Education and its Consequences*, Oxon: Routledge, in Oxenham, M., *op. cit.*, pp. 1-51.
14. M. Oxenham, *op. cit.*, pp. 1-51.
15. Ibid.
16. Ibid.
17. Ibid.
18. Visiting Research Professor Program (VRPP) includes: D.D. Kosambi Visiting Professorship in Interdisciplinary Studies – Professors Romila Thapar, Madhav Gadgil and Sudhir Kakar; Dayanand Bandodkar Visiting Professorship in Political Economy – Professors Amit Bhaduri, Ashok Chandra and Lord Meghnad Desai; Kavivarya Bakibab Borkar Visiting Research Professorship in Comparative Literature – Jeet Thayil, Ashok Vajpeyi; Mario Miranda Visiting Research Professorship in fine art/painting /illustrative cartooning – Professor Jyotindra Jain,

Orijit Sengupta and Atul Dodiya; Anthony Gonsalves Visiting Professorship in Western Music – Professor Santiago Lusardi Girell and group; Nana Shirgaonkar Visiting Research Professorship in traditional music –Shuba Mudgal.

19. http://gulibrary.weebly.com.
20. A.A.S. Benadict, (2002), *Corporate Disclosure Practice in India - an Empirical Study*; Garge, Anil Kumar G. (2009). *Valuation of futures in Indian Stock Market – An Empirical Analysis*; John, M. (2009). *Corporate Governance in Selected Industries*; Khanapuri, H. (2009). *Dynamics of Returns in Emerging Markets: Evidence from Asian and Indian Stock Markets*; Madiwal, G. (2008). *Performance Analysis of Co-operative Sugar Factories in Maharashtra, Karnataka and Goa (A Comparative Study of Select Units)*; Nambiar, B. (2008). *An Evaluation of HRD Practices in Financial Services Sector of India*; Nath, G. C. (2004). *Long Memory and Linkage Dynamics Between Equity and Foreign Exchange Markets in India.–An Empirical Evidence*; Patil, M. R. (1999). *A Study on Performance Evalutation of Urban Cooperative Banks in Goa*; Patkar, S. B. (2004). *Factoring and Mutual Fund Services of SBI and Can Bank: A Comparative Study*; Raju, A. (2002). *Mutual Fund Prices and NAV: An Empirical Analysis of Discounts in Indian Context*; Rebello, R.W. (2009). *Corporate Earnings and Stock Returns in India: An Empirical Study*; Rodrigues, A. P. (2002). *Accounting and Financial Practices of Small Scale Industry*; Sebastin, A. (2008). *Financial Applications of Entropy Theory*; Shanbhogue, S. (2010). *Socio-economic impact of public finance in Goa: a critical Evaluation*; Shashikant, U. (1998). *Portfolio Investments in Emerging Markets (An Empirical Analysis of Diversification Benefits)*; Torcato, S. (2006). *Study on Vocational Education Programme and its Impact on Entrepreneurship Development and Employment Opportunities in Goa.*
21. N. Abreu, (2004), *Women and Employment (A Study of Employment of Women in Selected Industries in Industrial Estates of Goa)*; Chandan, B.P.S. (2009). *Economic Impact of Regional Trade Agreements: A Study of ASEAN and its Implications on India*; De Souza, C.A.M. (2009). *Labour Welfare and Job Satisfaction: A Comparative Study of Indian Pharmaceutical Companies and Multinational Pharmaceutical Companies in Goa*; Dias, A.A.D. (2004). *A Critical Evaluation of DWCRA - Development of Women and Children in Rural areas and ICDS (Integrated Child Development Services) Programmes in Goa*; Fernandes, A.R.F. (2009). *Marketing Practice and Problems of Pharmaceutical Companies Registered in Goa*; Kamat, M.M. (2009). *Goa's Iron Ore Exports: An Empirical*

Investigation into Growth, Contribution and Competitiveness; Karmali, D. P. (2006). *Factors Determining International Trade in Services: An Econometric Analysis Using Country Level Panel Data;* Mascarenhas, B.R.C.S.E.F. (2009). *Trade Unions in Goa – A Comparative Study;* Nagvenkar, H.T. (1999). *Salt and Goan Economy (A Study of Goa's Salt Industry and Salt Trade in 19th and 20th Centuries During Portuguese Rule);* Nayak, R.S. (2008). *Regional Disparities in Economic Development of Goa: A Talukawise Sectoral Analysis;* Reddiah, R. (1997). *Evolution of An Eco-Development Strategy for Coastal Area Case Study of Sindhudurg Dist. Maharashtra;* Rizvi, H.S. (1997). *Economics Structure, Foreign Trade and Balance of Payments: A Case Study of India, 1970-71 to 1990-91;* Urankar, G.R. (2008). *Economic Growth of Goa: A Sectoral and Structural Analysis with Special Reference to Service Sector.*

22. A.C.M. Aradhana, (2003), *Understanding of Complaining Behaviour and Handling of Complaints in Hotels of Goa – A Managerial Perspective;* Colvalkar, T.M. (2009). *Impact of Service Channel on Consumer Satisfaction – A Study in Health Care Services;* Dayanand, M.S. (2003). *Tourism Attraction Development: A Comparative Study of Development of Small and Medium Tourism Attractions in Goa and Portugal;* Desai, P.G.H. (2004). *Determinants of Expeditious Complaint Redressal in Banks;* Fernandes, C.F.V. (2008). *Impact of Personal and Job/Organizational Factors on Organizational Role Stress (An Empirical Study of Private and Public Bank Officers);* Fernandes, K. (2003). *Index Fund Implementation in India;* George, B.P. (2004). *Holiday attachment: construct measure, and its Relation with Customer Loyalty;* Hegde, S. G. (1996). *Study of Complaints and Complaining Behaviour of Customers of Public Sector Commercial Banks in Goa;* Mallya, P.D. (2004). *Performance Measurement and Evaluation in Banks;* Nattuvathuekal, B. (2009). *Impact of Structural Variables (Autonomy Decentralization and Formalization) on Market Orientation and Organizational Performance: A Study in Indian Retail Banking Sector;* Pathak, J.P. (1993). *Information System Auditing and Distributed Data Processing;* Raykar, V. (1997). *Consequences of Violence: An Exploratory Study on Industries of Goa;* Salgaonkar, P. B. (2004). *Determinants of Loyalty: An Exploratory Empirical Study in Health Care Service.*
23. A.J. Abreo, (2003), *Co-Curricular Activities in Different Types of Secondary Schools of Goa: A Study;* Almeida, R. F. (1991). *Teacher-Pupil Relationship and its Impact on Learning in School and at Home of High School Students in Goa;* Caldeira, M. (2006). *An Evaluation*

of Centrally Sponsored Scheme of Vocationalisation of Education at Higher Secondary Stage in Goa; De Souza, S. (1993). *Standardization of Norms for Physical Fitness Tests for Girls in Age Group of 13 to 16 Years in State of Goa*; DSouza, R. (2006). *Leadership Behaviour of Principals in High and Low Performing Secondary Schools of Goa in Relation to Certain Relevant Variables*; Gonsalves, E.N.B. (2003). *Cost Analysis in Higher Education in Goa*; Iyer, G.M. (2001). *A Psycho-Social Study of First Generation Learners*; Mendez, B. (1996). *Qualitative Study of Impact of Rational Emotive Therapy on High School Girls Exhibiting Emotionally Ddisturbed Behaviour*; Paily, M.U. (1999). *Development of Critical Thinking Among Secondary School Students in Relation to Some Psycho – Contextual Variables*; Vernal, Louis. (1999). *Image of School in Goa - A Study at Higher Secondary Stage*.

24. H. Joharpurkar, (1995), *Prachin Marathi Jain Aakhyankavyancha Abhyas*; Kajrekar, G.G. (2009). *Rajan Gawas Yanche Kathatma Sahitya: Ek Chikistak Abhyas*; Kale, G. (1999). *Meghdutache Marathi Avatar-Ek Chikistak Abhyas (Critical Analysis)*; Kale, G. R. (1992). *Bodhlikambari (Sant Mankoji Bodhale) Ek Tapashilwar Abhyas*; Kandolkar, S. (1998). *Nature and Manner of Self-Expression in Personal Essay in Marathi (1930-1990)*; Kanolkar, B.G. (2002). *Prof. Laxmanrao Sardesai Yanche Kathalekhan: Ek Abhyas*; Mangutkar, Ashok D. (2006). *Critical Study of Novels of Subhash Bhende*; Pandit, A.A. (1999). *Pandit Mahadevshastri Joshi Yanche Kathavishwa*; Prabhudesai, V.V. (1999). *Gomantakiya Marathi Kadambari*; Sadre, K.M. (1996). *A Critical Study of Modernity and Modernism in Marathi Poetry (With SP. ref. to B.S. Mardhekar, P.S. Rege, Vinda Karandikar, Dilip Chitre and Arun Kolatkan): A Critical Study*; Tadkodkar, S.M. (1995). *Critical Study of Contribution of Prof. Anant Kakba Priolkar to Marathi Literature*.
25. A. Aga, (1992), *Northrop Frye As A Literary Critic*; Bhandare, Sandhya. (2000). *Plays of James Reaney and Pundalik Naik: A Comparative Study*; Bhandary, S. (2004). *Canadian Native Narratives: A Study of Four Women Novelists*; Bodade, C. (2006). *Shashi Deshpande's Women Characters are they Empowered Women or do they Define a Mask of Tranquil Feminity? or Creative Feminity?'*; Budkuley, K.J. (1994). *Golding's Novel: A Study of William Golding's Fictional Work*; Caldeira, N. (1998). *Multiculturalism and Marginalized Psyche in Select Representative Fiction of Canada*; Dennis, I.I. (1995). *Malcolm Lowry: A Critique of His Writings*; D'lima, E. J. (2004). *Creative and Critical Writing of Armando Menezes*; Fernandes, A. R. (2004). *Tiatro – A Critical*

Study; Fernandes, C. (2004). *Fiction of Alice Munro: A Study*; Fernandes, L. M. (1999). *Canadian Fiction of Margaret Lawrence: A Study*; Fernandes, S. (2006). *Landscape of Realism in Selected Plays of Arthur Miller: A Study*; Gomes, M. C. (2006). *Fictional World of Peter Carey*; Guha, T. (2009). *A Post-Colonial Critique of Nirad C. Chaudhuri's Writings*; Kulkarni, M.M. (1994). *Sri Aurobindo, S Savitri - A Study of Epic as a Twentieth Century Indian Specimen of Apocalyptic Literature*; Menezes, R.L. (2008). *Immigrant Women in Fiction of Willa Cather*; Miranda, E. de Jesus, (1995). *Literatura Indo-Portuguesa Dos Seculos xix e xx: Um Estudo De Temas Principais No Contexto Socio-Historico*; Rocha, P.A. (2008). *Salman Rushdie: A Critical Study of his Novels*; Sardesai, M. (2006). *A Comparative Linguistic and Cultural Study of Lexical Influences on Konkani*; Tabassum, R. (2009). *Gender, Female Sexuality, Power and Family Relationships in Novel of Mulk Raj Anand, R.K. Narayan and Raja Rao: A Critical Study*; Vas, M.I.S.R. (2008). *Performing Change: A Study of Theatre in Context of Social Transformation in Three Asian Cultures in Twentieth Century*.

26. M.V. Bharne, (1992), *Hermeneutics in science*; Desai, M.B. (1996). *A Critical Study of Karl Popper's Theory of Falsificationism: A Semantic Approach*; Geevarghese, I.V. (2005). *Environmental Ethics: Problems and Approaches*; Kunkolienkar, K.R. (1992). *Perspectives on Mind and Consciousness: A Critical Evaluation*; Menezes, M.E. (1996). *Reinterpreting J. Krishnamurti: Towards A Comprehensive Theory of Education*; Menezes, M.N. (1996). *Quest for Human Subjectivity: An Essay in Philosophical Anthropology*; Padmaja, L.V. (1993). *A Philosophical Probe into Feminine Life-World*; Rodrigues, R.R. (2009). *Understanding Linguistics and Hermeneutical Foundations of Genetic Epistemology*; Vernekar, S.D.P. (1998). *Understanding Medical Thought and Practice. (An Essay on Ethics of Informed Consent)*.
27. R. Braganza, (2001), *Goa-Karnataka Relations 1763-1857 (A Political and Economic Study*; Chandran, K. (1989). *Working Class Movement in Travancore (1922-1949)*; Chauhan, R.S. (1993). *Siddis of Janjira and Portuguese*; Costa, M.M.L. de. (2002). *History of Trade and Commerce in Goa: 1878-1961*; D'Cruz, S.J. (2003). *Franciscans in Goa*; Desai, K. (1993). *Trade Union Movement in Goa 1936-1986*; Dias, A.D.R, (2004). *Socio-Economic History of Goa with Special Reference to Communidade System: 1750-1910*; D'souza, A.M. (2008). *Reconstructing Urban Maritime History of Goa: A Study of Port-Capital of Chrandrapur, Gopakapattana and Ella*; Gracias, M.F.L.T. Da Silva. (1992). *Health and Hygiene in*

Goa 1510-1961; Kamat, V.V. (1996). *Socio-Political and Religious Life in Goa (1900 to 1946)*; Kumar, N.D. (1996). *History of Police in Goa*; Martins, X.M. (1994). *Portuguese Shipping and Ship Building in Goa 1510-1780*; Mishra, R. (2004). *History of Press in Goa*; Mitragotri, V.R. (1992). *A Socio-Cultural History of Goa from Bhojas to Vijayanagara*; Phaldesai, P.R. (2003). *Cultural History of Canacona Taluka of Goa*; Radhakrishnan, N. (1994). *Dayanand Balkrishnan Bandodkar: Architect of Modern*; Rao, N. E. (2001). *Craft Production and Trade in South Kanara: A. D. 1000-1763*; Rao, V.G. (2003). *Temples of Goa - An Architectural Study*; Risbud, S.S. (2002). *Goa Struggle for Freedom, 1946-1961: Contribution of National Congress-Goa and Azad Gomantak.*

28. A. de. Sa, (1994), *Some Aspects of Social Justice in India*; Desai, A.A.R. (2003). *Voices in Liberation Struggle Case of Goa-1947-1961*; Desai, N.B. (2002). *Politics of Script: Case of Konkani (1961-1992)*; Fernandes, A.F. (1995). *Cabinet Government in Goa Since Liberation 1961-(1993)*; John, P.K. (1994). *Development and Critical Evaluation of Fire Services in India*; Rodrigues, M. do Ceu. (1996). *Opinion Poll in Goa - An Evaluation of Method to Settle Controversy*; Salgaonkar, S.P. (2000). *Women, Political Power and State in Goa.*
29. G.S. Desai, (2008), *Shenoy Goybabalem Konkani Sahitya Ani Samajik Chetana*; Naik, J. (2004). *Konkani Lokvedantali Bailenchi Pratima (Ek Samajik-Samskrutik Abbhas*; Vazrikar, P. (2006). *Konkani Kadambaryantalem Samaj Darshan.*
29. A.M. Botelho, *Language and Early Schooling in Goa*; D'souza, M.S. (2008), *Reproductive Health and Quality of Life (A Sociological Study of Women in Mining and Non-mining Regions)*; Gomes, M.B. (1993). *Ethnomedicine and Healing Practices in Goa (Kunnbi Case)*; Gonsalves, J. (2007). *Food and Foodways in Transition (A Socio-Cultural Study of Domestic Dinning in Goa)*; Kurian, C. (1991). *A Sociological Study of Schizophrenic Patients in Goa*; Mangalekar, R.S. (2006). *Development, Displacement and Rehabilation (A Sociological Case Study of Sea Bird Project, Karwar)*; Mascarenhas, M.N. (1993). *Social Construction of Powerless Woman*; Monteiro, A. (1993). *State Subject and Text Construction of Meaning in Television*; Pereia, B.V. (2007). *Cultural Location of Alcoholic Beverage in Goan Society*; Pereira, J.G. (2010). *Language and Public Sphere (A Sociological Study of Language Question in Goa Since 1987)*; Ruiz, G.A. (2010). *Youth in Contemporary Goan Society (A Study in Sociology of Youth)*; Sa, B.J.W. de. (2001). *Role of Christian Organisation in Upliftment of Poor and Helpless in Goan Society*; Sequeira, R. (2009). *Mitagars of Goa: A Sociological Study of A*

Community in Transition; Somajaji, G. (1997). *Udupi, Hoteliers in Goa (A Sociological Study in Occupational Mobility)*; Sowrabha, C. (2004). *Liberalisation and Enterprise: A Study in Sociology of Work Culture*; Thakur, M.K. (2003). *State, Development and Village: A Sociological Study of Rural Development Institutions*; Thomas, L. (2002). *Religion and Society: Indigenisation of Roman Catholicism in South India*; Tombat, N. (1995). *Tristao De Braganza-Cunha (1891-1958) and Rise of Nationalist Consciousness in Goa.*

30. Teotonio R. de, Souza, (1990), *Goa Through the Ages: An Economic History*, Vol. II, New Delhi: Concept Pub.
31. A few of the very critical and well researched articles included in the volume are: Kamat, P.P. *Historical Geography and Natural Resources*, pp. 1-54; Srivastava, H.C. *Demographic History and Human Resources*, pp. 55-77; Souza, Teotonio R. de, *Rural Economy and Life*, pp. 78-116; Gune, V.T. *Goa's Coastal and Overseas Trade – from Earliest Times to 1510 AD*, pp. 117-136; Mathew, K.S. *Trade and Commerce in Sixteenth Century Goa*, pp. 137-145; Pearson, M.N. *Goa based Seaborne Trade (17th - 18th Century)*, pp. 146-167; Souza, Teotonio R. De & Borges C.J. *Transport and Communication*, pp. 227-247; Mascarenhas-Keyes, S. *International migration – its development, reproduction and Economic Impact on Goa Up to* 1961, pp. 242-261, all in Souza, Teotonio R. De (ed.), *Goa Through the Ages: An Economic History*, Vol. II, New Delhi: Concept Pub., 1990.
32. International Seminars on Indo-Portuguese History (ISIPH) was first convoked in 1978 in Goa, which seminar heralded a new approach to the subject and one which brought to light wealth of sources on Indo-Portuguese History. ISIPH-2 was held in Lisbon (1980) and ISIPH-3 was conducted again in Goa (1982). The first two International Seminars deliberated on sources and problems of Indo-Portuguese History. The first seminar in October 1978 was attended by many renowned scholars from the world. Important papers presented at the seminar are published in a work by Correa-Afonso, John. (ed.) (1981). *Indo-Portuguese History: Sources and Problems*, Bombay: OUP. The volume contains many valuable studies, important among them being John Correia-Afonso's account of the Jesuit records found at Lisbon's Torre de Tombo. There is also a contribution by Luis F.R. Thomaz on Portuguese sources for sixteenth century Indian economic history. The volume also includes a survey of writings on Indo-Portuguese History by C. R. Boxer, A.R. Disney's land orientation for Indo-Portuguese studies, and

Teotonio R. de Souza's passionate plea at course correction by writing history of common man in Goa. G. Bouchon also outlines uses and problems of Portuguese documents for sixteenth century Goa. See for details, Pearson, M.N. (1981, reprint 2004). *Coastal Western India – Studies from the Portuguese Records*, New Delhi: Concept Pub.

33. ISIPH-3 focused on navigation, trade and cultural exchanges, all old issues but subjected to new questions. The papers (20 in number) have been published in a volume by Souza Teotonio R. de (ed.) (9185). *Indo-Portuguese History: Old issues, New Questions*, New Delhi: Concept Pub.. Internationally renowned scholars like Steensgaard, N. *The Teturn Vargoes of the Varreira in the 16th and Rarly 17th Ventury*, pp. 13-31, and *Asian Yrade and Eorld Rconomy from the 15th to the 18th Venturies*, pp. 225-236; Bouchon, G. *Glimpses of the Neginnings of the Carreira da India*, pp. 40-55; Mathew, K.S. *Indian Merchants and the Portuguese Trade on the Malabar Coast During the Sixteenth Century*, pp. 1-12; Blussé, L. & Winus, G. *The Origin and Rhythm of Dutch Aggression Against the Estado da India*, pp. 73-83; Correia-Afonso, J. *Manuel Godinho's Alternative to the Carreira da India*, pp. 84-89; Kulkarni, A.R. *Portuguese in the Deccan Politics: A Study of New Portuguese Documents from Lisbon*, pp. 114-122; Bacelar. J.P. e Oliveira, *Arrest, Spoliation and Exile of the Goa Jesuits According to Father Caeiro's de Exilio*, pp. 123-132, were among the Contributors to the Volume. Souza, Teotonio R. de, has Written Seminar Paper Titled *Capital Inputs in Goa's Freedom Struggle: The Bombay Connection*, pp. 102-113.
34. B.S. Shastry, (1987), *Goan Society Through the Ages*, New Delhi: Asian Pub. Services. Critically researched articles in volume include: Read, Kamat, N.K. *Gopakapattana Through the* Ages, pp. *49-55*; Borges, C.J. *Christianization of the Caste System in*, pp. 251-269; Chauhan, R.R.S. *Marketing in Goa During the 16th Century*, pp. 154-177; Kale, P. *Konkani Tiatr: An Expression of Popular Culture*, pp. 236-247.; Shastry, B.S., *Sources of Income and Items of Expenditure of the Churches in Goa (c. 1510-1800 a.d.): a note*, pp. 35-47.
35. M.N. Pearson, (1987), *Cambridge History of India 1.1 the Portuguese in India*, Cambridge: CUP, pp. 1-7.
36. M.N. Pearson, (1981 reprint 2004), *Coastal Western India – Studies from the Portuguese Records*, New Delhi: Concept Pub., pp. 1-17.
37. Ibid., pp. 1-2.
38. Souza, Teotonio R. de, (2014), *Goa Outgrowing Postcolonialisml*

Historical Explorations, CreateSpace Independent Publishing Platform.

39. Fundação Oriente – Panjim, has also on its own been undertaking various restoration works of architectural importance of heritage sites in Goa.
40. B.S. Shastry & Navelkar, V. R. (1989), *Bibliography of Dr. Pissurlencar's Collection*, Vol. I-III, Bambolim: Goa University Pub. In the three volumes the editors give a descriptive sketch of Dr. Pissurlencar's biography and historical works, a complete list of books and other historical material which he donated to the university, and reproduce letters which he received from eminent contemporary scholars and academicians. Goa University also has a vast collection gifted by the family of and Nuno Gonsalves, besides other families. Navelkar, V.R. (1997). *Bibliography of Dr. Uuno Gonsalves Collection*, Taleigao Plateau: Goa University Publication.
41. M. B. Afonso (2007), *Language and Early Schooling in Goa*, PhD submitted to Goa University, pp. 291-323.
42. Ibid.
43. Ibid.
44. Pereira, J.G. (2010), *Language and Public Sphere (A sociological Study of Language Question in Goa Since 1987)*, pp. 246-260.
45. D'souza, S.M. (2009), *Reproductive Health and Quality of Life. (A Sociological Study of Women in Mining and Non-mining Regions)*, PhD submitted to Goa University, pp. 239-250.
46. Ibid.
47. Ibid.
48. G.A. Ruiz, (2010), *Youth in Contemporary Goan Society (A Study in Sociology of Youth)*, PhD submitted to Goa University, pp. 228-334.
49. R. D'Souza, (2006), *Leadership Behaviour of Principals in High and Low Performing Secondary Schools of Goa in Relation to Certain Relevant Variables*, PhD Submitted to Goa University, pp. 235-274.
50. R. Dias, 'Quality Assurance in Higher Education: Role of the Stakeholders', in Dias R. (ed.), (2006), *Changing Scenario of Our Higher Education – Enhancement and Sustenance of Quality Assurance*, Quepem: Govt. College Quepem Pub. pp. 238-254.
51. A.R. Ferrao, Fernandes, (2009), *Marketing Practice and Problems of Pharmaceutical Companies Registered in Goa*, PhD Submitted to Goa University, pp. 242-262.
52. M.M. Kamat, (2009), *Goa's Iron Ore Exports: An Empirical*

Investigation into Growth, Contribution and Competitiveness, PhD submitted to Goa University, pp. 204-230.

53. D.P. Karmali, (2006), *Factors Determining International Trade in Services: An Econometric Analysis Using Country Level Panel Data*, PhD submitted to Goa University, pp. 202-216.
54. Savio P. Fallero, da Piedade, (2011), *Economic Implications of HIV/AIDS on Individuals and Households in Goa*, PhD submitted to Goa University, 269-298.
55. A.K.G. Garag, (2009), *Valuation of Futures in Indian Stock Market–An Empirical Analysis*, PhD submitted to Goa University, 179-192.
56. H. Khanapuri, (2009), *Dynamics of Returns in Emerging Markets: Evidence from Asian and Indian Stock Markets*, PhD submitted to Goa University, 172-187.
57. S. Shanbhogue, (2010), *Socio-Economic Impact of Public Finance in Goa: A Critical Evaluation*, PhD submitted to Goa University, 243-251.
58. C. Bodade, (2006), *Shashi Deshpande's Women Characters are They Empowered Women or Do They Define A Mask of Tranquil Feminity? or Creative Feminity?*, PhD submitted to Goa University, 241-269.
59. M.I.S.R. Vas, (2008), *Performing Change: A Study of Theatre in Context of Social Transformation in Three Asian Cultures in Twentieth Century*, PhD submitted to Goa University, 269-286.
60. P.A. Rocha, (2008), *Salman Rushdie: A Critical Study of his Novels*, PhD submitted to Goa University, 237-253.
61. R. Tabassi, (2009), *Gender, Female Sexuality Power and Family Relationships in Novel of Mulk Raj Anand, R.K. Narayan and Raja Rao: A Critical Study*, PhD submitted to Goa University, 254-278.
62. Devi, Prasad, B., 'Content analysis: a method in social science research', in Lal Das, D. K & Bhaskaran, V. (eds.). (2008), *Research Methods for Social Work*, New Delhi: Rawat, pp. 173-193.
63. K. Lewin, (1946), Action Research and Minority Problems, *Journal of Social Issues*, 4 (2), pp. 34-46.
64. M. Limoges, Gibbons, C., Nowotny, H., Schwartzman, S., Scott, P. & Martin Trow, *The New Production of Knowledge: The Dynamics of Science and Research in Contemporary Societies*. London: Sage, 1994.
65. M. Petticrew & Roberts, H. (2006), *Systematic Reviews in Social Sciences: A Practical Guide*, UK: Blackwell Publishing, pp. 1-27

8

Understanding History as a Concrete Science

Marzbaan Jaal

> The revisionists show that it is precisely the dialectic that must be removed if one wishes to found a thorough-going opportunist theory, a theory of 'evolution' without revolution and of 'natural development' into Socialism without conflict.
>
> Georg Lukács, *History and Class Consciousness.*

> Before Marx, two continents only had been opened up to scientific knowledge by sustained epistemological breaks: the continent of Mathematic with the Greeks (by Thales) and the continent of Physics (by Galileo and his successors). Marx has opened up to scientific knowledge a new, third scientific continent, the continent of history, by an epistemological break, whose first still uncertain strokes are still inscribed in The German Ideology, after having announced in the Theses on Feuerbach.
>
> Louis Althusser, *Lenin and Philosophy.*

It is indeed an irony when one is beginning an exploration on the social sciences when one is taking the views of thinkers whose epistemic positions stand totally in opposition to one another. Lukács, as we all know it was the philosophical founder of the historicist and humanist school within Marxism (along with Antonio Gramsci), whilst Althusser was the founder of the structuralist school. Both, as we again know it, are totally in antagonism to one another—the historicist and humanist school postulated a theory of "history with a subject", whilst structuralism was totally against it when they argued for a theory of "history as a process without the subject". What we are doing in starting with this opposition: humanism vs. structuralism in order to situate ourselves in the social sciences in India.

It is without doubts that though there is an abundance of excellent social scientific research being carried out in India, there is in the last resort some sort of what I would like to call an: "unhappy crisis" within the social sciences. The idea of an "unhappy crisis" I am deriving from Hegel's idea of the "unhappy consciousness" that he conceptualized in his *Phenomenology of Mind*, coupled with the theory of crisis in the sciences that Georg Lukács in *History and Class Consciousness* and Edmund Husserl talked of in his *The Crisis of the European Sciences*. In this sense we are in opposition to Althusser's position to the idea of the crisis of the sciences.[1] According to Althusser:

> There are phenomena, which we are beginning to understand, When certain sciences undergo important revolutions (at that time Mathematics and Physics), there will always be professional *philosophers*, to proclaim that the 'crisis in science', or mathematics, or physics, has begun. These philosophers' proclamations are, if I may say so, normal: for a whole category of philosophers spend their time predicting, i.e. awaiting, the last gasp of the sciences, in order to administer them the last rites of philosophy, *ad majorem gloriam Dei*.[2]

Despite this Althusserean intervention we shall be discussing the problem of the crisis of the sciences. Science cannot be taken in an uncritical way that Althusser certainly suggested, a science that is somehow beyond critique. And though I shall be discussing the problems raised by Husserl followed by the formulation of the Frankfurt School, it is Lukács' critique that remains the basis of our essay. It must be said that not only did "Western Marxism" (as Merlau-Ponty had called the non-Soviet discourse emanating in the shadows of Lukács' *History and Class Consciousness*) develop from Lukács, but also by and large a number of social scientific school developed after the Lukácsean inspiration. The Frankfurt School, as we all know it, was one such school of thought. Theodor Adorno, Walter Benjamin, Herbert Marcuse, Erich Fromm and Jürgen Habermas all sprang from this radical critique.

The questions however emerge: "What is so special to Lukács that different schools of the social sciences developed in Europe in the 20th century?" "How would this help in the development of the social sciences in India?" Keeping these questions in mind, I will like to state that one intends to create a radical social science for India, and thus be able to relate the above stated themes with radical Indian thinkers, most notable, Jyotiba Phule and B.R. Ambedkar. What I also intend to do is to bring the ideas of modernity and the critique of ritual which both sets of thinkers had conceptualized.

There are multiple understandings of the social sciences. One form follows the Weberian logic where science is understood as vocation. Neo-liberalism however has transformed this understanding of science as vocation into the understanding off science as business. But there is a third perspective that lies rather buried and this is the theme of science as a revolutionary endeavor. This essay is on the third perspective of the social sciences especially in Western India. And considering that there has been a shift to the right in Indian politics where serious sciences are now being confused with fascist mythopoetics, the very idea of science is now being devalued.

This third idea of science is basically a Marxist idea, but it is an idea that was also a part of the foundation of the education in India. It was J.P. Naik who had talked of beginning a Revolution with a Revolution. Now this idea of education in India in the first moments of India's independence as a revolutionary endeavor was against both the ideas of education as vocation and education as business. It was J.P. Naik who had talked of beginning a Revolution with a Revolution in his seminal essay 'To begin a Revolution with a Revolution'. This theme of Revolution with a Revolution is basically an idea that emerged in the French Revolution, a theme that Slavoj Žižek keeps central to his philosophical discourse. But this theme is also a theme that is central to the works of Jyotiba Phule and B.R. Ambedkar. Science is not something innocent, nor is it a commodity that can be bought in the global market.

However with the triumph of the fascist forces in the 2014 elections, followed by the victory in the state elections in Maharashtra and Haryana, and also with the now fascistization of education by the RSS, the role of the social sciences has totally changed. Science as vocation and business will now be subservient to the fascist forces. Unfortunately studies in fascism in India in particular and Asia in general have not taken centre stage of academic imagination. One could point to Jairus Banaji's works on fascism that have raised the issue of fascism. However the finer details in the Asiatic mode of production and the role of caste hegemony have not been brought out in his works. In a way then one can say that radical social sciences are struck by the specter of Eurocentric discourses. The main point is then to look into an alternative discourse of the social sciences in India. In 2006 Syed Farid Alatas published his *Alternative Discourses in the Asian Social Sciences: Responses to Eurocentrism* where he argued for an alternative model which is neither caught up in abstract particularism (the natavist discourses), nor in abstract universalism (Eurocentrism). What Alatas claims is that Western imperialism has systematically created what he calls the "captive mind" where the sciences in non-Western countries are subservient to the interests of imperialism. In this sense by and large the social sciences in Asia are under the grip of what we know as the "imperialism of categories".

The counterpoint to this is the decolonization of the education that thinkers like Paulo Freire, Frantz Fanon and Pierre Bourdeieu talked of. In this sense we are directly in opposition to the old Weberian thesis of science as vocation and the neo-liberal ideology of science as big business. What one does is that one directly confronts educational and scientific orthodoxy. For understanding this a little history of the crisis of the sciences in the twentieth century is necessary. One will have to go to the Critical Theory of the Frankfurt School in order to understand that the sciences cannot be taken uncritically, but they have to undergo a radical critique. Searching for the epistemic roots of critical theory is an extremely complex affair. Whilst Max Horkheimer and Theodor Adorno were influenced by their teacher Hans Cornelius in the 1920's—Horkheimer received his doctorate on the topic : *Zur Antinomie der teleologischen Urteilskraft* (1922) and his *Habilitationsschrift* titled *Kants Kritik der Urteilskraft als Bindeglied zwischen theoretischer und praktischer Philosophie* (1925) both were completed under Cornelius's direction, whilst Adorno's doctorate under Cornelius was on transcendental phenomenology titled *Die Transzendenz des Dinglichen und Noematischen in Husserl's Phänonenologie* (1924)—Herbert Marcuse's teachers included Husserl and Heidegger. However it is Husserl and Lukács's critiques of the European sciences that would form the epistemological basis for both Critical Theory's entire *oeuvre* as well as our investigation into the question of the status of the social sciences in India. It must be noted that the reception of Husserl and Lukács in twentieth-first century India, would pose the question: *"What is one to do with the social sciences when they were already stated to be crisis ridden a century earlier?"* It must be noted that both Husserl's and Lukács's works emerged in the gory and aftermath of the first imperialist world war (Lukács wrote these essays comprising his main text immediately after the 1917 Bolshevik revolution, whilst Husserl's text was composed in the thirties, the first part being published in 1936, the second part was published posthumously only in 1956-59), the intellectual climate of that period raised the question of the *relation between science and society. Is science then an autonomous, objectivistic system of knowledge or a social project closely related to the ruling ideology of that period? What are the specific characteristic of the modern sciences and if they are crises ridden, would the traditional sciences be a solution to the problem? What is the relation between modernity and the modern sciences?*

Now if not Husserl's *Crisis* at least Lukács's *History and Class Consciousness* (as well as Critical Theory emerging a few years later) has a pre-history based on the methodological dispute *(Methodenstreit)* in the social sciences in Germany and the question of the nature and relation between the natural sciences *(Naturwissenschaften)* and the social sciences *(Geisteswissenschaften)*. One only needs to recall Willhelm Dilthey's *Einleitung in die Geisteswissenschaften (Introduction to the Social Sciences,* 1883) and *Dië Entstehung der Hermeneutick (Origin of Hermeneutics,* 1900) to understand the rigorous line of demarcation to be drawn between the *Geistewissenschaften* and the *Naturwissenschaften.* One also recalls the neo-Kantian Wilhelm Windelbland's war of attrition raised against positivism in his 1894 rector's address at Strasbourg. And it is this hermeneutics of suspicion unleashed on the natural sciences (the tradition would be carried by Windelbland's student Heinrich Rickert and Georg Simmel) that would soon be embedded in Lukács's *History and Class Consciousness.* One cannot, as Lukács claims "seek refuge in the methods of natural science and use it as an ideal model of knowledge". According to Lukács, though he is said to be a Hegelian in the period of writing the *History and Class Consciousness,* there is also a hidden neo-Kantianism in his epistemic formulation. Consider this:

> When the ideal of scientific knowledge is applied to nature it simply furthers the progress of science. But when applied to society it turns out to be an ideological weapon of the bourgeoisie.[3]

What he suggests (after the general theory of neo-Kantianism) is that since there is said to be a radical difference between nature and society, the natural sciences have to be totally distinct from the social sciences. Nature deals with matter, with hard core facts; its method is quantified methodology where truth should be measurable. That which cannot be measured (according to this theme) is not scientific. But society deals with people who cannot be governed with the same method. The central part of humanity is the act (and not the fact). To put it in a nutshell: natural sciences deal with facts, social sciences deal with acts.

And so Lukács suggests a double bound critique: not only is something rotten in the state of the natural sciences (according to him the natural sciences are formal quantified sciences and not dialectical), but an archaeology of the natural sciences reveals the manipulative social structure that produces a false episteme. One could then call it what Louis Althusser called after Lenin as *der Holzweg der Holzwege*: the falsest of all false paths. But besides the apparent neo-Kantian dualism in Lukács' critique, there is indeed something more profound than a mere Kantian reside in his work. It is thus not merely the case that he is applying a Webeian *Verstehen* method in Marxism.

What he is saying is that the natural scientific method in its bourgeoisie form presents an estranged supra-historical signifier studying as if the eternal laws of nature. There are five basic characteristics of Lukács's critique of this estranged-reified model. It must be noted that Lukács prefers to use the term reification *(Verdinglichung)*: (1) loss of totality, (2) rationalized objectivism (3) pure quantification, (4) fetishization of facts and (5) abstract formalism, culminating in anti-historicism and the repression of radical praxis. It is with the exposition of these fundamental characteristics of the modern sciences that its crisis can be understood. Now the crisis of the modern sciences (both the natural and social) is understood in the perspective of the reduction of science to quantified rationalism based on a false and fragmented or what Lukács after Marx calls a "ghostly objectivity". And this spectral objectivity falsely presents itself as a "pure fact". What seems to be a "fact" is actually the estranged world appearing in a delusory form. And this delusory mode of appearance conceals reality. Concealed reality appearing in delusory form is what is described as a "fact". Not only is the mode of appearance delusory, it is also fragmented, and this fragmentation appears as "scientific truth". Thus the alleged facticity of the sciences is actually a monadic interpretation of reality which studies only surface structures. It does not proceed into the deep structure. It does not ask: how and why has the world been fragmented? Why does reality appear only in "object form" *(Form des Objects)*? What is this strange "form of appearance" *(Erscheinungsform)* of the object form of reality? And thus Lukács claims that science has "torn the real world into shreds and ha(s) lost its vision of the whole". It is this paradigm that locates the reified consciousness of the modern sciences which " will turn its back on the ontological problems of its own sphere of influence and eliminate them from the realm where it has achieved some insight. The more highly developed it becomes and the more scientific, the more it will become a formally closed system of partial laws. It will then find that the world lying beyond its confines, and in particular the material base which it is its task to understand, *its own concrete underlying reality* lies, methodologically and in principle, *beyond its grasp."*. In the same vein Husserl claimed that:

> Science has nothing to say to us. It excludes in principle precisely the questions which man, given over in our unhappy times to the most portentious upheavals, finds the most burning : questions of the meaning or meaninglessness of the whole of this human existence ... Scientific, objective truth is exclusively a matter of establishing what the world, the physical as well as the spiritual world is in fact. But can the world, and human existence in it, truthfully have a meaning if the sciences recognize as true only what is objectively established in this fashion, and if history has nothing more to teach us than all the shapes of the spiritual world, all the conditions of life, ideals, norms upon which man relies, form and dissolve themselves like fleeting waves, that is always was and ever will be so, that again and again reason must turn into nonsense and well-being into misery?[4]

It is in this way that the crisis-ridden character of the modern-bourgeois sciences appeared to Husserl and Lukács. It must be noted that whilst for Husserl modern sciences is rooted in Descartes and Galileo (he called Galileo "a discovering and a concealing genius"), for Lukács the modern sciences include the natural sciences, political economy, philosophy and law. Critical theory of the Frankfurt School would continue this Lukácsian rendering. Secondly, Husserl and Lukács disagree on the basis of the crises of the sciences—for Husserl it is based on "the attitude", for Lukács the crisis is deeply embedded in the history of commodity production and the reification of conscious thereof. The modern sciences have to be understood as the mimesis of the actual social structures of estrangement and reification. Commodity production and estrangement are the 'roots' of the five above-mentioned features of Lukács's critique of the modern sciences. It is this binding: estrangement/modern-capitalist sciences which serves as a model from which Critical Theory's reading of the crisis of the modern sciences would soon emerge. Whilst Lukács himself at no given time was sympathetic to the philosophy of Friedrich Nietzsche, Critical Theory would borrow heavily from his thinking. Consider Nietzsche's *The Will to Power* who had said "In the formation of reason, logic, the categories, it was need that was authoritative: the need not to 'know', but to subsume, to schematize, for the purpose of intelligibility and calculation.[5]

This is the summary and the leitmotiv of Critical Theory, the conversion of the will to knowledge to the will to power. But where has this will to power to be located? Can one find a historical space wherein this will emerge? What is the relation between the will to power and the modern sciences? Reading Critical Theory, especially Adorno a theme continuously recurs to haunt the reader, the theme of calculation and control. The modern sciences thus have at its underlying epistemic base, the theme of calculation and control. Science thus no longer wants to know nature—it wants to *control* it. The modern sciences are thus constituted within this peculiar fusion of technology and domination, rationality and oppression." The earlier theme of quantified rationalism and the question of modern science's act of concealment would reappear again. There are two important and intertwined questions with respect to the social sciences in India. The first deals with the question of Marxism as a rigorous social science, especially in its applicability in India in particular and other South Bloc nations in the periphery of global capital accumulation. This question deals with an alternative view of Marxism—a Marxism that is different than the one practiced by the Established Left's politics of history that follows the unilinear model of progress and development. This alternative Marxism brings in the scientific thinking of non-western societies where the study of social formations is not determined by Eurocentric understanding that is also determined by a form of economism what one may call "classicist" reductionism, where class in the form of political economy of Western Europe is imposed on Indian conditions. This brings to the social sciences the question of caste, its relation to both the Asiatic mode of production and modern capitalist class system

But there is another question that emerges. If an alternative form of Marxism is possible which keeps the caste system as the central part of its discourse, then where would one put the works of Phule and Ambekkar. Would this alternative Marxism also involve another question: "Can there be a rigorous science called Ambedkarism?" How would Phule's critique of ritual be related to the idea of ritual proposed by Walter Benjamin in his The Work of Art in the Age of Mechanical Reproduction? Or how would ritual of both Phule and Benjamin be related to the psychoanalytic ideas of neurosis and psychosis? Could we say that Freud's ideas of neurosis and psychosis as forms of different stages of mental disturbance is now superseded for a new mental disturbance called "neurosis-psychosis"? Would fascism be the manifestation of this "neurosis-psychosis"? Would we be able to create a New Critical Theory for India? How would this new theory—I would like to call this the "New Physics" in the Indian social sciences—relate with the original Marxist idea of historical materialism? And how would this new critical historical materialism be essentially humanistic in both form and content?

Louis Althusser in *Lenin and Philosophy* had talked of Marx discovering a new continent of history. And Marx himself had talked on there being a unified science—he calls it "one science in *Economic and Philosophical Manuscripts of 1844* and *The German Ideology*—the science of history. Accordingly this one science of history has two sides—that of nature and the other of human society. Whilst both had captured the attention of Marx, it was the second that was essential for his revolutionary repertoire. In it is this line of thinking that we borrow from Lenin's *Marxism and Insurrection* where he had talked of understanding insurrection as an art form. This insurrection as an art form is what we call after Žižek the arousal of "the sublime feeling of revolutionary enthusiasm". Marxism as a unified science goes back to the classical philosophical concerns of the true, the good and the beautiful. And since fascism is false, evil and ugly Marxism will have to necessarily confront it. This shall be the immediate future of the social sciences in India.

Notes

1. Louis Althusser, *Lenin and Philosophy and Other Essays*, trans. Ben Brewster (Delhi: Aakar Books, 2006), p. 12.
2. Ibid.
3. Georg Lukás, *History and Class Consciousness*, trans. Rodney Livingstone (London: Merlin Prsee1983), p. 10.
4. Edmund Husserl, *Crisis of the European Sciences and Transcendental Phenomenology*, trans. David Carr (Evaston. IU : Northwestern University Press, 1970), pp. 6-7.
5. Friedrich Nietzsche, *The Will to Power*, trans. and ed. Walter Kaufmann (New York: Vintage Books, 1968), p. 278.

9

Issues of Theorisation and Data Validation

Need for New Paradigms in Research in Political Science

Mrudul Nile

The growth of political science, its concepts and the ideas have always been a part of the social constructions. Political science thrived upon these social constructions which have relied for its development of the political events. Thus, I would like to begin with my first argument that the political variables are always influenced by social developments. These social developments have a causal relationship with other variables like the economic and cultural. Political variables tend to combine these variables and present them as a holistic systemic entity. One can argue this with the help of an illustration that the "social construction essentially depends on the needs which are governed by the economic considerations but the instincts of the individual are more political while accessing these economic considerations.

Concepts and themes like sovereignty once constituted the basic foundation and the fundamental ideas around which the discipline of political science revolved. Ideals and norms also constituted the central theme of the subject. Many studies have been conducted on ideologies, and probably this is the only subject which is very well grounded with the theoretical aspects of the cultural, economic and political construction of the social order. These theories are still serving as the common platform to understand the social relations and economic priorities in any nation state. The ideas of identity and nationalism have grown in this background. The fact remains that the people across the continents have not thought of theories of political science as theories of politics alone but understood them from the point of view of social discourse.

In fact, this may be one of the reasons that political philosophies were born before political theories. This would then mean that philosophies were more prescriptive in nature and based on observations than any empirical analysis of outcomes. The nature of scientific knowledge is not absolute because it is influenced by the practice and perspective of human agents. Scientific Perspectivism argues that the acts of observing and theorizing are both perspectival, and this nature makes scientific knowledge contingent. Nevertheless, today when we look at those philosophies and attempt to understand the society in the context of its prescriptive nature, we attempt to test those philosophies which have graduated to, or assumed the nature of theories. For example, the theories of Social Contract. These theories are put to practice in the sphere of the current governmental systems and the social relations are in a way structured in the same manner as prescribed. Further, it also encourages debates regarding the idea of legitimacy in a "democracy prone world "One also need to understand here that, neither the time when these ideas (philosophical constructions) were made the social relations were prescribed or emerged on their own and then they were analysed. But we may absolutely be sure that these relations are perceived from that philosophical (now theoretical) perspectives.

The initial studies were more normative and concerned with issues like how the state ought to be and the like. Most of these studies were influenced byreligion and moral philosophy, therefore the concept of ecclesiastical laws dominated the whole discourse of the formation of state and the concept of rule of law. The concept of Rule of Law during this time was non secular and drew a lot from the religion. Initially these trends dominated the study of political science.

By the end of the 19th century, we experienced the wave of social movements not only in the sphere of state but also in the realm of economy, society and culture too. Very broadly, these movements may be put under the title of renaissance and reformation. These movements dealt with unequal distribution of resources and social stratification that prevailed in Europe in those days. The natural consequence of these movements was that the later studies in political science focused on rationality and secularism and the separation of state from the church. Ideas of Liberty, Equality and Justice paved the way for a more open society and the studies also had a dominant impact of these ideas on the nature of State. It is these ideas that were responsible for the emancipation of the constantly discriminated communities and societies, both in the Europe and the other subcontinents. People all across the world attempted to assert themselves for a more equitable society and percolation of resources to those who were deprived of for a very long time. Finally, this also led to the independence of many Afro-Asian countries.

Scholasticism in Political Science

Parallel to this, newer thought processes formed the basis for contemporary political theory. Broadly, these theories are Marxism, Communitarianism, Feminism, Multiculturalism and Civic Republicanism. These theories have grown due to the socio- economic cultural and political developments in the society and the need for the newer thoughts. The most important aspect of the emergence of these ideas is that mostly, they were constructed on the basis of the empirical studies conducted and the forecasting done on the basis of strong culture of theory building The essence of this essentially means that the contemporary political ideas which have assumed the status of theory are empirically tested. For this purpose a very highly specialised tools of research methodologies must have been used. This also proves our first argument that the "social developments have a causal relationship with other variables like the economic and cultural. However, political variables tend to combine these variables and present them as a holistic systemic entity".

The second argument rests on the interdependence of research methodologies in the political science. "there is a higher predictive sense and methodological rigor leads to better understanding of the political processes". Since early 1930 one may trace major changes in the study of political science. The emergence of political sociology and political economy embarks upon the new techniques of the study of political science where there were studies, methodologies and theories borrowed directly for the discipline of sociology, anthropology, psychology, mathematics, statistics and other natural sciences. It is always assumed that anthropology had developed better tools of scientific enquiry of its subject. Political science initially was developed on the basis of observations which lead to the theory building. After the first world war, a need was felt to understand the social and political shifts among various States and communities. There were competing ideologies which stood against eachother and there were many recognised forms of government. Therefore a need was felt to quantify the changes and with respect to the applicability for a better governmental system. The behavioural school of the political science too attempted to understand the processes based on the empirical studies conducted with the help of psychology, mathematics and statistics. It was at this time it was agreed by the scientists that the quantifiable inputs were more accepted to determine the socio-political orientations and thus newer empirical theorisation of the human problem could be studied scientifically. These studies facilitated to understand the emerging phenomenon of politics and social construction. The reason why the studies got highly interdisciplinary is because it started asking questions of human existence and survival. These question never fell into the core subject matters of either political science, sociology, economics or psychology. Hence not only there was a growth of the parameters of the study but also the techniques and models adopted by each other to understand the phenomenon in their own core subject areas.

Problems of Indigenous Political Theory building and Research Inadequacies:

> Political theory is the study of the concepts and principles that people use to describe, explain, and evaluate political events and institutions. Traditionally, the discipline of political theory has approached this study from two different perspectives: the history of political thought, and contemporary political philosophy.

Political theory is engaged with current political issues and is self-reflective about political life. It has a strong ethical component and develops alternative conceptualizations of how we might organize social and political relations. Theory thus is understood, as an aspect of the whole discipline, interwoven with each concentration; it also has its own tradition of discourse, from ancient to contemporary theorists. The tradition focuses on the ethical bases for relationships of authority among individuals, those invested with legitimate and non-legitimate power. It studies the forces that expand and limit human potential. In Western political theory, theorists tend to have research specialties in one or more of the three periods: ancient (the Golden Age of Greece and Rome); modern (from Machiavelli and Hobbes through Marx and Nietzsche); and contemporary. Theorists also read and teach broadly across these historical periods.

The current theoretical constructions in the realm of political theory is based more on the current challenges in the political environment in the world, the decade of 1970s and 80 did act more in the sphere of social wellbeing and social welfare. The nations that developed in those days adopted a more centrist line of ideological thought and also tried do good to its people. This may be understood in the context of Rousseaus 'General Will' which can be seen in operational nature of the state in countries like United Kingdom, Canada, France and other European Countries.

Recently, in the more globalised world, which is entrenched with the notion of competition, meanings of sovereignty and democracy haschanged the structure of the world order. Inspite of tall claims of strong nationalism and democracy more than half of the world is suffering from poverty, hunger and violence, some African countries like Nigeria, Sudan, Pakistan, Syria, Iraq, are war torn countries, some are failed states and many others are striving hard to give its people the basic minimum. These ideas were very well spelt out by Samuel Huntington in his Clash of Civilisations.

On the other hand the largest democracies like India and the United States of America have fallen prey to the antagonistic politics and the politics of 'Selective Nationalism'. By selective nationalism I mean, Nationalism for the few who form the part of the larger caucus of politics. It also means that the government defines what constitutes nationalism and there can be a nationalism of the state or 'State Nationalism'and 'other nationalism' which may not necessarily be defined in the same manner as the 'ruling elites' may define. This nationalism also helps identify or draw clear lines of demarcations of ideological allegiance. Therefore it also assumes that those who are not a part of this selective nationalism are anti nationals. This politics of vendetta needs a better theoretical understandings. It is imperative to seek explanation for questions like, is it that the people all across the world look forward to a new world order and a changed economic systems every twenty to fifty years, or is it the big corporations who decide upon the system of states they want to govern. The problems are many; therefore, it is essential to connect these contours to make sense of the world. There is a dire need for the logical solutions to these problems.

The research inadequacies in political theory have brought the world to the brink of a doomsday. The problems of terrorism, nuclear war, communal conflicts and freedom movements are unavoidable. Post World War II, the world saw some peace and development for some time, it was essentially because the nations which were at wars did not have enough resources to fight more wars. Hence, the economy of abundance certainly makes the world more and more unsafe. Further, the nations are now retracting itself from duties of nation building and welfare activities (which was the case in the pre war world) and concentrating only on the sovereign principles of the state thus bringing the state and its people to a position of conflicting goals.

It is essential that we work towards making political science adaptive to the development of the subject in the other parts of the world like United States of America and Europe. Of course, it will take some time for culture of political science to attain those heights in India. But an initiation towards following the trend can bring some important changes in the way we approach political science in our country and more specifically, in the western India. The subject seems to be more mature in the American Universities and institutions like the Princeton University, Chicago School or the Frankfurt School; they have a recognised style of their own. This style is not only restricted to the research but a higher quality of theorisation is being continuously developed. On the contrary, research in India is still in a nascent stage. Baring some stray instances of good research seen in some parts of the country like the universities in Delhi, few humanities departments in IITs, and certain other institutes where advanced research takes place, largely we are far away from attaining the quality research culture. This problem in my opinion may be due to the maximum concentration on international relations and security and strategic studies, where scholars of political science are engaged more in analysing the international events than theorising the problem. If at all theorising is carried out the component is minimal.

Political science research in India especially in western India suffers too many inconsistencies. In western India there are hardly any specialised centres of theory and research. Still most of the universities are involved in the traditional or classical research with the old tools of research. Barring some centres or universities, most researchers and scholars rely on the library research or if at all they conduct some empirical studies, they are essentially concerned with the basic statistical methods like the mean, median and mode. Most studies that use some field work component for their doctoral work seem to use the average to ascertain and validate their propositions.

Though many scholars have made an attempt to contribute to the social theory in a political perspective, these kind of works are very few and limited to a smaller areas of study. Unfortunately, the reason for this set back can be attributed to the very nature of the study one conducts. Most of the political science scholars are engaged into more of a generalised study of a particular phenomenon than really building theories. These studies are more or less to concern the political participation of women in Panchayati Raj Institutions, or analysing a social movement or understanding the trajectory of an international event. The construction of social models is ostensibly missing. Further, these models are also not properly constructed to understand the relationship between the social, political and economic indicators. The theoretical understanding of the problem looks weak and therefore theory based work also suffers some amount low concentration that has led to meagre direction to the entire discourse of theory building in western India. In fact western India could have been the most fertile ground for the process for theory building as it is a home for major social reform movements in India. If at any major theoretical work been done it is mostly with regard to social and political assertion of weaker sections of the society which were influenced by the studies undertaken by Dr. Ambedkar and the scholars belonging to leftist school. Scholars like Ghanshyam Shah, Jayant Lele, Rajani Kothari, Suhas Palshilar and V.M Sirsikar have been conducting some studies especially in the area of political process. Apart from these names which have been a rich source of academic enquiry, other scholars have not really made a mark to that extent. These studies examined the relationship between caste/ class and politics that is social and political variables. They also tried to build models in the regional context. If at all, any theory exist in any research work, it is more of the available data/theoretical interpretations but the process of theory building, in a way analysing a problem from the theoretical perspective is a seems a distant.

Methodology and Perspectives of political science studies in India should aim to attain similar strature as that of the universities in the United States of America. Political science has long aspired to emulate both the objective research methods of the natural sciences and their practical success in controlling their objects of study. These studies right from the world war II have been very specialised. Scholars have been experimenting with the communities and identifying the problems of social cohesion. Therefore, today in American societies it is easy to identify patterns of behaviours and these patterns during certain political events like elections have been more or less predictable. These prediction of certain political behaviours are also present in the Indian scenario but the distinctness and a clear identification becomes difficult. The reason for this identification in the United States of America, which can be understood as a phenomenon is due to the strong theoretical structures available for interpretation. For example the concept of 'swing states' in American Presidential Elections often decide (depending upon how they vote), who would become President of United States. Hence, it becomes very imperative and essential that as we claim that the Indian society is distinct and different, we must also develop certain theoretical structures which will be a ready reference points of analysis for some studies to be undertaken.

Estimating the Research Potentials

It is essential that emphasis of the study should shift from formal institutions to the behaviours of the structures. Generally the study of political science concentrates on studying institutions and their structures in the historical and functional aspects. It is essential that the under currents of these institutions are studied. These structures behave in a particular manner which is governed by the socio-cultural determinants.

Further, it is also imperative to understand the behaviour of individuals and their relations with the structures in which these individuals operate, it becomes essential to prove it scientifically. To understand these relationships, there is a need to undertake correlation study between the two variables. Both individuals and structures here, would be understood as variables. For instance in an Indian society, we must attempt to look at how people coming from various caste groups or religious groups would behave in very prestigious corporate or any social organisation like the newly formed NGO? Here we may consider organisation to be static variable or a constant variable till the individuals from various castes/communities enter these organisations. It will be but obvious that the individuals coming from various backgrounds for instance, rural, urban, metropolitan, rich, poor, in a higher, middle or an lower income group would occupy spaces as per the cultural categories constructed and accepted over a long period of time. In this kind of a situation, a brahamin coming from a metropolitan, rich, convent educated, would occupy dominant (geographically closer to the centre of power or where the power emanates) spaces of that organisation as he has been subconsciously trained in that manner. Whereas a person coming from a dalit community, from a metropolitan and rich background may not essentially occupy the dominant spaces unless he has one more attribute to himself and that of assertion. Once these spaces are defined by the individuals themselves, the organisation starts reacting with these individuals and thus a system is developed in the organisation. This system over the period attains the capacity of distribution of resources, including the social status.

This can be analysed by observation but a correct relationship between the individuals and institutions or organisations cannot be ascertained unless some scientific tools are employed. To understand this relationship, it is first essential to understand if the two variables are internally consistent which is related to reliability. Once it is clear that the two variables are internally consistent with each other, correlation is employed.

Quantitative analysis is faced with some criticisms. Healy and Perru (2002) for example, qualitative methods are flexible, inductive and multifaceted whereas the quantitative methods are often characterised as inflexible and forced. Moreover, most qualitative research views quantitative methods as characteristic of a positivist paradigm. Some scholars are of the opinion that "doing quantitative research entails commitment to a particular ontology and specifically to a belief in a single objective reality that can be described by universal laws".

However, quantitative analysis should not be synonymous with the positivist paradigm because statistical inference is concerned with probabilistic as opposed to deterministic conclusions. Statisticians do not believe in a universal law measured free from error

The distinction between objective research and subjective research in political science also appears to emerge in qualitative versus quantitative debate. Statisticians are viewed as neutral investigators and are detached from the personal biases. The quantitative researchers while interpreting the facts may be influenced by personal choices of ideology and likings (miller 2008).

Validity and Reliability

The recent studies conducted in politics are based more on scientific deduction and verifiable conclusions. More and more scholars are adopting to use the above mentioned models and abstractions to verify the assertions made in many studies. Along with these, more theory based models; some very positivistic studies pertaining to the psephology are also conducted by scholars. These studies have changed the methodology and content of the study and are considered to be more and more in use in recent times.

The notion of measurement is of pivotal importance to any study that claims empirical analysis and a scientific outlook. However, in India till recently we have not acknowledged the importance of good measurement. Therefore a general approach to measurement in political science is yet to develop. This use and development of measurement is essential for the political science as the abstractions that are being developed be tested scientifically.

Measurement may be defined as "the process of linking abstract concepts to empirical indicators"(Zeller and Carmines, 1979) as a process involving "explicit, organised plan for classifying and often quantifying a particular sense data at hand-the indicants- in terms of general concept in researcher's mind (Riley, 1963, quoted in Carmines and Zeller, 1979). This definition makes it clear that measurement is a process involving both theoretical as well as empirical considerations. Measurement, for that matter focuses on the crucial relationship between the empirically grounded indicators that is observable responses and the underlying unobservable concepts.

In other words, it is an attempt to define the abstract concepts on various scales of understanding and prioritising them. For example, we may say an abstract concept of political behaviour can be empirically tested using some scales of measurements. There are a lot of studies conducted on political behaviour of voters and it may not really be considered as an abstract concept for that matter. But in political science, it can be defined as an abstract concept which is laden with theory to some extent. This essentially needs to be understood from the perspective of the kind of study being conducted at a given point. Hence, while using the measurement techniques, it is essential to define what exactly does one mean by voting behaviour and how that behaviour is manifested. Therefore, a researcher attempts to define the manifestations of their behaviour in the context of the theoretical interpretations of political behaviour. The researcher also assumes various indicators of behaviour in a given circumstances. Therefore another variable becomes essential and that may be political (electoral) process in a democratic setup. This would then mean that an attempt is being made to understand the political behaviour in an electoral process. Taking into consideration this relationship an abstraction may be developed which will attempt to answer the question like "Electoral process positively influences the voting behaviour". This expression of abstraction now can be measured as to what extent electoral process affects the voting behaviour, or how much positively, or otherwise, does it affect the voting behaviour?

Generally three kinds of validity are used for measurement and assessment of a particular phenomenon. These are Criterion Validity, Content validity and Construct Validity. Criterion validity and content validity is not so central to the study of political process. Construct validity is the one that is and can be used predominantly for the study of political behaviour and processes. Fundamentally construct validity is concerned with the extent to which a particular measure relates to other measures consistent with theoretically derived hypothesis concerning the concepts (or constructs) that are being measured.

Construct validity involves three distinct steps. First, the theoretical relationship between the concepts themselves must be specified, second, the empirical relationship between the measures if the concept must be examined and the empirical evidence must be interpreted in terms of how it clarifies the construct validity of a particular measure.

To measure values or variables normally two indicators are used. These are reliability and validity. Reliability essentially means the extent to which an experiment, test or any measuring procedure yields the same result on repeated trials. Reliability plays an important role to acknowledge that when repeatedly some variables are endowed they tend to give similar results. Though, in any social sciences especially political science, cannot give results that may not vary. Hence, it becomes essential to understand the consistency of these results of measurements. This tendency of consistency among variables found in repeated measurements of the same phenomenon is referred to as reliability. When repeatedly the same results appear, it means there is a higher level of reliability in measuring the themes.

Reliability tests are generally of four types. The Test-retest reliability, Parallel Forms Reliability, internal consistency reliability and inter-rater reliability.

These kind of tests are of great importance to conduct some study of political science. The Test-retest reliability is one of the best ways to measure the political programme of a contestant. This test essentially means that the tests are conducted over a period of time. Generally, this test can be used to undertake studies concerning the satisfaction levels of voters and in a particular constituency.

Parallel-forms reliability evaluates different questions and question sets that seek to assess the same construct. This can be employed to understand a particular phenomenon. Here two sets of questions can be asked to the same set of individuals to assess their perceptions regarding a particular phenomenon. These studies can be carried out to assess the political satisfaction or efficacy of the political programmes of the party in power.

Inter-rater reliability thus evaluates reliability across different people. Here to understand a particular phenomenon, or a political decision, say a plebiscite or to take a referendum, all the people with different socio-political, economic and cultural backgrounds may be administered a questionnaire to assess if majority or consents to a particular process. Hence, studies based on reliability and validity are utmost importance to arrive at empirically testes results. These kind of studies must be employed more and more to enrich the discipline.

It is essential for political science to do away with the old ways of study where most of the studies were based on observation methods or general theory prepositions. The dynamic nature of the state and the relationship with the individuals in the state is drawn from various political and social phenomenon. These phenomenon must be studied empirically to reach to goals that majority of the society intends and cherishes.

Use of Models

The idea of model should be central to the study of politics. These models can be used for generating testable predictions that can subsequently serve as hypothesis in data analysis. These models can be examined empirically and one can actually see the models working or not working according to the data and the logical positioning or arrangements of the variables

To some scholars models may mean the following, a

theory on the semantic view is a collection of models. Salmon (1988, 6) writes that a theory is "a set of models;" Da Costa and French (1990, 249) write that a scientific theory "can be considered in terms of a description of its set of models;" Downes (1992, 143) writes that scientific theories "consist of families of (mathematical) models," and Giere (1984, 83) writes that a scientific theory is the "conjunction" of claims regarding models and natural systems. (Quoted in Clarke and Primo, 2007). What emerges from these discussions of theory under the semantic view is the central role played by models. Giving a precise answer to the question "what is a theory" has even been argued, by a leading proponent of the semantic view, to be unimportant (Suppes 1967, quoted in Clarke and Primo, 2007).

To summarise, a model is a kind of system whose characteristics are specified by an explicit (and sometimes elaborate) definition. As a model is characterized by a definition, by construction it cannot be falsified.

As models should be assessed for their usefulness for a specific purpose, it is therefore necessary to detail the purposes to which a model can be put and how we can judge whether or not a model is useful. At the most basic level, models can serve in any one (or more) of five different roles: foundational, structural, generative, explicative, and predictive. These models serve the actual way we perceive of these models and the way they may be used for various purpose. The first and foremost purpose of the model is that of prediction. Though of course models may seldom be used for predictive purpose, if we design a model in a particular way, it can serve as a model for prediction. For instance, the model created by the author for the doctoral degree is that of a set of independent variables namely; ***Social Political and Economic Inequalities,*** the mediating variables being the ***Decentralisation, Privileging Dissent, and Privileging Rights*** and the Dependent variables identified were that of ***Access, Accountability and Transparency***. The argument in the thesis revolved around the idea that if there exist Social, Political and Economic inequalities, and they undergo say for instance, the processes of decentralisation, there will be chances of higher degree of Access, Accountability and Transparency. Hence, it is suggestive or predictive that greater decentralisation would bring more transparent government and socio-political economic inequalities will to some extent gradually erode.

Models play an organisational or structural role. This type of models provides a framework where in information may be defined, collected and ordered. One purpose of such a model might be to collect a group of disparate empirical generalizations or known facts under a single framework.

Models may also have generative functions. This essentially means that the models may generate hypothesis or generalisations. It is quite likely that they may produce non-obvious directions for further study.

In politics especially in the study of psephology, this kind of models do help. In the Indian context, we generally assume that all the politicians know their constituencies well, in the current scenario of political uncertainty these models may play in important role. All the poll alliances generally are developed on the basis of these models. These alliances serve as the prospective redistribution model and therefore they often become successful. For example the alliance between the RJD and JDU which is considered as the most successful model may be an explanation of this process. Further, as Guteno Mosca mentions the term 'Political Formula' is nothing but a political model.

This would essentially mean theory building and theory testing. With the enlarged boundaries of political science one has to understand that both theory building and theory testing has gained importance. The new wave of political process with the ever changing social relations has paved the way for newer research approaches, which largely depend on the two concepts of theory building and theory testing.

Both theory building and theory testing may begin from the same point. The point may be drawing some abstractions. These abstractions are developed to understand the causal relationship between variables. Further, these abstractions are deliberatively developed to understand the logical explanation of arrangements of the variables.

Most abstractions work on the idea of perceptions. These relationships can be tested by building logically accepted theories and understanding the perceptions of people. Therefore major work in this regard is based on the ideas, views and perceptions which are negated or accepted and hence a model is accepted or rejected.

A theoretical hypothesis asserts a relationship between a model and a real world system. In other words, a theoretical hypothesis asserts that an object, a system known as a model, is similar, in some respect and for some purpose, to another object, a real-world system.

References

Bernard, H. R. (2012), "The science in social science". *Proceedings of the National Academy of Sciences of the United States of America,* 20796-20799.

Bluhm, W. T. (1986), "Polis and Praxis: Exercises in Contemporary Political Theory by Fred R. Dallmayr." *The American Political Science Review,* Vol. 80, 297-298.

Carmines, E., & Zeller, R. (1979), "Reliability and Validity Assessment." *Series: Quantitative Applications in the Social Sciences,* 1-57.

Catlin, G. E. (1-13), Thomas Hobbes and Contemporary Political Theory. *Political Science Quarterly,* 1967.

Churchman, C. W. (1973), Reliability of Models in the Social Sciences. *Interfaces,* Vol. 4, No. 1, 1-12.

Clarke, K., & Primo, D. "Modernising Political Science: A Model-Based Approach." *Perspectives on Politics, 5* (4), 741-753.

Cooper, B. (1979), "Reason & Interpretation in Contemporary Political Theory." *Polity,* 387-399.

Dallmayr, L. A., & Dallmayr, P.A. (1986), "James Buchanan." *The Journal of Religion,* Vol. 66, No. 4, 461-462.

Deutsch, K. L. (1974), "Beyond Positivism." *The Review of Politics,* 461-464.

Germino, D. (1964), "Eric Voegelin's Contribution to Contemporary Political Theory." *The Review of Politics,* 378-402.

Goetz, M. D. (1982), "Problems of Reliability and Validity in

Ethnographic Research." *Review of Educational Research, Vol. 52, No. 1,* 31-60.

Graham Jr., George J. (1975), "Political Theory and Practice. by Bernard Crick; The Dilemma of Contemporary Political Theory: Toward a Post-Behavioral Science of Politics." by Thomas A. Spragens. *The Journal of Politics,* Vol. 37, No. 1, 284-286.

Gurjar, L. R. (2007), "Trends of Contemporary Political Theory." *The Indian Journal of Political Science,* 827-834.

Harvey C. Mansfield, J. (1980), "Liberalism and the Modern Polity: Essays in Contemporary Political Theory" by Michael J. Gargar Mcgrath. *The American Political Science Review,* Vol. 74, No. 1, 172-173.

Hedrick, A. K. (2013), "An Introduction to Implicit Attitudes in Political Science Research." *Political Science and Politics,* Vol. 46, No. 3, 525-531.

Healy, M., & Perry, C. (2000), "Comprehensive criteria to judge validity and reliability of qualitative research within the realism paradigm." *Qualitative Market Research: An International Journal, 3* (3), 118-126.

John M. Geringer, C.K. (2004), "A Fifteen-Year History of the Continuous Response Digital Interface: Issues Relating toValidity and Reliability." *Bulletin of the Council for Research in Music Education,* No. 160, 1-15.

Lupia, A. (2002), "New Ideas in Experimental Political Science." *Political Analysis,* Vol. 10, No. 4, *Special Issue on Experimental Methods in PoliticalScience,* 319-324.

McDermott, R. (2002), "Experimental Methodology in Political Science." *Political Analysis,* 325-342.

Monroe, C.E. (1998), "Réjean Landry." *Canadian Journal of Political Science,* 424-426.

Ogburn, W.F. (1934), "Trends in Social Science." *Science, New Series,* 257-262.

Peardon, T.P. (1955), "Two Currents in Contemporary English Political Theory." *The American Political Science Review,* Vol. 49, No. 2, 487-495.

RATHORE, L. S. (1978), "Leo Strauss and The Contemporary Political Theory: Critical Reflections." *The Indian Journal of Political Science,* 17-27.

Rathore, L. S. & Bhati, P. S. (1979), "Hannah Arendt's Contribution to Contemporary Political Theory." *The Indian Journal of Political Science,* 367-379. "Reliability of Models in the Social Sciences." (n.d.), *Interfaces,* Vol. 4, No. 1 (Nov., 1973), pp. 1-12.

Sarat, A. (1990), "Off to Meet the Wizard: Beyond Validity and Reliability in the Search for a Post-Empiricist Sociology of Law." *Law & Social Inquiry*, 155-170.

Spitz, D. (1966), "Democracy and the Majority Principle: A Study in TwelveContemporary Political Theories by Elias Berg." *The Annals of the American Academy of Political and Social Science*, 219-220.

Taylor, R.S. (2013), "Advancing the Enlightenment in Contemporary Political Theory by Nicholas Tampio." *Perspectives on Politics*, 631-632.

Young, I. M. (2001), "Political Theory and Feminist Social Criticism (Contemporary PoliticalTheory) by Brooke A. Ackerly." *The American Political Science Review*, Vol. 95, No. 3, 713.

Zimmerman, D. W. (1998), "How Should Classical Test Theory Have Defined Validity?" *Social Indicators Research*, Vol. 45, No. 1/3, *Validity Theory and the Methods Usedin Validation: Perspectives from Social and Behavioral Sciences*, 233-251

10

Current Research Trends in Anthropology in Western India

Anjali Kurane

Anthropology traces its roots to ancient Greek historical and philosophical writings around 400 BC about human nature and the organization of human society. Toward the end of the 19th century anthropologists began to take academic positions in colleges and universities, emerged as a serious professional and scientific discipline beginning in the 1920s. American anthropologists of the 20th century went on to establish anthropology departments at universities throughout the country. Anthropological research developed in different ways in the United States and Europe, to work in professional positions. They endorsed anthropological data, knowledge for as political, commercial, and humanitarian value.

In its early stages during the 19th century, Anthropology was principally concerned with the non-Western isolated cultures, which were frequently regarded as exotic and primitive. Consequently, enormous ethnographic, ethnological and monographic record of the tribes of the world was built up. Later on as simpler societies started getting increasingly involved into Urban societies, Anthropologists shifted their attention from simpler cultures to more complex cultures. The expansion of Urban anthropology, sub-discipline of anthropology, a relatively new and developing field in the 1960s, concerned with issues of rural-urban migration, urbanization, urban adaptation, ethnicity, poverty, village communities, cultural systems in Urban area and neoliberalism reflects the recognition that traditional target groups, such as tribal and peasant people, became increasingly integrated into the urbanized world. Anthropologists are in progress in the research and development relating to contemporary societies. In the 1970s many anthropologists, motivated towards looking the meanings of particular important cultural symbols and rituals within cultures themselves to demonstrate how this one symbol or ritual shapes or reflects an entire culture and to understood the culture of the people by examining important rituals. Development Anthropology is recent in origin, which views development from a *critical* perspective.

In India, Anthropology developed in the late 1940s. Sarana (2007), Srivastava (2007), Davis (2007), Sharma (2007), In India, Anthropological research endeavour had its beginning from the western colonial encounter. Misra (2010); Sinha (1957); Mujumdar (1957); Vidyarthi (1976) Foundation of the Asiatic Society of Bengal by Sir william Jones and the commenement of the Asiatic Research, in the 1784 mark the beginning of the Anthropological research in India. In the late 19th century, British colonial had a systematic approach to collect ethnographic information of the Indian communities as they had to administer them. In the beginning of 1807 the east India Company made formal decision to obtain Anthropological information of India for administrative significance. Misra (2003:33) has noted that the 'colonial Anthropologists' were agents of the colonial power and main objective of their ethnography on South Asian communities were expansion, consolidations, mopping up of resources for the development of home industry and keeping a tight control over the indigenous people'. Srivastava (1990) The English educated Indian Anthropologists reviewed the writings of the colonial masters and thus began a dichotomy of 'Practice of and Practice in' Anthropology. The Practice of

Anthropology was mainly for the exploitation of the natives and practice in mode shifted towards a concern for human welfare and development incorporating the people's perspectives. In this transition of colonial Anthropology to Nationalist Anthropology in the subfield of Socio-cultural Anthropologist, the major argument bust out had far reaching consequence among the Anthropologists in India, even today. The Argument is on the 'Policy for tribes of India'. In the opposition of nationalists approach G.S. Ghurye (1959) argued that they have rejected the 'aboriginality' status of the tribes of India and treated them as 'uncivilised, fringe communities at the periphery of the Hindu Society' and he advocated a policy of deliberate assimilation. While Verrier Elwin advocated the policy of 'No Changer' for the tribes.

The twentieth century is the era of the development in the Indian Anthropology. Sarana (2007:309) 'The predominant trends are marked by a shift of focus from tribes to castes and more than fifteen years long engagement with village studies'. During the period, late 1940s and 1950s, Anthropologists devoted to Indian research were focused on village and institutional studies. One of the dominant trend emerged during that period was holistic sense in combining both Physical and Cultural Anthropology. Sarana (2007) noted that D.N. Mujumdar, Iravati Karve combined Physical and Cultural Anthropology in their research. Many individual scholars such as Sarat Chandra Roy, M.N. Srinivas, Iravati Karve, L.P. Vidyarthi, Nirmal Kumar Bose, Shyama Charan Dube, Govind Ghurye, T.N. Madan, Verrier Elwin and others contributed development of Anthropology and created a impression in, and cause of development of Indian Anthropology. Many new concepts such as 'sanskritization', 'westernization', 'Universalization', 'Parochialization', 'Great tradition', 'little tradition', Sacred Complex', 'Nature–man-spirit complex', 'Brahmanisation', 'Rajputisation', 'Dominant Caste' and so on are emerged out of individual study and proved to be valuable concepts for study and contribution in Anthropology, in Indian Social Science in General and Indian Anthropology in Particular. During the period, late 1940s and 1950s,

Anthropologists devoted to Indian research were focused on village and institutional studies, and concepts such as the "great" and "little" traditions of Hindu culture, developed through this effort.

S.C. Dube (1962) referred to three phases of development of Social Anthropology in India: 1st phase – compilation and publication of volumes on Tribes and brief, sketchy accounts of the castes and their divergent customs and practices. 2nd phase – detailed monographic studies of the individual tribes through personal observations. 3rd phase – after Independence, considerable advancement and some qualitative achievements. Later on Nirmal Kumar Bose (1963) summarize in following three phases (1) encyclopaedia of tribes and castes; (2) descriptive monographs; (3) analytical studies of village, marriage and family, caste, civilisation. D. N. Majumdar (1956) was the foremost Anthropologist, who divided course of developments according to dominant trend in the historical period. He borrowed the terms and concepts of T.K. Penniman (A Hundred years of anthropology 1935). Later on same was reinforced with modification, suggestion, and agreed to chronological landmark in the course of development of Indian Anthropology by L.P. Vidyarthi (1966, 1975, 1978), Gautam Kumar Bera (1995), Vijoy Sahay and Pradip Kumar Singh (1997), Vijoy Sahay (2008). The four phases are (1) Formative Period (1784-1919); (2) Constructive Period (1920-1945); (3) Empirical Period (1946-1978); (4) Developmental Period (1979–onwards)

Anthropology as a curriculum of academic study begun in the University of Calcutta in 1920 under the patronage of Ananathakrishna Aiyer. In the same year was started in the University of Bombay under the patronage of Patrick Geddes and Govind Ghurey where social Anthropology also thought. Today almost all the states have Anthropology Departments in their respective Universities. Anthropological Survey of India established in 1947 and today it is largest Anthropological research institute of the world. Tribal research and training institute were also formed in different state to carry out Anthropological researches, and assist the National Planning.

Western India

This essay concerns the development, over the last 25 years, with several broad recent trends in anthropology and more specifically in socio-cultural Anthropological research and Studies in Western India, It must be noted at the outset that the limitations of the Anthropology Departments in the Western India make it quite impossible to compilation of data of the entire sub-disciplines of Anthropology.

All over India so as in Western India Anthropological researches whether at individual level, department level and institutional level focussed 'tribe' as their core area for study to understand Indian society and culture and developed monographs on various tribes. It was a general view that Anthropologists study only ethnic groups and tribes.

Although initially in Western India scholars focussed only on tribal cultures, in 1970s there was inclination to study process of urbanisation and urban growth from various dimensions by some scholars. From 1990s onwards some of the researches areas have major within the broader field of urban studies and urban policies. A significant trend in the Anthropology is anthropological study of the city. Currently, anthropologists are focusing their study of societies from the perspective of the city. This crossover was instrumental in the development of urban anthropology in Western India. Urban anthropology is an expansive and continuously evolving area of research. The concentration on study of cities has formally and officially endorsed once again the traditional claim of anthropology to concern itself with a variety of human cultures and societies". Recent studies emphasis on Anthropology of urbanization that is centre on studying rural-urban migrations, impact of urbanisation, immigrants' identity, and adjustments, adaptations, accommodations to their new environments focusing on the alteration of social structure in the context of the social change, interpersonal ties, and collective identities in the city, migration-urbanisation, and migration-development, community studies, ethnicity and urbanisation, urban adaptation, ethnicity, and poverty, modern city lifestyles, social mobility among the urban women with reference to specific communities, changing life style among urban women, and so on.

'Ethnicity' and 'Ethnic Conflict' have been key concepts in anthropology to understand intercultural interaction within a plural society and became central focus for research in 1990s in western India. Anthropological studies of ethnicity concentrated on relationship between the groups and role of ethnicity and ethnic identity in achieving mobility. Punekar (1974) following Francis (1947) and Gordon (1964) defines ethnicity /ethnic identity as 'the sense of peoplehood or we feeling shared by members of the group', Anjali Kurane (1999) defines ethnic identity as 'sense of belonging and has socio – cultural political dimensions, plays crucial role in bringing about social mobility of the community'. The current researches areas focus on ethnic identity and social mobility, ethnicity and urbanisation, ethnic conflict, ethnic movements, ethnic politics, ethnic separatism, situational ethnicity, resources competition and so on. The researches focus more on understanding the causes of ethnic conflicts, tribal economy, livelihood and how it closely tied to tribal culture and tribal identity.

Concurrently the interest in the researches in development anthropology is also increasing more rapidly. Today, India being a developing nation passing through the unstable state, experiencing rapid changes in every aspects of cultures, and is facing conflicts, pressures, inconsistency and chaotic situations. N. K. Gouraha (2012) "Exploitative tendency, public indecency, sub-human concepts and social disorder are the explicit symptoms of a retarded development. Today, unfortunately this has become basic pattern of Indian cultures and our cultural ideas. India is gripped with numerous social problems. We have problem of communal riots, backwardness of Schedule caste and tribe, problems of women and weaker sections, child labour, dowry and many more. All our efforts directed towards solving these problems have only made the problems more serious and contemptible". Anthropology and Anthropologists can play major role in understanding the root of the problems as they understand human societies theoretically as well as empirically. Eswarappa (2006a) "Development represents an increase in the capacities of a society to organise for its own objectives and carry out its programmes more effectively. The essential element here is organization. Anthropologically speaking, when one society is developed and another underdeveloped, the former is, by comparison with the latter, able to make much more complicated decisions and do more complicated things". Ashraf Ali (2009) 'Anthropology has a rich Methodological tradition in Understanding complex cultural variations, situated meanings and connotations of various social phenomena defined by local people in their own cultural context. Ethnographic fieldwork is the central not only to understand human cultures but also it develops general conceptions for guiding the resolutions of human problems'.

The current dominant research trend in development anthropology directly related to development issues and problems of tribes, dalits, dalit women, women, trafficking children, livelihood, health, malnutrition, education, gender discrimination, social exclusion and poverty, casteism and role of governments, NGOs, international development organisations in the process of development, anthropology and policy, process of policy development, modernisation and so on. Recently, Dr. Babasaheb Ambedkar, Mahatma Jyotirao Phule, Savitribai Phule, Shahu Maharaj have been included in the post graduates, and Ph.D. Syllabus as an Indian anthropologists.

Gardner and Lewis (1996) "Anthropologists for their part, face difficult questions when they become involved in the development. Because government or any donor agencies still see economic progress as real benchmark for development. It is perhaps for this reason there is tendency to bring in the anthropologist only when things begin to go wrong, rather than having them involved from the start".

As since the beginning Religion has always fascinated anthropologists. Simultaneously few scholars are also focussing on Anthropology of religion, role of pilgrimage in preserving and spreading culture, socio-cultural study of the cult. The tendency of studying folklore, village study is still active among some researcher. Socio-cultural change and continuity among the converted castes & migrated communities, social movements are as well popular areas of investigation. Few are exploring the problems of prostitution and sex workers. Few are interested in ageing population. The field of social organization, kinship and family, however, is still the strongest.

The anthropological study of symbolism developed in the 1960s to investigate what symbols stand for and the processes by which meaning is attributed to them. Symbolism is the use of symbols to convey different meanings. The existing trend appear to be symbolic studies of the communities in urban, and tribal areas, to demonstrate how this one symbol or ritual shapes or reflects an entire culture and to understood the culture of the people by examining important rituals, Such as Symbolism of Naga Handlooms, House decoration, and so on.

In the area of growth and nutrition, researchers are engaged in the anthropometric studies for assessment of nutritional status of some tribal groups, adolescent obesity, maternal nutrition, settlement studies, nutrition and diseases of the tribes from Ethno-Archaeological approach. Few studies were undertaken in Dental Anthropology. There is also emerging trend of researches in Molecular Anthropology, emphasis on mitochondrial DNA diversity, skin pigmentation.

To sum up, I say that in Western India current thrust areas and trends of researches are in Urban Anthropology, Development Anthropology, Cultural Anthropology, Symbolic Anthropology, Medical Anthropology, Growth and Nutrition and emerging trend in Molecular Anthropology.

As the study of the communities is the basic theme of the Anthropology, we should look how Anthropologists can make positive contribution to multiple socio-cultural problems that communities face in the process of development. Contemporary anthropology should focus on restoring social health of the communities and planning for welfare of the people. Certainly during the colonial period anthropology helped administrators and served to reduce the conflict between ruled and the ruler. Anthropology and anthropologists should emerge as a means for people's wellbeing and development. Eswarappa (2006b) "More than any other social scientists anthropologists are aware of the gap between the general theory and broad interpretations on the one hand, and empirical, down to the earth interpretations on the other". Sillitoe (2007) 'An anthropological training gives the analytical means to understand the heterogeneity of local actors and their interests to see the multiple links in their social lives and appreciate everyday strategies, to tap into local understandings and comprehend resistance to perceive outside interference'.

In recent years anthropology, particularly socio-cultural Anthropology, in Western India has taken lead in its diverse contributions to the Society and Humanity with an aim to promote a just humane society. Researches are trying to encounter human culture, society with its complexity as of today. This inventiveness may be potential in all over India. The academic dissertations and records are based on the contemporary realities, wants and needs of the people to promote socio-cultural, economic, political development of the people of Western India. However, number of crucial issues such as livelihood, identity, violation of human rights, violation against women, discriminations, casteism, stigmatization, social exclusion of ethnic minorities groups has remained to be unanswered. Satya Pal (2011) "Anthropologists help to carry out the policies but they do not make or criticize policy. Indian Anthropology unlike Western Anthropology visualizes there has been far too much concern with the problems of Indian society". Scholars from the different fields have understood the importance of anthropology to as fundamental discipline to know humanity in its entirety. Grillo (1985) "There is a reasonable chance that the application of anthropological knowledge will moderate the bad and enhance the good". Vinod Mudgal (2012) "Anthropology has bridged the gulf between developed and the underdeveloped (now called developing) societies by way of studying little known or not known cultures of the world. Thus the problems of human relations were highlighted by the anthropologists... There would be no exaggeration in saying, anthropology contributed a lot in guiding and developing a definite strategy of development in the world". Government departments, Non Government Organisations, research institutes, university departments, educationists, social activists, development planning agents, managements experts are have started involving anthropologists in their committee to have a humanistic and positive approach while planning for policies for tribal and rural as well as in industrial and urban planning and development and the humanity. Humanity is compatible with science; that science without humanity is a monster and social science without humanity is a fiend. Anthropology is both humanistic and scientific endeavour and subject matter of Anthropology is as eternal and as interesting as humanity itself.

References

Aidan Southall, (1974), *Urban Anthropology: Cross Cultural Studies of Urbanization*, Oxford University Press, London.

Al-Zubaidi, Layla, (1998), *Disciplines and Sub-disciplines: Urban Anthropology.*

Ashraf Ali, H.M., (2009), *Anthropology and the changing world: How can Anthropologists Serve Humanity?*

Bera, Gautam Kumar, K. Jose SVD, Edited, (2013), *Anthropology in India*, Abhijeet Publications, New Delhi 110002.

Bose, Nirmal Kumar, (1966), 'Studies in Indian Anthropology' (Ed.), *Calcutta: Indian Studies: Past and Present.*

Davis, Julie, (2007), 'The We-They Distinction in Anthropology', *Eastern Anthropologist*, 60:3-4, pp.373-381.

Dube, S.C., (1962), 'Social Anthropology in India', In T.N. Madan and Gopal Sarana, eds. *Indian Anthropology: Essays in Memory of D.N. Majumdar*, Bombay: Asia Publishers

Eswarappa, K., (2006a), 'Sericulture as a Case of Development in the context of Globalisation: A Village Study from Andhra Pradesh,' in Ajay Kumar Sahoo, Sadanand Sahoo and G. Nagaraju (Eds.) *Trends in Sociology: Education, Development, and Diaspora*, New Delhi: Abhijeet Publisher, pp. 113-139.

Eswarappa, K., (2006b), 'Sericulture and Community Development in the context of Globalisation: An Empirical Evidence of a Village,' in Chinta Ganesh (Ed) *Rural Development in the Era of Globalization*, Hyderabad: Department of Sociology, Osmania University, pp. 250-274.

Gardner, K. and D. Lewis, (1996), *Anthropology, Development and the Post modern Challenge*, Pluto Press.

Ghurey, G.S. (1959), The Scheduled Tribes, Bombay Popular Book Depot, first published 1953.

Grillo, R., (1985), 'Applied Anthropology in the 1980s: Retrospect and Prospect'. In G. Grillo, and A, Re eds. *Social Anthropology and Development Policy*. Cambridge University Press.

John, Gulick, *Urban Anthropology.*

Majumdar, D.N. (1956), 'Special Report on the teaching of Social Anthropology', *The Teaching of Social Science in India*, Paris: UNESCO Publications.

Majumdar, D.N. (1957), *A Tribe in Transition*. London, Longmans Green and Company.

Misra, K.K. (2010), 'Academic colonialism, Indigenization and production of knowledge in Indian Anthropology', in A.K. Danda and Dipali G. Danda eds. *Anthropology in India: Current Epistemologies and Future Challenges*, 13 INCAA Occasional papers. Jhargram INCAA, and Bhopal IGRMS.

Misra, P.K. (2010), 'Anthropology in India in Deep Crisis', in A.K. Danda and Dipali G. Danda eds. *Anthropology in India: Current Epistemologies and Future Challenges*, 13 INCAA Occasional papers. Jhargram INCAA, and Bhopal IGRMS.

Misra, Pramod Kumar, (2003), 'J.H.Hutton and the North East' in T.B. Subba and G.C. Ghosh (Ed.) The Anthropology of North East India—A Text Book. New Delhi. Orient Longman.

Penniman, T.K., (1935), *A Hundred years of Anthropology*, London: Gerald Duckworth and Company.

Richard, G. Fox, (1977), *Urban Anthropology: Cities in their Cultural Settings*, Prentice Hall, Inc. New Jersey.

Sarana, Gopala, (2007), 'Indian Society Cultural Anthropology: A Brief Review', *Eastern Anthropologists*, 60:3-4. pp 307-325.

Satya Pal, P. D., (2011), 'Activism and Anthropological Enterprise in India', Paper presented in the Seminar at Anthropological Survey of India, Mysore.

Sharma, K.N. (2007), 'Problemtique of Certification of Social Sciences', *Eastern Anthropologist*, 60: 3-4, pp. 273-289.

Sillitoe, P., (2007), 'Anthropologists Only Need Apply: Challenges of Applied Anthropology', *Journal of the Royal Anthropological*

Institute, 13, pp. 147-165.

Srivastava, Vinay Kumar, (1990), 'Practice of and Practice in Anthropology', *Annual Teview of Anthropology*, 5:209-225.

Srivastava, Vinay Kumar, (2007), 'Some Thoughts on Anthropology in India', *Eastern Anthropologists*, 60:3-4. pp. 291-305.

Mudgal, Vinod, (2012), 'Contribution of Anthropology to Contemporary Societies with Special Reference to Central India' in a *Anthropology in Contemporary Societies* Ed. by A. N. Sharma, S. K. Rawat.

Vidyarthi, L.P., (1976), *The Tribal Cultures of India*, New Delhi, Concept Publishing House.

Weaver, Thomas & White Duglas, (1972), *Anthropology of Urban Environment*.

PART II

Themes and Issues of Enquiry in Social Sciences

11

Trends in Women's Studies in Western India

Vibhuti Patel

Introduction

The dialectical relationship between 'pedagogy' and 'praxis', vis-à-vis the 'women's question', has been a matter of great concern for pioneers of Women's Studies (WS) in Western India. The need to study women's issues in academic institutions and to conduct research based on experiential material and affirmative action had begun to be discussed among Indian women's studies scholars by the early eighties. The discourse on this subject has proved to be a fruitful exercise for activists, academics, researchers, policy planners and the UN system. This paper tries to examine the following issues: the genesis of interaction between WS and the WM in India; the contribution of WS to mainstream academia-economics, political science, sociology, literature, history, education, philosophy, psychology; the analytical tools and the theoretical insights provided by WS and the WM in the Western India; the research methodology and agenda of the WS, ongoing debates on the scope and limitations of WS within institutionalised structures, the shift of focus from WS to gender studies; the economics and politics of funding, consultancy and priorities in research.

Pioneers of WS in India defined it as an academic discipline that involved research, documentation, teaching, training and action. Women's studies start with the premise that women have subordinate status in our society so the knowledge-base created by WS should be used for empowerment of women. Thus WS has a transformative potential in terms of changing the gender based power relations.

Evolution of WS in India

WS in India evolved as a result of state patronage after the declaration of the United Nations International Women's Year (UN-IWY). Publication by the Government of India in 1975, of the Report of the Status of Women Committee, TOWARDS EQUALITY, reopened the debate on the women's question. The Report revealed the deteriorating conditions of women. It highlighted the phenomena of the adverse and declining sex-ratio, marginalisation of women from the economy and gender-based discrimination in family laws (Desai and Patel, 1990). The Towards Equality report was translated into Marathi and Gujarati and widely circulated and discussed by state and non-state actors during and International Women's Year, 1975 and International women's Decade (1975-1985).

In the pre-independence period, academics in the Western India were concerned with the status of women in the higher castes and classes (Desai, 78). The reasons for widow-burning, child-marriage, purdah and illiteracy among women found extensive references in their works (Desai, 1977). In the post-independence period, two distinct periods can be discerned: that up to 1974 and the years thereafter. Before 1974, the focus of scholars interested in women's question was on the role-conflict of middle class women. Very few studies situated the problems of Indian women in the context of the macro forces of the developmental process. The only exceptions were the scholarly works of Neera Desai (1954) and D.R. Gadgil (1965). Neera Desai's work got recognition in the 1970s and was printed as a volume in 1977.

Towards Equality was prepared by the scholars with an interdisciplinary perspective and was presented in Parliament, where it received a tremendous response from the decision-making bodies, the state apparatus and the print media. Principal research bodies, like the Indian Council of Social Science Research (ICSSR), provided financial support to scholars committed to the women's cause, to conduct research into problems faced by women in poverty.

The Genesis of Women's Movement in India

The birth of the women's liberation movement in Western India was a result of the radicalisation of Indian politics in the late 1960s and the early 1970s. In the late 1960s there was an upsurge internationally of the black movement, the women's movement, the anti-war movement and the working class movement. These were independent, self-determining and democratic movements, which questioned all hierarchical structures. In Gujarat and Maharashtra, young people of that period, faced with multiple crises: - economic, social and political, together with corruption, drought, inflation, unemployment, pauperisation of the rural poor - the disenchanted youth responded with protest. Widespread, open discontent, was expressed in action and consolidation of the action developed into powerful organisations throughout the country. These movements raised a number of diverse issues-land-rights, wages, employment security, water availability, destruction of nature, oppression and exploitation of the Dalits, tribals and the working masses (Desai, 2006). Many women participated in these struggles with enthusiasm, responsibility and creativity.

The UN Declaration of 1975 as an International Women's Year coincided with the Emergency Rule in India. By the time the Emergency was lifted in 1977, several women's groups had developed around democratic rights issues in Pune, Mumbai, Panjim, Vadodara (Omvedt, 1978). The press swung into "action" after the imposed silence of nearly two years. Atrocities committed against women during the Emergency were openly documented and reported in the press. These atrocities struck a chord in most women's own experience of life in the family, in the streets, in the workplace and in political groups (Gandhi & Shah, 1992). The culmination of this process was reached in 1980 when many women's groups took to the street to protest. During the 1980s the issue of women's oppression was depicted not only in discussion forums, seminars and `serious' articles but also in the popular media (Patel, 1988). Women, who had on their own identified the sources of their problems and indignity, began to acquire a language, an organisational platform, a collective identity and a legitimacy they did not have earlier. Many activists of women's movement played pivotal role in development of women's studies (Desai and Patel, 1990).

Dialogue between WS and WM

When analysing the origin, development and direction of women's studies (WS) in India; it is important to understand its relationship with the Indian women's movement (WM).

It was in the early 1980s that women's studies' centres, functioning autonomously or within the university system, started accepting empirical and experimental evidence from the women's movement. It was a time when participatory research, action research and subaltern studies were gaining ground in the field of social sciences (Krishnaraj, 1988). This process indirectly facilitated the interaction of WS and the WM.

In the first National Conference of Women's Studies in 1981, a wide variety of issues were discussed by activists, researchers, academicians and policy makers. These included the developmental process which bypassed women, the gender bias in textbooks, sexism in the media, gender blindness in science and technology, legal reforms, health needs of women and violence against them (rape, domestic violence and prostitution). The general consensus among the participants (both women and men) was that WS was pro-women and not neutral. It was seen that WS would build a knowledge base for empowering women by pressing for change at policy level and in curriculum development, by criticising gender-blindness as well as gender-bias within mainstream academia, by creating alternative analytical tools and visions and by advocacy for women's developmental needs in the economy and in society. This Conference established a new trend by which, gradually, women activists were invited, as resource persons and participants, to academic seminars, consultations and training workshops (Patel, 2013).

Activist Researchers

During the 1980s, an increasing number of women's rights activists became involved in WS either as independent researchers, consultants, trainers and resource-persons for seminars and workshops - or as guest faculty members in higher education institutions which specialised in mass communication or government training. Anveshi in Hyderabad and Alochana in Pune and women's library (Kolkata) were formed by women activists collectively as platforms for promotion of WS outside the academic institutions. Anveshi made a major contribution through its collective research project, "Women's Writings in India" (1990), was based on women's creative writing in more than a dozen languages, mostly from India's diverse folk tradition, from 600 B.C. to the present. Women's studies scholars from Gujarat and Maharashtra also made valuable contributions by sourcing and translating creative poetry and prose in Gujarati and Marathi. Rigorous research on land rights of women (Velayudhan, 2009), women in governance (Thakkar, 1997), girls & girlhoods (Patel, 2010), women in science (Shah & Chahdha, 2002) were conducted by scholars actively involved in the women's movement.

The dual roles of theory and praxis or academic exercise and action in WS have been articulated by the past president of Indian Association of Women's Studies (IAWS): "Women's studies provide contextualisation of knowledge in the process of both understanding and changing women's reality. As a movement it emphasizes the need for providing material basis for equality and independence of women." (Krishnaraj, 1986).

This approach accepts the dual role of WS as a discourse and as a movement. There have been critics of this approach who think that if WS has to be part of the educational system, it should retain its dispassionate features of rigorous intellectual activity and objectivity. But IAWS counters this argument and stresses that rigour can be retained even if WS takes an interventionist approach. It is this contact with the real situation, which provides insights, which, may not be obtained by sitting in a 'distant' university chair. Hence IAWS provides a platform to discuss the issues confronting contemporary reality.

Curriculum Development

In the last 35 years, the principal body of higher education, the University Grants Commission (UGC), has given primary attention to WS. SNDT Women's University in Bombay was the first to establish a WS unit, in 1974. Now it has a fully established Research Centre for Women's Studies (RCWS) and the UGC has accorded it the status of a Centre for Advanced Research in Women's Studies. During 1975-2013, the UGC has supported over 100 universities in different parts of the country in starting WS centres. The National Policy for Education, 1987 (NPE) also incorporated WS in its curriculum development. Mainstream disciplines now are introducing optional or compulsory papers. National Council for Education, Research and Training (NCERT) is promoting gender sensitivity in the school curriculum and school text books. Gender Economics, Sociology of Women, Women and Development, Women and Literature, Women and Psychology, Women and Education, Women in History, Reproductive Rights of Women are being offered in all premier universities of India. SNDT Women's University was the first to introduce a foundation course, "Women's Rights in Changing India" as a compulsory paper for all undergraduate students in each discipline.

The response of academics to WS in mainstream academia

is mixed. Interest in studying women from a feminist perspective has been more of a concern to some individuals in the university system. The majority of sociologists continue with the structural functional theory and consensual model; economists continue with their neo-classical paradigm and psychologists continue with quantitative analyses that have misogynist implications. Even radical historiography/ subaltern studies are not immune from stereotypical representation of women (Desai and Patel, 1993).

In this context, the IAWS, which was established in 1981, has been a torchbearer as it has provided an arena for brainstorming and discussing women's issues, new perspectives, innovative methodologies and theoretical insights. Contributions made at its biannual conferences include task forces like "Education for Women's Equality" in the NPE (1986), "The Role of Science and Technology", "Reviewing and Planning WS" for the UGC, collective multi-centric research projects by WS centres on "Girl Child and the Family", building of archives for women' studies. These have resulted in a vast body of literature for classroom teaching as well as for policy dialogue.

The Search for a New Paradigm

An approach was accepted which considers that WS is both for understanding the situation of women's lives and consciousness-raising for social change. This resulted in a serious search for a new paradigm. The first step in this direction was to make women visible in various disciplines, highlighting their role and contribution and capturing their experience. By creating legitimacy for WS as a 'researchable' area, efforts were made to break the silence surrounding the role of women and the silence of women themselves. Thus WS became a process of unfoldment of women. Making women visible is not an additive process where earlier women were not seen but are now visible — a kind of tokenism that exists in the power structures or some history textbooks. The WS approach implies challenging the dominant notion of knowledge, methodology and data sources based on class, ethnic/caste/religious and gender biases. Another related problem with visibility is about new indicators, new standards and new criteria for visibility creation. WS makes women visible not as sex-objects but as active agents in socio-economic, cultural and political processes. WS looks at gender not as a set of psychological traits but as a basic element of social structure especially of sexual division of labour which is tied to gender division and male dominance. WS attempt towards visibility of women in statistics and indicators by questioning the concepts of 'work', 'productive labour', 'head of the household' led to the process of deconstructing patriarchy (Dewan, 1995).

WS and the Construction of Knowledge

Radical scholars in various disciplines-sociology, history, economics, psychology, political science and literature have raised questions about objectivity, value neutrality, consensual model, demystification with survey research and quantitative analysis, the elitist bias of the disciplines and other such issues. However, they have ignored women's dimension. Hence, the need for WS to go beyond both the mainstream and male critiques of the mainstream disciplines.

Sociology of Women

WS Sociologists in Western India made pioneering contribution by challenging structural functional analysis that predominated researches on women. They also enriched debate on caste question by bringing intersectionality of caste, class and gender with perspective of stand-point theory in their researches (Ganesh, 1993; Rege, 1998, 2003, 2008; Tambe, 2009). Very comprehensive examination of gender implications of mass scale displacement and relocation of toiling poor has been done with specific focus on Mumbai with action research methodology by several scholars (Gopal, Contractor, Madhiwala, 2006).

Gender Economics

For the construction of knowledge, WS in India began by re-examining prevalent concepts on household, economic activity, work-force and using new concepts such as patriarchy, sex-segregation, gender, oppression and exploitation. Several studies pointed to the biases and lacunae in the existing methods of data-collection, faulty definitions and ideological constraints especially in the large-scale sample surveys and in the census. Women's studies have evolved a new source of data-base and a new approach of analysing the existing data-base (Mahadevia & Hiraway, 1996). WS scholarship has analysed the interaction between women's productive and reproductive roles in the market economy as well as in the subsistence production by unearthing cultural, historical and social contexts of construction of female identity and reorganisation of gender-based division of labour (Patel, 1989; Hiraway and Antonopoulos, 2009). Gender economists have examined serious gender implications of liberalisation, privatisation and economic globalisation at macro, meso ad micro levels (Jhabwala & Sinha, 2002; Patel, 2002). Tribal women have been most neglected by WS researches. Very few scholars have worked on tribal women's survival struggles with WS perspective (Talmaki, 2012).

Demography of Gender

Contributions of women's studies scholars towards demography of gender impacted highly-acclaimed National Family Health Surveys I, II, III (Bhende & Kanitkar, 1978; Karkal, 1991). As a result reproductive health issues of women got their place of prominence in the discourse on demography (Radkar and Parasuranam, 2007). This was a paradigm shift as focus shifted from 'reproductive control' to 'reproductive health'. NFHS focused on much neglected areas such as maternal mortality, maternal morbidity, anaemia, iron deficiency, nutrition and overall health needs of women (Khanna, 2005). Scrutiny of new reproductive technologies harming women thro' contraceptives, sex selective abortions of female fetuses, gender blindness of biomedical research were brought to fore by feminist health researchers (Ravindra, 1986; Lingam, 1998). Impact of HIV-AIDS on gender relations has been a crucial area of examination in WS (Anand, 2005).

Gender and History

WS historians have looked at non-conventional data sources like reinterpretation of mythologies, scanning of short-stories, autobiographies, biographies, novels, poems and folk-songs (Kosambi, 2000). Attempts at rewriting the history of women in ancient India raise serious questions as to why was there marginalised representation of women? Was it due to limited concerns of traditional historian or was it due to the kind of tools employed? Why there is a heavy reliance on literary texts? In India, the early literary sources being literary texts, the problem is further compounded (Desai, 2006; Bhave, 1988; Bhagwat, 1995). Poonacha has imaginatively used both archival and primary sources to focus on women in marriage and kinship networks. (Poonacha, 2004). Here the attempt has been to use a non-Brahminical source. Lata Mani uses historical documents to question the motives of the British rulers in enacting the law of Sati (Mani, *EPW*, April, 1986).

Feminist Literary Criticism and Media Studies

Deconstruction of print and audio visual media portrayal of women has been made by women studies scholars in the region (Desai, 2009). Identification and removal of sexist-bias in the textbooks and formulation of gender-just curriculum development have been a major concern of women's studies scholar. In psychology, discourse analysis and qualitative analysis have contributed new insights to understand complexities of gender relations (Joshi, 1991). In the field of literary criticism new inroads have been made by women's studies scholars who have examined the mainstream literature with women's perspective and generated a new theoretical understanding to capture intricacy of man-woman relationship (Harish, 2003; Shukla, 1991).

Engendering of Human Rights Discourse

WS has been successful in mainstreaming gender concerns in human rights discourse. As there is acceptance of the fact that Women's rights are human rights, several renowned scholars have worked on various aspects of violence against women and women's resistance to violence (Poonacha, 2007). Thus women are not seen as mere victims of violence but also as survivors (Kudchedkar and Al Issa, 1998; Pandey & Poonacha, 2000). Intersectionality of identity politics, cultural nationalism and gender has been an area of keen scrutiny in the western India during last 2 decades (Patel, 2005). Even the discipline of social work has been engendered and there has been a paradigm shift in perspective, from 'philanthropy' to 'right based approach' that concerns itself with right to food, shelter, education, safe environment, livelihood, safety in life, freedom from sexual violence, dignified existence.

New Tools of Analysis

Women's studies begin by re-examining concepts and using new concepts to understand women. Role theory as used in conventional researches in sociology to study working women, has been questioned as it concentrates more on women rather than men and role conflict indicates a fact and not explanation. Further it confirms the role relationships but does not question it (Krishnaraj, EPW, 1986). Similarly conventional concepts of household, family, housework, and male-headship have been modified while understanding women's reality. In the earlier sections of review of substantive researches various illustrations of such modifications and even radical departures have been mentioned (Poonacha, 2004).

WS scholars have started using the concepts of patriarchy, sex-segregation, discrimination and gender in their various studies. Several studies point to the biases and lacunae in existing methods of data collection, especially in large-scale sample surveys and in the census (Hiraway and Autonopoulos, 2009)

Case Studies

The WS researchers have been quite adept in using the case history or case study methods. When researchers found that secondary sources were unable to provide insights into the problem, case studies were taken up. For a long time it was thought that case study is a method used by the anthropologists, to study in detail the tribal life situations. Neera Desai has described how she proceeds with case study when she wanted to understand the life of 100 women activists in Gujarat, Maharashtra and Goa (Desai, 2006).

Similarly those who are involved in ICSSR studies on the family strategies have used case studies method to understand how families try to cope with the larger needs of survival through the control or promotion of women's education and works. In one of the studies in Gujarat, case studies not only helped understand the strategies but how caste norms affected family decisions were brought out in the in-depth interviews. Similarly, the participation of the tribal women in the earlier protest struggle surfaced during the discussion. (Desai and Patel, 1993).

Oral History : Case History

When written records to grapple with the experiences of women are not available, oral testimonies of women's experiences have been very useful. (Sparrow's audio visual documentation of women who made mark in the field of politics, women's movement, people's movement, fine-arts, crafts). The folk literature, particularly proverbs, myths, songs and folk tales are beginning to be used by WS researchers to understand the inner stirrings of women and society's attitude to women. Leela Dube has very ably used the folk material to examine social construction of gender (Sparrow, 1990). C. S. Lakshmi believes that in WS, the use of oral history is convenient because while dealing with illiterate and semiliterate women, it helps the latter to become articulate, thereby enabling the researcher to obtain information and perception (Lakshmi, 2000 & 2003).

Autobiographies, Biographies and the 3 Generation Studies

The study of autobiographies, biographies and the 3 generation studies have proved to be useful to understand how some of the women grew from traditional background to forming their own identities. For getting authenticity and first person perception, autobiographies and diaries prove very useful. Autobiographies, of course, have to be cautiously handled, as many a times, romanticised picture is portrayed or certain vital facts are omitted because they might bring stigma to the person. Nostalgic memories of the past are many a times seen in romantic perspective (Gawankar, 2003). A study of 20 autobiographies of Maharashtrian women analyses the issues like child marriage, widow remarriage, family conflicts, struggle for education, participation in the nationalist movement and even opting for unconventional careers like cineartists have been covered. (Sparrow, Mumbai has a massive collection of visual, audio and print archives).

Quite a few seminars have been held where the focus of discussion is oral history, study of autobiographies and use of photographs and three generational studies to evolve an understanding of women's identity. Unfortunately the papers of such seminars are not available, with the result that much useful material and experience fail to reach larger community.

Content Analysis

WS has been using content analysis, particularly for media studies. Almost all researches on media (including in the literature) have tried to understand society's perception of women through the content analysis of film, television serial, tabloid journals, radio programmes, advertisements and dramas. Content analysis of literature has also been used to understand the motives of the ruling class, the ideology of social reformers and philosophies such as liberalism and feminism.

Participatory Technique

Participatory technique is more used in training

development personnel and organising awareness programmes. Action being an important constituent of WS, this technique is used to conduct researches on the existing movements and developmental projects. Those who have been working with women at grass- roots have felt the need of using various techniques to break the silence of women, to get their participation and eventually generate a climate of equality. The hiatus between the trainer and the trainee, needs to be obliterated; the gap between producer of knowledge and user of knowledge has to be removed.

In WS, we have been saying that women's voices have to be heard; how they perceive dowry or a violent situation is very crucial. While studying objective reality and micro forces, WS also examines subjective reactions, psycho related issues. To understand social oppression, personal involvement provides a deeper understanding of the problem (D'mello, 1988; Agnes & Ghosh, 2012). Hence WS recognises the role of personal data and personal accounts in highlighting the dynamics of women's oppression in situations like draught, communal riots, caste riots, Bhopal gas tragedy, ecological policies and others. (Omvedt, 1978; Patel, 1988).

A nagging question invariably crops up whether these individual accounts are sufficient to infer general trends? Whether they have really helped in understanding women's lives? Whether the rigour in the studies could be maintained when subjective experiences are used as data sources?

WS in India has been a decade old phenomenon. It is too early to evaluate the efficacy of the tools and methods. What is very significant is that, after the eighties, more and more innovative approaches are being used by WS scholars. Information on experiences in various facets of life is growing. At a future date, effort will have to be made to provide a cohesive or not so cohesive picture of a woman's life as manifested in different spheres. Importantly enough it is recognised by researchers that subjective tools have to be handled very cautiously and they need constant checking and rechecking through other evidences. Further it is also accepted that WS by definition is interdisciplinary, hence it will have to borrow tools and methods from various disciplines. Further a versatile mind and not a specialist approach to grasp the problems of women is necessary. It is important to note that studies based on experimenting with new tools or new concepts have yet to emerge.

Research and Action

During the decade for quite some time researches on women and action on women were moving parallel. After the eighties the chasm between the researcher and the activist sharpened, as funds started pouring into women's research. The government through its ministries, such as labour, Rural Development and Social Welfare sponsored studies initially to academics, which might have resulted into a hierarchical situation. Simultaneously with the growth of grassroots work and autonomous women's groups organising campaigns and lobbying for political action, a necessity to study the problem arose. Foreign funders started supporting such actions or activists resulted in debates on whether one should take foreign fund or not? It was believed to have implications of unequal power dimensions, apart from the fact that research priorities might be determined (Gothoskar, 1997, 2000, 2013).

Another dimension of this issue is concerning role of the researcher. If women's studies are both understanding and action, then commitment to social change is essential. Women's oppressive reality has not to be merely studied in a classroom but has to be eliminated (Gupte, Awasthi & Chickerur, 2012).The logic of adopting innovative techniques like life history, autobiography, experiential data is self-awareness and then the need to change. Articulation of one's experiences in terms of oppression or growing identity on the one hand indicates a changed situation wherein a woman is able to frankly and honestly express her inner turbulations and a critique of the most private relationship. On the other hand this realisation some day ought to lead to action for changing this relationship. It could come more rapidly if there is support available through the women's movement. Of course, there are levels and levels of action, but activity and empathy are of prime significance in women's studies.

From Descriptive to Analytical Approach

Absence of analytical approach has been due to very faulty research training and lack of perspective. In women's studies, we have been shouting from the housetops that we do not wish to sacrifice rigour, nor do we want women's studies to be a 'soft discipline'. Frequent workshops on training in methodology and exposure to more and more innovative techniques will be prerequisites for making women's studies researches more analytical and not superficial. (Ganesh, 1993)

Institutionalising Women's Studies : A Few Hurdles

With the UGC legitimising women's studies by encouraging the building up of centres, cells, programmes, courses in the university system; many concerned WS protagonists have been anxious about implications of such steps. On the one hand, unless women's studies get into the mainstream of education, the transformation in attitude, behaviour or perception is not possible. Apart from the danger of using Women's Studies as spring board for one's own career promotion, there is also a serious danger of supporting status-quo, through mystical and ideological explanations. By highlighting the 'inner strength' or 'shakti' of women, contending that 'fire' is a purifier or eulogising 'mother earth' and 'motherhood', the scholars many times hide the acceptance of women's oppressive situation. Similarly, attempts are also made to justify sex selective abortions of female foetuses on the ground that it will end ill-treatment and discrimination of female child, which leads eventually to female mortality. There is a very thin line between understanding women's oppressive situation and recommending adjustment to the situation in the name of 'purity', 'inner strength' or 'lesser evil'.

Contribution at Policy Levels

WS scholars have contributed base papers for Human Development Reports of Gujarat, Maharashtra and Mumbai.

State profile for multi-centric research on crucial areas such as child care, abortion, working women's hostels, etc. Have been prepared. Status reports prepared by WS scholars have has great impact on formulation of policies, programmes and schemes (Engineer, 1995; Datar, 2003; Devashali et al, 2012). All women's studies in the Western India have conducted impact analysis of self help groups of women and microfinance to draw policy implications (Parthasarathy, Thekkekara & Poonacha, 2011)

Shift in the Thrust-Areas during 21st Century

With more and more data coming out emphasising marginalisation of women in the development activities, employment is no guarantee against ill-treatment of women as revealed in dowry deaths, wife-beating, sexual harassment and attitude to girl child, explorations into the causes for such occurrences, the role of superstructure and ideology is realised. Patriarchal overtones in the institutional structures of family, education, economy, law and others are being examined. Induction of educated, computer literate women in the Information Technology Sector has encouraged researches on the labour processes and labour relations in BPOs and KPOs and Corporate World. Women working in the night shifts in service sector of the economy have to deal with issues concerning their safety. Currently major focus of women's studies is on problem of sexual harassment at workplace and sexual assault in the streets and community. Globalisation, flexibalisation of labour and informalisation of workforce, feminisation of poverty and impact of slow down of economy, gender implications of agrarian crisis and farmers suicide are crucial concerns of women's studies.

From WS to Gender Studies

A move from women's studies to gender studies has been a demand of the day in the mainstream academia. While justifying WS as a felt-need for a new epistemology, the basic understanding was that male dominant ideology and sexism in the social sciences and humanities were unable to capture women's perceptions and it was necessary to decentre a patriarchal discourse. Justification for Gender Studies comes from an understanding that both men and women are constructed and constrained by the unequal power relations based on class, caste/race/ethnicity and gender. While WS focuses on patriarchal control over women's sexuality, fertility and labour, gender studies focuses on power relations that are socially constructed and result into subordination-domination relationship between men and women in a multilayered manner resulting from class, caste, location, race, ethnicity and religion.

Discourse on Women's Studies versus Gender Studies

Several women's studies scholars have raised their doubts as regards using 'gender' as an analytical category as they aver that the use of the term gender fails to focus on subordination of women as a result of women's oppression and exploitation, injustice and structural patriarchal violence. According to them, GS is responsible for depoliticizing of feminist scholarship. To them, even using gender as a category to study men, women's perspectives, actions, and concerns can be omitted and the idea that men are the central actors in human societies and women the passive receptors of their actions is reinforced.

Old guards in women's studies consider Gender Studies was a retreat from more radical women's studies. Feminists think that Women's Studies were a compromise itself as a name, more innocuous than say Feminist Studies. Somehow it seems less threatening to say well we are studying women, without specifying that one is studying women from a feminist perspective. But since most WS programs have a "Feminist Theory" course, it would seem that most remain committed to some kind of feminist analysis. There are feminist scholars who think that Gender Studies was more radical since it held men accountable for their privilege and made them responsible for change along with women. But, at the same time, they would be opposed to the word feminist. Many male faculties have no problem with gender studies program because "it is not "feminist."

Gender, in academic terms, reflects a broad concept that goes beyond "women's studies". It includes all kinds of genders, which has been the principle of feminist inclusiveness. In GS Women as an oppressed group that we can research and study disappears. All we have in gender studies becomes different groups or cultures within cultures within a mainstream culture. Women's studies exist to study women. While, "gender studies," accommodates men. Women's Studies scholars strongly believe that until they have equal inter-disciplinary research that is truly gender free, they must study women and not gender, so that they can catch up intellectually, theoretically, and of course, politically.

Women and Gender Studies

Women's and Gender Studies course have been promoted in several Asian counties (in spite of its unweildiness) because it encapsulates a conflict within the field and allows the conflict to get stated up front to students rather than being part of a hidden agenda. It allows work to proceed on the idea of gender as a relational system in which, in good structuralist fashion, change in one part of the system requires change in another (i.e. women's state will not change unless men's does), allows us to explore gingerly the area of "men's studies," and still maintain a place in the curriculum to view these issues through women's perspective. In Women's and Gender Studies, the study women and men, the relations between women, between men and between the two are done from a woman's perspective. This maintains a significant and important balance. This view includes both 'mainstreaming gender' and 'women's room' approaches.

Scholars promoting GS find it impossible to discuss women as separate from social practices such as power inequities, differences in the role of "mother" vs. "father", etc. According to them GS allows looking at gender as a verb in terms of the interpersonal and societal practices that create or construct women's and men's behavior. Gender studies helps in examining the unequal distribution of power. While women's studies help in deconstructing patriarchy, as a dominant structure in our society, cannot be 'escaped" in any simple way. Only by revealing the inadequacies of patriarchy can we begin to forge an alternate conception of gender. This argument provides justification for women and gender studies—that incorporates the two major strands of feminist theory structuring programs today; the gynocentric, essentialist view that we must focus on women, women's language, women's work, women's agency, etc. and the poststructuralist/Marxist view that we can only forge political change by deconstructing traditional gender, an act of questioning traditional constructions.

Feminist Studies

The difference between Women's Studies and Feminist Studies lies in the ideological framework. Women's studies are about women, may or may not have a feminist perspective. Focusing on women still means seeing gender as a relational term and making comparisons to men. The strength of feminist studies lies in its challenge to androcentric frameworks and generalizations in scholarship and women-centered inquiry remains critical to analytic vision. For many people (and many departments), Women's Studies is already a euphemism for Feminist Studies; a Dept. of Feminist Studies could/would study the whole world from the vantage point you get from assuming that the existing society is an oppressive patriarchy, and that this oppression causes social pathologies of far-reaching consequences, affecting everything from economic systems to child-raising to beliefs about God and meaning. It would include the study of men and boys as well as of women and girls, but would not have to "sneak in" a tendency to use feminist text as basic while using text such as Sigmund Freud more as subject matter to be analyzed and subjected to critique for its patriarchal distortions and how they have affected the fields of patriarchal study that have relied upon him, etc, etc.

Gender Studies comes about because there is plenty of social behavior to be analyzed in terms of gender (especially from a feminist perspective) that is not specifically about WOMEN. It also arises from non-feminist or possibly anti-feminist intentions to reopen gender issues from perspectives that are more easily taught by men or by either men or women who have no interest or familiarity with feminist viewpoints. The label Women's Studies, if applied to a program or department that is essentially interested in doing comprehensive study of gender from feminist viewpoints, can make it hard to argue against such changes; and changes that start off as mere changes in program title can lead to changes in content and in personnel later on.

The traditional curriculum teaches us all to see the world through the eyes of privileged, white, European males and to adopt their interests and perspective as our own. It calls books by middle-class, white, male writers 'literature' and honors them as timeless and universal, while treating the literature produced by everyone else as idiosyncratic and transitory. The traditional curriculum introduces the (mythical) white, middle-class, patriarchal, heterosexual family and its values and calls it 'Introduction to Psychology.' It teaches the values of white men of property and position and calls it 'Introduction to Ethics.' It reduces the true majority of people in this society to 'women and minorities' and calls it 'political science.' It teaches the art produced by privileged white men in the West and calls it 'art history'.

Conclusion

Women's Studies, by design, are about transformation. Women's studies have been critical to unmasking androcentric assumptions that make men the human norm. The idea that gender studies holds men accountable for gender inequalities in power while women's studies does not is contradicted by the volumes of women's studies scholarship that precisely do point to men's part in the constructions of these systems. Part of the dispute may center in the various definitions of gender that appear in scholarship. They range from the social relations of the sexes (usually analyzed in terms of power inequalities) to "a vocabulary for power". Given that most of the curriculum and scholarship focus on men, whether gender is used as an analytic framework or not, programs focusing on the study of women are critically necessary.

The state of art profile of researches in WS in the Western India at the end of this exercise is not neat and clear, as women's life is also not simple. It is full of contradictions. The research activity and the debates generated have reached the levels of compensatory research where women's perspective has been added to the conventional discipline. We need more systematic work to challenge the mainstream academic disciplines, build new paradigms and provide significant theoretical understanding.

A move from women's studies to gender studies is gaining ground in the mainstream academia among the WS scholars in the Western India. While justifying WS as a felt-need for a new epistemology, the basic understanding was that, that male dominant ideology and sexism in the social sciences and humanities were unable to capture women's perceptions and it was necessary to decentre a patriarchal discourse (Patel, 2002). Justification for Gender Studies comes from an understanding that both men and women are constructed and constrained by the unequal power relations based on class, caste/race/ethnicity and gender. The WSCs are the nodal centres to galvanise mainstream academic disciplines into integrating women's concerns in the curricular, co-curricular and research activities. Existing WSCs in Maharashtra, Gujarat and Goa, recognised and partially supported by the UGC are at a crossroad and every crossroad leads to a new road. Let that road be of scientific understanding of gender relations leading to gender-justice.

In the final analysis, both Women's Studies and Gender Studies challenge patriarchal, hierarchical order and facilitate the process of mainstreaming women's concerns. Pitting WS against GS serves the interest of dominant patriarchy which is oppressive for all women, men and children.

REFERENCES

Agnes, Flavia and Shobha V. Ghosh (2012), *Legal Domains, Gender Concerns and Community Constructs*, Delhi: Oxford University Press.

Anand, Vaijayanta (2005), *HIV/AIDS and Intervention at the Workplace*, Mumbai: Perspectives in Social Work, April.

Bhave, Sumitra (1988), *Pan on Fire: Eight Dalit Women Tell their Story*, New Delhi: Indian Social Institute.

Bhagwat, Vidyut (1995), 'Marathi Literature as a Source for Contemporary Feminism', *Economic & Political Weekly, Review of Women & Studies*, Vol. XXX, No. 17, April 29.

Bhende, Asha and Tara Kanitkar (1978) *Principles of Population Studies*, Mumbai: Himalaya Publishing House.

Datar, Chhaya 2003, *Status of Women in Maharashtra*, Mumbai: Tata Institute of Social Sciences.

Deosthali, Padma Bhate, T.K. Sundari Ravindran, and U. Vindhya (2012), "Addressing Domestic Violence within Healthcare Settings", Mumbai: *Economic and Political Weekly, Review of Women's Studies*, Vol - XLVII No. 17, April 28, 2012.

Desai, Mira K. and B. C. Agrawal (2009), *Television and Cultural Change: Analysis of Transnational Television in India*, New Delhi: Concept.

Desai, Neera (1977), *Women in Modern India*, Vora & Co, Bombay.

Desai, Neera (1978), *Social Change in Gujarat: A Study of Nineteenth Century Gujarati Society*, Bombay: Vora & Co.

Desai, Neera (2006), *Feminism as Experience: Thought and Narratives*, Mumbai: Sparrow.

Desai, Neera and Patel, Vibhuti (1990), *Indian Women: Change and Challenge*, Bombay: Popular Publications.

Desai, Neera and Patel, Vibhuti, 1993, *Critical Evaluation of Women's Studies Researches in India, 1974-1993*, Mumbai: Research Centre for Women's Studies (RCWS), SNDT Women's University (SNDTWU).

Dewan, Ritu (1995), "Gender in Neoclassical Economics-Conceptual Overview", Mumbai: *Economic and Political Weekly, Review of Women's Studies*, Vol. XXX No. 17, April 29.

D'mello, Flavia (1988), "Our Fight against Wife beating" in Ghadiali, Rehana (ed.) *Women in Indian Society: A Reader*, New Delhi: Sage Publications.

Engineer, Asghar Ali (1995), *Problems of Muslim Women in India*, Hyderabad: Orient Longman.

Gadgil, D. R., (1965), *Women in the Working Force in India,* Delhi: University of Delhi.

Gandhi, Nandita and Nandita Shah (1992), *The Issues at Stake*, Delhi: Kali for Women.

Ganesh, Kamala (1993), *Boundary Walls: Caste and Women in a Tamil Community,* Delhi: Hindustan Publishing Corporation.

Gawankar, Rohini (2003), *Mrinal Gore,* Mumbai: SPARROW.

Gopal, Meena, Qudsiya Contractor and Neha Madhiwalla (2006), *Uprooted Homes, Uprooted Lives: A Study of the Impact of Involuntary Resettlement of a Slum Community in Mumbai,* Mumbai: Cehat Publication.

Gothoskar, Sujata (1997), *Struggles of Women at Work,* Delhi: Sangam Books.

Gothoskar, Sujata (2000), "Teleworking and Gender", Mumbai: *Economic and Political Weekly,* Vol. XXXV, No. 26, June 24.

Gothoskar, Sujata (2013), "The Plight of Domestic Workers: Confluence of Gender, Class and Caste Hierarchy", Mumbai: *Economic and Political Weekly,* Vol. XLVIII, No. 22, June 01.

Gupte, Manisha, Ramesh Awasthi and Shraddha Chickerur (2012), *Honour and Women's Rights: South Asian Perspectives,* Pune: MASUM.

Harish, Ranjana (2003), *Shakti: Multidisciplinary Perspective on Women Empowerment on India,* Delhi: Rawat Publications.

Hiraway, Indira and Rania Antonopoulos (2009), *Unpaid Work and the Economy: Gender, Time Use and Poverty in the Global South,* Palgrave Macmillan, UK.

Jhabwala, Renana and Shalini Sinha (2002), "Liberalisation and the Woman Worker", Mumbai: *Economic and Political Weekly,* Vol. XXXVII, No. 21, May 25.

Joshi, Ila (1991), *Women Dimension on Television: Policy, Personnel and Programme,* Delhi: Concept Publishing Co.

Karkal, Malini (1991), Studies *on Women and Population: A Critique Unknown Binding,* Mumbai: International Institute of Population Sciences.

Kosambi, Meera (2000), *Pandita Ramabai through Her Own Words,* edited and part translated, Delhi: Oxford University Press, *2000*

Khanna, Renu (2005), "Obstetrics and Gynecology", Mumbai: *Economics and Political Weekly,* Vol. XL, No. 18, April 30, 2005.

Krishnaraj, Maithreyi (1986), *Women's Studies in India - Some Perspectives,* Bombay, Popular Prakashan.

Krishnaraj, Maithreyi and Joy Deshmukh (eds.) (1988), *Evolving New Methodologies in Research on Women's Studies, Contributions to*

Women Studies, Mumbai: RCWS, SNDTWU.

Kudchedkar, Shirin and Sabiha Al-Issa (1998), *Violence against Women: Women against Violence*, Delhi: Pencraft International.

Lakshmi, C. S. (2000), Seven *Seas & Seven Mountains*: *Volume 1: the Singer and the Song: Conversations with Women Musicians*, Delhi: Kali for Women.

Lakshmi, C.S. (2003), *Seven Seas & Seven Mountains: Volume 2: Mirrors and Gestures – Conversations with Women Dancers*, Delhi: Kali for Women.

Lingam, Lakshmi (ed.) (1998), *Understanding Women's Health Issues*: A Reader, New Delhi: Kali for Women.

Mahadevia, Darshini and Indira Hirway (1996), "Critique of Gender Development Index-Towards an Alternative, Mumbai: *Economic and Political Weekly*, Vol. XXXI, No. 43, October 26, 1996 *Review of Women's Studies.*

Omvedt, Gail (1978), *We Shall Smash This Prison*, Delhi: Orient Longman.

Pandey, Divya and Veena Poonacha (2000), "Responses to Domestic Violence", Mumbai: *Economic and Political Weekly*, Vol. XXXV, No. 07, February 12.

Parthsarathy, D., Thekkekara, Thanksay and Poonacha, Veena (Ed.) (2011), *Women's Self Help Groups: Restructuring Socio-economic Development*, New Delhi: Dominant Publication.

Poonacha, Veena (2007), "Gender in Human Rights Discourse," Mumbai: *RCWS*, SNDTWU.

Poonacha, Veena (2004), "Recovering Women's Histories: An Enquiry into Methodological Questions and Challenges", Delhi: *Indian Journal of Gender Studies*, September-/December, Vol. 11, No. 3.

Patel, Vibhuti (1988), "Emergence and Proliferation of Autonomous Women's Organisations in India" in Ghadiali, Rehana (ed.) *Women in Indian Society*, Delhi: Sage Publications.

Patel, Vibhuti (1989), "Recent Debates on Concepts of Paid-Unpaid Work, Domestic Work and Employment of Women", *UN-INSTRAW and SNDT Women's University*, Bombay.

Patel, Vibhuti (2002), *Women's Challenges of the New Millennium*, Delhi: Gyan Publishing House.

Patel, Vibhuti (2005), "Fundamentalism, Communalism and Gender Justice" in Ram Puniyani (ed), *Religion, Power and Violence*, Delhi: Sage Publications.

Patel, Vibhuti (2009), *Discourse on Women and Empowerment*, Delhi: The Women Press.

Patel, Vibhuti (ed.) (2010), *Girls and Girlhoods at Threshold of Youth and Gender*, Delhi: The Women Press.

Patel, Vibhuti (2013), "The Dynamics of Women's Studies in India", Mysore: Samruddhi Foundation, Monograph Series-1.

Radkar, Anjali and Sulabha Parasuraman (2007), "Maternal Deaths in India: An Exploration", Mumbai: *Economic and Political Weekly*, Vol. XLII No. 31, August 04.

Ravindra, R.P. (1986), The *Scarce Half: A Report on Amniocentesis and other Sex-determination Techniques, Sex Pre-Selection and New Reproductive Technologies*, Mumbai: Centre for Education and Documentation.

Rege, Sharmila (1998), "Dalit Women Talk Differently—A Critique of Difference and Towards a Dalit Feminist Standpoint Position", Mumbai: *Economic and Political Weekly*, Review of Women's Studies, Vol. XXXIII, No. 44, October 31.

Rege, Sharmila (2003), "More than Just Tacking Women on to the 'Macro picture'", Mumbai: *Economic and Political Weekly*, Vol. XXXVIII, No. 43, October 25.

Rege, Sharmila (2010), "Education as *Trutiya Ratna*: Towards Phule-Ambedkarite Feminist Pedagogical Practice", Mumbai: *Economic and Political Weekly*, Vol. XLV, No. 44-45, October 30.

Shukla, Sonal (1991), "Cultivating Minds-19th Century Gujarati Women's Journals", Mumbai: *Economic and Political Weekly, Review of Women's Studies*, Vol. XXVI, No. 43, October 26.

Talmaki, Rekha (2012), *Socio-Economic Development of Tribal Women–Changes and Challenges*, Delhi: The Women Press.

Tambe, Anagha (2009), "Reading Devadasi Practice through Popular Marathi Literature", Mumbai: *Economic and Political Weekly*, Review of Women's Studies, Vol. XLIV, No. 17, April 25.

Velayudhan, Meera (2009), "Women's Land Rights in South Asia: Struggles and Diverse Contexts", Mumbai: *Economic and Political Weekly*, Vol. XLIV, No. 44, October 31.

Shah, Chayanika and Gita Chadha (2002), "Teaching Feminist Science Studies in India", *episteme4.hbcse.tifr.res.in/proceedings/strand.../shah-and-**chadha**.*

Thakkar, Usha (1997), "Engendering Politics for Good Governance: Advocacy by Women for Social and Political Change", *www.istr.org/resource/resmgr/working_papers_cape./**thakkar**.pdf*

12

Critical Engagements with Research in Psychology in Western India

Gautam Gawali

In India, psychology as an independent subject at the post-graduate level, that is, at the Master of Arts level, was first started in 1916 at the Calcutta University under the direction of Dr. N.N. Sengupta who had his doctoral training under Hugo Munsterberg at Harvard. This was followed by the University of Mysore, which commenced its undergraduate and post-graduate courses in 1924. Teaching of experimental psychology not as an independent subject but as part of the philosophy program was started in Dacca in 1921, in Aligarh in 1932, in Patna in 1934 and in Lucknow in 1929. Psychological laboratories were also set up at the universities of Punjab and Banaras during this period. It should be noted that the Calcutta University's Department of Applied Psychology was the only pre-war attempt for setting up institutional facilities for conducting research on guidance and mental health testing problems in the fields of industry and education (Bose, 1938; Sinha, 1963). The first department of psychology came into existence in the western part of India in the year 1950 in Savitribai Phule Pune University (earlier known as Pune University) and was named as the department of experimental psychology. The Department of Applied Psychology of the University of Mumbai was established as early as 1959, about 56 years ago. This was at a time when the field of Psychology was just grounding its roots in India and was in its infancy in Mumbai.

In our country, the discipline and practice of psychology as a behavioral science has never faced greater challenges than in the existing environment. Funding for psychology education and training is inadequate, there is a shortage of psychology personnel, and Indian researchers in the field of psychology are yet to perform at par with the standards of their international counterparts. The psychological literacy of our country continues to lag behind. Thus, we need to address these challenges from various platforms, perspectives and at the level of professional bodies, which are committed towards building the importance of the science of the discipline of psychology, which are the essential initial steps.

It is noteworthy that the old school of psychology essentially treats experimental psychology as the most important and the only field that studies human behavior in the most empirical way. Experimental psychology for a long time has been considered as a super specialized field; almost like 'econometrics' is considered as an elite subfield of economics. This view, which accords priority to a particular branch of knowledge, affects adversely the growth of the discipline.

The research in field of psychology carried out in the western part of India at specialized centers and universities reflected primarily the needs of the industry as their relevance. This could be observed by looking at the knowledge imparting practices worked through syllabus making; moreover, the discipline was also influenced substantially by the liberal economic changes of the year 1991. Thus the concerns of markets become priority of the social science research practice. These changes have influenced the area of research in psychology a great deal. Hence, the studies conducted in psychology were behavioral and became more individualistic in nature, and by implication, the 'social' orientation was compromised.

The nature of society, social composition and the aspirations of the social groups, are changing and are being impacted by diverse forces including traditional ethos, the market led economic changes as well as the democratic ethos and system of governance we have adopted. The patterns of land distribution, educational attainment, and government employment to the socially disadvantaged groups like the oppressed and exploited castes, tribes, women in general, other backward classes, minorities and marginalized communities shows their continuous deprivation. Any attempt on their part to exercise their social and democratic rights, their attempts of sharing social goods and resources to which they have legitimate right, however, are perceived as challenge to the dominance of the privileged communities which have over the years established exclusive control over these resources. There are divergent perceptions of these new social constructs. Therefore, problems of caste atrocities, communal violence pose challenge to the fabric of a democratic and peaceful society. Hence, it becomes imperative that we lay emphasis on research in social psychology as prerequisite for change in the social mindset and for working towards bringing harmony in the society.

It could have been more pertinent to study social movements by the scholars in the field of psychology to understand social psychology in an empirical way. It is ironical that instead of being an agent of social change, where the traditional hierarchies become redundant, the discipline of psychology itself is subjected to the new hierarchies. While examining the problem, unfortunately, an unexplained hierarchy is seen being established in psychology beginning with counseling and industrial psychology and social psychology finds its place only on the last pedestal of the ladder of this discipline.

The Three Problems

There are three major problems faced by most of the departments of psychology in India, all stemming from inadequate financing and physical facilities. Many of the departments who are known for their academic contribution are housed in old buildings or houses, and lack sufficient classrooms, laboratory and office space. Library facilities are also inadequate. Most departments have their own small psychological library. Libraries also lack sufficient subscriptions to current psychological journals. Testing materials and other equipment are in short supply. The second major problem faced by Indian university departments is lack of full-time teachers. Most of the departments are functioning with less than a half of the sanctioned faculty strengths. The opportunity for individual student-teacher contact is simply insufficient. Similarly, time for research in the department is severely limited due to frequent changes at policy level and assessment system. What little time the professor has is used up by the teaching demands of ever increasing enrollments. Inadequate budget allocation for the entire university makes the struggle further difficult.

A third major problem is the lack of internship facilities/ fieldwork facilities. In many areas of psychology, such as counseling, career guidance and counseling, clinical, social, and industrial—a period of closely supervised actual work experience is considered essential to the preparation of professional psychologists. This internship is usually done in hospitals, clinics, schools, factories and NGOs etc., under the supervision of the teachers/psychologists working in that institution. Since there's a marked shortage of qualified psychologists in India and extremely limited psychological services, it implies that internship opportunities are few. Most departments allocate internships to too many students for only brief periods of time. Supervision in these work settings is frequently inadequate and at some places nonexistent; this burden falls back on the faculty of the department. Since the faculty is already overworked and hard pressed for time; the student is likely to receive little individual supervision from any source. The nine months or one academic year paid internship supervised by a qualified practicing psychologist is indeed a rarity in India. Frequently, students must find their own opportunities to gain practical experience and do the best they can without supervision.

Adair, Pandey, Begam, Puhan, and Vora (1995) conducted a study on 64 Indian psychologists through a mailed questionnaire. The survey revealed three major impediments to research productivity: (a) lack of supportive intellectual climate, (b) poor professional support, and (c) inadequate research funding.

Universities in Western India

In western India, the focus of psychological research was more on experimental psychology. When researchers realized that the application of experimental psychology in actual practice and particularly in industry as a source of employment is very limited; they started working on other areas of psychology specially applied psychology. In further scrutiny of the masters program conducted in various universities of western part of India shows their major thrust as experimental psychology, experimental personality research, five-factor model of personality, mathematical psychology, clinical psychology, educational psychology, industrial and organizational psychology, psychology of stress, gender related issues, business psychology, gender equality, social psychology, counseling psychology, clinical psychology and industrial psychology, multicultural psychology, rehabilitation psychology, evolutionary psychology.

Review of research shows that Western theories and concepts constitute the core backbone of research and teaching programs in all the universities in India. It will not be an exaggeration to expect from psychologists in India and researchers to gear up to develop further psychology as an academic discipline in India.

Psychologist being a social scientist, engaging with socially relevant research topics means that they must first of all engage with themselves. In India, like other countries in transition, knowledge needs to be gathered to enable us to better understand the problems and the direction of the social changes faced by these countries. In authoritarian functioning governance, the political administration seeks to control the production of socially relevant knowledge. They politicize research and use it as an instrument to achieve their own hidden social agendas. The social scientists thus should consider it as part of their ethical and moral responsibility to reflect on the conditions of a free and democratic society, because it is a prerequisite for the very existence of freedom of social research. In brief, social scientists must maintain certain distance from their socio-political surroundings (biases and prejudices) and take care to protect their academic and personal autonomy. The psychologists being social scientists must further point out that the benefit of psychology lies in the fact that the psychology as a discipline does not serve the interests of particular religion, politics or the economic system, but instead analyze psycho-societal problems and the current issues from their psychosocial perspective, supported by sophisticated research methods.

Understanding Mental Health Needs of Culturally Diverse Groups

World Health Organization has defined health as "a state of complete physical, mental and social well-being and not merely the absence of disease or infirmity." The fundamental goal of life is happiness. Many researchers, scientists and even lay people struggle to find what happiness is and how to identify the factors that produce it. In our country, we have 190 religions and 4635 communities. They have been staying in 29 states and 7 union territories and they talk in 1625 languages. Out of these, a significant population belongs to minorities and socially disadvantaged groups and they are subjected to social discrimination and prejudice (Gawali, 2014). Therefore, their happiness and wellbeing fluctuate along lines of community and group membership. The fulfillment of basic needs for connectedness sometimes is not satisfied due to the underestimation of importance of personal connection. Prejudice is a key factor in creating stress that adversely affects mental health of socially disadvantaged, women and minorities. In chastise rationalization the variability in functioning is attributed to biological differences. However, no genetic research has supported this explanation.

The book-view of Hindu Social Order does not only mention the hierarchical position of the four *Varnas*, they have also prescribed various socio-economic, political, educational and religious functions of each Varna (Kakar, 1992). A fifth group, the outcastes or Untouchables, which are found in every part of India, was traditionally relegated to occupations associated with "organic waste, filth, ritual pollution, death, evil spirits, or various menial tasks" (Deliege, 1999; p. 25).

This has created caste as well as gender bias in occupational fields, which are against the basic principles of human resource development and management of modern psychology. There is enough evidence that religion is a major divider of humanity. For thousands of years, religion has kept people apart, creating deep 'us-v/s-them' divisions that have kept men and women from marrying one another, eating together, being buried beside one another, letting their kids play with one another, etc. For religious Hindu, all so called low caste Hindus are *other*. The same goes for how Hindus view all non-Hindus. For believing Christians, you're either Saved or Damned, and throughout history, the consequences of this distinction have been savage. For faithful Catholics, non-Catholics are not to be wed, among other things. Muslims consider all non-Muslims as kafir, and the internal rift between Sunni and Shiite Muslims continues to result in bloodshed.

Contemporary Research Issues

Casteism in all its horrific forms is transmitted across generations and is manifested in individual behaviors, institutional norms and practices, and cultural values and patterns. Casteism serves simultaneously both to rationalize the hierarchical domination of one group over other group(s), and maintain psychological, social and material advantages for the dominant group. Both active casteism and passive acceptance of caste-based concession disrupt the mental health and psychological functioning of both victims and perpetrators of caste injustice.

A study of various religious practices of the world makes it clear that only the Hindu religion sanctions the most horrible form of discrimination based on one's birth. May be some followers of other religions also practice some sort of caste discrimination. However, their religious texts do not approve of the caste discrimination. Hindus derive the caste system directly from their scriptures and their scriptures sanction Caste discrimination.

Non-Hindu research scholars do not actively address caste system in India and its harmful psychosocial consequences. Any such attempt would warrant essentially analysis of Hindu social and religious practices. The practice of psychology that is uninformed by such critical engagement of caste based social order results in implying a tacit legitimizing of discriminatory and oppressive society. Moreover, it is observed that researchers who have an access to research funding have attempted to bring in religious dimensions as a basis of building 'Indian' psychology. On the other hand social scientists struggling to understand Indian society from diverse/ multicultural perspectives have stove to bring diverse and located, even subjugated, voices to fore in psychological research practice.

Since 1970s the developments in social sciences shows a quest to address the contextual challenges, while remaining rooted in the universal ethos. There are a number of larger psychosocial factors such as structural inequality, abject poverty, gender based discrimination and domestic violence; caste discrimination all contributing towards disturbing the mental health of our society. Thus critical engagement with these is a necessary condition for Indian psychologists and researchers, to be relevant to the needs of our people and our context. We need to change the way we teach and practice psychology. There is also need to emphasize on preventative rather than mere curative approach. For us this means working towards prevention and reducing of inequalities and discrimination as structural reasons for mental illness.

Social Psychology

The discipline emerged in America and later travelled to Europe. In the beginning, especially in America and Europe the areas of studies and the research conducted in the discipline were essentially very objective and were based on experimental psychology, akin to the needs of the larger social benefit. In terms of the studies conducted in India under the sub-branch of Social Psychology, one often observes that a new vista of 'Indian (social) Psychology' a localized terminology being developed over a long period of time. This school of thought essentially argues and links psychology to the mainstream culture. Attempts have been made to derive the essence from the religio-cultural perspectives. The other problem that one may witness in such kind of labeling is that, if at all one argues about Indian content, very much visible in terms of writings of yoga gurus and other mythological personalities, one must also very broadly look at the 'other Indian' psychology in terms of Buddhist practices or Sufi tradition in terms of school for the actualization of divine ethics, so also, Sikhism, or Jainism which teaches about the control of body and mind.

The hierarchization of the subject can be seen in the discipline of psychology too. Prioritization of studying branches of the discipline is very much visible. A definite hierarchy is established in the discipline where clinical and industrial psychology assumes the top position and social psychology is at the bottom of the hierarchy. The reasons attributed to this kind of prioritization / hierarchisation is that a myth is developed around social psychology with respect to dealing with marginalized, discriminated population, which is not an area of interest of 'elite' psychologist.

The perspective of Social Psychology challenges social structure/institutions and practices including the discipline of psychology directly or indirectly may contribute to various forms of inequality, negative discrimination, injustice and oppression. Researchers should suggest psychologists to position themselves and work within society and develop a critical attitude towards such forces or discipline and its functions. The diagnostic function that psychologists are expected to perform in society with regard to peace building–reconciliation, reconstruction, and development, power structures, and all forms of inequalities and discrimination etc. To increase the acceptance of Indian psychology they need to systematically study the social structure of caste and gender discrimination and differentiate between structural disadvantages, which imply large, pervasive and systemic effects, and incidental disadvantages, which imply suddenly, imposed conditions requiring adaptation to a novel situation.

Positive Psychology

Martin Seligman and Mihaly Csikszentmihalyi introduced the field of Positive Psychology, in 2000, in an effort to shift away from the disease or deficit model of human functioning that has dominated the field of psychology since World War II. Instead of emphasizing psychopathology, positive psychology focuses on human prospering and helping individuals live happier lives (Seligman & Csikszentmihalyi, 2000). This new field of psychology emerged at a pivotal time, as the discipline of psychology also recognized that current psychological approaches were not adequately addressing the needs of racial and ethnic minorities and that, in many cases, we were failing to understand culture-specific strengths. In recognition of this bias in the mental health system, the APA (2003) called for cultural competence in the practice of psychology. With its strength-based approach and its reliance on empiricism and objectivity, positive psychology was ideally suited to address these disparities and to lead psychology in the 21st century.

Within the framework positive psychology; new theories, constructs and interventions have been developed. As a relatively recent framework, however, positive psychology still has much to gain from new ideas, approaches and assessment instruments (Richardson and Guignon 2008).

Positive psychology has become an exciting, well-regarded field of study, and an influential tool for clinicians.

But, for many years, the research in areas relevant to positive psychology, such as happiness, subjective well-being, and emotional intelligence, has been based on research findings from non-ethnic community. Now, researchers in the field of positive psychology have started providing a comprehensive reference that focuses specifically on how a culturally-informed approach to positive psychology can help capitalize on the strengths of socio-culturally and economically marginalized groups and have a greater potential to positively impact their psychological well-being.

Researchers in various disciplines have been increasingly involved in the investigation of one of the most complex and universally debated issues: the pursuit and achievement of the good life. New entries of discipline become acceptable largely due to the failure of present /existing discipline.

It is time that the psychologists from India integrate their understanding of behavior and society and find ways of how they can contribute in co-creating a more harmonious society. Community mental health interventions that look at preventive mental health care interventions such as life skills education programs, using techniques of conflict management to resolve intra-familial conflict—are some ways which can make a difference to make individuals, families and communities more resilient.

Women

During recent decades, women and girls of diverse ethnicities, social classes, sexual orientations, and life experiences have encountered dramatic and complex changes in education, health, work, reproductive and caregiving roles, and personal relationships. Although many of these changes have resulted in increased equality, opportunity, and quality of life, girls and women are also at risk for a variety of health concerns and life stresses (National Healthcare Disparities Report, 2005). Stressors in the lives of women and girls include interpersonal victimization and violence, unrealistic media images of girls and women, discrimination and oppression, devaluation, limited economic resources, role overload, relationship disruptions, and work inequities. Violence against girls and women is often predicated in sexism, racism, classism, and homophobia (Glick & Fiske, 1997; Koss, Heise, & Russo, 1994; West, 2002).

In India, women are victims of social order like other marginalized groups. A full participation in social and economic life is central to women's freedom and sense of self. Thus, fulltime employment/work of women should be considered as an opportunity for them to express their self and also for their social and emotional liberation. Therefore, researchers need to focus on career development of women in contemporary society. One must assume that at all levels, but especially at the higher occupational levels or in nontraditional careers women will exhibit more conflict than men, will experience differences in job-seeking pattern, and will have to overcome more obstacles to career advancement (Leviton and Whitely, 1981).

The implication for career counseling, as the number of working women in this country continues to increase, it seems reasonable to assume that the sex-role attitudes of women will continue to be more liberal, and work will play an important role in the lives of the female population in the country. The rapid and continuing growth in the number of working women will create a growing need for career counseling services focused on. However, based on the recent writings on women and work, it seems that counselors are often not adequately prepared either personally or professionally, to provide these services (Fitzgerald and Crites 1979).

It is the burgeoning field of women studies that has pointed to the need for considering gender as an analytical category in research. The concept of gender has been recognized as cultural and distinct from sex, which is merely biological. Gender is created by the social structure and should be seen as a system of relationships rather than as a set of psychological traits. Kalpagam (1986) highlighting this view stresses that, "the division between female and male is socially created and is deeply woven into the organization of institutions and of everyday life" (p. 59). Psychological research, both in the west and in India, which treats gender, as primarily a collection of dispositional traits stemming from the biological fact of sex then cannot go beyond documenting sex differences in various dimensions. It is thus the feminist recognition of gender as a cultural creation with its various social, political and personal ramifications that is likely to shift the perspective in our research and yield new insights. As Lott (1985) has pointed out, gender differences then, will center only around the few "biological imperatives of sex".

Community Need Based and Humanistic Psychology Research

Needs, can be defined as the gap between what is and what should be. An individual, a group, or an entire community can feel a need. It can be as concrete as the need for food and water or as abstract as improved community cohesiveness. An obvious example might be the need for public transportation in a community where older adults have no means of getting around town. More important to these same adults, however, might be a need to be valued for their knowledge and experience. Examining situations closely helps uncover what is truly needed, and leads toward future improvement.

There should be growing interest among social scientists to involve in community-based research in communities and institutions of higher learning around the country. In Indian community the humanistic approach of study encourages a proactive stand of activism, advocacy, and social justice that promotes awareness, wisdom, purpose, respect, interdependence, and peace. There should be serious concern for those who experience multiple levels of discrimination and exploitation, much of which is barbaric, degrading, horrifically violent and totally inhumane.

"An assumption unusual in psychology today is that the subjective human being has an important value which is basic; that no matter how he may be labeled and evaluated he is a human person first of all, and most deeply." Carl Rogers, 1962.

Today, the concepts central to humanistic psychology can be seen in many disciplines including other branches of psychology, education, therapy, political movements and other areas. For example, transpersonal psychology and positive psychology both draw heavily on humanist influences.

The goals of humanistic psychology remain as relevant today as they were in the 1940s and 1950s. As Maureen O'Hara, former president of the Association of Humanistic Psychology, explained, "As the world's people demand freedom and self-determination, it is urgent that we learn how diverse communities of empowered individuals, with freedom to construct their own stories and identities, might live together in mutual peace. Perhaps it is not a vain hope that is life in such communities might lead to the advance in human consciousness beyond anything we have yet experienced."

Role of Psychologist in Democratization Process

Psychology in India is confronted by many challenges. It is observed that the Indian psychologists work within a highly politicized climate in which political struggle has become part of popular culture. The typical Indian youth discuss cricket, movies and politics most frequently. Furthermore, despite political change and reform, Indian psychologists are still faced with international academic and professional isolation. Many communities and community organizations appear to question the relevance of psychology in a world where material struggle takes precedence. In this context, some practitioners are attempting to make psychology more relevant. Many are seeking to play a constructive role. Being a social scientist, it is expected from the psychologist that they should participate in criticizing and improving the existing social order.

In a democratic process, the psychologists should therefore be encouraged to align themselves with the forces that are attempting to create a more just Social and economic order in India. Importantly, because real change within psychology and other spheres of society is a slow process, psychologists need to ensure that change happens. The biggest challenge in a multicultural society like India is that how can we best manage cultural diversity and intergroup conflict and terrorism of different nature in this fast-changing world.

In recent years, a number of prominent thinkers have argued that democratic arrangements tend to favor the flourishing of toleration among groups with radically different comprehensive worldviews. The democratization means advancing caste and gender equality, social, political and economic inclusion. The researchers working in this field needs to identify different conflicting areas in Indian society and should suggest possible psychosocial interventions. The major conflicting areas like marital, interpersonal, social, religious conflicts can be managed by incorporating psychosocial perspective in democratization process. The families are to be built as laboratories for getting introduced to democratic values. Some serious Social scientists need to seriously understand how slavery to a large extent got eradicated because it was not a part of their religion but in Indian context gender, caste inequality and negative discrimination is not getting eradicated; on the contrary it is further intensified. In India, ex-untouchable castes and several tribal groups continue to be subjected to discrimination, economic and social exclusion and a stigmatized identity (e.g. Thorat 1979; Deshpande 2011; Navsarjan Trust 2010). Psychologists in India need to make serious efforts in understanding socially disadvantaged people and through research they should join their struggle for reclaiming human personality.

Psychologists should challenge unjust social structure/ institutions and practices – including the discipline of psychology – those directly or indirectly contribute to various forms of inequality, injustice and oppression. Researchers in social sciences should suggest psychologists to position themselves and their work within society and develop a critical attitude towards such psychological knowledge and its functions. This can be labeled as – 'social psychological perspective'. Largely Indian psychology appears as adopting an elitist ideological position that may promote the interests of the powerful that is upper castes male institution and hence may contribute to the exploitation and oppression of down trodden and females in general.

Scientific Temper

In India, people with mental illnesses frequently turn to temples and shrines, not to doctors. It is believed that the symptoms of mental illness are caused by visitations and wrath of spirits, demons and ghosts. As a result, it is believed that religious, magical and other traditional methods by God, men and customary healers can elevate the symptoms. The basis of these formations has to be examined in the background of the oppressive social structures in which there is widespread, unawareness and irrationality.

Cultivating a scientific attitude among Indian youth is not only a challenge and opportunities but it is also need of the hour. The scientific attitude encourages an individual to look at the world without distorting it. Such a person can intelligently appreciate and understand the wonders of nature. The scientific attitude necessitates appreciation of good and also bad without ascribing them to external or supernatural forces. In Indian social context, especially our youth should not go around by formulating a fixed view on life or a situation or a topic, but rather be open to new information. Researchers should study how excessive religious teaching can hamper perceptual plasticity. The nature and nurturing both may not comply due to such continuous teaching and therefore, nurturing the scientific attitude among Indian children and youth limits the cognitive development.

Growth and development of psychology in India is depending upon scientific stand taken by them to address the Indian psychosocial issues in a reformist's role. Mental health of our community depends upon how much scientific temper you introduced in Indian masses

The role of reason is to apply scientific knowledge to problems, to grapple with them through the method of scientific inquiry and to work for social transformation inspired by Scientific Temper. After having outlined the essential elements of Scientific Temper, even despite Pandit Jawaharlal Nehru's advocacy of Scientific Temper and In 1976, India also became the first country to include in its Constitution 'Scientific Temper with humanism' as a fundamental duty of all citizens of the country [Article 51-A (h)], we are witnessing a phenomenal growth of superstitious beliefs and obscurantist practices. The influence of a variety of god men and miracle makers is increasing alarmingly. The modern tools of mass/ social media and communication are especially created for social change and work intensively on issues like caste, gender discriminations etc.; but it is mostly being used instead to give an impression that there exist instant and magical solutions for the psychosocial problems that confront our people. The psychologists through their research should try and increase the internal standards of our masses so that the irrational external forces having effect on their behavior can be minimized an also uphold the principles of justice, democracy, science and responsibility.

"The understanding of the social phenomena and human behavior, knowledge about the social process and its determinants, are essential for designing policies to promote social change and to produce a dynamic society capable of absorbing and utilizing the scientific and technological developments for the welfare of human beings" (VKRV Rao).

Emancipatory Disability Research

Percentage of Persons with Disability (PWD) in India has increased both in rural and urban areas during the last decade. Proportion of disabled population is higher in rural areas decadal increase in proportion is significant in urban areas. The total population of persons with disability 2.13 in 2001 whereas 2.21 in 2011. 2.21 was the rural population of PWD in 2001 but 2011 it has increased to 2.24

Proportion of Disabled Population,
Type of Disability, India: 2011

Type of Disability	*Persons*	*Males*	*Females*
Total	100.0	100.0	100.0
In Seeing	18.8	17.6	20.2
In Hearing	18.9	17.9	20.2
In Speech	7.5	7.5	7.4
In Movement	20.3	22.5	17.5
Mental Retardation	5.6	5.8	5.4
Mental Illness	2.7	2.8	2.6
Any Other	18.4	18.2	18.6
Multiple Disability	7.9	7.8	8.1

Source: C-Series, Table C-20, Census of India 2001 and 2011

As per the UN convention of the rights of the persons with disabilities article, 1 "Person with Disabilities include those who have long term physical, mental, intellectual or sensory impairments may hinder their full and effective participation in society on an equal basis with others". As per the world disability report 2011, about 15 per cent of the population in the world has disability and among them 2 to 4 per cent is suffering from severe disabilities.

In India as per the National Census 2011, the disabled population is 2.1 per cent that comes 2, 68, 10557 and the male female ratio is 58:42.The Planning Commission of India in the 11th Five Year Plan estimates that 5 to 6 % of the population have disabilities. The above figures show that in India a considerable number of populations are having disabilities. The psychosocial and vocational rehabilitation of people with disability is a biggest challenge before the rehabilitation psychologists. In the rehabilitation process of PWD they have to face society's attitudinal barriers, which is the biggest hurdle in rehabilitation process.

The Emancipatory disability research refers to a radical new approach to researching disability (Oliver, 1992). Since then, there has been much discussion in the UK about whether such an approach is a 'realistic goal' or an impossible dream'

(Oliver, 1997). As per the definition one can judge emancipatory disability research by its ability to empower disabled people through the research process, but whether this is achievable is a highly argumentative issue. Unlike the abled bodies, Persons with Disabilities are a heterogeneous group. Emancipatory research must resonate with abled bodies to empower the disabled population

Social Justice and Counseling Psychology

Several reasons exist regarding the need to infuse the Advocacy Competencies into counseling practice. One reason is related to the prevalence of oppression in society and the negative impact it has on human development. To illustrate, Jacobs (1994) asserted that environmental factors such as generational poverty can often lead to increased depression, low self-esteem, and a lack of educational and career opportunities.

There is a growing movement calling on counselors to implement the social justice advocacy strategies and interventions into counseling practices (Kiselica & Robinson, 2001; Ratts, D'Andrea, & Arredondo, 2004; Toporek, Gerstein, Fouad, Roysircar, & Israel, 2006). Calls for counseling professionals to be the change agents and advocates for social justice are reflected in the school counseling (Bemak & Chung, 2005; House, 2004; Stone & Dahir, 2006), critical psychology (Fox & Prilleltensky, 1997; Prilleltensky & Nelson, 1997; Prilleltensky & Prilleltensky, 2003) feminist and multicultural counseling literature (Goodman et al., 2004). There is a need to make social justice advocacy needs to make a clearer presence in the field, and reconnect the profession with its roots, is primarily fuelled by a desire to more adequately address systems of oppression that negatively affect client/ student development (Lee, 2007). The belief is that helping professionals can no longer operate solely from the comfort of their offices if they wish to better serve their constituencies. This perspective is echoed by Goodman et al. (2004), who added that "unless fundamental change occurs within our neighborhoods, schools, media, culture, and religious, political, and social institutions, our work with individuals is destined to be, at best, only partially successful" (p. 797). For this reason, counselors need to expand their roles to include social justice advocacy (Lee & Walz, 1998)

Social justice can be referred to as fair and equitable allocation of bargaining power, resources, and burdens in society. Without social justice, an indispensable building block of the good or ideal society is missing, putting the whole edifice at risk of collapse (Prilletensky, I., Nelson, G. (1997).

Social justice is a multifaceted approach to counseling in which practitioners strive to simultaneously promote human development and common good through addressing challenges related to both individual and distributive justice, social justice counseling includes empowerment of individual as well as active confrontation of injustice and inequality in society as they impact clientele as well as those in their systematic context. While doing so, the social justice counselor's direct attention to the promotion of four critical principles that guide their work: equity, access, participation, and harmony. From this perspective, equity is the fair distribution of resources, rights and responsibilities to all members of society. Access is a key to a socially just world. It includes access to resources, services, power, information and understanding crucial to realizing a standard of living that allows for self-determination and human development. Participation principle describes the right of every person in society to contribute in and be consulted on decisions that impact their lives as well as the lives of other people in their contexts and systems. Harmony is a principle of social adjustment wherein the actions revolving around the self-interests of any individual or group ultimately produces results that afford the best possible outcomes for the community as a whole.

Ratts (2009) contended that social justice "'is related to a growing need to connect human development issues with toxic environmental conditions" (p.163) and added: Environmental factors such as racism, heterosexism, and classism, can delay peoples' growth and development and hinders peoples' ability to react their potential??. This especially is true for clients who have been historically marginalized society such as people of color, those in poverty, and individuals who are LGBT. Helping clients recognize the presence of oppressive factors is important because it prevents them from blaming themselves for their plight.

Impact of Unemployment and Mental Health Issues of Youth in India

Unemployment is known to have a negative effect on the subjective well-being. The unemployment blues manifest themselves in a variety of psychological and psychophysical symptoms, such as worry, fatigue, lack of concentration, sleeplessness, listlessness, feelings of loneliness and boredom among others. Psychological deprivation is produced by the prolonged experience of unemployment

The United Nations International Labour Organisation (ILO) released its 2017 World Employment and Social Outlook report in which it has been predicted that there would be a rise in unemployment and worsening social inequality throughout 2017.

Definition of Youth

Youth are defined as those aged 15 to 29 in the national youth policy (2014). This age group constitutes 27.5% of India's population. The 2011 Census counted 563 million young people from 10 to 35, according to the 12th Five-Year Plan Vol. II (2013).

Youth must develop skills that are relevant to employment needs, in order to ensure employability and to prevent labour demand-supply mismatches. This can be achieved by measures such as quality improvements in formal education, vocational education, and specialized skills training and by ensuring sufficient income-generation opportunities commensurate to their skills. Also, the National Occupation Standards need to be defined and the training and skill development programs need to be aligned to such standards. In order to promote employment of youth, GOI has taken a two-pronged approach, namely, (i) enabling skill development and (ii) implementing direct employment programs for lower skilled individuals (NYP-2014). We must reaffirm our commitment to investing in youth as a development strategy. India will have one of the youngest workforces in the world by 2020. The Vision aims to cash in on this demographic dividend by educating and building the skills of its population.

Youth is a period of multiple transitions, physical, cognitive, sexual, emotional, and social. Adolescence, in particular, represents a time when "lifelong health behaviors are formed, when pathways of opportunity or risk emerge, and when the future life course begins to take shape" (McCarthy, Brady, & Hallman, 2016).

Youth development is critical for young people to realize their capabilities to pursue gainful and decent employment, education opportunities, health and wellbeing, as well as civic and political empowerment (The Commonwealth, 2013).

When we support healthy transitions to adulthood—by meeting the unique developmental needs of youth, by safeguarding their rights, and by protecting them against being prematurely thrust into adult roles—we are investing when it counts. When we engage youth meaningfully as partners in development, we are laying the foundation of an inclusive and empowered society.

Positive Youth Development (PYD) and Youth Service engagement

The goal of positive youth development is to build and strengthen assets that enable youth to grow and flourish throughout life. Many youth development programs try to prevent or intervene in the development of problem behaviors by building character strengths such as social intelligence, morality, self-control, and spirituality (Weissberg and O'Brien. 2004')

According to Lerner and colleagues' seminal Five Cs model of PYD, young people who exhibit competence in cognitive, social, academic, and vocational domains; confidence in their abilities and an overall sense of self-worth; connection to positive people and institutions; moral character; and compassion towards others are more likely to make positive self, family, community, and broader societal contributions in the future (Lerner et al., 2005; Lerner et al., 2014).

Trends in Technology are Changing the Way Work is Done: We are becoming increasingly reliant on technology and automation that will likely change and, possibly eliminate some jobs. What does that mean for the work that your organization does? Will you need fewer employees in the future? Will they need different skills? What will your workforce look like? Are you planning for those changes in the way that you are currently hiring and training your employees? I-O psychologists as well as career counseling psychologists can work with organizations to envision the impact that technology and automation will have on business in the future and help identify the skills your workforce will need to be successful in that world.

Conclusion

Psychologists in India need to unlearn to some extent their self glorified ancient past for effective international engagement, which is not automatic but it can be learned. The effective international engagement always requires listening, observing, and testing assumptions by using validated scientific methods.

The world of psychology is continuously becoming large and diverse. It is easy to be remaining in our own discipline geographically and as well as content wise but to begin actual scientific journey in the field of psychology some psychologists in India should come out of their self drawn boundaries.

In the era of globalization, merely going to a new place, culture and visiting different language group is not going to provide us an international status. It is important to scientifically understand the context, issues and local vulnerabilities. We have to go further to remember the innermost biases of human perception and cognition. If you take a serious review of research conducted in India particularly in the field of Indian psychology we may find that researchers trying to find out the confirming evidence of what they think and know, in brief they are trying to justify what is quoted and observed in their ancient mostly religious literature/ sculpture. On the contrary to be effective international psychologists we are required to figure out how to look around our religious and cultural lens, and try to see the word from more diverse and scientific perspectives.

Legally speaking discrimination is a violation of human dignity directed specifically at marginalized groups1. However most of the discrimination at an organizational level isn't obvious and direct but indirect discrimination. Indirect discrimination happens when an employer treats all workers in the same way but a particular marginalized group (i.e. women, racial minorities, religious group, and the handicapped) is disadvantaged.

Higher education funding models must be reviewed and shaped to best support current and future requirements of psychology, education and training. For the good of our discipline and profession, and our local and global communities, psychological scientists, educators and practitioners need to seize every opportunity to increase the psychological literacy of the general public. Psychological literacy is the capacity to intentionally use psychological knowledge and skills to achieve personal, professional and societal goals (Cranney & Dunn, 2011), the process of making things uniform or similar. "The fear of cultural homogenization is a barrier to some multinational businesses"

Need to Incorporate Multiple Perspectives

It is being realized that social psychology does not constitute a single theoretical perspective. These perspectives are complementary rather than competitive. It would be theoretically relevant and fruitful for applications if we could approach the perspectives from an open mind. Over enthusiasm for any given perspective may obscure the generative potential of theories. Sensitivity to different perspectives may enhance the range of social psychological discourse (Dalal, 2002).

References

Adair, J.G., Pandey, J., Begam, H.A., Puhan, B.N., & Vora, N. (1995), "Indigenization and development of the discipline: Perceptions and opinions of Indian and Bangladeshi Psychologists." *Journal of Cross-Cultural Psychology, 26,* 392-407.

American Psychological Association. (2003), "Guidelines on multicultural education, training, research, practice, and organizational change for psychologists." *American Psychologist,* 58, 377–402.

Bemak, F., & Chung, R.C.Y. (2005), "Advocacy as a critical role for urban school counselors: Working toward equity and social justice." *Professional School Counseling,* 8, 196–202.

Bose, G. (1938), *Progress of psychology in India during the past twenty-five years. In the progress of science in India during the past twenty-five years.* Calcutta: Indian Science Congress Association (pp. 336-352).

Dalal, A.K. (2002), "Psychology in India: A historical introduction." in G. Misra & A.K. Mohanty (Eds), *Perspectives on Indigenous Psychology* (pp. 79–107). New Delhi: Concept.

Deshpande, A. (2011), *The Grammar of Caste: Economic Discrimination in Contemporary India.* New Delhi: Oxford University Press.

Fitzgerald, L.F., & Crites, J. O. (1979), "Career Counseling for Women." *Counseling Psychologist,* 8.

Fox, D., & Prilleltensky, I. (Eds.), (1997), *Critical Psychology: An Introduction.* Thousand Oaks, CA: Sage.

Goodman, L. A., Liang, B., Helms, J. E., Latta, R. E., Sparks, E. & Weintrab, S. R. (2004), "Training counseling psychologists as social justice agents: Feminist and multicultural principles in action." *The Counseling Psychologist,* 32, 793–837.

House, R. (2004), "School counselors working as social justice advocates." *Oregon Professional School Counselor Journal,* 1, 1–6.

Jacobs, D.H. (1994), "Environmental failure: Oppression is the only cause of psychopathology." *Journal of Mind and Behavior*, 15, 1–18.

Kakkar, S. (ed.), 1992, *Identity and Adulthood*, Oxford University Press, New Delhi.

Kalpagam, U. (1986), "Gender in Economics: The Indian Experience." *Economic and Political Weekly*, October 25, 59-65.

Kiselica, M. S., & Robinson, M. (2001), "Bringing advocacy counseling to life: The history, issues, and human dramas of social justice work in counseling." *Journal of Counseling & Development*, 79, 387–398.

Lee, C. C., & Walz, G. R. (Eds.), (1998), *Social Action: A Mandate for Counselors*. Alexandria, VA: American Counseling Association and Educational Resources Information Center Counseling and Student Services Clearinghouse.

Lee, C. C. (Ed.), (2007), *Counseling for Social Justice* (2nd Ed). Alexandria, VA: American Counseling Association.

Lerner, R. M., Lerner, J.V., Almerigi, J. B., Theokas, C., Phelps, E., Gestsdottir, S., ... von Eye, A. (2005), "Positive youth development, participation in community youth development programs, and community contributions of fifth-grade adolescents: Findings from the first wave of the 4-H study of positive youth development." *The Journal of Early Adolescence*, 25(17), 17–71. doi:10.1177/ 0272431604272461

Lerner, R. M., Wang, J., Chase, P. A., Guiterrez, A. S., Harris, E. M., Rubin, R. O., & Yalin, C. (2014), "Using relational developmental systems theory to link program goals, activities, and outcomes: The sample case of the 4-H study of positive youth development." *New Directions for Youth Development*, 14, 17–30. doi:1002/yd.20110

Leviton, L. C., & Whieley, S. E. (1981), "Job seeking patterns of female and male Ph.D. recipient." *Psychology of Women*, Quarterly, 5 (5), 690-701.

Lott, B. (1985), "The potential enrichment of social/personality psychology through feminist research and vice-versa." *American Psychologist*, 40, 155-164.

McCarthy, K., Brady, M., & Hallman, K. (2016), "Investing when it vounts: Reviewing the evidence and charting a course of research and action for very Young adolescents." *Population Council*. New York.

Navsarjan Trust, (2010), *Understanding Untouchability: A Comprehensive Study of Practices and Conditions in 1589 Villages*.

Veemaraja, N. (2015), "Impact of Caste System in Indian Democracy,"

International Journal of Management Research and Social Science (IJMRSS) Volume 2, Issue (Print),

Oliver, M. (1992), "Changing the social relations of research production." *Disability, Handicap and Society*, 7 (2), 101-114.

Oliver, M. (1997), "Emancipatory research: realistic goal or impossible dream?" In C. Barnes & G. Mercer (Eds.), *Doing Disability Research, Leeds: The Disability Press*. Retrieved from: http://www.leeds.ac.uk/disability-studies/archiveuk/index.html

Prilleltensky, I., & Nelson, G. (1997), *Doing Psychology Critically: Making a Difference in Diverse Settings*. New York: Macmillan.

Prilletensky, I. & Nelson, G. (1997), "Community Psychology: Reclaiming Social Justice," in Fox, D., and Prilletensky, I. (Eds.) *Critical Psychology an Introduction*, Sage Publication, California.

Prilleltensky, I., & Prilleltensky, O. (2003), "Towards a Critical Psychology Practice. *Journal of Health Psychology*, 8, 197–210.

Ratts, M., D'Andrea, M., & Arredondo, P. (2004), "Social justice counseling: 'Fifth Force'" in field, *Counseling Today* (pp. 28–30).

Ratt, M. J. (2009), "Social justice counseling: Toward the development of a 'Fifth Force among counseling paradigms." *Journal of Humanistic Counseling, Education and Development* 48, 160-172.

Richardson, F.C. & Guignon, C.B. (2008), "Positive Psychology and Philosophy of Social Science." *Theory and Psychology*, 18(5), 605-6

Rogers, C.R. (1951), *Client-centred Therapy*. Boston: Houghton Miffin.

Rothman, S. (1973), *Women's Proper Place: A History of Changing Ideas and Practices, 1870 to the Present*. New York: Basic Books.

Seligman, M.E.P., & Csikszentmihalyi, M. (2000), "Positive psychology: An Introduction." *American Psychologist*, 55(1), 5-14. DOI: http://dx.doi.org/10.1037/0003-066X.55.1.5

Sen, A. (1992), *Inequality re-examined*. Oxford: Oxford University.

Shaffer, J. B. P. (1978), *Humanistic Psychology*. Englewood Cliff, NJ: Prentice Hall.

Sinha, S. (1963), *Fifty Years of Science in India: Progress of Psychology*. Calcutta: Indian Science Congress Association.

Stone, C.B. & Dahir, C. A. (2006), *The Transformed School Counselor*. Boston: Lahaska Press.

Thorat, S. (1979), "Passage to Adulthood: Perceptions from Below." In Sudhir Kakar, (Ed.), *Identity and Adulthood*, New Delhi: Oxford University Press.

Toporek, R., Gerstein, L., Fouad, N., Roysircar, G., & Israel, T. (Eds.), (2006), *Handbook for Social Justice in Counseling Psychology:*

Leadership, Vision, and Action, Thousand Oaks, CA: Sage.

Van Zomeren, M., Postmes, T., & Spears, R. (2008), "Toward an integrative social identity model of collective action: A quantitative research synthesis of three socio-psychological perspectives," *Psychological Bulletin*, 134(4), 504-535.

Weissberg, R.P. & O'Brien, M.U. (2004), "What works in school-based social and emotional learning programs for positive youth development." *The Annals of the American Academy of Political and Social Science*, 591, 86-97.

13

Changing Perspectives of Disabilities
Trends in Research

Varsha Gathoo, Kasturi Kulkarni & Jignya Shah

In the present Millennium the word 'inclusion' has become fashionable. We often use the term 'inclusion' as shorthand to talk about a series of complex social processes indicating that we antagonize exclusion of all marginalized that includes class, income, education, gender, habitation and bodily functions. The term inclusion has different interpretations in various countries. It is sometimes associated with those students living in marginalized or poor contexts, but frequently it is related to the participation of the disabled or those with special educational needs in mainstream society & education (UNESCO, 2008). Disability estimates varies across the different countries as nations diverge in defining and recognizing various categories listed in the legal frameworks. On an average the World Health Organization (WHO) estimates that 10 per cent of any population is disabled (Thomas, 2005). In addition, approximately 85 per cent of the world's children with disabilities under 15 live in developing countries.

Demographic details of disability in India

Disability was referred to as 'infirmity' in India until 1993 and finds a mention in the report that dates back to 1872. The rate of infirmity per one lakh population varied between 228 to 369 during 1881 and 1931 i.e. approximately 0.23 per cent to 0.37 per cent of the population. The infirmities included insanity, deaf-muteness, blindness and leprosy. It was only in 2001 that Independent India began a comprehensive Census enumeration of people with disability. Census 2001 revealed over 21 million people in India to be suffering from one or the other kind of disability. This was equivalent to 2.1 per cent of the total population. Other demographic details documents note that 75 per cent of persons with disabilities live in rural areas. The literacy rates amongst disabled were found to be less than the national average as only 49 per cent of disabled population was reported to be literate out of whom only 34 per cent were employed. Among the five types of disabilities on which data was collected, visual disability emerged as the top category at 48.5 per cent. Others in sequence were: Disability in movement (27.9%), mental (10.3%), in speech (7.5%), and in hearing (5.8%). The disabled by sex followed a similar pattern except that the proportion of disabled females was higher in the category of visual and hearing disability.

The Census (2011) is seen to have extended data on eight types of disabilities namely, disability 'In Seeing', 'In Hearing', 'In Speech', 'In Movement', 'Mental retardation', 'Mental Illness', 'Any Other' and 'Multiple Disability'. There seems to be just a marginal increase in percentage of disabled population as Census (2001) reported 2.13 per cent of the total population while Census (2011) reports 2.21 per cent of the total population facing some form of disability. There is an overall increase in the size of the disabled persons in the rural & urban areas with 2.21 per cent of the disabled persons in rural areas & 1.93 per cent of the disabled persons in urban areas respectively. Amongst the eight types of disabilities, disability in movement (27.9%) emerged as the top category, followed by sensory disabilities and the multiple disabled. There is a trivial increase in disability among percentage of males with disability as reported by Census (2011) as 2.41 per cent as compared to 2.37 per cent of Census 2001. Females with disability on the other hand show a decline from 2.01 per cent in Census 2001 to 1.87 per cent of 2011.

The affirmative features of NSSO (2002) with respect to disability statistics is seen in terms of drop in the age of identification and intervention of disability, enrolment in primary education, diminution in out of school children, enrolment in higher education and corresponding employment rates. The number of years lived by disability also seems to have increased in congruence to averages of population with ought (Kinsella & Wan He, 2009).

Factors contributing to the changing demography of persons with disabilities in India

Political Will

According to the World Bank Report of 2007, India has a vibrant and growing disability rights movement and has one of the more progressive disability policy frameworks in the developing world. A yearning desire to cater to the needs of the disabled in mainstream schools is evident in very early recommendations of the Sargent report in 1944 followed by the recommendations of Kothari Commission in 1964. The launch of the District Primary Education Programme (DPEP) in 1994 provided a great impetus for the integrated education. With India becoming signatory to the Salamanca Statement (UNESCO, 1994) the 1990s saw the rapid incorporation of the term 'inclusive education'. Three landmark legislations have been instrumental in carving the progress of Persons with Disabilities in India namely; The Rehabilitation Council Act (1992), The Persons with Disability (PWD) Act for Equal Opportunities, Protection of Rights and Full Participation (1995) & The National Trust Act (National Trust for the Welfare of Persons with Autism, Cerebral Palsy, Mental Retardation and Multiple Disability), (1999). Following closely to these, the Government of India launched a flagship programme of Sarva Shiksha Abhiyan (SSA) in 2000 for achievement of

Universalization of Elementary Education (UEE) in a time bound manner, as mandated by 86th amendment to the Constitution of India making free and compulsory Education to the Children of 6-14 years age group, a Fundamental Right. The legal mandates further helped to shape the comprehensive National Action Plan for Inclusion in Education of the Children and Persons with Disabilities (MHRD, 2005), the National Policy for Persons with Disabilities (MSJE 2006) and the most recent Right to Education Act (2009) directing inclusion of the marginalized children by endorsing the concept of strengthening the neighborhood schools and 'one school for all'. India is also a signatory for the United Nations Convention on the Rights of Persons with Disabilities UNCRPD (2009) which mandates a human rights approach to all aspects of disability ranging from education to employment.

Technological advancements & support

Disability policies both national & international over the past several years have been based on the assertion that individuals with disabilities are entitled to: (a) equality of opportunity, (b) full participation in society, (c) opportunities for independent living, and (d) participation in activities that will enable economic self-sufficiency (Silverstein, 2000). Several provisions involving technology in the UNCRPD have resulted in the real and substantive inclusive approaches to communication technologies, policy and its implementation at the infrastructural level. Rapid advances in technology have not only transformed the process of rehabilitation, but have also substantially brought down the cost of process of rehabilitation in India. Online screening, research & development in aids and assistive devices like cochlear implants for the hearing impaired, software such as Jaws for the visually impaired and text to speech and speech to text technology has in fact opened the floodgates of information for persons with disabilities in India. There has been an enormous progress in access to information and services for prevention, early identification and intervention of disability coupled with use of educational technology in the form of ICT in India (Vanaja,

2012). Technology especially for education and employment of persons with disabilities has proved to be the most significant dividend to the changes in demographic trends in India.

Human resource development

Education and human resource development of and for persons with disabilities has always been impacted by the philosophical approach of special vs. inclusive education. India is one of the few countries world over, where the education of children with special needs exists parallel under two Ministries. The special education model is under the administrative control of the Ministry of Social Justice & Empowerment (MSJE) and the mainstream education is under the control of Department of Education in the Ministry of Human Resource Development (MHRD) of the Govt. of India. The Rehabilitation Council of India (RCI) is the statutory body mandated to develop, recognize and regulate the human resource development for rehabilitation of persons with disabilities. Approximately 18 Diploma, 11 Degree & 14 Post graduate courses catering to single and multiple disabilities are recognized and being conducted under affiliation of RCI. The Universities across India & the National Institutes along with NGOs under MSJE have been primarily responsible for conducting the Long term & Short term training for developing professionals such as Special Educators, Speech therapists, Audiologists, Occupational therapists, Mobility instructors, Sign language interpreters etc. In the general teacher education diplomas and degrees available nationwide, there exists an optional 'special needs' paper to train and 'prepare' teachers to identify and diagnose disability. In order to meet the demand of inclusive classrooms and bridge the gap of demand and supply, the RCI has also initiated Foundation Courses for general education teachers to address the needs of children with disabilities. To develop curriculum for special education and its inclusion in general teacher preparation programmes, RCI made a historic collaboration with NCTE in January 2005(Kumar & Khagendra (2007). This has been one of the significant proactive step in upholding the mandate of RTE (2009) for education of all children in the most appropriate environment.

Advocacy for Disability

While attitudes which are deep-rooted in cultural assumptions are probably the most difficult aspect of change, they have influence across the board, ranging from community, to school, to government (INTEMAS Report, 2007). This suggests that attitudinal change is an integral part of any programme or plan for rehabilitation of persons with disabilities. Disability Advocacy is about speaking up and ensures that the human and legal rights of people with disabilities are promoted and protected so that people with disabilities can fully participate in the community. Disability support workers have an important role to play in creating awareness, curbing discrimination and help the disabled to live life with dignity.

Advocacy has been instrumental in changing the way disability is viewed and defined in the modern concept. The World Health Organization (WHO) had developed the International Classification of Impairments, Disabilities and Handicaps (ICIDH) in 1980. It was based on the assumption that similar disease processes produce similar disabilities which vary with the individual's health history and environment (Wood, 1975). This classification is based on medical model because; it views disability as arising from health issues. The concept has undergone change in the perspective and disability is now looked from the lens of participation.

ICF (2001) puts the notions of 'health' and 'disability' in a new light. It acknowledges that every human being can experience a decrement in health and thereby experience some disability. This is not something that happens to only a minority of humanity. ICF thus 'mainstreams' the experience of disability and recognizes it as a universal human experience.

Advocacy initiatives in India include setting up of a grievance cell and redressal forums. The Office of the Chief Commissioner for Persons with Disabilities (Chapter XII of the PWD Act,1995) has been set up under Section 57 of the PWD Act of 1995 for safeguarding the rights of persons with disabilities in India. The Indian Copyright Act, 1957, was also amended to introduce one of the most progressive provisions ever in the history of global copyright law. These amendments seek to foster access to copyrighted works for the disabled by providing for the conversion and distribution of copyrighted works without the risk of copyright. The National Policy for Persons with Disabilities (2006) advocates that sign language of the deaf should be recognized as an independent language. Following this mandate, University Grants Commission has directed Universities to the cause of establishing Sign language cells and Departments of Disability Studies fostering a social acceptance & participation.

Outcomes Resulting into Change in the Perspectives

Education of children with disabilities initiated from a journey from extreme neglect to segregation where children with particular difficulties have been put together with other children whose needs were similar. This type of educational setting has been critiqued by advocates as Frederickson and Cline (2002) contend that the creation of special facilities segregating children with Special Educational Needs (SEN) from other children of their own age can be stigmatizing; it also restricts access to important educational opportunities. The political will helped children with disabilities gain access to mainstream and now the inclusive schools. The approach of education in natural environment is mandated globally. Hence residential schools for children with disabilities have slowly weaning giving way to neighborhood schools. Family being the most important stake holder is considered to be an equal partner in rehabilitation and hence the shift has been to provide intervention in the natural environment as opposed to the clinical settings used conventionally. The most significant outcome of the change in the perspective is probably the shift of approach from normalization to the strength based approach. While normalization implied making people "normal" – forcing them to conform to societal norms, the current 'strength based model' respects, values and welcomes diversity. Hence there has been a shift from Medical to the present preference of Social model in viewing and addressing disability. The Medical Model held that disability results from an individual person's physical or mental limitations – a 'sickness' that is largely unconnected to their social or environmental context. The model placed the source of the problem within the impaired person, and concludes that solutions are found by focusing on the individual. Inevitably, finding a cure became difficult because disabled people were not necessarily 'sick'. The Medical model which dominated the formulation of disability policy for years steadily gave way to the Social model which views disability as a consequence of environmental, social and attitudinal barriers that prevent people with impairments from maximum participation in society. Disability is now seen to stem from the failure of society to adjust to meet the needs and aspirations of a disabled minority. It reiterates that if the problem lies with society and the environment, then society and environment must change. This model implies that the removal of attitudinal, physical and institutional barriers will improve the lives of disabled people, giving them the same opportunities as others on an equitable basis. The strength of the Social model lies in placing the onus upon society and not the individual and this is perhaps the revolutionary outcome in terms of changing perspective of disability in the modern era.

Rationale for the Investigation

There has been a paradigm shift in policy towards Persons with Disabilities since the Ninth Five Year Plan, from the earlier welfare based approach to a rights-based approach. The Tenth Five Year Plan focused on effective implementation of various provisions of legislation and National Policy for Persons with Disabilities. It advocated a multi-sectoral and multi-collaborative approach. The Eleventh Five Year Plan (2007–12) had aimed at inclusive growth. It was expected to achieve inclusiveness through significant improvements in literacy/

education, health, greater employment opportunities and sharper focus on disadvantaged groups. The Twelfth Five Year Plan has outlined obligations on States to respect, protect and promote the right of the Persons with Disabilities. The Draft Rights of Persons with Disabilities Bill, 2014 being ratified is based on guidelines of UNCRPD and hence envisages fostering a Social model of disability. Since research practices and evidenced based practices are known to shape policies and practices, a general curiosity arose to ascertain if simultaneous changes have ensue in research being conducted in the field of disability parallel to the societal outlook.

Statement of Purpose

The main purpose of the present investigation was to ascertain the research trends in the field of disability undertaken by lead Institutions in Western India and to study whether the trend is in congruence with the prevailing change in the perception of model of disability.

Questions Investigated

1. Which parameters of the medical model of disability have been extensively studied?
2. Which parameters of the social model of disability need attention for future research?
3. Are the trends in research congruent with the changing models of disability in western India?

Method & Design: Mixed method research of the Exploratory Sequential Design (Creswell, 2012) was used for the present study. This design involves gathering qualitative data to explore a phenomenon, and then collecting quantitative data to explain relationships found in the qualitative data. At the beginning, document analysis of 202 research studies was conducted and later the abstracts of these research studies were classified on the basis of five parameters of medical and social models respectively.

Sample, Site & Data Analysis: A total number of 202 documents (research studies) were obtained from four lead institutions in Western India working in the field of disability rehabilitation. These included Ali Yavar Jung National Institute for the Hearing Handicapped, Mumbai, Tata Institute of Social Sciences, Mumbai, SNDT Women's University Mumbai, and MS University, Gujarat. Document analysis was undertaken on the identified parameters of medical & social model. The same have been adapted from Mason & Rieser (1990) and is given below:

Parameters of the Medical Model

M1—Sample: Medical model focuses on the disability first and the person later. It focuses on the impairment in a person. The studies focusing on the needs, issues, skills, etc of persons with disabilities were listed under this category for e.g. A study of emergent literacy skills of children with hearing impairment.

M2—Special or segregated contexts: Medical model views disability as a condition that can be treated. Hence, the person with disability is segregated from the mainstream society for treatment. Efforts are undertaken to normalize the individual and integrate into to the society. Studies undertaken in the segregated set ups like special schools were included under this parameter.

M3—Health Issues of the Persons with disabilities (PWDs): Since the medical model deals with both physical and mental health, studies undertaken on these conditions were listed under a common parameter of health. Example of physical heath includes Impact of otitis media on school attendance and an example of mental health includes study of stress factors related to visual impairment.

M4—Assistive devices & assessment tools: Medical model emphasizes assessment and treatment using devices. Hence studies focusing on use of devices of rehabilitation such as audiometers, hearing aids or assessment tools such as GAEL-P or BERA were categorized under this parameter.

M5—Training Programmes: Medical model views person with disabilities as having a deficient and hence outlines therapy or treatment schedules. Hence studies undertaken for training programmes or manuals developed specifically for persons with disabilities were listed under this parameter.

Parameters of the social model

S1—Samples: Social models includes acceptance, adjustment of environment which primarily includes people around the individual. Hence studies based on stakeholders like the parents, teachers, special teachers, administrators, policy makers, etc were categorized under this parameter.

S2—Inclusive set up: Inclusion is the characteristic of a social model. Studies involving sites of inclusive set ups such as SSA programs inclusive schools, corporate offices, etc. were listed under this parameter.

S3—Support: Scaffolding is a social phenomenon. Hence studies attempting to explore the support extended to the PWDs in the form of family support, legal support, and financial support were listed under this parameter.

S4—Barriers & Access: Participation being the main feature of a social model studies involving facilitators and hindrances of Persons with disabilities were grouped under this parameter.

S5—Training programmes for the stakeholders: Since social model views disability as emerging from the negative attitudes and barriers of the society, studies involving development of training programmes, manuals for developing a positive attitude amongst stakeholders were clubbed under this parameter.

Results of the Investigation

Result 1: Extensively studied parameters of medical model

Table 1 and Fig. 1 indicates that extensive studies i.e. about 57 out of a total of 117 studies had persons or children with disabilities as the samples for the study. 21 studies focused on devices and tools and almost equal number about 20 studies were conducted in segregated special set ups. Less attention seems to have been caught in the research pertaining to training of persons with disabilities and least no of studies i.e. about 9 focused on either physical or mental health of persons with disabilities.

TABLE 1
Distribution of studies across different parameters of Medical model

Parameters of Medical Model					*Total*
M1 *Sample: PWDs. Focus on studying their needs, issues, attitudes.*	*M2* *Special/ segregated contexts/ specialized teaching methods*	*M3* *Treatment to bring Health Back to normal*	*M4* *Assistive devices, technology for correcting disabilities*	*M5* *Training programmes, therapies, manuals for PWDs*	
57	20	9	21	10	117

Figure 1: Parameter wise distribution of research studies based on medical model of disability

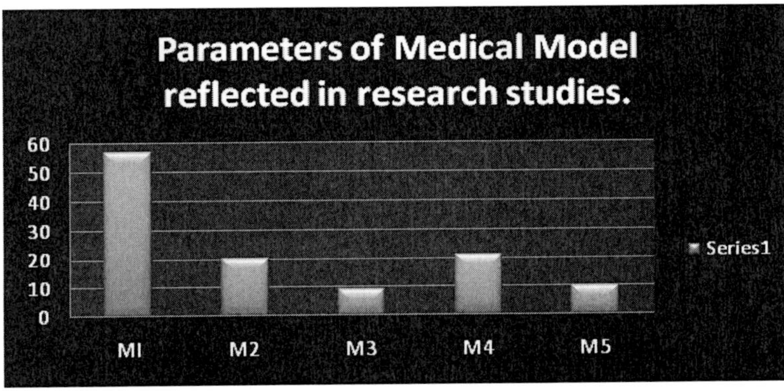

Result 2: Parameters of social model requiring attention

Figure 2: Parameter wise distribution of research studies based on social model of disability

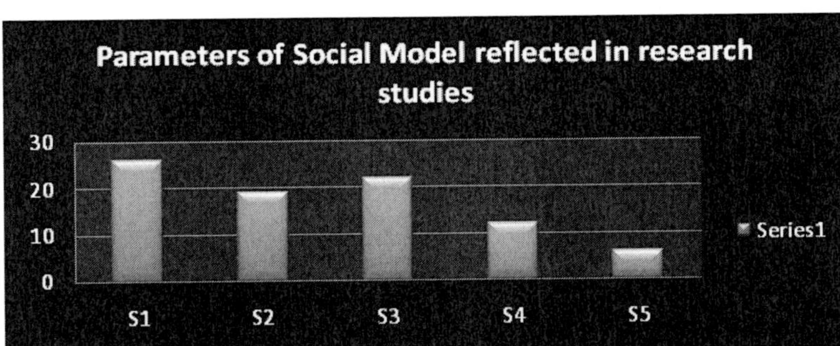

Table 2 & Figure 2 indicates that the almost 26 studies had stakeholders (parents, special teachers, mainstream teachers, etc) as the samples for the study. 19 studies were conducted in inclusive set ups, 22 studies involved provision of support services (legal support, family support and financial support) to PWDs, 12 studies studied barriers or accessibility issues for PWDs. The parameter of social model requiring attention was found to be training to stakeholders of PWDs like parents, teachers, administrators, etc for increasing

TABLE 2

Distribution of studies across different parameters of Social model

Parameters of Social Model					*Total*
S1. Sample : Stakeholders (Parents, teachers, administrators,etc)	*S2 Inclusive set ups for all persons*	*S3 Support in the form of (legal, attitudinal, family, finacial,etc) provided to PWDs*	*S4 Barriers/ accessibility for PWDs*	*S5 Training progs, therapies,manuals for Stakeholders (parents,teachers,etc)*	
26	19	22	12	6	85

participation as only 6 studies were reported under this parameter.

Result 3: Trends in research

Figure 3: Disability model wise distribution of research studies

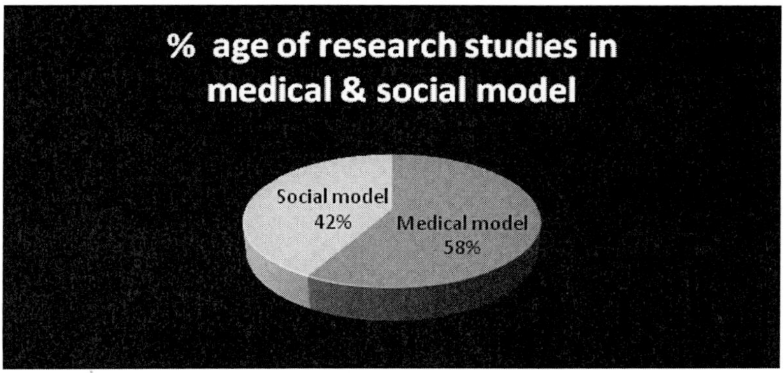

Fig. 3 indicates that medical model is still a preferred area of research and is dominant over the social model. This is in spite of the technological advances, political will, legislations, capacity building and intense advocacy for disability related issues.

Conclusion

The present investigation brings to a conclusion that in spite of the change in the overall perspective of disability the research undertaken is not in congruence with the trend. A newer trend of mixed model researches has also been emerging in the present investigation including issues of disability in denotified tribes, unemployment, livelihood, job opportunities, job satisfaction, marital expectations so also transgender issues, homeless children, feminism etc. Out of the total of 202 abstracts investigated 14 were pertaining could be categorized under this trend.

Acknowledgements

- *Ali Yavar Jung National Institute for the Hearing*

Handicapped, Bandra, Mumbai.

- *Tata Institute of Social Sciences, Deonar, Mumbai.*
- *S.N.D.T Women's University, Juhu, Mumbai.*
- *Maharaja Sayajirao University of Baroda, Gujarat.*
- *Mr. Premal Desai, Lecturer, Akshar Trust, Baroda, Gujarat.*

References

Census of India (2001), Retrieved on 15/8/2014, Available from: http://www.censusindia.gov.in/2011common/CensusDataSummary.html.

Census of India (2011), Retrieved on 12/6/2014, Available from: http://www.censusindia.gov.in/2011-prov results/indiaatglance.html

Creswell, J.W (2012), (4th Ed), *Educational Research. Planning, Conducting and Evaluating Quantitative and Qualitative Research.* Pearson :New Delhi

Eleventh Five Year Plan (2007-12), *Inclusive Growth Volume-1,* Planning Commission.GOI.Retrieved on4/11/2014.Available from http://planningcommission.nic.in/plans/planrel/fiveyr/11th/11_v1/11th_vol1.pdf.

Frederickson, N & Cline.T (2002), "Learning Difficulties." (pp. 231-260). In. J. Swain & S. French (Eds.). *Therapy and Learning Difficulties: Advocacy, Participation and Partnership.* Oxford:Butterworth-Heinemann.

GOI (2005) *Ministry of Social Justice and Empowerment Annual Report* 2004-05, New Delhi: Government of India

INTEMAS Report (2007), *Inclusion and Education in European Countries. Retrieved on 5/11/2014.* Available on http://www.pedz.uni-mannheim.de/daten/edz-b/gdbk/09/Inclusion_education_hungary6_en.pdf

Kinsella, K. & Wan He (2009), *An Ageing World.* Retrieved on 5/8/2014. Available from http://www.census.gov/prod/2009pubs/p95-09-1.pdf

Kumar, S. & Khagendra, K. (2007), "Inclusive Education in India." *Electronic Journal of Inclusive Education.* Vol. 2(2).

Ministry of Human Resource Development (2004), *Education for all: India marches ahead.* New Delhi: Governmentof India.

Ministry of Social Justice and Empowerment (2007), "Disability Policy and Programs: Experiences and Prospects for Future

Presentation made at the People with Disabilities in India: Status, Challenges and Prospects workshop held at World Bank. New Delhi: India

National Sample Survey Organization.(2002), *Disabled persons in India, NSS 58th round (July December 2002) Report no. 485 (58/ 26/ 1)*. New Delhi: National Sample Survey Organization, Ministry of Statistics and Programme Implementation, Government of India

National Trust Act (1999), Retrieved on 12/8/2014. Available from http://socialjustice.nic.in/pdf/ntact1999.pdf

National Policy for Persons with Disabilities (2006), Retrieved on / 10/2014.Available from: http://www.indg.in/india/sitemap-1/primary-education/education-as-fundamental-human-right/national_policy_for_persons_with_disability.pdf

Nikora, L. W., Guerin, B., Rua, M., &Te Awekotuku, N. (2004), *Moving away from home: Some social consequences for Tuhoe migrating to theWaikato*. New Zealand Population Review, 30(1&2), 95-112

Persons with Disabilities (Equal Opportunities, Protection of Rights and Full Participation) Act, (1995), In *National Policy for Persons with Disabilities, 2006. Retrieved on 3/11/2014. Available from :* RCI Act (1992), *Rehabilitation Council of India*. Retrieved on 13/ 6/2014, Available from http://rehabcouncil.nic.in/engweb/ rciact.pdf

Rieser, R. & Mason, M. (1990), *Disability Equality in the Classroom: A Human Rights Issue*. London/ ILEA/DEE. Retrieved on 4/7/ 14. Available from www.diseed.org.uk

Rights of the Persons with Disabilities Bill (2014), Retrieved on 4/ 11/2014. Available from http://www.prsindia.org/billtrack/ the-right-of-persons-with-disabilities-bill-2014-3122/ Right to education (2010), *In Right of Children to Free and Compulsory Education Act- Wikipedia-the free encyclopaedia*. Retrieved on 4/ 7/2014. Available from: http://en.wikipedia.org/wiki/Right_of_Children_to_Free_and_Compulsory_Education_Act

Silverstein, Robert. (2000), *Emerging Disability Policy Framework: A Guidepost for Analyzing Public Policy*. *Iowa Law Review* 85(5). SSA(2000). *Sarva Shiksha Abjiyan-Education for all Spotlight: National Portal of India* Retrived on 9/5/2014, Available from: http://www.india.gov.in/spotlight/spotlight_archive.php?id=31

Thomas, P. (2005), *Disability, Poverty and Millenium Development Goals: Relevance, Challenges and Opportunities for DFID*. Retrieved on 5/10/2014. Available from http://digitalcommons.ilr.cornell.edu/cgi/viewcontent.cgi?article=1257&context=gladnetcollect

UNCRPD (2006), *Convention on the Rights of Persons with Disabilities.* Retrieved on August, 5th 2012, Available from: http://www.un.org/disabilities/convention/conventionfull.shtml

UNESCO (2008), *Inclusive education: The way of the future.* In International Conference on Education. Retrieved on 2/11/2014. Available from http://www.ibe.unesco.org/fileadmin/user_upload/Policy_Dialogue/48th_ICE/CONFINTED_48_Inf_2__English.pdf

UNESCO (1994), *The Salamanca Statement and Framework for Action on Special Needs Education.* Madrid: UNESCO/Ministry of Education and Science.

Vanaja, C.S. (2012), *The Status of Disability in India.* RCI : New Delhi.

World Bank Report (2007), *People with disabilities in India:From commitments to outcomes.* Retrieved on 22/10/2014. Available from http://siteresources.worldbank.org/INDIAEXTN/Resources/295583-1220435937125/Philip_Okeefe_1_1a.pdf

Wood, P.H.N. (1975), *Classification of im-pairments and handicaps.* Document WHO/1 CDO/REV.CONF/75.15. Geneva: World Health Organization.

World Health Organization (2002), *Towards a common language for functioning, disability and health ICF.* Retrieved on 4/11/2014. Available from

http://www.who.int/classifications/icf/training/icfbeginnersguide.pdf

14

Dalits and Sociology in India

Resisting the Cognitive Blackout and Beyond

Ramesh Kamble

Introduction

The year 2016 marks a centenary of Dr. Ambedkar's essay titled 'Castes in India: Their Mechanism, Genesis and Development' (1989b/1916). This important essay which was presented in May 1916 at the 21 Golden Weiser's Seminar in University of Columbia, was the first serious attempt by an Indian social scientist to grapple with the question of caste, which Dr. Ambedkar saw as intersecting with women's subjugation. Subsequently, he wrote anthropological works such as "Who Were Shudras"? and, "Who Were the Untouchables". Yet, till a few years ago, Dr. Ambedkar was glaringly rendered invisible in the sociological/anthropological discourses in India. In fact a cursory glance at the history of the development of sociology in India, especially at the Bombay school, suggests institutionalized closure towards the Dalit social experience, Dalit quest and movement for equal humanity and justice; as well as silencing of contribution made by Dr. Ambedkar, which much prior to that of prominent Indian sociologists such as Ghurye, towards making of sociology in India: neither the dalit social lives and their movement were of issues of academic engagements in the Bombay school, nor Ambedkar's contribution towards theorizing caste and untouchability was recognized as important sociological engagements. Thus there is scope to say that the sociological knowledge practice operating through institutional structures made dalit movement redundant to the imagination of sociology and practiced organized forms of silencing that rendered Ambedkar's scholarship in sociology as unworthy to the narrative of sociology. Hence, the Ambedkar's contribution to sociology and his struggle against Untouchability was rendered "untouchable" in the institutionalized practice of sociology in the Bombay School. Moreover, while the Bombay School contributed to the nationalist discourse, it remained apathetic towards Dalit struggle for freedom from the slavery of caste and Untouchability, much like the elite, dominant narrative of nationalism in India. (Ghurye's passing reference to the 'problem' of Scheduled castes and Scheduled tribes, shows his prescription (authoritative at that) of assimilating them — 'accommodating' them — within the dominant Hindu society).

This paper attempts to investigate as to how and why the leading scholars of Bombay School of sociology, through organized, institutionalized knowledge-practice, practiced such a closure. We draw on Foucault's articulation of knowledge/ power to analyze this closure witnessed in the Bombay School knowledge engagement. The reason to invoke Foucault here arises from the need to critically interrogate the institutional sociological knowledge practice, which either made the Dalit subject, and the experiential location that emerges from this location, redundant to the making of sociology or constituted the Dalit sociality through the knowledge practice that was external/alien to Dalit subjectivity. While a lot has been written both by and on Foucault, this discussion may sound unnecessary. However for our analysis of practice of scientific sociology at the Bombay School and implication of this practice for the Dalit subjects, it would not wrong to mention a few main articulations of Foucault.

I

The Object and Subject of Knowledge: Invoking Foucault

The detail systematic analysis of different modes of objectification of the human subject, through discursive practices, operating at the institutional knowledge structures has been at the centre of Foucault's work. He points out, "my objective...has been to create a history of the different modes by which, in our culture, human beings are made subjects" (quoted in Robinow, 1984:7). Analyzing the processes of objectification of subject he suggests three modes; a) "dividing practices", 'scientific classification', and the processes of 'subjectification'—"way a human being turns him-or herself into a subject" (Robinow: 1984: 11). Elaborating on 'dividing practices' in his works such as Madness and Civilization, The Birth of the Clinic, and Discipline and Punish, Foucault states that in different ways, through use of diverse procedures, "the subject is objectified by a process of division either within himself or from others" (ibid: 8). That, in these processes of social objectification and categorization human being receives both a social and personal identity. The 'dividing practices' therefore modes of manipulation that combines the mediation of and practice of exclusion. Furthermore, the 'dividing practices' are interconnected with formation of social sciences. There is also rationalization of these knowledge practices–modes of classification, control and containment – (developed through sophisticated conceptual apparatus and efficient analysis) as required for reform and progress.

Another mode of objectification of subject is "scientific classification". This mode of objectification results from " the mode of enquiry which try to give themselves the status of sciences; for example, the objectivizing of the speaking subject in *grammairegenerale*, philology, and linguistics...[or] the objectivizing of the productive subject, the subject who labours, in the analysis of wealth and economics. Or...the objectivizing of the sheer fact of being alive in natural history or biology" (quoted in Ibid.: 9). Foucault shows further, in his works such as The Order of things, as to how "the discourses of life, labour and language were structured into disciplines; and how they achieved a high degree of internal autonomy and coherence, and lead to formation of the universals of human social life" (Ibid.) Elaborating this Foucault states that "various human experiences, such as madness or sexuality, become the objects of intense analysis and scrutiny. They are discursively (re)constituted within rationalist and scientific frames of reference, within the discourses of modern knowledge, and thereby made accessible for administration and control. Since the eighteenth century, there has been a discursive explosion whereby all human behaviour has come under the 'imperialism' of modern discourse and regimes of power/ knowledge. The task of the Enlightenment, Foucault argues, "was to multiply 'reason's political power' and disseminate it throughout the social field, eventually saturating the spaces of everyday life" (Steven Best and Douglas Kellner, 1991: 43). The mode of scientific classification realized through elaborate procedures and systematic analysis in human sciences thus leads to subjecting the subject to meticulous administration, manipulation and control and thereby constituting the subject.

The mode of objectification of the subject to which Foucault draws our attention is seen in both the passive objectification as well as in the processes of 'subjectification'— "way a human being turns him-or herself into a subject". Unlike the other two modes of objectification which render the subject as passive and constrained and subjected to manipulation and control, the third mode indicates processes of self-formation where the subject is active. Foucault analyzes the techniques of an active self-formation draws attention to complicated genealogy, unfolding in "operations on [people's] own bodies, on their own souls, on their own thoughts, on their own conduct (Robinow: 1984: 11).

Foucault's theory of subject thus articulates three major modes through which human subjects become either objects or subjects. The first two modes – dividing practices as well as scientific classifications — construct human subject as passive objects, meaningful only through discursive practices; and the third mode of subjectification, the way human being turn themselves in to subjects with self-formation and self-understanding also exhibiting the subjection to external authority expressed in scientific discourses. Thus whereas the modern theories tend to see knowledge and truth to be neutral, objective, universal, or vehicles of progress and emancipation, Foucault analyzes them as integral components of power and domination (Best and Kellner,1991:43).

This articulation of theory of subject offered by Foucault renders an inescapable character to subject under the modern condition. In his *Order of Things: An Archaeology of the Human* (1973) Foucault describes emergence of the human sciences by engaging in analysis of the underlying rules, assumptions and ordering procedures present in renaissance, classical and modern eras and shows that under the modern era human being becomes the object of modern scientific investigation, a finite and historically determined being to be studies in its living, laboring and speaking capacities (Ibid: 46). This view of objectification of human subject analyzed by Foucault, leads to the charge that his analysis denying politics (a capacity of resistance). However Foucault also describes how modern philosophical construct of 'man' (as an object and subject of knowledge) exhibits "a series of unstable 'doublets': the cogito/unthought doublet whereby Man is determined by external forces yet aware of this determination and able to free himself from it; the retreat-and-return-of-the-origin doublet whereby history precedes Man but he is the phenomenological source from which history unfolds; and the transcendental/empirical doublet whereby Man both constitutes and is constituted by the external world... In each of these doublets, humanist thought attempts to recuperate the primacy and autonomy of the thinking subject... "(Steven best and Douglas Kellner, Ibid).

In the above pages we have described some aspects of Foucault's theory of subject and alluded to his analysis of the discursive construct of 'man' for a number of reasons: Firstly, it helps us to look critically at the practice of sociology at Bombay School critically. Second, it helps us to investigate as to how the margins in general and Dalits in particular figured in this practice and also to analyze the sociological practices that exhibits both construction of Dalit knowledge-subject by that practice, as well as Dalit knowledge-subject critically becoming aware of the knowledge/power operating at the institutional settings of making of sociology. Thirdly, Foucauldian perspective also helps us to understand the various attempts on the part of Dalit knowledge-subjects in recuperating the primacy and autonomy of themselves as thinking beings and thereby intervening into and attempting to reconstitute that practice.

II

Sociology at the Bombay School: the 'Colonial' modernity and 'reverse' Colonized sociology?

In introduction to her edited volume on Doing Sociology in India, Patel draws attention to the link between colonialism, anthropology and sociology in India. Drawing on worksof Beteille, Uberoi and Oommen, she suggests that the division between the two disciplines of sociology and anthropology emerged in the West and for pragmatic reasons, though asserts that such a division was rooted in political project of colonialism (Patel, 2011:XIV), and that, more specifically in the case of Anthropology, its research agenda, theories and methodologies were linked to the needs and policies of the colonial state (Ibid. XV)–the explicit link between institutionalized knowledge engagement and power. Furthermore, extending this insight (knowledge/power) from the practice of anthropology, she raises questions about the development and practice of sociology in India as directed by the colonial anthropology.

Looking at the close links with nationalism and sociological tradition in India, Patel asserts that "sociologists in India saw their project as that which analyses one's own society (India) in one's (indigenous) 'own terms' without colonial and now neo-colonial tutelage." (Ibid: XXIV). The post-colonial development of sociology witnessed shift from the 'book-view' to the 'field-view' and fostered participant observation as an insider's perspective' of doing sociology (XXV).

This brief review of development of sociology in India and in Bombay raises some fundamental questions: While sociologists were committed to the cause of nationalism, did they question or critique the nature of this nationalist fervor (as Ambedkar did)? Did they critically approach the articulation of nation as privileging of a few nations in nationalist struggle? Furthermore, was the project of analyzing one's own society, in one's (indigenous) 'own terms', questioned the nature and characterization of 'one's own'? (In other words, what constituted the idea of 'one's own'?) Did this not lead to denying the diverse "one's" and the diverse notions of 'society", and thereby abrogating the space to define the nature and content of "one's own" and "society"? What constituted 'insider's perspective' in doing sociology? Which "insiders" had privilege to conceptualize the notion of "inside" and to articulate the nature and validity of the "perspective" emerging from that location? Whose conceptualization, or knowledge emerging from which social locations legitimately became "indigenous" in character, and thereby articulation of a new direction in sociology? Whose voices, emerging from which social locations had prerogative of articulating the "new" directions in sociology? Looking at the institutionalized practice of sociology in India and the key knowledge actors involved in producing and legitimizing sociological knowledge shows that this knowledge practice was exclusive domain of the upper castes, and the upper caste knowledge actors were instrumental in laying down the rules and procedures in articulating appropriate 'subject matter, appropriate 'sources' of knowledge, appropriate methods of enquiry, the forms of interpretations and producing objective knowledge about the "Indian" social experience. Thus the 'objective' sociology the privileged knowledge actors practice was in fact rooted in their experiences of the world, based on their assumptions, and ways of interpretations and validation rooted in that privileged social location. Let us illustrate this by looking at the practice of sociology in India.

Critically investigating into the birth of sociology in Bombay, Manorama Savur has pointed out that Ghurye's training in Sanskrit and Indology led to articulation of appropriate approach to sociology in India. She quotes Ghurye to show that for him, "anthropological approach to sociology is the most appropriate" and that his stress on anthropology as guiding development of sociology led to perpetuation of 'anthropolised' sociology in Bombay (Savur, 2011:17). Savur also brings out another implication of his work and approach to formation of sociology, which is important for our concern. She points out that "his major contribution is Aborigines so Called and Their Future, where one also sees his reactionary fears of Christian Missionaries, but fails to take note of the Hindu exploiters…"(Ibid:18). Moreover, despite being father of "Indian" sociology, Ghurye practiced and propagated Hinduised sociology. (This pointhas been argued strongly by T. K. Oommen in his 'Scheduled Castes and Scheduled Tribes: Situating Ghurye'). It is only after A. R. Desai assumed the charge of Bombay department of sociology that sociology came into its own. Desai, a Marxist scholar-activist took sociology, observes Savur, outside classroom, in people's struggles and in his lectures "gave a broad sweep human history…he posed questions, raised issues, presented diverse view points and encourage one to think and choose…he spoke about massive slave labour, the galley slave to build the glorious civilization" (Ibid:21), and that he trained students to integrate theory and practice and to participate in seminars and raise questions. Thus with Desai assuming charge of the Bombay department of sociology became a radical engagement of theory and practice, brought working classes and discussion of Marxism at the forefront of sociological analysis, which further led to sociology becoming a part of 'public' intellectual exercise. One glaring omission in this narrative of radical sociology practiced by Desai (and his students) was the invisibility of critical analysis of caste and Untouchability, and unconcern towards understanding caste and Untouchability from the perspectives of those the perspective of those who were enslaved on account of these structures of social and material relations exploitation and oppression. The Dalits struggles against this slavery (both material as well as social), and later radical Dalit assertion by Dalit panthers in Bombay, was all lost on the radicalized sociology in Bombay. Thus, if Dalits were (as sources for building sociological knowledge) unworthy candidates for Hinduised sociology of Ghurye, they, and the struggles they waged, were irrelevant for radical sociology championed by Desai.

III

Post-colonial 'colonization' of sociology

Patel in the above cited work alludes to recognition on part of the anthropologists in the North that sees their discipline as firmly associated with the colonial project, and the nature of knowledge they created and organized, institutionalized practices they engaged in reflects 'othering', and thus anthropology becoming a "handmaiden of colonialism" (Ibid:XIV). That the making of social sciences in the colonial context in India thus reflects power/knowledge both in its social relevance as well as the supremacy of western philosophical systems (Ibid: 77). The stress on study of India through scriptures — Indological approach – resulted in privileging Brahmins as 'indigenous intellectuals', and formation of sociology and anthropology mediated and constituted by these native intellectuals (Ibid:78). The colonial modernity therefore led to "local colonialism" or 'colonialism of the upper caste locals' as regards to setting up appropriate research questions, methods of enquiry, and proprieties of interpretations and validation of truth claims. Since the '*Samaj* was...conceptualized in Hindu, high caste gentry...terms' (Sumit Sarkar, quoted in Ibid.), the upper caste perspectives constituted the 'objective' character of sociological and anthropological knowledge'. The nature of objective knowledge about Indian society, the authentic knowledge of

Indian society based on 'insider's perspectives' arrived at through intensive field-work, the methodological and theoretical proprieties to pursue knowledge and advance knowledge claims were rooted in upper caste experiences of 'religion', 'community', 'caste', and 'class' even 'India' and their perspectives emerging from their social locations in India. The commitment to the principle of objectivity, the quest for insider's accounts thus demanded commitment to upper caste perspectives, and their reproduction, as authentic and appropriate sociological and anthropological knowledge practice. Patel's critical appraisal of M. N. Srinivas' Anthropology/sociology illustrates this. Reviewing Srinivas' work, especially his understanding of 'Varna' and 'Jati', 'social change' and 'social mobility', and the methodological shift his work (field-view' resulting from ethnography as opposed to 'book-view' emerging from Indology), and the functionalist paradigm as an appropriate approach to the study of Indian society which become prominent through prominence of Srinivas in academia, resulted in institutionalization of the*Savarna* vision of India (Ibid: 84). The practice of sociology and anthropology in India thus presents *colonization* of these disciplines by the upper castes in the post-colonial times by constituting upper castes' perspectives translating into authoritative (arrogant) account of knowledge of Indian society. Thus doing sociology in India was to remain committed to and to reproduce the upper caste perspectives on Indian society. Moreover, under these pursuits of knowledge, though 'caste', 'community' 'religion', 'culture' and 'nation' were important categories and context of knowledge formation, those who suffered denial and violence on account of caste system and religion, or those who were denied the membership of human community through practice of Untouchability, or those did not count in articulation of nation were neither objects of this knowledge, nor their perspectives (on caste, community or nation) had any place in knowledge production.

IV

Dalits as Objects of Knowledge and Dalits as Knowledge subject-actors

The sociological and anthropological knowledge was built independent Dalits, their life experiences or their perspectives on their lived experiences. Thus while Foucault's theory of subject views objectification and constitution of subject through discursive knowledge practices, we are faced with a situation where Dalits were either irrelevant objects in understanding categories of caste, community and nation, or if they were 'studied' (few studies do make them 'object' of knowledge), they were viewed from the perspectives of the dominant upper castes. We should also note here that the possibilities of taking up Dalits as objects of knowledge became possible only when Dalit scholars, both as students and later academics, had opportunity to gain entry into academia. This section attempts to discuss two issues: a) the nature of sociological studies on Dalits by Dalit-Bahujan scholars and implications for understanding Dalit-Bahujan social experiences, and, b) the perspectives adopted by the Dalit-Bahujan knowledge actors in interrogating the dominant perspectives and their attempts to construct alternative knowledge of Dalit condition and thereby assume agency in knowledge production. Of course it is not only Dalits who have advanced critique of existing dominant knowledge practices. Following Dalits' attempts at critical knowledge engagements, other scholars writing on dalit experiences and arguing for knowledge based on those experiences and addressing issue of epistemology, methodology and perspectives are important part of new scholarship that centres Dalit experience as basis of producing critical knowledge. The last section of this paper will discuss these new efforts on part of both Dalit scholars and scholars who regard primacy of Dalit experience as necessary requirement for producing critical knowledge, which could be termed broadly as "Dalit Studies". Before we delve into the question Dalits and object of knowledge and Dalits as subjective knowledge-actors, it would be useful to describe broad strands in Dalit scholarship. (We wish to make it clear that this is not the exhaustive or thorough description of Dalit scholarship. We are only mentioning some attempts to illustrate our concern of understanding this scholarship in terms of Dalits as objects of study and Dalits as subjective knowledge actors. The exhaustive review of Dalit scholarship is warranted to understand the dalit knowledge engagements, but that needs to an independent concern of a full length study, which is not possible in this limited space).

Three dimensions of Dalit and Dalit-Bahujan scholarship:

(a) Critical evaluation of the state policies in terms of the nature and processes of their (non) implementation and their impact on changing socio-economic conditions of Dalits.
(b) The nature and unfolding of Dalit movements, their historical trajectories, the issues they addressed, the ideological framework in which they articulated their struggle and consequences of these movements in understanding the category 'Dalit'.
(c) The question of Dalit Identities, both as representation and reclaiming witnessed in Dalit literature and serious studies of these as sources of knowledge and knowledge claims, even literature as a knowledge claim.
(d) Critical assessment of existing methodological and theoretical proprieties their implications for understanding the category 'Dalit' leading to basic rejection of existing concepts (such as 'De-brahmanisation', 'De-sanskrtisation') and recovery of Dalit-Bahujan social experiences and social practices as legitimate sources of building knowledge, raising the questions of epistemology, and recovering Dalits as knowledge-actors, as opposed to merely objects of analysis and theorization external their social experiences.

V

Dalit Scholarship: Making Dalits as 'objects' of knowledge

It is only though the entry of Dalit scholars, both as students and later as faculty members in academia, that Dalits and Dalit social and material experience became a matter of serious study, or object of study. Of course this recognition of the dalit as subject matter of knowledge, the legitimacy of the knowledge claims these attempts advanced, had to be rooted in the strong commitment to the methodological and theoretical proprieties determined by the existing knowledge practice. Thus while Dalits did become objects of sociological analysis, their personal and social being had to be made sense of within the dominant framework of "objective" knowledge proprieties, the institutional sites of which were dominated by the upper caste knowledge actors, who were acting as both producers and regulators of 'value neutral', 'objective' knowledge practice.

Within the framework of the value neutral, "objective" social science (rooted in epistemological claims based on 'measurement' as a source of knowledge), the studies of by dalit scholars have attempted to understand the nature of state policies and their impact on changing social and economic status of Dalits. The study by S. L. Gaikwad titled 'Protective Discrimination Policy and Social Change: An Analytical Study of State Action on Scheduled Castes in Aurangabad', and by G. G. Wankhede 'Social Mobility and Scheduled Castes: Receding Horizons', for instance, attempts to critically evaluate the state policies and show that while the policy of protective discrimination has been an important factor for mobility and social change among the Scheduled Castes, its implementation is not rigourous and effective. Both these studies are empirical in nature and have followed the conventional research practice and quantitative data as a source of critical understanding. Another study by S.M. Dahiwale, 'Emerging Entrepreneurship among Scheduled Castes of Contemporary India : A Study of Kolhapur City', also based on quantitative data, focuses attention not on the state policies and their impact but, on the attempts of self-employment, initiatives of entrepreneurship on part of the ex-Untouchables (four major scheduled castes in Maharashtra), and analyses social background of respondents and other motivational in understanding their choice of self-employment. A mention must be made of a study of new middle class among the Scheduled Caste by Nandu Ram, undertaken much before the current engagement with Indian middle class. Recently a study by Sukhadeo Thorat and Katherine Newman titled, 'Blocked by Caste: an Economic Discrimination in Modern India', though also based on conventional research practice of quantitative data drawn by large scale surveys, shows the importance of extra-economic factors such as discrimination based on caste and attitudinal orientation based on caste as important factors in understanding poverty, inequality and access to basic resources to realize once own human potential. It shows as to how social and economic exclusion leads to unequal access to business, wage-earning, health status, and educational attainments.

Apart from critical studies of state policies, there have also been studies on the nature of Dalit social movement, their impact on Dalits' social life and the challenge they have posed to the social universe of India. The study by P. G. Jogdand on Dalit movement in Maharashtra merits attention. This study attempts to historicize Dalit movement and explore the nature of protest it waged. It also raises a sociological question: is Dalit movement a social movement within the framework of sociology of social movements. While this study is an important contribution to the study of Dalit movement, it draws on the theory of relative deprivation, which has been questioned strongly in contemporary times. The above short discussion indicates that while Dalits became legitimate objects of knowledge, such 'visibility' of Dalits in knowledge engagement also indicates commitment to the dominant theoretical and methodological proprieties as a necessary condition for introducing 'Dalit' as a category in academic knowledge. Thus the Dalit knowledge-subjects did help in bringing Dalit as a category for social science analysis, however, the primacy of the existing theoretical and methodological proprieties meant subjugation of Dalit knowledge-subjects to the dominant epistemologies.

***Dalit Scholarship: Dalits as Subjects and Knowledge-actors*:**

The recent studies (since last decade) have shown departure from the earlier attempts of bringing dalit as a legitimate object of knowledge practice. They have viewed Dalits as subjects critiquing and transforming social practices and claiming universality. 'Dalits and Democratic Revolution' by Gail Omvedt, thus rejects the characterization Dalit movement as merely 'social' in nature and points out it is a political movement aimed at democratization of Indian society. Likewise the study of Untouchables' attempts of challenging the practice of Untouchability, by G. K. Karanth and Simon Charlsey has brought in academic discussion the Dalit subjectivity in oppressive social spaces, hence, the need of new ways of theorizing Dalit social experiences. The prominence of the discourse and engagement with human rights has provided impetus to understand Dalits' marginalization and deprivation within the universal framework of human right discourse merit mention.

Apart from the above attempts of articulating Dalits as a category as subjective and critical, some recent studies have attempted to arrive at new methodological practices as basis of producing valid knowledge and have raised issues of politics of knowledge. Witnessed in these attempts is also a quest for new conceptualization of Dalit Experiences. KanchaIlaiah's works such as 'Why I am Not a Hindu: a Shudra Critique of Hindutva, Philosophy, Culture and Political Economy (Samya, 1996)' and' Post-Hindu India: A Discourse on Dalit Bahujan Socio-Spiritual and Scientific Revolution (Sage. 2009) ', thus makes Dalit Bahujan experiences as basis of (valid) knowledge, and introduces the terminologies evolved in these experiences as concepts for understanding that experience. The quest for Dalits' everyday social experiences of subordination, discrimination as well contestations as basis of critical knowledge is present in Ramesh Kamble's work on

Dalits in Urban context of Bombay. His work also exhibits the quest for alternative concepts in understanding dalit experiences of atrocities. He has articulated a new concept, "Shame and Rage" as a tool to explain Dalits' experiences of brutal violence by the dominant castes. A mention must be made to the *Dalit Intellectual Collective*, a forum of Dalit scholars that has brought to fore critical discussion on the important issues such as the relationship among caste and class, the question of validity of using the term 'Dalit' as a universal category to examine social experiences of groups variedly known as Scheduled Castes, *Pichade, MagasJati* ; the nature and relevance of Dalit knowledge in understanding not only Dalits' social universe but also the nature of Indian society.

An important aspect and consequence of the recent Dalit scholarship has been the visibility of the category 'Dalit' in sociological pedagogical practice. Though the struggle to make visible the category 'Dalit' as an autonomous analytical category to analyze social processes and to assert the importance of Ambedkar's contribution to the making of the discipline of sociology has been challenging, today it is certain that the sociological knowledge and pedagogy is incomplete and even irrelevant without referring to the category 'Dalit' and Ambedkar. This paper is one such modest attempt to highlight and herald the Dalit arrival in sociology.

Notes

1. See B.R. Ambedkar 1916 (1989) – 'Castes in India: Their Mechanism, Genesis and Development', in Moon Vasant (ed.) *Dr. Babasaheb Ambedkar's Writings and Speeches* Vol. 1, Mumbai: Education Department, Government of Maharashtra; also refer to Dr. Ambedkar's Who Were the Shudras? (availableat:http://www.ambedkar.org/ambcd/38A.%20Who%20were%20the%20Shudras%20Preface.htm), and "The Untouchables: Who were They and Why They became Untouchables?, (available at: http://www.ambedkar.org/ambcd/39A.Untouchables%20who%20were% 20they_ why%20they%20became%20PART%20I.htm)

2. See T.K. Oommen, 2005, 'Understanding Indian Society: The Relevance of the Perspective from Below', in Dahiwale, S.M. *Understanding Indian Society: The Non-Brahminic Perspective*, Jaipur, Rawat.
3. See, S.P. Punalekar, 2001, "Dalit Literature and Dalit Identity", in Ghanashyam Shah (ed.) Dalit Identity and Politics, New Delhi: Sage, pp. 216-41.

References

Ambedkar, B.R. (1936) (1989), "Annihilation of Caste," in Vasant Moon, (ed.) *Dr. Babasaheb Ambedkar's Writing and Speeches*, Vol.1, Mumbai: Education Department, Government of Maharashtra.

Best, Steven and Kellner, Douglas, 1991, *Postmodern Theory: Critical Interrogations*, New York: Macmillan.

Dahiwale, S.M. (1989), *Emerging Entrepreneurship among Scheduled Castes of Contemporary India : A Study of Kolhapur City*, Rawat: Jaipur.

Dhanagare, D.N. (2011), "Legacy and Rigour: The Bombay School of Sociology and Its Impact in Universities of Maharashtra", Patel Sujata (ed.), *Doing Sociology in India: Genealogies, Locations, and Practices*, New Delhi: Oxford.

Gaikwad, S.L. (1996), *Protective Discrimination Policy and Social Change: An Analytical Study of State Action on Scheduled Castes in Aurangabad City*, Rawat: Jaipur.

Ghurye, G.S. (1979), *Caste and Race in India*, Bombay: Popular Prakashan.

Guru, G. and V. Githa, (2000), "New Phase of Dalit-Bahujan Intellectual Activity", *Economic and Political Weekly*, Vol. 35, No. 3: Mumbai.

Jafferlot, Christophe (2005), *Dr. Ambedkar and Untouchability: Analysing and Fighting Caste*, New Delhi: Permanent Black.

Jogdand, P.G., (1991), *Dalit Movement in Maharashtra*, New Delhi: Kanak Publications.

Kamble, Ramesh, (2000), *"Untouchability in Urban Setting"* in Ghanshyam Shah (ed.) *Dalits and the State*, New Delhi: Concept.

———(2010), "Understanding Dalit Movements: Trajectories and concerns" Occasional paper series 7, Mumbai: Department of Sociology, University of Mumbai.

Karanth, G.K. and Simon Charlsey (1998), *Challenging Untouchability: Dalit Initiative and Experience from Karnataka*, New Delhi: Sage.

Kancha Ilaiah (1996), *Why I am Not a Hindu: a Sudra Critique of Hindutva, Philosophy, Culture and Political Economy, Kolkatta: Samya.*

———(2009), *Post-Hindu India: A discourse on Dalit Bahujan Socio-Spiritual and Scientific Revolution*, New Delhi: Sage.

Oommen, T. K. (2005), "Understanding Indian Society: The Relevance of the Perspective from Below", in S.M. Dahiwale, *Understanding Indian Society: The Non-Brahminic Perspective*, Jaipur: Rawat.

———(2011), "Scheduled Castes, Scheduled Tribes and the Nation: Situating G.S. Ghurye", Occasional paper No. 7, Mumbai: Department of Sociology, University of Mumbai.

Omvedt, Gail, (1994), *Dalits and Democratic Revolution: Dr. Ambedkar and Dalit Movement in Colonial India*, New Delhi: Sage.

Patel, Sujata (ed.) (2011), Introduction in *Doing Sociology in India: Genealogies, Locations, and Practices*, New Delhi: Oxford.

———(2011), "Social Anthropology or Marxist Sociology? Assessing the Contesting sociological Traditions", in *Doing Sociology in India: Genealogies, Locations, and Practices*, New Delhi: Oxford.

Pradhan, G.R. (1938), *Untouchable Workers of Bombay City*, Bombay: Karnatak Publishing House.

Punalekar, S.P. (2001), "Dalit Literature and Dalit Identity", in Ghanashyam Shah (ed.) *Dalit Identity and Politics*, New Delhi: Sage, pp. 216-41.

Ram, Nandu (1988), *The Mobile Scheduled Caste: Rise of a New Middle Class*, New Delhi: Hindustan.

Robinow, Paul, (1984), *The Foucault Reader*, New York : Penguin.

Rodrigues, Valerian (2002), *The Essential Writings of B. R. Ambedkar*, New Delhi: OUP.

Savur, Manorama (2011), "Sociology: the Genealogy of the Discipline in Bombay", in Sujata Patel (ed.) *Doing Sociology in India: Genealogies, Locations, and Practices*, New Delhi: Oxford.

Srinivas, M.N. (1996), *Caste, its Twentieth Century Avatar*, New Delhi: Penguin Books.

Thorat, Sukhadeo and Katherine Newman (eds.), (2009), *Blocked by Caste: an Economic Discrimination in Modern India*, New Delhi: Oxford

Wankhede, G.G. (1999), *Social Mobility and Scheduled Castes: Receding Horizons*, Jaipur: Rawat Publications

15

(Up) Rooted Through Routes
Understanding the Impact of Diaspora on Gender

Preeti Shirodkar

The late Twentieth and early Twenty First centuries have seen an increasingly blurring approach to scholarship and an attempt to address and resolve the concerns, emerging from the socio-cultural milieu. And, while the former has given rise to a larger thrust being placed on interdisciplinary studies, the latter has attempted to draw upon literature, as a subaltern record of history, since a scrutiny of it can offer alternative perspectives to pressing concerns and forestall repeating the mistakes of history, while also serving to forewarn about the pitfalls, that emerging realities may impose upon unwary generations.

A prominent among varied realities and concerns that are currently dogging nations and its people and will continue to do so for a long time to come is the condition of diaspora that has no doubt been a lived reality of the socio-cultural fabric, since many centuries, but is one that is gaining in complexity, both in the context of globalisation and the dissolution of boundaries, on the one hand and their paradoxical deeper entrenchment, on the other. This has further deepened the debates on identity, belonging and home that are emerging as prominent dilemmas, in the context of the identity of both the individual and the nation state, whether they choose to call themselves multicultural or plural.

Moreover, considering the length of time that 'diaspora' as a lived reality has been in existence, the constitutive identity has been further problematised by the overlapping, yet exclusive, issues that are brought into focus by the dynamics of gender and its contribution to diasporic identity. Terming this 'intersectionality', Avtar Brah – a prominent thinker in the diasporic space, asserts the need to provide due consideration to this unique identity. Explaining 'intersectionality' as the interlinking/crossing of the diasporic space, with that of gender, she argues that the dilemmas arising from this have not been given the consideration that is due to them, which may result in subsuming a doubly marginalised identity, that of women diasporics in the larger diasporic identity, which in turn may result in homogenising it, at the cost of burying its unique subalternity.

In this context, issues that become a part of the overlapping space, while nevertheless demanding a gaze that is informed by dynamics of gender, and those that are unique to women need to be delineated.

Diaspora by its very nature, as a scattering, involves a 'movement', which brings along with it a spacio-temporal distancing from the homeland that may be at times out of choice or at other times enforced by the emerging realities of the socio-political milieu. Nevertheless, this distancing creates its own dynamics and problematic that, even though imagined, may not be envisaged in its totality or then not thought about at all. In either case, this is a reality that becomes a challenge to cope with, given its vast and varied expectations and nature.

In turn, this results in issues that are diverse and multiple, which according to Jha, arise because Indian diasporic women are caught between the two extremes of nativity and naivety, tradition and modernity, and the past and the present.

As regards women, in the early stages of diaspora, one of the chief reasons that they migrate is for marriage and settling, something, that they have more often than not, not envisaged and which is sprung upon them in the context of an arranged marriage, as can be seen through the experience of Ji Bai from Vassanji's *The Gunny Sack*, making it a reality that is doubly traumatising - that of accepting their changed status, from being a girl to becoming a woman, while simultaneously having to adjust to the new weather and environment, the latter, which is in a context that is both physical and cultural.

Moreover, along with the suddenness of this change that is both imposed and one which is more or less permanent, given that women then and often even now rarely have the hope of 'returning' to their childhood home, if something were to go wrong, is the uncertainty of the future and the trauma of having to adapt to and adopt newer habits that may be expected from or thrust upon them in the 'hostland'. Often, chief among these is the nightmare of most women that of having to accept a man who has already lived with/been married to another and having fathered a child – a 'chotara' with this other woman, a woman who was often offered to diasporic men who had gone for trade especially to African countries as a comfort for the 'lonely' and 'alien' nights – as discovered by Fatima from *The Gunny Sack*, whose husband Dhanji Govindji has already fathered Huseni – a half caste with Bibi Tarantibu.

This sense of a loss of roots creates in them especially in the early diasporic women a deep sense of alienation, rootlessness and displacement, as more often than not this is a not only a condition they are not prepared for but proves to be one that involves compromises that engulf even their dream that of finding an ideal partner without an adequate support system that can help them cope with it. In fact as Anita Desai, they feel alienated from both worlds one that they cannot acclimatise themselves to and the other they are expected to leave far behind though they feel an essential connect to it.

Additionally, women, who by their very nature are receptacles of memories and are expected to be repositories of culture, face greater emotional upheaval, both in trying to maintain cultural and religious purity, while attempting to blend in with the demands of the new place, whether in their own context or that of their family, especially the younger generations, which often being born and largely brought up in the land of settlement, have divided/changed loyalties, resulting in inter-generational conflicts. While some of these may be more easy to deal with like a change in food and clothing, at times proving shocking for their first generation male counterparts, as experienced and expressed by Nurdin in Vassanji's *No New Land,* others like the practice of faith, intermarriages, intercommensality and cultural change become far more difficult to adjust to, themes explored by Jhumpa Lahiri through her writing.

Countering this, are also the reactions of the natives/the original inhabitants, who often view diasporics suspiciously or react in a vituperative manner, perceiving the diasporics as outsiders, who are a threat to them, resulting in racist and fascist attacks, that affect at times their family for whom they fear and at others themselves, though in the initial stages the latter is rare, as women rarely move out at all, let alone by themselves, as explored on the one hand by varied stories in Bharati Mukherjee's *Darkness,* though her later writing depicted women emerging stronger and more independent as a result of the diasporic experience, while on the other through the writing of Vassanji.

While it is interesting to understand the perspective of men about women in the diasporic context and how the men portray their experiences, as recorded in the writing of male diasporics, what one cannot deny and needs to be watchful for, is falling prey to the male gaze, as defined by Berger in his seminal text *Ways of Seeing*. No doubt, leaning on the other extreme, denying this gaze, will result in the pitfalls engendered by radical feminism. This makes it important to record the overlapping areas and the perspectives of both in approaching them; so as to observe the similarities, while valuing the differences.

Over and above these intersecting areas are those that are chiefly recorded and discussed by women at length, as against men, who if they refer to them at all may do so in passing. However, given their impact on the physical/mental space of women, they tend to dwell upon these more at length, if also from a different perspective. While some of these concerns are fairly superficial and are touched upon in one way or another by most women, some others are major markers of change that, though not necessitated by cultural uprooting, form an option that women choose to exercise, making them that much more significant and deep rooted, with implications that my serve to be more vibrant and deep; and yet, ironically, these do not find widespread expression. One among such area is that of sexuality that Bharati Mukherjee explores at length, not surprisingly evoking the comment that her usage of sexual content can be unnerving.

What most other women writers explore at length, as a related issue, though is that of marriage moving from it being an arranged marriage and the resultant adjustments as well as concerns of maintaining religious purity etc., to love marriages, especially among those studying together and finally inter-caste marriages and the reactions to it (a theme explored by, among others, Bapsi Sidhwa in *An American Brat*) and a prime aspect related to marriage – separation/divorce and subsequent return that may prove equally traumatic as experienced by the protagonist of Bharati Mukherjee's *The Tiger's Daughter*.

More interesting however are the choices that women are seen making both as regards maintaining family ties, since they are envisaged as receptacles of traditions, to making a choice of deviating from a tradition that they might otherwise have followed, as is seen in the case of Runu from the collection *Arranged Marriage*, who prefers to remain abroad for her delivery, rather than travelling to her mother's home, as the former would give her the freedom to have her husband in the delivery room, as she goes into labour, a choice which she prefers to going to her maternal home as per the traditions, subtly reflecting the changing mindset of women in diaspora, seen through the choices they make and the reasons behind making them.

Along with these choices, women are seen exercising others as basic as dressing, where they change their attire both for comfort and blending in as well as at times out of necessity, like for example, to deal with the climate, which, however minor, basic and superficial a change, evokes at times extreme reactions from men, who are not used to women having even that much freedom and see it both as a threat to tradition and as an affront to their being, imagining what others would think of them.

Another challenge, which though basic is much deeper, is that of language. Constituting expression and the power that comes with it, it is also emblematic of the paradox that underlines women, who are largely not given a voice or whose voice is often written off and yet the language of expression is known as the mother tongue, since the child first acquires it from his/her mother and then often turns it against her. Constituting a dilemma for the diasporic women is learning another tongue that of the place they have moved to, as it will be a source of their assimilation or even power in the new home, as witnessed and expressed by Meena Alexander, as also how to continue instilling the mother tongue in succeeding generations, as the language can evoke with it an entire universe and culture.

An offshoot of the language dilemma is also that faced by diasporic women writing in their mother tongue and whom they are writing for, the small group from their own community, who are in diaspora, or the larger group back home, who might not get an easy access to their writing or then might rebuff them for being a miniscule and negligible minority and therefore not authentic, an angle explored by Telugu Sireesha in her book *Diasporic Indian Women Writers Quest for Identity in Their Short Stories*. What one needs to rethink and examine though, in debating the merits of the mother and the other tongue, in the context of the diasporic consciousness, is whether or not is will enable the rise of a female Caliban, who will learn/has learned to curse in the master's own tongue.

Contrasted to these debates that women's diasporic writing explores/raises are implications of decisions like those of women taking up a job or being the only people getting one, with men being brought out of their traditional comfort zone, by having to assist them in household chores, if they are running a 'traditional woman based business from home' or taking over the chores totally, if they do not have a job and are relying on the woman to bring home the money or then even seeking their help in running a male dominated business that the men have set up, situations that Vassanji has recorded in various books.

Though rare, women writers are also seen building upon and engaging the imagination, by weaving a world of magic from the mundane world of womanhood that revolves around the traditionally entrenched chores of cooking, cleaning and managing the house, by creating a world that draws upon the mundane to transform it into the exotic world of the mysterious and enigmatic that offers power both through itself and by serving to create an opportunity for a woman to work, by drawing upon her strength, an aspect that Chitra Banerjee Divakaruni superbly explores in *Mistress of Spices.* Taking on spices that become the world, to a woman, serving as an aide in her various roles as she cooks or attempts to nurse a loved one, Divakaruni makes it a magical world that is in the power of women, reversing the dynamics of enslavement by the spices, to being the force that can assess and harness their power.

Though subtle, intricate and rare these extended metaphors add a unique flavour and dimension to the writing of diasporic women, by defamiliarising the familiar and making it border on the magical, a trend very different from the way magical realism is seen interwoven in the male strand of diasporic writing.

What is also interesting is the attempt, though not frequent, to unearth the palimpsest, by rewriting mythology to not merely liberate its women from the shackles of the past, but also from the male gaze that essentially confined them to it. And, while this has been done by women writers from within the home (like Mahasweta Devi), making it a voice of resistance, its expression and attempt from the space of diasporic womanhood, as in Divakaruni's *Palace of Illusions,* offers it a different direction, raising questions (like why do women feel compelled to explore these themes from that distance, do they still feel the shackles of time, even if freed from those of space, or are they able to offer a divergent perspectives made possible by distance or are they less afraid of censure and therefore more open), while also intertwining the strands of women's writing liberating it from the chains of time and space.

For this however one needs to get over the resistance of looking upon diaspora as merely one additional experience added to the consciousness of the individual and society or as a reality that encompasses a few or an issue, which is receiving an unfair focus, at times resulting in a warp that in meting justice makes a mockery of it, by replacing the writing of native writers by those of diasporics of the same land, in the halls of academic limelight and study.

Ironically though, diaspora studies is still considered an upcoming field that is becoming increasingly interdisciplinary; and one would not be wrong in asserting the importance of keeping one's focus on the place and value of women's voice in it, as an expression of a subalternity that is defined by both place and gender and, in that, is one that constitutes the voice of the doubly marginalised that may get subsumed in the glitz, glamour and clamour of creating and noting history, resulting in mistakes, which, if repeated, would become difficult to control, as regards both the depth and spread of their effects.

And, while some women in diaspora themselves would not like to be confined by or would even like to outright reject the label, with others trying to stretch its margins to find refuge within its parameters; as also while acknowledging that like all other experiences, the intersectional spaces occupied by diasporic women would themselves be open to varied sub categories and groups and homogenising them would dilute their diversity as those of their experiences, what needs to be noted is that this intersectional space occupied by women, who have been (up)rooted, through routes, is one that needs to be carefully considered, researched and documented, for what it has to offer.

No doubt giving in to the temptation of keeping each of

these strands apart would be great, given the rising obsession with exclusivity, but what is also important is to appreciate that though the manifestations of most of the issues faced by diasporic women would be unique, based on innumerable variations that feature both time and space, the underlying concerns that afflict them would have an underlying force that unifies its strands, which if forced apart may result in losing out more than it seeks to offer by the way of a gain.

What is important is to account for the effect of intersectionality on the diasporic space, at a time when neither the (up)rooting nor the routes can be denied, so that it becomes an experience that is recounted with a sigh of relief and not of pain, in a world in which it has become an undeniable marker of identity – whether that of the individual or the nation state.

References

Alexander, Meena, *Poems of Meena Alexander*. www.poemhunter.com

Brah, Avtar (2014), *Multiple Axis of Power: Articulations of Diaspora and Intersectionality,* University of Mumbai. Inaugural Address. 17 January 2014.

Brah, Avtar, (1996), *Cartographies of Diaspora: Contesting Identities.* London and New York: Routledge.

Divakaruni, Chitra Banerjee, (1995), *Arranged Marriage,* London: Black Swan Books.

Divakaruni, Chitra Banerjee, (1997), *Mistress of Spices,* London: Black Swan Books.

Divakaruni, Chitra Banerjee, (2008), *Palace of Illusions,* London: MacMillan.

Jain, Ravindra K., (2010), *Nation, Diaspora, Trans Nation Reflections from India,* New Delhi: Routledge.

Jayaram, N. (2011), Understanding Diversities in the Indian Diaspora in N. Jayaram (Ed.), *Diversities in the Indian Diaspora: Nature, Implications, Responses,* India: Oxford University Press.

Jayaram, N. (Ed.), (2004), *The Indian Diaspora: Dynamics of Migration.* India: Sage Publications.

Jha, Gauri Shankar, (2013), *Indian Diaspora: Women English Writers.* Jaipur: Yking Books.

Kadekar, Laxmi Narayan, (2012), "Global Indian Diaspora: A Brief

History." in Ajaya Kumar Sahoo and Laxmi Narayan Kadekar (Eds.). *Global Indian Diaspora: History, Culture and Identity.* India: Rawat Publications.

Kamath, A.P. (1999), "Women Writers of Indian Diaspora Create A Big Impact." *rediff news,* 23 Aug. 1999. http://www.rediff.com/news/1999/aug/23us1.htm,.

Lahiri, Jhumpa, (2003), *The Namesake,* USA: Houghton Mifflin.

Mukherjee, Bharati. (1973). *The Tiger's Daughter,* London, Chatto and Windus.

Mukherjee, Bharati, (1985), *Darkness.* Toronto: Penguin.

Raju, Saraswati (ed.). (2011), *Gendered Geographies: Space and Place in South Asia,* New Delhi: Oxford University Press.

Sidhwa, Bapsi. (1993), *An American Brat.* USA: Milkweed Editions.

Spivak, Gayatri Chakravorty, (1994), "Can the Subaltern Speak?" in Patrick Williams and Laura Chrisman (Eds.). *Colonial Discourse and Postcolonial Theory: A Reader,* New York: Columbia University Press.

Telugu, Sireesha. (2009), *Diasporic Indian Women Writers: Quest for Identity in Their Short Stories,* New Delhi: Prestige Books.

Vassanji, M.G. (1989), *The Gunny Sack,* India: Penguin Viking.

Vassanji, M.G. (1995), *The Book of Secrets,* India: Penguin Books.

Vassanji, M.G. (2007), *The Assassin's Song,* India: Penguin Viking.

Vassanji, M.G. (1991), *No New Land,* India: Penguin Books.

Vassanji, M.G. (1999), *Amriika.* India: Harper Collins.

Viswanathan, Gauri, (1989), *Masks of Conquest: Literary Studies and British Rule in India,* London: Faber and Faber.

Visweswaran, Kamala, (1994), *Fictions of Feminist Ethnography,* Minnneapolis: University of Minnesota Press.

16

Dalit Studies in Maharashtra
Priorities and Concerns

Pralhad G. Jogdand

This research article aims at reviewing studies carried out in the area of sociology of Dalit studies/weaker sections in Maharashtra state. An attempt is made to unfold the major issues addressed by the researchers in their respective research works. Roughly, the following themes have been addressed—social mobility, protective discrimination policy, conversion to Buddhism, dalit literature, community studies (Ex-Mahar/Neo-Buddhists, Mangs, Chambhars and Scavengers), Dalit movements, Dalit entrepreneurship, Dalit women, New Economic Policy and Dalits, Educational enrollment of the Dalit students, Dalit identity etc.

The research carried out in the last 20-25 years in Maharashtra provides some valuable insights and also show emerging trends in this area. The different facets of the Dalits have been unfolded by the scholars/writers. Most of the studies were empirical analyzing different processes and currents at work at the grassroots level.

Inspite of all this, a few important themes/areas have not been probed as yet.

I, therefore, intend to identity the unexplored areas for

further studies to be undertaken.

This article aims at reviewing the studies carried out in the area of sociology of Dalit studies or underprivileged in Maharashtra State in order to identify the gaps in research and indicate new areas which may be examined by the scholars in future.

Roughly, sociology of weaker sections or dalit studies emerged as an area of specialization in the eighties. A large number of studies were undertaken and a few studies have been published in the last two decades in the country. Maharashtra is not exception to the studies under reference. Sociology of weaker sections or sociology of Dalit studies is now a common course (optional course at few places) taught in almost all the Universities in the state of Maharashtra and other parts of the country. Dalit studies meaning 'writings on Dalits'. Dalit studies is knowledge about Dalits produced both by Dalits and non-Dalits. Further, Dalit studies is not just a new body of knowledge about Dalits and that. It is a new perspective to study Indian society and to redefine the existing disciplines.

This paper is focused on 'Dalit Studies'. Thus it is concerned with lives of the 'oppressed' and 'exploited' stratas who are living a day to day sub-human existence after 66 years of Independence. After Independence, an illusion was created and hope generated that the path of development pursued by the leaders and policy panners of India will take off the country from a backward to a prosperous and egalitarian society eliminating all sorts of inequalities. After 60 years of our planning and all that what has been the trend of our development? What is the reality? The contradictions of socio-economic order remain almost the same. Half a century is a considerable time in the history of a society to correct its mistakes and imbalances but even at the twenty first century neither the society nor the state has been able to resolve its contradictions. On the contrary, the vast majority of the Indian population is subjected to multiple deprivations. The Dalits have yet to experience the so-called fruits of development.

The Dalits are not happy with the kind of development

that we have been witnessing. Hence, they are questioning the development paradigm which resulted in perpetrating atrocities on them. These people are asserting on every possible fronts viz, grassroots, socio-political etc. They are conscious now. They are waging protest movements. They have discarded old identities (*Harijans*, Untouchables) and have constructed a new name i.e. 'Dalit'. Dalit is not a caste but a symbol of change. It is the expression of the powerless and voiceless. This category has a greater capacity to reach out to a larger sections of people. However, from practical point of view this category has number of problems. Hence, we come across the categories like Hindu Dalits, Neo-Buddhists Dalits, Christian Dalits etc.

It is in the light of these assertations among the Dalits at the grassroots level, it is the proper time to take a critical review of the studies undertaken by the scholars (Dalits and others) in Maharashtra.

Roughly, the following areas or themes on which studies on Dalits have been done. Social mobility, impact of protective discrimination policy, conversion issue, Dalit literature, community studies (Ex-Mahars, Mangs, Chambhars), Dr. Ambedkar, Dalit movements, Dalit entrepreneurship, Dalit women, educational enrollment of the Dalit students, impact of globalization etc.

As stated earlier, the Dalits are not happy with their wretched (ascribed) status, hence they are trying to go for new kind of status. With a view to change the degraded status, the Dalits have used a Sanskritisation formula. Sunanda Patwardhan has made an interesting study of the process of sanskritisation at work among the several scheduled castes groups in Maharashtra such as Ex-Mahars, Mangs, Chambhars, Dhors and Holars.

Patwardhan looks at the concept of identity from many angles. She believes, for every individual or a group there is always an individual or a group that becomes a reference whom he admires and whose life style he tries to adopt and imitate. Such groups referred to as 'reference group' which may be both 'positive' and 'negative'. She further says that for Mangs, Chambhars, Dhors and Holars, the positive reference group for cultural mobility is the Hindus and the negative reference group is the Mahar or Neo-Buddhist. For Neo-Buddhists Buddhism is the positive reference group and Hinduism negative reference group. While explaining the identity of Neo-Buddhists and rest of the Buddhists Patwardhan uses the terms such as primary or actual identity. The primary identity of Neo-Buddhists and rest of the Buddhists Patwardhan uses the terms such as primary or actual identity. The primary identity of Neo-Buddhist is with the converted group itself and their ideal identity is with the Buddhists at large. Thus, there is wider identity perceived by them in the Indian competitive political and economic system. Thus, there are overlapping circles of identity. She also brought out the fact that the conversion to Buddhism did not alter the condition of the Mahars materially as the stigma of untoughability still lingered. Y.B. Damle has done a micro study in the light of this process at Pune. "Reference Group Theory with regard to Mobility in the caste system in India" (1968). He exhibits as to how the Dalit students changed their surnames after Brahmins. According Damle this was an attempt to imitate the way of life of the Brahmins with a view to change their status. Over a period of time the Dalits realized the limitations of this process and started searching for other avenues.

Protective discrimination policy is one of the factors to bring about social mobility among the Dalits. Thus, there have been studies on this line. S.L. Gaikwad's study "Protective Discrimination Policy and Social Change: An Analytical Study of State Action with Special Reference to Aurangabad City" (1991) deals with the impact of PDP on the employees and the students those who get scholarship (GOI). R.N. Salve's Study "Impact of Government Welfare Measures for SCs: A Sociological Study" is also an empirical study. His sample was from Kolhapur District. This study analysed the impact of provisions in the areas such as employment and jobs. One of the significant findings of this study is that the beneficiaries feel that they are being isolated in every walks of life. They are being looked down upon. S.M. Dahiwale discusses "Occupational mobility among the persons from the Ex-untouchable castes in Kolhapur city" (1997).

Dalit movements and social change is yet another important theme on which considerable research has been done. The following studies examined the genesis, development and consequences of Dalit movements on the people at large. Elenor Zelliot (First Ph.D. on Dr. Ambedkar) has examined "Dr. Ambedkar and Mahar Movement" (1969); Lata Murugkar and Shridhar Balan have worked on "Dalit Panthers Movement of Maharashtra – A Sociological Appraisal", Dalit Panthers Movement in Maharashtra – Problems and Prospects", JNU (1977) respectively. P.G. Jogdand's work "Protest Movement and Social Change: A Study of Dalit Movement in Maharashtra" (1991) underlines the style of protests of the Dalits and the consequences of the same on the lives of the Dalits. This study has pointed out the limitations and has given future line to be adopted by the people involved in the movement. Gail Omvedt's study "Dalit and the Democratic Revolution: Dr. Ambedkar and the Dalit Movement in Colonial India" (1994), provides details as to how Dalit Movements arose in A.P., Karnataka and Maharashtra in Colonial period. "Ambedkarism: The Theory of Dalit Liberation" has been brilliantly portrays by Gail in this work. N.S. Vaidya's study "Dalit Chalwal Ani Sahitya Yanchatun Abhivakta Honari Dalitanchi Samajik Janiv" (1984) attempts to assess the emerging consciousness among the Dalits through Movement and Literature.

Apart from all these studies there are a few community studies especially on the Mangs and Chambhars. First full length study on 'Mang' is that of D.D. Kachole. "Mang Community in Transition" (1980). Followed by B.K. Khadse "A study of Mang caste with special reference to Social Change"(1982); Suresh Waghmare has worked on "Mang Community: A Sociological Study". All these studies focused on ethnographic descriptions of the Mang community. However, these studies made an attempt to take a review of life style and backwardness of this community. Recently, B.V.

Bhosale has done a study on "Sociological Study of Charmakar Community in Maharashtra" wherein he focused on the traditional occupation (leather), social status and role of Charmakars in politics and Dalit movements.

There have been attempts to analyse the consequences of conversion to Buddhism. The following scholars worked in this area. T. G. Meshram " A sociological study of Nav-Buddhists in Vidarbha" (1993); M.G. Kulkarni "The Scheduled Castes in Maharashtra – A study in social change with particular reference to Mahars (Buddhists) (1969); Gare and Limaye have done a good amount of work viz; 'Dalit Shod Ani Bodh' (1973) which has bearing on the topic under discussion. Uttara Shastri's work is very interesting. She worked on 'Neo-Buddhists as Marginalised Group'. It is on the basis of her sample, Neo-Buddhists living in Urban are, she shows that the Neo-Buddhists Elites are being marginalised on two grounds. These elites have not been uprooted from their Dalit community, on the one hand, and they have not been absorbed by the upper castes, on the other.

The tendency of revolt finds expression in creating writings of Dalit writers. It is through Dalit literature, the Dalits exhibited their suffering and dissatisfaction. Its language was new reflecting a new revolutionary consciousness and an ideological awakening. Dalit literature movements has been studied by Vidyadhar Pundlik and Kulkarni " Dalit Sahitya: Ek Samajik Sanskritik Abhyas" (1996); D.S. Manwar " A Sociological Study of Dalit Autobiographies; Bhoite and Bhoite " Dalit Sahitya Movement in Maharashtra" (1977); S.P. Punalekar "Sociology of Dalit Autobiography"(1993). These scholars tried to unfold the social, cultural and political facets of Dalits. Moreover, they underlined the relationship between self-narratives and sociology.

Dr. Ambedkar's contribution for the upliftment of the Dalits is amazing. He made the Dalits a political factor to reckonwtih. The use of the political means to change the condition of status of the Dalits was first made by him. Dr. Ambedkar's contribution was highlighted by a few scholars projecting him as a sociologist. Pradeep Aglawale's study "

Dr. B.R. Ambedkar: Ek Samajaik Vicharwant" takes a review of the work done by Ambedkar and situates him in the domain of Sociology. M.S. Gore's study " The Social context of an Ideology-Ambedkar's political and social thought" deals with an evolution of an ideology of protest envisaged by Ambedkar. He further analysed Ambedkar's ideology from the prespective of the sociology of idea systems (knowledge). Gore shows how ideology can influence historical interpretation and how ideology itself can be influenced by social context. Wilkinsan T.S. studied the impact of Dr. Ambedkar's conversion on the Dalits in his study viz, " Dr. Ambedkar and Neo-Buddhist Movement: Sociological Study"; Sharayu Anantram's Study "Ambedkar and Savarkar – Their social and political philosophy with special focus on Untouchability" (1992) gives us a panoramic views about origin and different facets of Untouchability envisaged both by Ambedkar and Savarkar.

Education is one of the principal factors of social mobility in our society. These people treated education as an agent of change. The degree of social mobility, educational enrollment of the Dalit students, drop outs, literacy etc. have been analysed by the following scholars. "Literacy and Educational Enrollment Among the SCs in Maharashtra"(1974); " A long way to go"(1981) by Suma Chitnis; "SC and Higher Education –A study of college students in Bombay"(1980) by Jacob Aikara; " Inequality in Higher Education – A case study of SCs in Maharashtra" (1987) by G.G. Wankhede; "Wastage and stagnation among the SCs" (Major Research Project) by Jude Henquires and G.G. Wankhede (1985).

Very recently a few studies have been undertaken on the plight of Dalit women. N.D. Jatratakar's study on "Devdasi in Belgaum District: A sociological study", deals with the Devdasi custom which literally means "female slaves of the deity" or girls dedicated to Yellamma goddess.

The girls who are forced to become Devdasi are from the Mahar, Mang, Holar castes especially from Maharashtra and Karnataka border. The Researcher highlighted the sexual exploitation of the Dalit women in the name of custom i.e.

Devdasi. P.G. Jogdand's work is an edited volume - "Dalit women: Issues and Perspectives" (1995) explains Dalit women as a category subjected to triple deprivations viz., caste, class and patriarchy. A collection of essays in this volume unfold the sorry state of Dalit women on different grounds. Padma Velaskar done a project on "Changing Social status of Dalit women in Maharashtra" (Times Fellowship 1997) wherein she focused on linkages between caste, untouchability and patriarchy for understanding the social situation and social condition of Dalit women. She further pointed out that the nature of subordination of Dalit women is profoundly different from that of the subordination of upper caste women. Sexual oppression is another crucial aspect of the Dalit women's subordination. Caste based sexual division of labour and also caste linked division of reproductive labour has been overlooked by feminist analysis, she maintained.

Sharmila Rege made a significant contribution for the theme under discussion. "Writing caste/writing Gender: Narrating Dalit Women's Testimonios" is a testimony of her contribution for constructing Dalit feminism. In this study Sharmila talks about the specific problems – caste, class and sexual exploitation – of the Dalit women.

Her work on the Dalit Feminist standpoint is groundbreaking in dismantling Dalit and gender as frameworks of identity and crafted a rich and productive challenge to mainstream sociology of gender and caste.

Of late a few studies carried out mapping the impact of globalization/New Economic Policy on Dalits - S.M. Dahiwale ' New Economic Policy and its Impact on Marginal segments', P.G. Jogdand (Ed) New Economic Policy and Dalits. The studies maintained that it is due to the process of privatization and commercialization the Dalits (SCs, STs, OBCs and Muslims) have been excluded from the project of development. Therefore, there is a demand for 'inclusive growth' from the concerned. The NEP has become a stumbling block in social sector such as education, health, employment, rural development and welfare.

Sukhadeo Thorat's work 'Dalits in India- Search for a

Common Destiny' is well researched attempt to explore the status of Dalits in India by presenting all – India and state level analysis of various human development and other correlated indicators. The work engages with various dimensions such as demography, gender, levels and patterns of urbanization, occupational pattern, ownership of agricultural land, rural labour, employment and unemployment rates, employment under reservation in the public sector, literacy and education etc. It brings to the surface pertinent facets regarding Dalits and thus sets out the agenda of engagement for the government as well as for civil society.

S.M. Michael's (edited) work 'Dalits in Modern India – vision and values' narrates the Dalit vision of Indian Society is different from that of the upper castes. The Dalits have become aware and are forging ahead to shape a new modern India.

To sum up, the research and writings done so far provide some valuable insights and elucidation on Dalits lives in Maharashtra. The Different facets of the Dalits have been unfolded by the scholars/writers. Most of the studies are empirical which analysed different processes and currents at work at the grassroots level. A few studies have attracted the attention of the policy planners and the leaders who have been trying to enlighten the people.

Priorities and Concerns

Inspite of all this, a few areas have not been probed as yet viz, violation of the Human Rights of the Dalits, Internal tensions between the four major Dalit Caste groups, no major break-through in the formulation of theory, role of educated elites and their role in social transformation. Such a study may bring out how the role of the caste organizations may have changed in recent decades. The relation between Dalits and other groups in rural areas has remained unexplored. Ambedkar's major project was to "Annihilate the caste". To what extent this has been actualized by the Dalits, could be one of the areas for research. Around 95 per cent studies have been done on Neo-Buddhists only whereas not a single study is there on Dhor and Holar communities. As mentioned above, there has been no attempt so far as theory building is concerned. However, some studies have made use of 'Non-Brahmanic perspective, perspective from below, Dalit – Bahujan perspective and Subaltern perspective though there is no consensus of all these perspectives among the researchers.

Dalit assertation in different forms, social exclusion in different spheres, growing humiliation and atrocities on Dalits, a critical appraisal of Dr. Ambedkar's work (situating him in a contemporary times), Dalits in urban and semi-urban settings, process of migration and mobility, marriage and family structures, DICCI, Dalits in changing village and caste systems, decline of Dalit movements etc. As the Dalit assertation is in constant dialogue with other it would be appropriate to study the 'others' or 'non-Dalit world'. It is required to investigate what the nation state has done for Dalits, what the nation state means to Dalits. Ambedkar charis in the different universities in Maharashtra reflect a token-response from the state, their performance and contribution have been quite dismal. One can take a research project on this issue.

Dalit activism, especially Dalit middle class activism needs to be examined. A variety of Dalit organizations and NGOs have cropped up – cultural groups, Dalit intelligentia, writers, Dalit employees, students and women organizations. What is the role of these organizations for the empowerment of Dalits at the grassroots level.

Conducting interdisciplinary research in this area is the need of the hour.

I think these are some of the priorities in which further studies should be undertaken.

References

Agalawe, Pradeep (1991), "Dr. B.R. Ambedkar : Ek Samajik Vicharwant", (Ph.D. Thesis) Nagpur University, Nagpur, 1991.

Aikara, Jocob (1990), *S.C. and Higher Education – A Study of College*

Students in Bombay.

Anantram, Sharayu (1992), "Ambedkar and Sawarkar – Their Social and Political Philosophy with Special Focus on Untouchability", (Ph.D Thesis), S.N.D.T. University, Mumbai, 1992.

Balan, Shridhar (1977), "Dalit Panthers Movement in Maharashtra" M.Phil Dissertation, J.N.U., New Delhi.

Bhoite, U. and Bhoite A. (1977), "Dalit Sahitya Movement in Maharashtra," *Sociological Bulletin*, Vol. 26, 1977.

Bhosale, B.V. (1998), *Sociological Study of Charmakar Community in Maharashtra*, Ph.D. Thesis, University of Pune, Pune.

Chitnis, Suma (1981), "Literacy and Educational Enrollment–Among the SCs in Maharashtra" A Long Way to Go, Popular Prakashan, Mumbai.

Dahiwale, S.M. (1987), "Occupational Mobility Among the Persons from the Ex- Untouchable Castes in Kolhapur city", Ph.D. Thesis Dr. B.A.M.U., Aurangabad.

Damle, Y.B. (1968), "Reference Group Theory with regard to Mobility" in James Silverberg (ed.), *Social Mobility in the Caste System in India*, Mouton, Hague.

Gaikwad, S.L. (1991), "Protective Discrimination Policy and Social Change: A Analytical Study of State Action with special Reference to Aurangabad city" Ph.D. thesis Dr. Babasaheb Ambedkar Marathwada University (Dr. B.A.M.U.) Aurangabad.

Gare and Limaye (1973), "Maharashtratil Dalit Sodha Ani Bodh" (in Marathi) Sahadhuyan Prakashan, Bombay

Gore, M.S. (1995), *The Social Context of an Ideology –Ambedkar's Political and Social Thought,* Sage Publicaiton.

Jatratkar, N.D. (1988), "Devdasi in Belgaum Distric: A Sociological Study" Ph.D. Thesis Shivaji University, Kolhapur.

Jogdand, P.G. (1995), "Dalit Movement in Maharashtra' Kanak Publications, New Delhi, 1991;" (ed) *Dalit Women: Issues and Perspectives*, Gyan Publication, Delhi. (Ed) *New Economic Policy and Dalits*, Rawat Publication, Jaipur, 2000.

—(2012), "New Economic Policy and its Impact on Marginal Segments" Occasional Paper No. 10, Department of Sociology, University of Mumbai.

Kachole, D.D. (1980), *Mang Community in Transition* (Ph.D. Thesis), B.A.M.U., Aurangabad,

Khadse, B.K. (1982), *A Study of Mang Caste with Special Reference to Social Change* Ph.D Thesis, Nagpur University, Nagpur.

Kulkarni, M.G. (1960), "The Scheduled Castes in Maharashtra–A Study in Social Change with Particular Reference to Mahars

(Buddhists)", *Marathwada University Journal*, July.

Manwar, D.S. (1997), *A Sociological Study of Dalit Autobiographies*, (Ph.D. Thesis), Dr. B.A.M.U. Aurangadab.

Meshram, T.G. (1993), *A Sociological Study of Nav-Buddhists in Vidarbha*, Ph.D. Thesis, Nagpur University, Nagpur.

Michael, S.M. (2007), *Dalits in Modern India – Vision and Values*, New Delhi: Sage Publications.

Murugkar Lata (1990), *Dalit Panther Movement of Maharashtra –A Sociological Appraisal*, Bombay: Popular Publication.

Omvedt, Gail, (1994), *Dalits and the Democratic Revolution: Dr. Ambedkar and the Dalit Movement in Colonial India*, Delhi: Sage Publications, 1994.

Patwardhan, Sunanda (1973), "Change Among India's Harijans Maharashtra—A Case Study, New Delhi, Orient Longman.

Punalekar, S.P. (1993), "Sociology of Dalit Autobiography", *Man and Development*, December.

Pundlik, V. and Kulkarni, *Dalit Sahitya : Ek Samajik Sanskritik Abhas*, Sugawa Publication, Pune.

Rege, Sharmila *Writing Caste/writing Gender: Narrating Dalit Womens*, Testimonios.

Salve, R.N. (1993), *Impact of Government Welfare Measures for Scheduled Castes: A Sociological Study*, Ph.D. Thesis, Dr. B.A.M.U., Aurangabad.

Shastri, Uttara (1983), *New-Buddhists : A Margianl Group in India*, (Ph.D. Thesis), University of Pune, Pune.

Thorat, Sukhadeo (2009), *Dalits in India – Search for a Common Destiny*, Sage Publicaitons, New Delhi.

Vaidya, N.S. (1984), *Dalit Chalwal Ani Sahitya Yanchataun Abhivakta Honari Dalitachi Samajik Janiv*, (Ph.D. in Marathi) 1984, Nagpur University, Nagpur.

Velaskar Padma (1086), *Inequality in Higher Education – A Study of SC Students in Medical Colleges*, Ph.D Thesis, TISS, Mumbai. (1997), "Changing Social Status of Dalit Women in Maharashtra" Project Work. Wankhede, G.G. (1984), *Social Determinants of Occupational Mobility —A Case Study of SCs in Maharashtra.*

Waghmare, Suresh (1987), *Mang Community : A Sociological Study*, Ph.D. Thesis Dr. B.A.M.U. Aurangabad.

Wankhede & Jude Henquires (1985), "Wastage and Stagnation Among the SCs" (Research Project), TISS.

Wilkinsan, T.S. *Dr. Ambedkar and New Buddhist Movement: Sociological Study*.

Zalliot, Eleanor (1969), "*Dr. Ambedkar and Mahar Movement*", Ph.D. thesis, University of Pennsylvania.

17

Gujarat Over Time
Progress Towards Growth, Development and Inclusiveness

Niti Mehta

1. Introduction

Gujarat has been a frontline state since the accelerated reforms began in 1992-93. The state enjoys an entrepreneurial culture and people's participation in the development process. Gujarat has a developed industrial economy and commercial nature of agriculture. The state is urbanizing at a rapid pace, its urban population increased to nearly 43 per cent in 2011, being considerably more urbanized than the rest of the nation. From the onset, the state made a clear choice of encouraging the secondary sector activities over the primary and tertiary sector activities and according priority to directly productive activities vis-à-vis creation of social overhead capital.

Development in Gujarat is aided by natural advantages that the state possesses, such as its location and presence of a long coastline. However, the economy also faces severe constraints, notably its location in the semi-arid region of the country, the relative deficiency and uneven distribution of natural resources. The state is also highly vulnerable to climatic variations. Agriculture is affected by erratic and uneven rainfall that often leads to scarcity conditions. Soils in Gujarat are generally rich, though water resources in the state are scarce and regional variations in rainfall availability are very high. The state has limited mineral base. The state faces severe environmental degradation in several regions, in the nature of declining vegetation, soil erosion, deforestation, water logging, increased salinity of land and water arising from over use of canal water and over drawl of ground water.

Up to the beginning of the last decade Gujarat was beset by large spatial imbalances in the levels of development (Mehta, 2006; Kashyap and Mehta, 2007). Development was biased in favour of areas having proximity to the urban corridors. The remote hilly areas in the east and to the south witnessed little growth of per capita income or employment. As a result, regional imbalances were glaring. The development gains trickled down unevenly among rural and urban areas, developed and backward pockets and among scheduled and non scheduled sections of population. Some aspects of social retrogression were also quite visible as seen from the discrepancies in key demographic variables. Education and health care facilities faced problems of delivery and access. The selective path of development posed major impediments to distributive justice.

The state witnessed considerable growth acceleration, beginning early 2000s, fuelled by unprecedented agricultural and industrial growth. Under the circumstances, the optimal use of resources for realizing full potential of the economy requires a careful re-appraisal to ascertain whether growth acceleration ushered in equitable and inclusive development outcomes or not. Gujarat's economic development has been often acclaimed as a highly effective growth and private sector driven model. In fact, the average growth rate of GDP in Gujarat over the last two decades has been higher than the national average, and more balanced than the other high growth rate states, primarily because of improved performance across sectors, especially that of agriculture and industry. However, in terms of overall social development,

Gujarat has miles to cover in ensuring that the economic growth translates into improved human development.

Though Gujarat is a highly industrialized state, industrial development is largely capital intensive and labour displacing. The traditionally uneven pattern of industrial growth has been further reinforced in the post-reform regime. Industrial investments mostly flow to talukas that are close to some major industrial concentration or trunk routes or near ports, thereby suggesting an element of polarity (Awasthi and Kashyap, 2008). Northern Gujarat seems to have been bypassed by the industrialization process. Evidence points to the skewed and lopsided nature of industrial growth with the resource rich South and Central Gujarat spearheading and maintaining the lead in industrial growth. This selective path of development followed poses major impediments to distributive justice (Mehta, 2013).

The paper is divided in five sections. The next (2) section traces the economic growth experience of Gujarat in the decade of 2000s. The third section deals with "business as usual" approach vis-à-vis an alternate vision of development and distributive growth. The fourth section highlights aspects that have faced neglect due to growth oriented approach and stresses the need for a more inclusive vision for the future development path. The last section concludes with a brief discussion on how to operationalize an alternate vision.

2. Growth Experience

Gujarat has in recent years earned the tag of "most favoured state" with investors. In the eighties, Gujarat lagged behind the nation in nearly all sectors. In the 1990s (beginning 1993-94) it grew at around 6.5 percent per annum (against all India rate of 5.9 % / annum); this was in fact the highest recorded amongst the major states (Kohli, 2006; Awasthi and Kashyap, 2008). Productive labour force, stable industrial relations and a prolonged record of pro-business government were the initial advantages that triggered a growth spurt in the 90s over the 80s decade. With regard to inter-sectoral pattern of growth, the agriculture sector did not register much growth in the 80s (0.34 %) and the slow growth continued in the 90s, leading to overall deterioration of the primary sector. Volatility in Gujarat's economic growth owed chiefly to the primary sector, particularly agriculture. Its sectoral share (in the NSDP) declined from 40.8 per cent in 1980-81 down to 15 per cent in 2000-01, indicating significant structural changes in Gujarat's economy.

Liberalization process had considerable impact on the state's economy. It resulted in growth acceleration especially in the secondary sector to around seven percent (1990s), of which manufacturing grew at nearly six percent. Tertiary sector witnessed a faster growth pattern (9% / annum) with transport, storage, communication, trade and public administration recording the fastest growth. This growth pattern led to consistently higher than national average of per capita income and growth, increasing to 4.7 % in 1990s from three percent in the 1980s. In late 1990s the per capita income in Gujarat was 38% more than the national average, and with a declining level of income inequality in the rural areas (Puri, 2003). Experience of growth in the 90s decade showed that Gujarat had developed capabilities to absorb the large adverse shock in its primary sector. This was manifested in the growth of the non-primary sectors, even though agriculture and the allied sectors did not witness significant positive impact. Moreover within the manufacturing sector, registered manufacturing showed growth acceleration.

Official statistics revealed a high growth in agriculture since the early years of 2000 decade. The agricultural growth rate in Gujarat accelerated at rate of nearly 10 per cent. This was in sharp contrast to the growth of three per cent for agriculture and allied sector recorded at the national level. It was also in contrast to Gujarat's own highly volatile agricultural performance during the decades before 2000s. The primacy of agricultural sector in growth acceleration of Gujarat's domestic product during the previous decade has been established. The secondary sector and manufacturing sectors also grew at 11 % / annum in the 2000s decade. Tertiary sector registered a growth acceleration to 10.3 per cent / annum. At the end of the last decade the share of primary sector in NSDP had further dwindled to 14 per cent, while secondary and tertiary sectors contributed 33 per cent and 50 per cent respectively to the NSDP. Inter-sectoral growth variations persist, pointing towards unbalanced nature of economic growth in the state. It is well known that industry-led growth has a much higher chance of long term sustainability. Most of the demand for services is linked to expansion of industry and growth inducing effects of manufacturing sector that are larger than that of services.

Despite declining share in state income as well as steep fall in share of workers employed in it, primary sector continues to be a major source of labour absorption in the state. Share of workforce engaged in this sector is the highest at 49.3 per cent (NSS 68th Round, 2011-12, UPSS). The fall in primary sector's share to total labour force is not as steep as in the case of income from it. Any downswing in the agriculture and allied activities is bound to have severe consequences for a large segment of the population. A crucial variable in this respect is the relative sectoral product per worker (RSPW). RSPW (being the ratio between income share of a sector in NSDP and its share in the workforce) for primary sector (largely agriculture and allied sectors) in 1983-84 was 0.61. Since then there is a rapid decline (Table 1) at 0.43 in 1993-94 to 0.35 in 1999-2000. The index for 2004-05, based on estimates of NSDP (at 1993-94 prices) revealed considerable improvement of the RSPW for the primary sector at 0.46, perhaps due to a sharp decline in the labour force dependent on cultivation and related activities (NSS 61st Round, Employment & Unemployment Survey, UPSS). Favorable weather conditions in Gujarat in the initial years of the 2000 decade led to an upswing in the growth rate of the agriculture sector.

In 2011-12, the RSPW has again taken a severe beating, declining to 0.30, this being the lowest ever. Despite decline in the share of output from the primary sector, it is noteworthy that people employed in the sector have recorded an increase over 2004-05. Declining RSPW obviously implies rapid fall in the relative labour productivity in the primary sector and a sharpening of rural-urban inequalities. This is likely to have negative implications for the cause of equity and inclusiveness.

Other forms of inequalities are manifest in the state. The development path followed by the state so far has led to a reversal of the equalization process. The coefficient of variation in the incidence of rural poverty in 1993-94 between the geographical sub regions of Gujarat was 0.23; and for urban poverty it was 0.16. The coefficients rose in 1999-00 to 0.26 (rural) and 0.25 (urban). By 2009-10 the coefficient of variation for rural areas increased further to 0.41, though it declined for urban areas to 0.19. Apparently the reforms process and the growth spurt in the last decade have failed to make any significant dent on reduction in spatial variations, as regional imbalances have further increased. Inter-regional and inter-sectoral inequality limited the spread of growth in consumption expenditure.

TABLE 1
Relative Sectoral Product per Worker

Year	*Primary Sector*	*Non Primary Sectors*
1993-94		
Share in total workforce (%)	55.6	44.4
Share in NSDP (%)	23.7	76.3
RSPW	0.43	1.72
1999-00		
Share in total workforce (%)	56.4	43.6
Share in NSDP (%)	19.4	81.7
RSPW	0.34	1.87
2004-05		
Share in total workforce (%)	46.0	54.0
Share in NSDP (%)	21.1	78.9
RSPW	0.46	1.46
2011-12		
Share in total workforce (%)	49.3	50.7
Share in NSDP (%)	14.7	85.3
RSPW	0.30	1.68

Source: CSO, Net State Domestic Product, Various Years; NSSO, *Employment & Unemployment in India, Various Rounds.*

3. "Business as Usual" Growth

In the past most important drivers of growth in Gujarat have been electricity, gas and water, storage and communication, construction, real estate and rainfall. In addition it was observed that during the nineties enterprises (own account and establishments) in manufacturing, electricity, gas and water, retail trade, storage and warehousing were shifting towards the urban areas. There was a decline in the importance of household based manufacturing activities (both in rural and urban areas). In the rural areas accelerated growth was observed in the 'sunrise sectors' of retail trade, construction, communications and personal services. Some of these activities are associated with deterioration in quality of employment; nonetheless these were operating as depository of surplus labour. This had significant implications for growth strategy and the state policies (Mehta and Kashyap, 2002). With the passage of time other factors important for the state economy have emerged. Sustaining an overall SDP growth of more than 10 per cent per annum achieved in the 2000s decade would require focusing on innovations, research and development, better management and organisation, skill improvement and fundamental changes in the structures of economic activities. This would imply shifting away from low productivity, traditional activities to high value, high productivity, modern activities (Dholakia, 2006). It would also result in entrepreneurial flexibility in resource shift and allocation and removal of technological, administrative and economic barriers to growth. Activities that are drawing the largest shares of workers outside agriculture require promotional efforts geared towards technological up gradation to enhance modernization, coupled with support towards credit, power etc. Disaggregated look at these sectors by their size, location and growth pattern is warranted.

The question is how far the economic growth process can relate to the human and social development aspects in the state, importance of which cannot be emphasized enough. The synergies between social and economic sectors are mutually reinforcing. Human development in itself is also a desirable goal as it provides people with equal opportunities to participate in the growth process. The social sector expenditure ratio to the GSDP is likely to have a bearing on the state of human development. Gujarat's position vis-à-vis the nation has not been very favourable and did not improve much till the late 90s. However, Gujarat witnessed a rising trend in the allocation of expenditure for the social sectors in 2000s compared to the late 1990s. For the period 1999 onwards the decline in capital expenditure in key social sectors like education and health was considered justifiable on grounds of increasing private sector participation, given the high level of fiscal deficit being experienced by the state (Puri, 2003). The ratio of the social sector expenditure to the GSDP between 2001-03 was around seven per cent, though it declined to 5.4 per cent in the period 2009-11.

The neo-classical economic growth accounting models do not lay adequate stress on aspects such as inter-regional inequalities and unequal distribution of gains or the crucial sustainability issues. On the other hand, it is becoming clear that human development efforts of the government have increasing returns while efforts on development of physical capital have started yielding diminishing returns in terms of basic welfare objectives of the government. The "business as usual" economic growth paths aiming at more returns and capital investments often lead to wasteful practices and negative externalities. Aspects of human, societal development and sustainability are not separate concerns in an expanding economy. These are believed to get automatically addressed when the growth momentum picks up. But often criucial areas of weaknesses abound (such as IMR, literacy). In the alternate case these concerns have to be integrated into the growth model for adequate and appropriate policy response. Gujarat needs to grow at a higher rate than 10 per cent / annum, but with a vision that encompasses all of the above concerns. This also subsumes a move towards ecologically friendly and broad based development pattern. Some of the crucial aspects that require focus of the future development strategy in the state are highlighted in the following paragraphs.

4. Vision for the Future

In this section we take note of some of the trends which are essential in the long term perspective of sustainable and inclusive growth. Gujarat being a front runner in economic growth in recent times and "Gujarat model" of development attracting attention necessitates careful monitoring, especially in areas where markets impose heavy social costs. Hence implications of high growth on poverty, bypassed regions (tribal and coastal areas), weaker sections (SC/ST, women) deserve serious attention. Policy interventions are also important so that unleashing of market forces does not destroy common property resources. A vision for inclusive agricultural development is also required. The approach paper for the Twelfth Plan lays emphasis on a high growth path regime but pledges that the growth needs to be inclusive and poverty reducing, particularly of the traditionally deprived groups, the SCs, STs, OBCs, minorities and wage labour and petty producers that are considered most vulnerable and poor. The progress in some of these trends during the high growth period of 2000s decade is analyzed.

(i) *Human Development:* High and robust economic growth is expected to have favourable outcomes for overall population growth, sex ratio and urbanisation. As compared to the early part of 2000s decade some of these ratios have recorded a noticeable improvement. The persistence of a skewed sex-ratio in Gujarat could possibly be the result of in-migration of male workers from neighboring states due to rapid industrialization. However, pending careful analysis nothing conclusive can be stated. Table 2 identifies some of the areas of concern. Phenomenon of social retrogression was evident particularly from the discrepancies in the sex ratio, both overall and juvenile ratios up to early 2000s. The reasons were- high child mortality among females, substantial loss of life associated with childbirth due to lack of health care, rising incidence of sex determination and abortion of female fetus. During the 2000 decade overall sex ratio remained unchanged, but the gap with national average has widened, implying that progress on this front in the state is slower. Child sex ratio shows improvement, but is still lower than the national average. Diseases and access to health care facilities also merit a perspective. Infant mortality rate is declining, though the substantial gulf between rural and urban still persists. Under-five mortality rates in the past were higher than the national average. Not only have these halved overall but the progress is faster than the country as a whole. Government's efforts in this direction have been noteworthy (GoG, 2014). Though even in this measure the rural areas lag behind the urban centres. The access to primary health care in rural areas continues to be a sore point, even though the state has made notable progress as compared to the national scenario.

The number of average deaths of women is falling (from 254 in 2004-06) and the state is favourably placed even in this regard. Maternal and child health care systems require special emphasis. Gujarat needs to make valiant efforts to emulate success of Kerala in terms of death rates and infant mortality rates.

TABLE 2

Comparison of Some Human Development Related Indicators

S. No.	*Indicator*	*Gujarat*	*India*
1.	Sex Ratio (females /000 males) (2011)	919	943
2.	Sex Ratio 0-6 years (females /000 males) (2011)	890	919
3.	Death Rate (per '000 population) (SRS 2012)	6.6	7.0
4.	Birth Rate (per'000 population (SRS 2012)	21.1	21.6
5.	IMR (per '000) (SRS 2011)		
	Total	41	44
	Rural	48	48
	Urban	27	29
6.	Under 5 Mortality Rate (SRS 2011)		
	Total	52	55
	Rural	60	61
	Urban	35	35
7.	MMR (deaths/lakh live births) (SRS 2011)	122	178
8.	Av. No. of Villages served by PHC (2011)	15	24

9.	Density of Schools/10sq.km (2011-12)		
	Primary	2.07	3.55
	Upper Primary	1.52	1.71
	Secondary	0.49	0.61
10.	Schools/000 child population (2011-12)		
	Primary	8	10
	Upper Primary	5	8
11.	Access of Households to tapped water supply (2011)		
	Rural	55.8	30.8
	Urban	85.6	70.6

Sources: Socio-Economic Review, Gujarat State, Various Years; Registrar General of India.

Gujarat had fared poorly in terms of social and human development indicators in the past. Quite evidently the state has shown noteworthy improvements on some of these counts. There is a wide rural-urban disparity in the access to safe drinking water. The same is true with reference to education. State's education system, including tertiary education requires considerable upgrading. Domestic supply of technical/ professional personnel is inadequate compared to the likely demand. Also, literacy gap over space (rural, urban) and gender for both rural and urban areas persists and is quite high (Table 2).

Although there has been significant improvement in terms of health and education infrastructure over the years, especially in urban areas, the challenge remains in further improving the access to health and education services of people living in remote rural areas. The main challenges faced by the state is the prevalence of high degree of child under nutrition, in addition to a slow pace of reduction in Infant Mortality Rate and Maternal Mortality Rate.

(ii) *Gender Concerns:* Gender issues have to occupy centre-stage in meeting the challenge of inclusivity. Working women in urban areas of Gujarat succumb to the dual strain of poverty and patriarchy. Women in general and rural women in particular face social and economic deprivation compared to their counter parts living in urban areas.

Table 3
Gender Differentials and Changes in Education Level in Gujarat (2004-05 to 2011-12)

Education Level	*Rural*			*Urban*		
2004-05	*Male*	*Female*	*Total*	*Male*	*Female*	*Total*
Not literate	30.7	53.1	41.5	15.3	26.4	20.5
Up to Primary	36.0	28.9	32.6	30.3	27.9	29.2
Middle	18.3	10.4	14.5	17.9	18.9	18.4
Secondary & Above	14.9	7.6	11.4	36.5	26.8	31.9
2011-12						
Not literate	27.9	43.5	35.3	13.9	22.1	17.7
Up to Primary	36.9	36.7	36.8	30.3	29.7	30.0
Middle	15.8	9.2	12.7	17.0	17.0	17.0
Secondary & Above	18.9	10.3	14.8	38.5	31.1	35.0

Source: NSS Survey of Employment-Unemployment, 61st and 68th Rounds, Reports No. 515 and 554.

Table 3 shows that nearly 44% of the women in rural areas of Gujarat are still illiterate; however in the recent past considerable progress has been achieved due to government's policies and programmes targeting education of females. Decline in female illiteracy is larger in rural than in urban areas. Among the population that is literate, the male-female and rural-urban differentials are yet glaring across all levels. The final outcome indicates that government has to make renewed efforts at retaining children in middle schools and inculcating importance of higher education across gender and space. Mother's education, it needs to be emphasized, apart from medical and maternity care, is an important factor that influences the IMR. Despite robust economic growth such weaknesses persist. The vision for demographic and population stability would include attaining close to half percent of annual growth rate of population. The social dimension of this vision would have to involve significant upgradation of the status of women in the society. Crucial variables to aim at would be women's education, enhanced participation in labour market and above all respect in society. Though progress over time is visible, the state has to accelerate the ongoing efforts.

Women's income and consumption levels, means of livelihood and their contribution in unpaid work deserve in-depth analysis. Gender equality will be achieved only by engendering the development model. A perspective is required that recognizes women as producers of marketable goods and services and that incorporates unpaid work as a macroeconomic variable. New institutional mechanisms and better public policy are needed to effectively engender the development process. Process of decentralized development and women empowerment deserve to be addressed on a firm footing.

(iii) *Poverty and Employment:* The head count ratio of poor in rural areas of Gujarat was below that of the country in the 70s and 80s, irrespective of the poverty line adopted and price indices used and continued to be so even in the 90s and 2000 decade. This has been explained in terms of high per capita income, reasonably high labour productivity and its growth. However urban poverty had been similar to the national average and was above the rural figures all through the 70s and 80s. The high incidence of urban poverty in the state could perhaps be explained in terms of high immigration from other states. Migration within the state from drought prone, tribal areas was also quite substantial. In the 90s and thereafter the urban poverty in the state has shown remarkable decline. In 2004-05 the incidence of urban poverty in Gujarat was nearly half of that for rural areas and considerably below the national average. In 2011-12, urban poverty declined by ten percentage points; in rural areas also poverty declined but at a slower pace. Overall poverty level in the state is quite low compared to the national figure.

In the recent period the annual decline in the head count ratio of poverty in the state suggests an optimistic picture. The decline between 1993-94 and 2004-05 was nearly double in urban Gujarat (-3.1%) than in rest of India (-1.9%). Between 2004-05 and 2011-12 the pace of decline in urban poverty quickened (-9.4%), and was still higher than the decline at India level. In rural Gujarat the pace of decline slowed down in 90s vis-à-vis the 80s period. Between 1993-05, the decline was nearly two times more in India (-1.6%) than the state (-0.9%). In the following period (2004-2011), the situation reversed and poverty in rural Gujarat declined more rapidly (8.2%) than in India (6.7%). If we consider the post liberalization period in its entirety, it can be seen that the annual decline in poverty in Gujarat (rural, urban and total) has kept above that in India (Table 4).

TABLE 4
Comparable Estimates of Poverty (%)
(Based on Mixed Reference period, Tendulkar methodology)

	Rural			*Urban*			*Total*		
	1993-94	*2004-05*	*2011-12*	*1993-94*	*2004-05*	*2011-12*	*1993-94*	*2004-05*	*2011-12*
Gujarat	43.3	39.1	21.5	28.3	20.1	10.1	38.4	31.6	16.6
India	50.1	41.8	25.7	31.8	25.7	13.7	45.3	37.2	21.9

Annual Average Decline (% per annum)

	1994-05	*2005-2011*	*1994-2011*
		Rural	
Gujarat	-0.9	-8.2	-3.8
India	-1.6	-6.7	-3.6
		Urban	
Gujarat	-3.1	-9.4	-5.6
India	-1.9	-8.6	-4.6
		Total	
Gujarat	-1.8	-8.8	-4.6
India	-1.8	-7.3	-4.0

Source: GoI (2013), Press Note on Poverty Estimates, 2011-12, Planning Commission.
Growth Rates are Author's Calculation.

The composition of rural poor reinforces the vulnerability faced by certain sections of the population. The high rate of growth of the Gujarat economy did not entirely percolate down to the weaker sections. Despite considerable growth in the state in the last decade, poverty in the state continues to be unevenly distributed amongst regions and various social groups. A typical poor household is subjected to social exclusion or is a tribal family residing in a backward or remote region. It is a reflection of the poor endowment of the productive assets, but also of lower educational standards or little access to any kind of regular employment. The economic situation of the STs in Gujarat is quite precarious vis-à-vis other groups (Table 5).

TABLE 5
Incidence of Poverty among Social Groups (2011-12)

	Rural			*Urban*		
	ST	*SC*	*All*	*ST*	*SC*	*All*
Gujarat	36.5	22.3	21.5	30.1	12.7	10.2
India	45.3	31.5	25.4	24.1	21.7	13.7
Rate of change 1994-2012 (% per annum)						
Gujarat	-2.1	-5.0	-3.8	-0.2	-7.3	-5.5
India	-2.1	-3.7	-3.7	-2.9	-4.7	-4.6

Source: Panagariya and More, 2013.

In Gujarat after the early nineties the fastest poverty decline amongst all the social groups was seen in case of the SCs. The state was also placed favourably vis-à-vis India in this regard. However, Gujarat faces a major task in reducing poverty and closing the poverty gap between STs and the remaining population. It calls for strong state support and public interventions that specifically target such households. Also included in the latter group would be women headed households, small and marginal farmers, agricultural labourers and rural artisans.

Volatility of the economy has important bearing on poverty in the state, which in turn hinges on the erratic nature of rainfall and its effect on agriculture. Growth in labour productivity and real wages hinges on stability of the economy. Analysis of time series data on poverty in Gujarat has shown that sectoral composition of growth mattered in overall rate of poverty reduction. Growth process has led to faster poverty reduction in urban areas vis-à-vis rural areas, which have double the poverty levels. Sustained growth in agriculture is likely to percolate to larger population, thereby making substantial dent on rural poverty. This signifies the need to view agricultural growth, employment generation, nutrition and poverty as interdependent phenomena. Rural occupational diversification has also emerged as an important factor bringing about changes in the rural economic structure and fostering urbanization. In this context public expenditure, public and private investments, and access to urban services deserve attention for the state economy.

TABLE 6A
Distribution of Workers across Rural and Urban areas, 2001-11 (% to total)

	2001			*2011*		
	Rural	*Urban*	*Total*	*Rural*	*Urban*	*Total*
Main Workers	65.3	34.1	100	58.3	41.7	100
Marginal Workers	91.8	8.2	100	83.8	16.1	100
Total workers	70.6	29.4	100	62.8	37.1	100

Source: Census of India, 2011

TABLE 6B
Worker Participation Rates (% to Population)

	2001		*2011*	
	Rural	*Urban*	*Rural*	*Urban*
Main Workers	35.0	31.2	34.3	33.0
Marginal Workers	12.2	1.9	10.7	2.8
Total workers	47.2	33.1	44.9	35.8

Source: Census of India, 2011.

Availability of remunerative employment is the most important determinant of material wellbeing. Equitable growth process is essentially related to the associated labour use pattern. Returns from employment depend not only on the sector of economic activity but also on the quality of work available. In Gujarat, the composition of workforce continues to be a cause for concern, which has implications on livelihoods and earnings. Evidence indicates an urban ward shift of work force (Table 6a). Census data showed that during 2001-2011 the percentage of main workers in rural areas fell by seven percent points (65% to 58%), the fall in the total workers was steeper by eight percentage points. The extent of marginal workers declined in rural areas by 12 percent points in nineties decade, the fall is slower to around eight percentage points in 2000 decade.

Lower work participation rates are due to retention in schools and higher education or the lack of employment opportunities, particularly for female workers. The worker participation rates (WPR) of rural marginal workers declined (12.4% in 2001 to 10.6% in 2011), while in urban areas it has doubled (from 1.9 to 2.8%) (Table 6b). Enhanced marginalisation of workforce in urban areas is a cause for concern. Currently, in rural areas the WPR of female marginal workers is three times that of males at 16 per cent. This has led to the considerably high female marginal worker participation rates. Apparently workers in the states are finding less remunerative jobs in rural areas. A policy perspective is required for the groups left out, such as, small and marginal farmers, unskilled casual (manual and agricultural) labourers so that they are enabled to have a reasonable standard of living. Labour intensity needs to be raised through research and development for appropriate technologies that ensure fair returns to labour.

(iv) Agriculture Development and Weather induced Vulnerabilities: Agriculture in Gujarat occupies a prominent position as it engages nearly half of the rural working population (52%) despite its declining share in the state net domestic product. An off-shoot of the process of liberalization in Gujarat was the distortion of the agriculture-industry linkages. However, relationship between the behavior of agriculture sector and that of NSDP has strengthened in recent times. Output after 2000 recorded an unprecedented growth,

leading to growth in land productivity at 7.5 per cent from 0.14 per cent recorded in 1990s decade. Thus early 2000s period can be considered a watershed (Mehta, 2012).

Since land is increasingly becoming a binding constraint to agricultural expansion, contribution of yield as a component of output growth picked up for most of the crops in the state. Liberalization period also boosted the process of agricultural commercialization. However, it is well known that freeing trade links the domestic commodity production to highly unstable global prices. Gujarat is now far more vulnerable in this respect owing to highly commercialized nature of its agriculture.

Analysis of crop sector has revealed that most of the crops in the state have either not shown enough growth or have a volatile production record. Nearly 58 per cent of the cultivated area in Gujarat is still rain fed. Sharp decline in yield levels has been observed during drought years. Rainfall is the major source of moisture for crop cultivation in Gujarat and explains to a large extent the fluctuations in production and yields (Mehta, 2013). Hence besides irrigation development, evolving and disseminating dry farming technologies should receive much higher priority in all future efforts, especially for resource poor farmers in the rain fed regions.

With the adoption of higher yielding varieties and now transgenic crop varieties, expansion of cultivation is happening on marginal lands with degraded and fragile soils and uncertain availability of irrigation facilities. This has rendered production far more sensitive than before even to small variations in natural phenomena. Institutional support to agriculture is rather weak in the state. Despite a well-functioning cooperative structure, it has not succeeded in ensuring adequate supply of credit for weaker sections. Of the total advances made by credit institutions in the state only 7.5 % have gone to the weaker sections (2011).

Agricultural development has to be integrated with the overall economic growth and with creation of livelihood opportunities in the rural sector. Although technical efficiency has distinctly improved in 2000s decade and state is witnessing technical progress, agriculture in Gujarat continues to show evidence of avoidable waste. Sustainability issues can be averted with adequate regulation and judicious use of key resources and Gujarat can be a torchbearer in this respect.

(v) Environment and Resource Base: Rapid economic development is often accompanied by a host of environmental problems. Gujarat is the second most industrialized state, but the distinction has come at a price. The pollution of land, air and water merit serious concern in the state. Coastal ecology is being threatened and extensive deforestation is affecting the livelihoods of the tribal communities. Industrial development has happened at the cost of considerable damage to air and water quality due to the concentration of industries and heavy emphasis on chemical based industries. Industrial pattern in the state has to become more diversified in terms of both location and product base so as to provide greater flexibility. The smaller urban centres and census towns have to be provided with civic amenities and infrastructure to arrest the deterioration of air and water quality and also to attract enterprise.

While development has turned the common property resources into open access resources on the one hand, on the other, ease in acquisition of land for industrial purposes has led to decline in the natural capital. The other noteworthy feature of the land-use pattern is that forests occupy only 9.7 per cent of the reported area in Gujarat as compared to the national average of 21 per cent.

Water resources in many parts of the State are under severe stress due to excessive exploitation. Over-exploitation of sub-surface water, falling water tables and deterioration of water quality is happening in some parts. The high cost of ground water irrigation is affecting profitability of agriculture in many areas. Needless to add, ground water over-exploitation with severely depleting water levels has serious equity implications. Injudicious use of surface sources of irrigation has raised the soil salinity in some areas. The pressing question is how to achieve sustainable development.

Sustainable management of hydrological system, which is under considerable threat, is the chief environmental issue which could avert a host of multi-faceted problems that require attention. Deterioration in land quality is also causing misgivings. Strategic interventions geared to specific locations are required. Space specific analysis of land resources and appropriate intervention for efficient use and management can enhance long term sustainability of the land resource.

A holistic and integrated approach for achievement of optimality in water and land resources would require participation of not only government agencies but also that of people's organizations, user groups and all stakeholders for effective implementation of different institutional mechanisms. Research initiatives would be required to evolve appropriate organizational forms to safeguard the state's environment and common property resources.

(vi) *Development Imbalances & Social Justice:* Despite the state having one of the highest per capita incomes in India, within the rural areas the social distance between the elite and rural poor has been widening due to changes in labour relations, educational background and residential location. An insight into the welfare aspects is required, especially in a situation where there are many factors hindering the trickle down of benefits (Shinoda, 2002).

The relative differences in human development related indicators as also poverty index between the tribal/backward communities and general population are glaring. The former enjoy much lower quality of life and have lower educational attainments. ST and SC sections constitute 14.8 per cent and 6.8 per cent of the state's population, yet about 36.5 per cent and 21.5 per cent of the rural poor in the state were concentrated in these two social groups. Lack of remunerative employment for large sections of the population determines their deprivation. Evidence from NSS indicates that WPRs in Gujarat are higher than those of the nation for all social groups. One could therefore argue that the state enjoys highest employment rates. The WPRs for both males and females in case of tribal population were the highest (47.1% in rural and

37.1 per cent in urban areas in 2009-10), closely followed by the OBCs and SCs. But it is the quality and type of employment as well as productive asset ownership which assume primacy. Table 7 has much to reveal in this respect. Literacy level among STs and SCs has shown improvement, however these groups continue to lag behind the OBCs and others in this respect. The disparity in educational attainment is starker in rural areas. A larger share of households are engaged in agriculture labour and other manual jobs amongst the SC and STs. "Others" category followed by OBCs are the main land owning groups. Clearly, SCs is the only category in Gujarat which is worse off than the tribal sections as far as economic status is concerned.

TABLE 7
Literacy and Employment Pattern of Households across Social Groups, Gujarat (2009-10)

Social Group	*Rural*					*Urban*			
	Self Employed		*Rural Labour*		*Others*	*Self Employed*	*Wage/ Salaried*	*Casual Labour*	*Others*
	Agri	*Non-agri*	*Agri labour*	*Other labour*					
ST	37.0	7.0	33.4	13.1	8.4	23.3	38.4	21.1	16.9
SC	17.1	13.7	36.9	22.1	10.3	26.2	39.4	25.1	9.2
OBC	34.1	17.2	23.3	14.0	11.4	36.8	35.0	17.1	11.1
Others	39.4	18.1	15.9	10.3	16.3	36.2	44.1	6.0	13.6
All	38.8	10.7	30.7	10.3	9.4	39.5	42.6	12.2	5.7

Literate Persons (%)

	Rural	*Urban*	*Total*
ST	62.6	90.1	64.4
SC	63.0	81.6	69.6
OBC	69.7	80.6	73.1
Others	79.4	91.1	86.8
All	69.3	87.0	76.3

Source: NSSO, Employment and Unemployment Situation among Social Groups in India, 66th Round.

In urban Gujarat too, the occurrence of self employment is much less amongst these groups, and are largely engaged as casual labour. Higher employment of SCs as wage/salaried workers is inevitably an outcome of reservation policy in government jobs, education and other areas and has helped in benefitting the SCs to march ahead. Out-migration from backward, resource poor and remote areas to urban centres in search of casual wage labour is a pressing issue in the state. Evidence also indicates that the economic vulnerability that characterizes backward social groups in terms of means of livelihood has not diminished over the years even when the rest of the state is forging ahead. Clearly life basis of weaker sections, particularly of tribals and dalits, is narrowing down. Safety net schemes have either failed or have had limited impact.

The other important characteristic of imbalances in growth in the state is the spatial distribution of poverty. There exists a wide variation in poverty levels within the state. The incidence of rural poverty continued to be high in the eastern and dry regions up to 2004-05 (Table 8). Between 2004-05 and 2009-10 the coefficient of variation increased from 0.35 to 0.47 indicating widening of regional variations in development. Change in the head count ratio was positive in all the regions, save the southern region. In the southern region the head-count ratio was 2.5 percentage points higher in 2009-10. Rural poverty declined fastest in the northern region. However, the increasing coefficient of variation is indicative of reversal of the equalization process. Apparently faster growth has exacerbated the spatial variations in development.

Comparison of urban poverty figures reveal regional variations have narrowed down. Urban poverty has deteriorated in southern region. The imported poverty from rural areas to urban may be the leading cause for such a trend. The above also indicates the considerable rural urban disparity prevailing in Gujarat in incidence of poverty. Despite faster rate of decline in rural poverty, the extent is still considerable more than the urban areas of the state.

TABLE 8
Regional level Head Count Ratio of Poverty

NSS Region	*Rural*		
	2004-05	*2009-10*	*Change (% / annum)*
Eastern	51.2	39.0	-12.2
Northern	38.0	19.0	-19.0
Southern	39.8	42.3	2.5
Dry Areas	48.3	35.0	-13.3
Saurashtra	16.7	10.9	-5.8
Coeff. of Var.	0.35	0.47	0.12
		Urban	
Eastern	24.9	14.3	-10.6
Northern	21.9	18.0	-3.9
Southern	14.1	23.9	9.8
Dry Areas	27.5	21.5	-6.0
Saurashtra	22.5	21.8	-0.7
Coeff. of Var.	0.23	0.19	-0.04

Source: Mishra (2014).

5. Nature of Policy Support & State's Role

It is apparent that the real challenge that Gujarat faces is to remain on a high growth trajectory and also usher in a people centered and inclusive development process that also envelopes equity and sustainability concerns. Despite high growth of the economy and rapid decline in poverty, Gujarat shows mounting pressure on natural resources, land and water, widening rural-urban and regional disparities. Certain sections of the population (weaker sections, asset less, women, poor) are being largely bypassed by the development process. Inter-sectoral growth disparities prevail. Falling relative share of the primary sector bodes ill for the largest share of the state's workers and the dependent population.

Gujarat has been a significant beneficiary of the liberalisation process and it has been one of the fastest growing states despite considerable shocks experienced in the form of natural and other calamities. But the development paradigm needs rethinking so that the benefits of growth reach out to the largest sections of its residents and sustainability aspects remain in place. The vision drivers in a people's centered approach of growth would be poverty alleviation, equity, empowerment of communities together with agricultural and industrial development. A vision has to have at its core a "non poor" state, elimination of ignorance, illiteracy, disease and inequalities of opportunities. The human resource base of a state is its greatest wealth. Rapid changes are bound to occur in all economic sectors, requiring rapid and continuous changes in the skill levels of the large numbers of people to enhance their core competencies. The state and private agencies would have to focus increasingly on providing easy credit and financing of the poor to come out of their economic impasse. This would have to be in the form of multi-pronged strategy that addresses the entire livelihood problem. Although the growth process has not been entirely inclusive, considerable progress is being made on some key fronts. In this context, redistribution of the government's revenue is required for including the marginalized groups and regions into the accelerated growth process.

Gujarat has seen the highest agricultural growth in the 2000 decade. This seems to be helping in reducing the poverty incidence of poor farmers and farm wage labour. However, greater investment in agricultural sector is needed to benefit rain fed areas and technology dissemination should benefit the entire farming community. Strengthening of wage employment programmes is also necessary to supplement the farm wage employment. This has to be linked with a comprehensive plan of water and land resource development (Thorat and Dubey, 2012). State needs to realize the complementarities of the wage employment programme and small farm development. A strategy with a focus on small and marginal farmers will need strengthening. The SC farmers who are asset poor will need special attention in supply of inputs and sale of farm output as they face constraints in both the factor and product markets.

Involvement of people in the development works needs to be given priority. Greater transparency, encouragement of self-help groups, WUAs and other local level organizational forms need to be ensured. In future, a perspective on the development methodology would have to articulate the altered economic and social reality, implying that as against supply based models the new approach would have to account for demand aspects and much enhanced role of markets. Analysis of externalities (positive and negative) arising as an outcome of unfettered markets would be important. State would be required to move from being hierarchal or authoritative to a gender sensitive and participative system.

Maximisation of productive employment rather than increasing the gross domestic product should be the objective of the state. Enhanced livelihoods and regular income are the keys towards ensuring welfare. Sufficient numbers of skilled persons are not being produced in the state to match the demands of the market. In this context the employers need to be involved in defining the skills required and also in training the young population. The political stability in the state should be leveraged for the creation of successful enterprises to benefit the weaker sections and the lagging regions. Access to capital and finance to facilitate growth of micro, small and medium enterprises has to be stepped up and lopsided industrial growth with continued emphasis on capital-intensive sectors should be reversed. State should facilitate creation of an enabling environment for markets to work for all sections, rather than allowing resources to be allocated to few sections. Dualism and rising inequalities that mark Gujarat's growth require to be addressed, as these will emerge as serious obstacles in the path of sustainable development.

In order to promote rapid but equitable development, the state government still needs to do much in transforming itself from being merely a controller of the economy. The state would have to play an important role as an efficiency creator, arbitrator for conflict resolution and as a guardian for the larger societal interests, particularly those of bypassed people and areas. Government will have to develop an ability to usher in an inclusive growth process, create infrastructure and also develop human resources. The state will have to take bold and innovative steps to finance the implementation of such a vision.

References

Awasthi, Dinesh N. and S.P. Kashyap (2008), "Emerging Industrialisation Process in Gujarat : Nature and Composition" in Swaminathan, R. (Ed.), *Gujarat Perspectives of the Future*, Observer Research Foundation, Academic Foundation, New Delhi.

Dholakia, Ravindra (2006), "Growth Acceleration and Potential in Gujarat" *Working Paper No. 2006-02-02*, Indian Institute of Management, Ahmedabad.

Government of Gujarat (2014). *Samajic Vikas Ej Manav Vikas -Gujarat*, Gujarat Social Infrastructure Development Society, GAD, Gandhinagar.

Kashyap, S.P. and N. Mehta (2007), "Growth of a Regional Economy: Perspectives for Human Resource Development," *Indian Journal of Public Audit & Accountability*, 1(2), April-June.

Kohli, Atul (2006), "Politics of Economic Growth in India, 1980-2005", *Economic & Political Weekly*, April 1-7.

Mehta, Niti and S.P. Kashyap (2002), "An Approach towards Identifying Sunrise Industries: A Regional Perspective", *Manpower Journal*, 38 (2&3).

Mehta, Niti (2006), "Imbalances in Development between Regions and Social Groups: Evidences from Gujarat", *Anvesak*, 36(1).

Mehta, Niti (2012), "Performance of Crop Sector in Gujarat during the High Growth Period: Some Explorations", *Agricultural Economics Research Review*. 25(2), July-December.

Mehta, Niti (2013), "An Investigation into Growth, Instability and Role of Weather in Gujarat Agriculture: 1981-2011", *Agricultural Economics Research Review*, 26 (Conference Number).

Mehta, Niti (2013), "Employability of Rural Labour in the Neo-liberal Era: A Study of Gujarat". *Indian Journal of Labour Economics*, 56 (2), April-June.

Mishra, Srijit (2014), "Incidence of Poverty and Poverty Risk in India across NSS regions for Rural and Urban areas, 2004-05 and 2009-10", *WP 2014-021*, IGIDR, Mumbai.

Panagariya, Arvind and Vishal More (2013), "Poverty by Social, Religious and Economic Groups in India and its Largest States, 1993-94 to 2011-12", *WP No. 2013-02*, Columbia University: Programme on Indian Economic Policies.

Puri, Mukesh (2003), "Gujarat Economy in the 1990s", *Anvesak*, 33(2).

Shinoda, Takashi (2002), *The Other Gujarat—Social Transformations Among Weaker Sections*, Popular Prakashan Pvt. Ltd, Mumbai.

Thorat, Sukhadeo and Amaresh Dubey (2012), "Has Growth Been Socially Inclusive during 1993-94–2009-10?", *Economic and Political Weekly*, 47(10).

18

Intersectoral Migration of Weaker Section Labourers in the Field of Sugarcane in Maharashtra

Balaji Kendre

Introduction

Social stability and social mobility are essential features of all human societies in the world. Migration plays vital role in these processes of societies. Migration of human population is age old phenomena and various reasons are responsible. Migration is also viewed as form of social and economic mobility in modern days societies.The process of industrialization paved the way to new economic system and as a result of that new social system emerged which is supportive to the model of capitalist development. The nature and extent of migration has undergone rapid changes in last three centuries when model of capitalist development forced on all societies to adopt its agenda by so called developed nations (capitalist) but unfortunately the exploitative aspects of migration process are rarely studied and highlighted in academic circle. The reason is most vulnerable sections such as Scheduled castes, Scheduled tribes, Denotified and nomadic tribes, special backward classes and women from these groups who most vulnerable of Indian society are the victims of this kind of capitalist model of development. Since the very term development is fascinating term where the 'hierarchy of needs' is at the center. Earning capital is not the need of capitalist,industrialist, profit maker, and rich but it has become greed which is responsible for violation of human rights and disappearance of feeling of human dignity. It is true that economic development, structural change in economic infrastructure, and economic reforms require changes in resource allocation at grassroot levels for human development but this agenda of development should not hurt the interests of weaker sections of society. Though we the people have solemnly resolved that we will contribute with all efforts to protect liberty, equality and dignity of all our fellow citizens. We have also resolved that we will try our best to maintain fraternity in everyday life but unfortunately it happens only within certain groups like same class and same social setting.Manifestations of these values in social relations is rare phenomena because of the of purity and pollution involved in social relations through caste. Caste system is a biggest hurdle to protect the basic human values enlisted in our constitution of India.

Migration Mobility and Indian Society

T.K. Oommen (2001) a visionary sociologist from India articulates Indian society in a different way according to him, 'like all societies Indian society too is *stratified* based on age, gender, rural-urban differences and class but unlike many of them Indian society is marked by considerable *cultural heterogeneity* too, particularly because of a large number of speech communities counting more than one thousand five hundred including some six hundred tribal communities. But India's *religious plurality* complicated by the uneasy co-existence of religions of Indic and non-Indic origin is a rare phenomenon in most contemporary societies. However, what is unique to India is the all pervasive *caste hierarchy* legitimized through the Hindu doctrine of Karma and Reincarnation'. Which is rare and unique characteristic of Indian society. According to Dr. Babasheb Ambedkar (1917), Indian caste system has character called graded inequality.

It is true that all human societies have their bottoms and the bottom layer in hierarchical societies is constituted on the basis of colour, sex and, poverty, but unfortunately in India it is formed on the basis of caste. Thus, the bottoms of all societies which are homogeneous and merely stratified are occupied by women, youth and the proletariat. There is growing feeling that nowadays because of democracy and freedom of expression bottom groups have questioned the knowledge produced by their counterparts- men,adults and bourgeoisie and in Indian context *Shudras, Atishudras* and *Adivasis* have questioned the Brahmnical set up of knowledge. This is also true that over a period of time, the specific role of each of these disadvantaged categories has come to be recognizable in the production of knowledge. In the case of culturally heterogeneous societies, if the constituted segments are equal, either because they are numerically small or economically weak or culturally backward or all of these, the tendency is to ignore them in the representations of reality. There are numerous instances when these ignored or marginalized communities demand to be represented in the process of knowledge production. There are thousands of marginalized groups and communities which are fighting for their dignified status in society which is historically denied to them.

Social stratification or division of labour is ubiquitous and natural phenomena in its origin which help to sustain and function society. The bases of social stratification in other than Indian society are liberal and dynamic in nature where as in India caste is considered as one of the important base of division of labour but according to Dr. B.R.Ambedkar (ibd) it is not division of labour but it is division of labourers. It has been reproduced with new changing order. It is fact that jobs which are vulnerable and with less payment or remuneration in informal sector are maintained for weaker sections of society such as Scheduled Castes, Scheduled Tribes and to some extent

Other Backward Communities. To maintain social stability upper caste think that lower caste person should stick to their traditional status during job. That happens in formal and informal sector of employment.

Migration in general and labour migration in particular is not new phenomena in the history of mankind and particularly in India but it is an integral part of all changing social structures. The importance of free migration is already known by visionary social scientist and they realized that it helps society to become more dynamic and so it must be promoted as a part of social agenda. The fact of the matter is that the constitution of India has also recognized the importance of free movement of its citizens as basic right. It helps to the state and nation to become more vibrant in all fields of human life.

Although, migration is an essential feature of developing and developed societies and it has been recognized by all modern social system. Migration in India takes place in the informal sector of economy is always considered as a result or outcome of poverty, drought, backwardness and some social and economic compulsion people migrate. Those who migrate they are considered as outsiders though legally they are not, most of the population in this group come from weaker sections of Indian society and migrate between rural to rural and rural urban stream. However, migration by the people from upper caste and class is always welcomed with open heart and mind, particularly from urban to urban migration. Why state is not proactive to protect the interest of migrant from weaker sections of Indian society. This tendency of indifference is found in mainstream social and political order. They feel migration of lower caste communities is something which is problematic for all and so the migration of labour is more victim of such ideology in India.

Seasonal migration of wage labourers in the field of sugarcane harvesting areas of Western Maharashtra is not age old phenomena but it has come into existence with the changes in agrarian policies of the government forced by capitalist agenda. Reforms in the sector of agriculture in Maharshtra is the result of capitalist agenda for making profit through the development of new seed technology, chemicals and fertilizers imported through established corporate links. Second factor which plays an important role in this capitalist setup is migrant labourers who are recruited through the established exploitative system of contractorship. Labourers come from backward areas of Marathwada and Vidharbha region as well as from western Maharashtra region but most of them come from Beed district of Marathwad which is also popularly known in maharshtra as the district of sugarcane cutters. The constitution of India has provision to ensure and reduce social and economic disparity among the groups and regions but fortunately people in power have no regret in continuing disparities in the state. The efforts of the state governments are not sufficient to ensure social and economic disparities.

There was desperate need to investigate this type of movement facilitated by the agenda of capitalist mode of development. The social and economic background of the migrant show that they are from historically neglected and marginalized groups and communities such as Scheduled Castes, Scheduled Tribes, De-notified and Nomadic Tribes and Other Backward Classes. The presence of uppercatse in this kind of labour is negligible. So this has become site of economic exploitation of labourers because they come from downtrodden section of Society.

Agricultural Reforms and Disparities

Agricultural and allied activities are source of income and livelihood of larger section of population of India. Two third of Indians depend on farm for their income and livelihood. It is unfortunate that even after more than 65 years of Independence from British colonial rule more than half of the countries cultivated areas do not have irrigation facilities. Reforms in the agriculture sector in north India were initiated under the pressure of corporate lobbies. We are paying price for the same now. However, no radical farm reforms yet formulated or implemented successfully by successive government in power, only under the name of reform healing touch offered. Because of Lack, of permanent employment in manufacture and Service sector unemployed at farm are migrating to other places for their survival. This has been one of the neglected areas in planning and policy of the government of Indian affecting the vulnerable section badly.

Regional Disparities and Migration in Maharashtra

Constitution of India has entrusted the responsibility of constitutional head of development board who has to ensure regional imbalance and regional disparity does not increase beyond certain point of limit. However, the grassroot level picture is entirely different, very rarely government of Maharashtra has shown the interest in implementing the orders issued by the head of development boards. Backlog in various sector of development has been been increasing day by day. It is affecting the chances of improving the quality of life in the regions of Marathwada and Vidharbha as compared to other regions. Why this must be happening? There must be some reasons for that one of them is, the representatives of these regions are always sidelined in power structure by mainstream politician. The heads of almost all political parties are not from Marathwada and Vidharbha Background. (GoM-2015).

Sugar Industry in Maharashtra

The beginning of commercial sugar industry in western Maharashtra is very recent phenomena and it is mostly run on cooperative basis. Sugar industry in Maharashtra is one of the organized industries in rural area of Maharashtra. Some scholars believe that the sugar sector has changed the agricultural life styles and outlook of agricultural development. The nature of sugar Industry can be understood by the number of sugar industries are set up in the state. Most of the units are established in politically dominant areas of western Maharashtra.There are some functional units exist in Marathwada and Vidharbha but the crushing capacity of these units is very weak as compared to western Maharashtra units because of regional backwardness. So that most of the labour force prefer to migrate to western Maharashtra to earn wages for long time. There are no formal figures available about seasonal migrant labourers anywhere that's why only estimates are made. Usually more than ten Lakh men and women migrate every year to western Maharashtra for sugarcane harvesting. It has also changed the socio-economic and political ethos of the rural life in certain parts of Maharashtra particularly of western Maharashtra. Sugar industry is mostly dependent on unorganized farm sector workers, almost known as cane harvesters and transport workers. These workers are migrating from drought zone of Maharashtra, particularly from Latur, Beed, Latur and Parbhani districts of the state. The nature of monsoon also affects the seasonal migration of labourers. Sometime migration decline due to the development activities in the original places and better monsoon too at the original places of migrants. This also illustrates the role of migration in the development of the sugar sector in the western Maharashtra.

Caste composition and social ranking among the migrant workers

The data with regard to the socio-economic background and working conditions at destination of migrant sugarcane cutters was collected by author for his doctoral work in 2009 and still he has touch with the happenings of field. The data about socio-economic background and their plight at destination clearly highlight that the rights of labour class are openly violated in all aspects. Minimum facilities like food, shelter and security of children and women from harassment by others are everyday phenomena which are unrecorded. Atrocities by local people and by middleman is their part of life. The caste system is responsible for all this because they cannot get united at destination because of caste background. The essence of caste hierarchy is the absence of equality among the units which form the whole. In this regard M.N. Srinivas (1969) great known sociologist in India observed through his field work that various castes in Rampura, do form hierarchy.

The caste units are separated by endogamy and commensality and they are associated with rank differences of dietary and occupation. Yet it is difficult if not impossible, to determine the exact, or even approximate place of each caste in hierarchal order. The caste generally represents a distinct ethnic group with its own history, traditions and identifications and each caste live in more or less separate quarter of village. Lewis (1969) in his study of Ranikhera Hindu Village of eleven hundred people, about fifteen miles from New Delhi, the national capital found that there are separate wells for Harrijans or Untouchables. Dining and smoking between higher and lower castes are still taboo. Low caste people will not sit together on the same Cot for village meeting. Same kind of exploitation and humiliation is associated with caste hierarchy system and exists almost all parts of India. All the castes continued to be endogamous and maintained specific social distances among them. Each caste had an occupation sanctioned by tradition and these occupations were monopolies not to be infringed, except in the case of agriculture, which all freely pursued.

Hiramani (1977) in his study on caste has observed that the caste, which has its roots in religion and has been reared by the socio-economic forces and recognized by the erstwhile political structure, had once occupied and even now occupies a pivotal place in the village social life. Naturally caste has been studied as religious, social, economic and political unit of the society, although all these aspects are interdependent. Recent studies have been able to register some changes in them and they have tried to correlate them with different social forces. The structure of caste hierarchy is shown by Hiramani (ibid) in his studies in Maharashtra society.

The heterogeneity of composition of migrant workers is reflected in the form of different castes. It is worth noting that none among the higher caste is in the category of migrant sugarcane cutters and transporting (bullock cart) workers. The middle caste is represented by Maratha, the lower middle caste represented by Kumbhar and Nhavi, the lower castes are represented by Vanjari, Dhangar, Hatkar and Lamani, whereas the lowest in the caste hierarchy is exhibited by the Chambhar, Mang, Bhil and Mahar. The proportion of migrant sugarcane cutting and transporting workers belonging to lowest as against, middle caste. This phenomenon is also reflected in the studies on migrant sugarcane cutting and transporting workers conducted by Kasar (1992) and Jugale (1997).The socio-economic conditions of the seasonal migrants seem more or less same in the Maharashtra (Guru 1989).

TABLE 1
Caste hierarchy and social ranking among migrant workers

Caste	*Rank*	*Percentage*
Brahman, Kshtrya, Vaishya	Higher-I	Nil
Maratha	Middle-II	29.5
Gujar, Kumbhar, Nhavi	Lower Middle-III	8.5
Vanjari, Dhangar, Hatkar, Lamani	Lower-IV	24.5
Chambhar, Mang, Bhil, Mahar	Lowest (Untouchables)-V	36.5
Kasab (Muslim)	Other	1.0
Total		100.0

It can be said while broadly speaking such hierarchies also operate throughout Maharashtra. The caste composition of migrant sugarcane cutters and transporting workers is mainly made up of middle, lower, and lowest castes (see Table 1). This is shown in the following way: caste hierarchy found in Maharashtra is still operating through its own way of superior and inferior status in social life. This kind of experience is found at place where workers settlements are made. Workers from scheduled castes were kept at outside of main settlements at factory site.

Table 2 reveals that the relationship between caste and reasons of migration. It is very clear that all different caste groups have different causes for migration which are highlithed. Both Marathas (45 cases) and Scheduled Castes (Mang, Mahar,) and Gujar and Dhangar are effected by absence

TABLE 2
Caste Composition and Reasons for Migration

Caste	*Migration Reasons*			*Total*
	Non economic expenditure and Underemployment	*No source of work for survival*	*Absence of source of irrigation*	
Maratha	10	45	4	59
Gujar	0	10	2	12
Kumbhar	0	2	1	3
Nhavi	2	0	0	2
Vanjari	12	6	0	18
Dhangar	7	9	2	18
Telangi	1	0	0	1
Hatkar	1	1	0	2
Lamani	1	9	0	10
Chambhar	1	3	1	5
Bhil	4	0	0	4
Mang	17	15	1	33
Mahar	16	14	1	31
Kasab (Muslim)	0	2	0	2
Total	72	116	12	200

Source: Field data collected by author

of source of irrigation in their native and infertility of land. No proper source for survival or no proper employment opportunities at native are dominant causes of migration. In few cases, it was reported that the reasons for migration are such as no irrigation facilities at native and good earning at destination.

For some migrants, place of destination is nothing more significant to satisfy the causes. Most of them were reluctant at native employment schemes such as employment guarantee scheme and others which possibly give guaranteed employment at native, because all rural public programmes are very vulnerable to corruption. It is generally relatively easy for the site managers to exaggerate the amount of earth work actually done, and the number of workers appeared on the muster roll. Long delays in the payment of wages to the workers are common. Caste-wise details are given in above table which reveals the fact that most of the workers are marginal farmers; they have come due to economic causes and underemployment at native place. Some of them listed causes like good earning, at destination and no irrigation facilities at native. However some workers have listed causes like no other proper source to survive. This paper highlights how regional disparity and intersectoral migration of weaker section people is neglected phenomena by civil society members. Labourers are the backbone of any kind of economic development and if we neglect the interest of these section, development cannot be sustainable.

References

Ambedkar, Babasheb (1917), "Castes in India: Their Mechanism, Genesis and Development". Anthropology Seminar of Dr. A. A. Goldenweizer at The Columbia University, New York, U.S.A. on 9th May 1916. Source: *Indian Antiquary*, May 1917, Vol. XLI. Republished by Government of Maharashtra as writing and Speeches of Dr. Babasheb Ambedkar (2010).

GoM.2015.http://rajbhavan.maharashtra.gov.in/Pages/frm_governer_resposibilities.aspx

Guru, Gopal (1989), "Cooperative Sugar Industry and Sugar Workers Movement in Maharashtra—A Study", in *Second Maharashtra Rajya Sugar Workers Conference*, Nifad, Nasik on 1 and 2 October.

Hiramani, A.B. (1977), *Social Change in Rural India: A Study of Two Villages in Maharashtra*. Delhi: B.R.Publishing Corporation.

Jugale, V.B., (1997), *Employment Wages and Industrial Relations*. New Delhi: Classical Publishing Company.

Kasar, D.V. (1992), *Economics of Seasonal Migration*. New Delhi: Classical Publishing Company.

Lewis, Oscar (1969), "Peasant Culture in India and Mexico: A Comparative Analysis," in McKim Marriott. (eds.), *Village India: Studies in the Little Community*, (145-170). Chicago and London: The University of Chicago Press.

Oommen, T.K. (2001), Understanding Indian Society: The Relevance of Perspective from Below. Occasional Paper Series-4. Department of sociology University of Pune Pune.

Srinivas, M.N. (1969), "The Social System of a Mysore Village," in Marriott, McKim (eds.) *Village India: Studies in the Little Community*, (1-35). Chicago and London: The University of Chicago Press.

19

Poverty, Malnutrition and Health Status of Tribal Population in North-western Part of Maharashtra

K. C. Ramotra

Introduction

In India the scheduled castes and the scheduled tribes are such communities, which are deemed as downtrodden communities; they are not only economically but also socially occupy the bottom position. The tribals are generally stricken with absolute poverty, not only in the economically backward state of Bihar, Orissa or Madhya Pradesh but also in an advance state like Maharashtra, which is one of the most industrialized and urbanized states in the country. It is astonishing to note that the tribals lagging much behind the non-tribals in terms of poverty and overall health status. The main focus of discourse is on tribal poverty, malnutrition and health that are very much interrelated and inter dependent. The word 'Tribe' denotes a group of people living in primitive or barbarous conditions. It is a social group with territorial affiliation of function. They have a head man or a chief who controls the activities of the group. The constitution of the Indian Union (Article 366) has defined 'Scheduled Tribes' as such tribes or tribal communities or parts of or groups within such tribes or tribal communities as are deemed under article 342 to be Scheduled Tribes for the purpose of Constitution (Desai, 1977, pp. 17-18). In tribal societies the relations of production are still homogenous barring a few those who have commenced sedentary agriculture or have migrated to urban area for earning their livelihood. It is easy to understand that tribal societies are un-stratified, their economy is underdeveloped, and specialization is absent wherein producers themselves are consumers (Beteille, 1977, p12).

Nutrition is defined as the science of food and its relationship to health. It is concerned primarily with the part played by nutrients in body growth, development and maintenance (Park, 526). Malnutrition has been defined by the World health organization (WHO) as "a pathological state resulting from a relative or absolute deficiency or excess of one or more essential nutrients. This state being clinically manifested or detected only either by biochemical anthropometric or physiologic test". Malnutrition is a general term for medical condition caused by an improper or insufficient diet. The immediate causes are inadequate dietary intake and infectious diseases, the underlying causes are household food insecurity, inadequate maternal and child care and inadequate health services and health environment, and the basic causes include formal and non-formal institutions, political and ideological superstructure, economic structure and political resources (World Bank, 2011). Malnutrition implies here the absence of freedom to lead a healthy life. Under-nutrition, the leading form of malnutrition in the South Asian countries, would further imply the absence of freedom to lead minimally healthy life (Sen, 1992:44). Amartya Sen (1999,36,19) has also developed the capability approach to development that means the essence of development as the expression of human capabilities rather than the maximization of utility or its proxy, income. Development requires the renewal of major resources. Any person, not only free from diseases but also mentally fit and capable to perform his duties or to do his work is called a healthy person. Generally it is a state of good condition of body and mind to be able to resist diseases. Quite a substantial proportion of tribals suffer from chronic energy deficiency indicated by body mass index (BMI) below 18.5. Among others, health depends upon the various parameters like adequate food with all necessary vitamins and proteins, housing condition, favourable environment conditions, state of mind, etc.

Poverty can be defined as social phenomena in which a section of the society is unable to fulfil its basic necessities of life. When a substantial segment of a society is deprived a minimum level of living and condition of substance level, that society is said to be plagued with mass poverty (Dutt and Sundram, 1982). Rath (2011:40) a well known economist quotes P.V. Sukhatame—that an average Indian (average age, sex, region, and work patterns), needed 2250 kilocalories per day. And D.T. Lakadawal in 1991 on the basis of the advice of nutrition experts, the expert committee adopted 2400 calories per day for rural persons and 2100 calories per head for urban persons as the norm. Any person who is unable to buy this is a poor.

Objective

The present study intends to measure poverty, malnutrition and body mass index (BMI) of the scheduled tribes to comprehend their overall health status in north western part of Maharashtra state.

Study Area

The area undertaken for the present study is north-western part of Maharashtra comprising four district viz. Nandurbar, Dhule, Nashik and Thane and 40 tahsils with on an average 43.09 per cent of the total tribal population in the state of Maharashtra, that lies between $22^0 06'$ and $18^0 42'$ North latitude and $72^0 45'$ and 75^0 $11'$ East longitude. As many as 25 tribal villages have been selected, which spread over the entire study area, that 10 villages from Dhule and 5 each from Nandurbar, Nashik and Thane districts. Near about 1066 or

23 per cent households were selected from the 25 villages wherein the proportion of the scheduled tribes was above 50 per cent, for collecting the primary data by conducting intensive fieldwork during 2006-09 to bring out the hidden grass-root reality which made us to comprehend the living conditions and their surrounding environment where they reside. The food what sort of they consume that includes food grains, pulses, vegetables, milk, eggs, meat, fish, fat, etc and as per the table given by Gopalan, et.al. (1972) for computing the caloric intake and accordingly it was computed. for adult tribals the average calorie requirement for moderate work with body weight about 60 kg considered 2875 kilocalories and for children up to the 6 age group was on an average 1465 kilocalories (Gopalan, et.al., 1972). The work which tribals pursue is mostly moderate to heavy, hence the average requirement of calories is considered for a moderate work.

The nutritional requirement is primarily concerned with the promotion, protection and maintenance of health in all groups of the population. They are reference standards of nutritional intake. For all nutrients, except energy, estimates of allowances are based on the defined "minimum requirements" plus safety margin, often generous, for individual variation and stresses of everyday life (Park, 2009: 547). Some calories (nearly 10%) are also lost while cooking the food. Hence, it needs to be added the standard mean to meet the needed requirement of an individual.

Body mass index (BMI) is one of the important indices to determine the health on the basis of weight and height and can be computed as follows:

$$\text{BMI: } \frac{\text{Weight in Kg}}{\text{Height in Metre}^2}$$

Whereas, BMI stands for Body Mass Index

Body mass index is a simple index of weight for height that is commonly used to classify underweight, overweight and obesity in adults (Park, 2009:347). For example, an adult who weight 64 kg and whose height is 1.65m will have BMI of

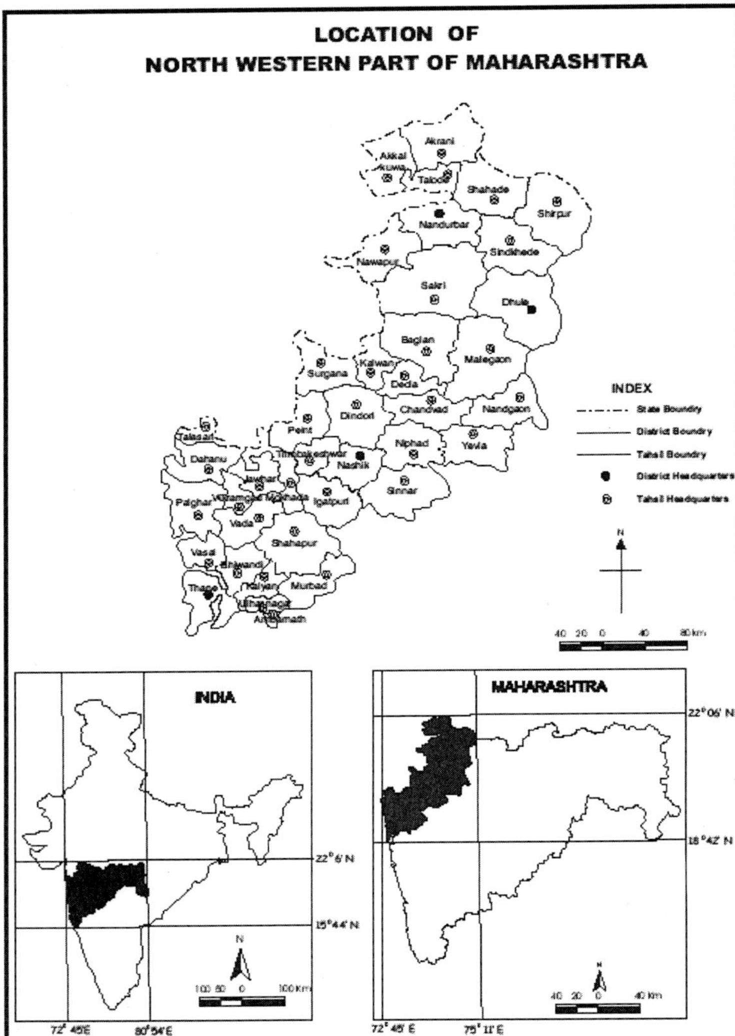

Fig. 1.1

23.5 with normal weight.

Attempts to measure the poverty in India dates back to pre-independence but since 1950s onwards a systematic effort has been made to define poverty line and then estimated the population of poor (Rath, 2011, p.4).

People below poverty line have been estimated on the basis of minimum required calorie an individual or house having. The D. T. Lakadawala committee in 1991 the planning commission appointed for calculating poverty line and submitted its report in 1993 on the advice of nutrition experts in 1993 adopted 2400 calories per day for rural person and 2100 calories per day for urban person.

Finally in 2009 the planning commission set up the expert committee under the chairmanship of Suresh D. Tendulkar who used the National Sample Survey organization for the year 2004-05 for computing the poverty. The Tendulkar committee originally calculated on the basis of a basket of food providing normative calories enabled the person or household to purchase that basket, the change in food consumption and calories was a matter of consumer choice that must be respected therefore, in this connection for the purpose of computing poverty among the tribals as per the Tahsildar office Nashik in 2008-09 any family with an average of four members with annual income (for all sources) below Rs 20,000/- or below Rs 5000/- per member of the family is deemed to be below poverty line (BPL) and those who were having income above Rs 20,000/- were considered as above poverty line (APL).

Malnutrition Among Tribal Children (Below 06)

The problem of malnutrition in India is a serious one since every third adult and 2/5ths of children are underweight due to malnutrition and more than 50 per cent of them die because of this problem (NFHS, 2005-06). The state of health of children, no doubt is serious one in Madhya Pradesh, Bihar, Uttar Pradesh, Orissa, etc. but it is astonishing to notice in Maharashtra, which is one of the advanced states in India in terms of industrialization, urbanization and per capita income.

The health and family welfare ministry (2010-11) estimated that 17 lakh children under the age of 5 die within first week. The main cause of deaths is malnutrition, diarrhoea, pneumonia and measles. This sort of serious problem of malnutrition in India is shame for country was well spelled out by the Prime Minister India in his speech on Jan 10, 2012 as India could not mitigate the level of malnutrition fast enough. This problem is very much related with poverty, hygiene-conditions, illiteracy, impure drinking water, no attention paid to mother during pre-delivery period, etc. the infant mortality has come down from 45 in 2001 to 31 in 2009 in the state of Maharashtra and hardly 10 to 15 per cent cases are of unsafe deliveries in the state. The state has been doing progress but at snails space.

Calorie Intake Index and Tribal Heath

The north-western part of Maharashtra comprises Nandurbar, Dhule, Nashik, and Thane, is the area undertaken for the present study where more than 43.09 per cent of the total tribal population in the state is concentrated having very serious problem of malnutrition and under-weight of children below the age of 0-6. As per our survey, (2006-09) it is found that on an average 56.03 per cent tribal children in this part suffer from insufficient calorie intake. They are so malnourished and under-weight that their poor health condition itself reflects from them. This insufficient intake of calorie problem is very much related to their extremely poverty stricken condition. In the entire study area, out of 25 sample villages this malnutrition problem varies from a minimum of 33.33 per cent in Lagadwal village in Sakri tahsil of Dhule district to a maximum of 96.55 per cent in Borvan in Dindori tahsil of Nashik district. In about six villages Lagadwal (33.33%), Kondaibari (34.50%), Bardipada (36.36%) and Raikot (38.46%) in Sakri tahsil of Dhule district, Nyahale (37.50%), Sulyachpada (37.50%) in Jawhar tahsil of Thane district where 30-40 per cent children were having food much less than what it was required (1465) calories although these villages have shown the better status as compared to other parts of study area. In about half a dozen villages, for instance, Dhaner, Amli, Umbaripada, Torankudi and Navagaon in Dhule district and Koch in Thane are such where 41 to less than 50 per cent children were not getting sufficient food. Five of these six villages fall in Sakri tahsil of Dhule district only and Koch in Mokhada tahsil of Thane district, having substantial problem of malnutrition and under-nutrition among children 0-6 age group. In about 13 villages 25 sample villages, this problem of malnutrition was evidently serious where 50 per cent or more were down with this problem. In about nine villages the proportion of children with insufficient availability of food has raised from 50 to 80 per cent. These villages are Ghatkarpada (50.00%) in Mokhada tahsil, Karamba (55.56%) in Jawhar tahsil of Thane district, Boratipada (66.92%) in Sakri tahsil of Dhule district, Surgas (67.74%), Bijaligavhan (75.61%) and Vegi (76.19%) in Akkalkuwa tahsil of Nandurbar district. The study has identified the villages with very serious problems of malnutrition (Table 1). These are four villages where almost all children were malnourished. The range of malnourished children is from above 80 per cent to above 96 per cent. For instance, Bardi (84.40%) and Pimpalkhuta (96.19%) in Akkalkuwa tahsil of Nandurbar district, Bhatode (93.33%) and Borvan (96.55%) in both of these villages in Dindori tahsil of Nashik district.

Overall Calori Intake Index

It is found that the overall calorie intake for the whole tribal population in the area under study was such that near about 56 per cent of the tribal population was having food much less than what it was required daily (2875 calories) for an adult man moderately active and 11 villages were above average condition of malnutrition. The difference between overall index and the index for 0-6 age group of children does not show much difference but in case of the children it is slightly high. This index explicitly shows that tribals in the north-western part of Maharashtra where they are highly concentrated are mostly malnourished as they hardly get adequate food to eat. This sort of problem is common in almost all tribal villages. The problem of malnutrition ranges from a minimum of 21.05 per cent in Amli village in Sakri tahsil of Dhule district to a maximum of 92.59 per cent in Borvan village in Dindori tahsil of Nashik district. The Table.1 vindicates that some of the villages in Nashik and Nandurbar district are highly affected with malnutrition problem.

The villages like Amli (21.05%), Dhaner (31.03%), Umbaripada (33.93%), Lagadwal (35.03%), in Sakri tahsil of Dhule district, Bhanwad (36.56%) in Dindori tahsil of Nashik district where 20 to 40 per cent tribal people fall in insufficient calorie intake index. It is further found that there were as many as five villages viz. Kondaibari (43.18%), Torankudi (47.50%), Boratipada (47.62%) and Raikot (47.92%) in Sakri tahsil of Dhule district and Koch (47.07%) in Mokhada tahsil of Thane district get insufficient food. In all there are 10 villages where about above 22 to less than 50 per cent tribals do not get the adequate calorie for their health maintenance in the north-western part of Maharashtra. In the remaining 15 villages out of 25 sample villages, which constituted of 60 per cent of total villages in which majority of tribals ranging above 50 per cent to about 93 per cent get insufficient food. As many as six villages for instance, Bardipada, Chandikapur, Ghatkarpada, Sulyachpada, Nyahale and Karamba fall in the range of above 50 to 60 per cent of insufficient food intake.

In about nine villages the condition is quite serious, for instance, Navagaon (60.00%) in Sakri tahsil of Dhule district, Phopsi (60.52%) in Dindori tahsil of Nashik district, Surgas (62.52%), Vegi (64.28%), Bijaligavhan (70.37%), Bardi (79.44%) and Pimpalkhuta (92.19%), Bhatode (86.36%) and Borvan (92.59%) in Dindori tahsil of Nashik district. It very clearly shows that Bhatode, Pimpalkhuta and Borvan are the villages where the problem of inadequate food supply and malnutrition is almost common of each household. The village Borvan has been identified the most serious one both in terms of child health as well as in overall health status of the tribal people in Dindori tahsil of Nashik district. In about 11 villages the proportion of tribals with insufficient food intake was above the average of 55.37 per cent of the study area.

Body Mass Index

Body Mass Index (BMI) is a simple index of weight-for-height which is commonly used by doctors to comprehend

TABLE 1

Overall Calorie Intake Index Of Scheduled Tribes in Sample Villages, 2006-09

Sr. No.	*Name of village*	*Name of Tahsils*	*Name of Dist*	*Total Household*		*0-6 Age Group*	
				Suffi-cient	*Insuffic-ient*	*Suffi-cient*	*Insuffi-cient*
1	Chandikapur	Dindori	Nashik	45.45	54.54	33.33	66.66
2	Bhanwad	Dindori	Nashik	63.46	36.53	37.03	62.96
3	Bhatode	Dindori	Nashik	13.63	86.36	6.66	93.33
4	Borvan	Dindori	Nashik	7.24	92.59	3.44	96.55
5	Popsi	Dindori	Nashik	39.47	60.52	23.07	76.92
6	Vegi	Akkalkuwa	Nandurbar	35.72	64.28	23.81	76.19
7	Bijaligavhan	Akkalkuwa	Nandurbar	29.83	70.37	24.39	75.61
8	Bardi	Akkalkuwa	Nandurbar	20.56	79.44	15.6	84.4
9	Surgas	Akkalkuwa	Nandurbar	37.25	62.75	32.26	67.74
10	Pimpalkhuta	Akkalkuwa	Nandurbar	7.81	92.19	3.85	96.15
11	Umbaripada	Sakri	Dhule	66.07	33.93	58.06	41.94
12	Dhaner	Sakri	Dhule	68.97	31.03	58.82	41.18
13	Amli	Sakri	Dhule	78.95	21.05	58.33	41.67
14	Navagaon	Sakri	Dhule	40.00	60.00	53.85	46.15
15	Raikot	Sakri	Dhule	52.08	47.92	61.54	38.46
16	Bardipada	Sakri	Dhule	47.69	52.31	63.64	36.36
17	Boratipada	Sakri	Dhule	52.38	47.62	33.33	66.67

18	Kondaibari	Sakri	Dhule	56.82	43.18	65.38	34.62
19	Torankudi	Sakri	Dhule	52.50	47.50	57.69	42.31
20	Lagadwal	Sakri	Dhule	64.79	35.21	66.67	33.33
21	Koch	Mokhada	Thane	52.94	47.06	58.82	41.18
22	Ghatkarpada	Mokhada	Thane	44.44	55.56	50.00	50.00
23	Nyahale	Jawhar	Thane	42.00	58.00	62.50	37.50
24	Karamba	Jawhar	Thane	41.67	58.33	44.44	55.56
25	Sulyachpada	Jawhar	Thane	44.44	55.56	62.50	37.50
	Average			44.25	55.75	43.97	56.03

Source: Fieldwork, 2006-09

the health of an individual whether he/she is underweight, overweight or obese and accordingly the treatment is given to the patient. It is defined as the weight in Kilograms (Kg) divided by the square of the height in metres (i.e. Kg/M^2) (Park, 2009). The classification of underweight, overweight (fat) and obesity is presented in Table 2. The scale determines that if the BMI value is below 18.5 then a person is considered underweight, from 18.5 – 21 is light underweight, index value 21-25 indicates normal weight, above 25 to 30 is overweight or fat and with index value over 30 is considered obese. The most crucial about a person is if the BMI is below 18.5 and over 30. In both the cases the health of an individual becomes alarming one as it can cause blood pressure, anaemia, coronary diseases, etc.

It is found that more than one-third of the tribal population was underweight with much below the BMI value of 18.5 in the north-western part of Maharashtra. The main health problem of tribals in this part is that where they are highly concentrated they are mostly poverty stricken and not capable to buy the food grains supplied by the government under Public Distribution System for them. Nearly 52 per cent (or13) villages out of 25 sample villages, tribals were extremely underweight as the BMI was much below 18.5 and the proportion of tribals with this severe condition was above the average (34.85%) for the study area. Above 29 per cent tribals were having light underweight with BMI 18.5-21. It means nearly two-thirds of them were underweight. This underweight problem is very much pertaining to the malnutrition and is quite serious in Akkalkuwa tahsil of Nandurbar district wherein village Vegi was with nearly 53 per cent tribals were extremely underweight closely followed by other villages like Bardi (47.1%), Pimpalkhuta (42.07%), Surgas (41.13%) and Bijaligavhan (40.5%) in Nandurbar district with above 65% tribal population is highly affected with malnutrition problem and causing high mortality rate. The district of Nandurbar in north-western part of the state was found worst hit with 1191 malnourished children in November, 2004 followed by Thane (793) and Nashik (717) district. Because of this severe malnutrition problem, they suffer from various diseases like Scabies and Stomach problems particularly among the children below 6. Tribal deaths especially the children occurred in Nandurbar and other water borne diseases particularly in monsoon season, the period during which neither they have sufficient food to eat and nor potable drinking water. Moreover, the transport and communication is very poor. Medical facilities are neither available nor accessible spatially as well as economically. In Dhule district as per our survey (2006-09) the underweight (< 18.5 BMI) population varied from about 25-30 per cent. Seriously affected villages were Umbaripada (46.86%), Navagaon (38.39%), Raikot (32.28%) and Dhaner (35.87%) in Sakari tahsil of Dhule district were the proportion is above the average of the study area (34.85%). Thane district which is an adjoining part of Mumbai metropolitan capital of the state, is also substantially affected with malnutrition problem as the proportion of tribals with underweight (below < 18.5 BMI) ranged between with a minimum of 27.53 per cent in Karamba village in Jawhar tahsil to a maximum of 40.68 per cent in Sulyachpada village in the same tahsil of the Thane district. Therefore, Sulyachapada (40.68%), Ghatkarpada (36.51%) and Koch (36.50%) were severely and Karamba (27.53%) was moderately affected with underweight problem of tribals in Dhule district. Being in the close proximity of Mumbai metropolitans, tribals are malnourished and dying away as they are not able to buy the food grains made available on Government *Rashan* Depots due to their crushing poverty condition.

Tribals with normal weight having to a certain extent normal health were hardly one-fourth of the tribal population. In about 10 of the 25 sample villages, the tribals found with normal weight were above the average of the study area (25.23%) and comparatively better in terms of their normal health were Boratipada (45.45%) Chandikapur (38.73%), Bardipada (36.56%), Lagadwal (33.71%), Kondaiwari (32.30%), Dhaner (30.53%), Raikot (29.27%), Bhanwad (26.58%), Nyahale (26.55%) and Vegi (25.64%) with BMI 21-25. Since the main problems of the tribals are poverty, malnutrition and

TABLE 2

Body Mass Index (BMI) of Scheduled Tribes in Sample Villages, 2006-09

Sr. No.	*Name of Village*	*Name of Tahsils*	*Name of Districts*	*Under weight below 18.5*	*Light Under -weight 18.5 to 21*	*Normal weight 21 to 25*	*Light Over weight 25to 30*	*Obese more than 30*
				%	%	%	%	%
1	Chandikapur	Dindori	Nashik	19.81	28.82	38.73	8.10	4.50
2	Bhanwad	Dindori	Nashik	29.76	26.01	26.58	10.11	7.51
3	Bhatode	Dindori	Nashik	36.64	22.90	22.9	9.16	8.39
4	Borvan	Dindori	Nashik	21.38	22.01	25.15	22.01	9.43
5	Popsi	Dindori	Nashik	32.43	24.87	23.17	12.92	6.58
6	Vegi	Akkalkuwa	Nandurbar	52.56	15.38	25.64	1.28	5.12
7	Bijaligavhan	Akkalkuwa	Nandurbar	40.5	30.37	21.57	4.43	3.16
8	Bardi	Akkalkuwa	Nandurbar	47.1	23.63	22.31	2.80	4.13
9	Surgas	Akkalkuwa	Nandurbar	41.13	29.74	23.73	3.79	1.58
10	Pimpalkhuta	Akkalkuwa	Nandurbar	42.07	28.04	20.73	3.65	5.48
11	Umbaripada	Sakri	Dhule	46.86	35.44	15.86	1.84	0.00
12	Dhaner	Sakri	Dhule	35.87	22.90	30.53	7.25	1.14
13	Amli	Sakri	Dhule	25.00	54.55	20.45	0.00	0.00
14	Navagaon	Sakri	Dhule	38.39	25.89	13.39	6.25	2.67
15	Raikot	Sakri	Dhule	38.28	27.47	29.27	4.95	0.00
16	Bardipada	Sakri	Dhule	31.56	23.43	36.56	8.43	0.00

17	Boratipada	Sakri	Dhule	32.92	21.59	45.45	0.00	0.00
18	Kondaibari	Sakri	Dhule	24.61	34.87	32.30	7.17	1.02
19	Torankudi	Sakri	Dhule	32.16	24.62	23.11	8.54	3.01
20	Lagadwal	Sakri	Dhule	30.00	31.71	33.71	5.14	0.00
21	Koch	Mokhada	Thane	36.50	36.5	18.51	5.82	2.64
22	Ghatkarpada	Mokhada	Thane	36.51	36.51	18.52	5.82	2.65
23	Nyahale	Jawhar	Thane	30.97	33.63	26.55	4.42	4.42
24	Karamba	Jawhar	Thane	27.53	35.63	24.29	6.48	6.07
25	Sulyachpada	Jawhar	Thane	40.68	38.98	11.86	4.24	4.24
	Average			34.85	29.42	25.23	6.18	3.35

Source: Fieldwork, 2006-09

underweight which form the vicious cycle of poverty, out of which they can't come out until external help is extended to them. Hardly 6.13 per cent and 3.35 per cent were with overweight (BMI 25-30) and above 30 respectively which is much less than the Maharashtra state as a whole wherein it ranged from in 12-15 per cent 15 to 49 age group (NFHS-3,2003-06, p. 19). They are mostly the people who are relatively well off as they have good cultivable fertile and irrigated land and or have been working in the nearby town or holding or held the position of *Sarpanch* (Head of the village) or something else. The severity in malnutrition of tribals is mainly due to their poverty and also due to the negligence of local administrative.

Tribal Poverty

The poverty stricken condition of a household affects the health of the entire family due to malnutrition, not that the food grains and other essential commodities are not available in the market, in fact, not able to buy. It is found that children of economically poor families failed to reach the development potential because of risk factors associated with poverty. The malnutrition is strongly associated with shorter adult height, less weight, less schooling and reduced economic productivity (Behman, 2009, p. 167). The incident of poverty among the scheduled tribes (45%) was much higher than what it was found among the scheduled castes (37%), Hindus (28%) and Muslims (33%) in 2004-05 in rural India (Thorat, 2011, p. 6 & 7). The overall poverty in the state of Maharashtra as computed by Tendulkar was 38.1 per cent in 2004-05 and has come down to 26.2 per cent in 2009-10 (Ahluwalia, 2011). It is found that, more than 51 per cent tribals in the tribal pockets were still below poverty line (in 2006-09) as per our field survey in 25 sample villages in north-western part of Maharashtra. Not only this, there are some tribal villages, which are identified with 100 poverty stricken, for instance, Pimpalkhuta and Surgas in Akkalkuwa tahsil of Nandurbar district, which are stricken with absolute poverty. Almost all the households were indicating their poverty from the outside structure of

TABLE 3
Proportion of BPL and Above BPL Households of Scheduled Tribes in Sample Villages, 2006-09

Sr. No.	*Name of village*	*Name of Tahsil*	*Name of District*	*Surveyed households*	*BPL*	*Above BPL*
1	Chandikapur	Dindori	Nashik	22	68.11	31.81
2	Bhanwad	Dindori	Nashik	52	59.61	40.38
3	Bhatode	Dindori	Nashik	22	68.18	31.81
4	Borvan	Dindori	Nashik	27	92.60	7.40
5	Popsi	Dindori	Nashik	76	68.42	37.57
6	Vegi	Akkalkuwa	Nandurbar	14	95.85	7.15
7	Bijaligavhan	Akkalkuwa	Nandurbar	27	96.29	3.71
8	Bardi	Akkalkuwa	Nandurbar	107	91.58	8.42
9	Surgas	Akkalkuwa	Nandurbar	51	100.00	0.00
10	Pimpalkhuta	Akkalkuwa	Nandurbar	64	100.00	0.00
11	Umbaripada	Sakri	Dhule	56	0.00	100.00
12	Dhaner	Sakri	Dhule	58	6.89	93.10
13	Amli	Sakri	Dhule	19	0.00	100.00
14	Navagaon	Sakri	Dhule	20	5.00	95.00
15	Raikot	Sakri	Dhule	48	8.33	91.67
16	Bardipada	Sakri	Dhule	65	7.69	92.30
17	Boratipada	Sakri	Dhule	21	0.00	100.00
18	Kondaibari	Sakri	Dhule	44	15.90	84.09
19	Torankudi	Sakri	Dhule	40	2.50	97.05

20	Lagadwal	Sakri	Dhule	71	11.26	88.72
21	Koch	Mokhada	Thane	34	73.52	26.47
22	Ghatkarpada	Mokhada	Thane	27	74.07	25.92
23	Nyahale	Jawhar	Thane	50	68.00	32.00
24	Karamba	Jawhar	Thane	24	91.66	8.33
25	Sulyachpada	Jawhar	Thane	27	74.07	25.92
	Average				50.47	49.53

Source: Fieldwork, 2006-09

TABLE 4

COL.NO	1	2	3	4	5	6	7	8	9	10	11
Sr.No	*Name of village*	*Total no. of surveyed house holds*	*No of house-holds with less than Rs 2500*	*%of less than 2500 per capita income*	*No of house-holds with Rs 2500 to 5000 per capita income*	*% of less than Rs 2500 to 5000 per capita income*	*Total of columns nos. (3+5)*	*% of column nos. (3+5)*	*No of house-holds with above Rs 5000 per capita income*	*% of house-hold with above Rs 5000 per capita income*	*Total % of income*
1	Chandikapur	22	2	9.09	14	63.63	16	72.72	6	27.27	100
2	Bhanwad	52	7	13.46	24	46.15	31	59.61	21	40.38	100
3	Bhatode	22	4	18.18	11	50.00	15	68.18	7	31.81	100
4	Borvan	27	14	51.85	5	18.51	19	70.37	8	29.62	100
5	Popsi	76	21	27.63	33	43.42	54	71.05	22	28.94	100
6	Vegi	14	12	85.71	1	7.15	13	95.85	1	7.15	100
7	Bijaligavhan	27	23	85.18	3	11.11	26	96.29	1	3.71	100
8	Bardi	107	78	72.89	20	18.69	98	91.58	9	8.42	100
9	Surgas	51	43	84.32	8	15.68	51	100	0	0	100
10	Pimpalkhuta	64	46	71.87	18	28.13	64	100	0	0	100
11	Umbaripada	56	0	0	0	0	0	0	56	100	100
12	Dhaner	58	2	3.44	2	3.44	4	6.89	54	93.10	100
13	Amli	19	0	0	0	0	0	0	19	100	100
14	Navagaon	20	0	0	1	5.00	1	5.00	19	95.00	100
15	Raikot	48	2	4.16	2	4.16	4	8.33	44	91.66	100
16	Bardipada	65	1	1.53	4	6.15	5	7.69	60	92.30	100
17	Boratipada	21	0	0.00	0	0.00	0	0.00	21	100	100
18	Kondaibari	44	0	0.00	7	15.90	7	15.90	37	84.09	100

19	Torankudi	40	1	2.50	0	0.00	1	2.50	39	97.05	100
20	Lagadwal	71	0	0.00	8	11.26	8	11.26	63	88.72	100
21	Koch	34	20	58.82	5	14.70	25	73.52	9	26.47	100
22	Ghatkarpada	27	17	62.96	3	11.11	20	74.07	7	25.92	100
23	Nyahale	50	22	44.00	12	24.00	34	68.00	16	32.00	100
24	Karamba	24	20	83.33	2	8.33	22	91.66	2	8.33	100
25	Sulyachpada	27	16	59.25	4	14.81	20	74.07	7	25.92	100
	Total	1066	351	32.93	538	17.35	538	50.47	528	49.53	100

VILLAGE LEVEL PER CAPITA INCOME, 2006-09

Source: Fieldwork, 2006-09

the house and in view of assets from inside. Not only this, there are some other villages where the poverty was very high, these are Borvan (92.60%) in Dindori tahsil of Nashik district, Vegi (95.85%), Bijaligavhan (96.29%), Bardi (91.58%) in Akkalkuwa tahsil of Nandurbar and Karamba (91.60%) in Jawhar tahsil of Thane district, more than 90 per cent tribals were stricken with poverty. In all there are seven villages ranged between above 90 and 100 per cent below poverty line. Some of the other villages like Chandikapur (68.11%), Bhanwad (59.61%), Batode (68.18%) and Pophsi (68.42%) in Dindori tahsil of Nashik district. Koch (73.52%) and Ghatakarpada (74.07%) in Mokhada tahsil of Thane district. Nyahale and Sulyachapada (74.07%) Jawhar tahsil of Thane district. The study investigated that out of 25 sample villages in 15 villages (i.e. 60% of villages) more than 51 per cent to 100 per cent tribals were below poverty line.

It is astonishing to note that almost all 10 villages like Umbaripada, Dhaner, Amli, Navagaon, Raikot, Bardipada, Boratipada, Kondaibari, Torankudi and Lagdwal in Sakri tahsil of Dhule district are such villages, which are mostly economically well off as nowhere, the proportion of tribals below poverty exceeds 10 per cent except Kondaibari (15.90%) and Lagdwal (11.26%). Within this, Dhaner, Amli and Boratipada have been identified with all households were above poverty line (APL).

It is concluded that, the tribal poverty is still at extreme, which can only be reduced by making the laws to bring back the lost resources like forest and land to them and provision of education, within the village or basic necessities of life have to be made available, which are within their reach.

Conclusion

It is inferred that malnutrition among the tribals in the north-western part of Maharashtra particularly among the children in the age group 0-6 is a serious one. It is found that 55.75 per cent tribal population was not getting adequate food as per our survey in 2006-09. In more than 15 sample villages the malnutrition was relatively very high as the calorie intake was much less than what it was required (2875) daily for a person who does moderately hard work.

Four villages like Borvan (92.59%), Bhatode (86.36%) in Dindori tahsil of Nashik district, Pimpalkhuta (92.19%) and Bardi (79.44%) in Akkalkuwa tahsil of Nandurbar district are identified with extremely serious problem of malnutrition.

In case of children in the age group 0-6, Bardi (84.4%) and Pimpalkhuta (96.15%) in Akkalkuwa tahsil of Nandurbar district, Bhatode (93.33%) and Borvan (96.55%) in Dindori tahsil of Nashik district having pitiable condition where the tribal children are trapped in a vicious circle of poverty and getting much low calorie intake than the required amount (1465). More than 56 per cent children in 0-6 age group suffer from malnutrition.

It is also found that about 35 per cent tribal population in north-western part of Maharashtra was underweight with BMI index value below 18.5, and above 29 cent with light under weight (18.5 to 21).

Nearly two-thirds of the tribal population was identified with underweight and one-fourth with normal weight (BMI 21 to 25).

Majority of tribals (50.47%) were stricken with poverty. Surgas and Pimpalkhuta villages are identified with absolutely 100 per cent below poverty line.

One-third of the tribal households in the study area were having per capita income below Rs 2500, considered extremely poor and 17.35 per cent moderately stricken with poverty as their per capita income was between Rs 2500 and Rs 5000. In all more than 50 per cent tribal population was below poverty line.

In comparison to planning commission of India (27.5%) and World Bank (41.6%) figures for population stricken with poverty, the proportion of tribal population with extreme poverty was much higher (above 50%).

The five villages extremely stricken with poverty are Borvan (92.60%), in Dindori tahsil of Nashik district. Bijaligavhan (96.29%), Vegi (95.85%), Bardi (91.88%) in Akkalkuwa tahsil of Nandurbar district and Karamba (91.66%)

in Jawahar tahsil of Thane district.

There is a strong correlation between poverty and malnutrition and significant at 1 % level. That means poverty leads to malnutrition and finally it affects the health of the tribals in general and their children more seriously in particular.

It is suggested that there is a dire need of basic infrastructural development. Pucca roads need to be constructed and bus service should be commenced immediately in this backward tribal area so as to have a good linkage between the tribal and advanced urban areas.

Provision of potable drinking water should be made available to all tribal areas in this pocket.

Provision of food grains on *Rashan* Depots in accordance with Public Distribution System has already made to a larger extent but the tribals hardly get the proper quantity and therefore it requires proper implementation so that needy people can get food grains as per the quantity per person is prescribed by the government.

Medical facility is an immediate requirement and should be provided with top priority to bring down the death rates in general and of tribal children due to malnutrition and other problems in particular.

It is also suggested that development of infrastructure in tribal areas should not lead their further exploitation. Their development is an uphill task but if it is being done honestly and sincerely and with political will, it will certainly bring development in tribal areas.

References

Ahluwalia, M. (2011), "Prospects and Policy Challenges in Twelfth Plan," *EPW*, Vol. XLVI, No. 2, pp. 88-105.

Behman, J. R. (2009), "Early Life Nutrition and Subsequent Education, Health, Wage and Intergeneration Effects" in Spencer, M and Lewis, M (eds), *Health and Growth*, The World Bank, Washington, D. C.

Beteille, Andhre (1977), "The Definition of Tribe", in Romesh Thapar, (ed), *Tribe, Caste and Religion in India*, Macmillan India Ltd., Delhi, p. 12.

Dasgupta, Rajaram (1989), *Nutritional Planning in India*, Navrang, New Delhi, p.1.

Desai, A.R. (1977), "Tribes in Transition" in Thapar, Romesh (ed), *Tribe, Caste and Religion in India*, Macmillan India Ltd., Delhi, pp.17-18.

Dutt, R. and Sundarm K. (1982), *Indian Economy*, S. Chand and Company Ltd, New Delhi.

Gopalan, C. et. al. (1977), *Nutritive Value of Indian Foods*, National Institute of Nutrition, Hyderabad, p. 1.

Hasnain, N. (1991), *Tribal India*, Palaka Prakashan, Delhi.

Mandal, B. Chattopadyah, M, and Gupta, R. (2005), "Economic Condition and Nutritional Status: A Micro Level Study among Tribal Population in Rural West Bengal, India," *Malnutrition*, 11 (2) 99-109.

National Family Health Survey (NFHS-3) - 2005-05, India (2008), Maharashtra, IIPS, Mumbai.

Park, K. (2009), "Textbook of Preventive and Social Medicine," Ms. Banarasidass Bharas Publisher, Jawalpur.

Rath, Nilakantha (2011), "Measurement of Poverty: In Retrospect and Prospect", *Economic and Political Weekly*, Vol. XLVI, No. 42, pp. 40-43.

Sen, A. (1992), *Inequality Re-examined*, Oxford University Press, New Delhi, p.44.

Sen, A. (1999), *Development as Freedom*, Oxford University Press, Oxford.

Thorat, Sukhadeo (2011), "Growth Inequality and Poverty Linkages During 1983-2005: Implications for Socially Inclusive Growth," *Indian Journal and Agricultural Economics*, Vol. 66, No. 1 (Jan-March), pp. 1-32.

White, Howard (2008), "The Measurement of Poverty" in Desai, Vandana and Potter, Robert B. (eds): The Companion to Development Studies (2nd editions), Hodder Education, London.

WHO (1986), "What it is, What it does, How it works", Geneva Quoted in Dasgupta,

Rajaram (1989), *Nutritional Planning in India*, Navrang, New Delhi, p.2.

World Bank/UNICEF (2011), Nutrition Assessment, Nutrition Section, Programme Division UNICEF, New York and Health Nutrition Population Unit, The World Bank, Washington D. C

20

Agricultural Priorities for Food Security in Western India

Vijay Laxmi Pandey & Niharika Venkatesh

I. Introduction

The Western region comprising of Gujarat, Maharashtra, Goa and Daman, together constituting approximately fifteen per cent of India's population and land area, contributes around twenty five per cent of the country's total GDP (Government of India (GoI), 2013). In the western region, Maharashtra and Gujarat together account for about ninety nine per cent of the population and 99.5 per cent of gross cropped area (Government of India, 2013; Ministry of Agriculture, 2014). The share of primary sector in total income of the region has reduced significantly, while the share of the secondary sector remained almost stagnant and the tertiary sector grew. In Maharashtra the share of agricultural sector has reduced from 24.7 per cent in 1980-1981 to 10.3 per cent in 2008-2009 while in Gujarat it has reduced from 37.2 per cent to 18.4 per cent. However, the number of people employed in agriculture has continuously increased. It has increased from 37.7 million in 2004-2005 to 38.9 million people in 2009-10 in Maharashtra and Gujarat (Ministry of Agriculture, 2014). Thus, agriculture is the major source of livelihood for more than fifty per cent of the population in the western region and more so in the rural areas, where incidence of poverty along with under-nutrition are high.

Intuitively one may expect that the higher economic growth would lead to better nutrition outcomes through increased income and food expenditures. On the contrary, the high economic growth in this region is not matched by the progress in human development and nutrition status. Except for Daman (which started off at a low base), the improvement in the health indicator (life expectancy at birth) and in Human Development Index (HDI) was quite below the national average (GoI, 2011). As per the IFPRI India State Hunger Index compiled for seventeen states, Gujarat and Maharashtra are at the bottom of the Hunger Index ranking, occupying thirteenth and tenth position respectively. These two states fall into the 'alarming' category, or second highest severity level in terms of hunger (Table 1). Maharashtra and Gujarat are also among the ten states having highest percentage of stunting in children below the age of five (46.3 per cent and 51.7 per cent respectively). Improvement in the prevalence of stunting over the period 1992-93 to 2005-06 has been lowest (Menon & Aguayo, 2011) in these two states.

Nutritional status can be measured through deficiencies in consumption of calories, vitamins and minerals. Chronic deficiencies in consumption of vitamins and minerals are called hidden hunger. Hidden hunger has no visible warning signs and therefore people who suffer from it may not even be aware of it. The focus of agricultural research on increasing production and profitability of the system was able to address calorie hunger but the issue of 'hidden hunger' has been relatively ignored (Das, Bhavani & Swaminathan, 2014).

Thus there is a greater need to emphasize the importance of the different aspects of food security from a policy perspective in order to speed up the progress. In the World Food Summit 1996, Food Security was defined as *"when all people at all times have access to sufficient, safe, nutritious food to maintain a healthy and active life"* (Food and Agriculture Organization, 2013). Thus the mainstays of food security are availability, access, stability and utilization. This paper deals with the research issues related to availability of balanced food in western region of India.

In this context the paper examines the issues related to food security in western region of India. Section II deals with the availability of balanced food, further divided into sub-sections (a) key focus areas of existing agricultural research (b) trend in area, productivity and yields of important crops and (c) consumption pattern in rural areas. Section III discusses the linkages between agriculture and nutrition and we conclude in section IV.

II. Availability of Balanced Food

Growth in agriculture has shown potential to address under-nutrition through its various direct and indirect linkages (Gillespie & Kadiyala, 2011) under conducive policy environment for right kind of priorities. These linkages are complex and they keep on evolving with changing agricultural policies, markets and consumer demand. Given the dependence of large percentage of population (almost 70 per cent) on agriculture in this region, it is imperative that focus of agricultural research and interventions shifts more towards availability of balanced food providing adequate amount of calories, protein, and micronutrients. This section deals with the key areas of research in this region, the cropping pattern change and the change in the consumption pattern.

II. a) Key focus areas of agricultural research

The agricultural research in this region has focused more on improving profitability and productivity of the system both through food and non-food crops. Most of the programs and policies in recent years were geared towards this goal, for example National Food Security Mission, Rashtrye Krishi Vikas Yojana, National Horticulture Mission etc. To an extent these interventions were quite successful as can be seen from the

TABLE 1

State Hunger Index, Human Development Index (HDI) and Gross State Domestic Product (GSDP)

State	*India State Hunger Index score (2008-2009)*	*India state hunger index rank*	*Consumption based HDI (2007-2008)*	*HDI rank*	*GSDP (2008-2009) in RsCrore*	*GSDP y-o-y growth rate (2008-09)*
Punjab	13.63	1	0.605	5	130,431	5.85
Kerala	17.63	2	0.79	1	162,659	5.56
Andhra Pradesh	19.53	3	0.473	15	327,731	6.88
Assam	19.83	4	0.444	16	64,033	5.72
Haryana	20	5	0.552	9	136,478	8.17
Tamil Nadu	20.87	6	0.57	8	321,793	5.45
Rajasthan	20.97	7	0.434	17	174,556	9.09
West Bengal	20.97	7	0.492	13	270,248	4.9
Uttar Pradesh	22.13	9	0.38	18	344,726	6.99
Maharashtra	22.8	10	0.572	7	610,191	2.58
Karnataka	23.73	11	0.519	12	244,421	7.11
Orissa	23.8	12	0.362	22	110,812	7.75
Gujarat	24.7	13	0.527	11	300,341	6.78
Chhattisgarh	26.63	14	0.358	23	68,982	8.39
Bihar	27.3	15	0.367	21	106,857	12.16
Jharkhand	28.67	16	0.376	19	70,129	-1.75
Madhya Pradesh	30.87	17	0.375	20	152,946	12.47
India [latest-2014]	17.8	55th (out of 120)	586 (latest: 0.2014 estimates for 2013)	135 (out of 187 countries)		

Source: Government of India, (2014a) and Menon, Deolikar & Bhaskar (2009)

Table 2 presenting agricultural GDP growth. The agricultural GDP growth of Maharashtra improved from 3.8 per cent during the period 1980-81 to 1989-90 to 4.8 per cent during 2000-01 to 2010-11. In Gujarat growth in agricultural GDP was remarkable as it improved from -1.0 per cent to 5.4 per cent during the same period (Table 2). For the period from 2000-01 to 2010-11 growth rates in these two states were much above the agricultural GDP growth at all India level. However, this was accompanied by a high level of instability in agricultural production in this region (Dev & Pandey, 2012). Due to increased availability and access, the number of people reporting lack of food has also reduced considerably from 3.1 per cent to 0.3 per cent in Gujarat and from 13 per cent to 1.1 per cent in Maharashtra from the year 1983 to 2004-05 (Deaton & Dreze, 2009).

Research focusing on diversification of agriculture towards high value agriculture and accelerating the growth through technological innovations were also given priority. One such example is adoption of Bt cotton in this region. To further boost the growth in agricultural sector marketing reforms were introduced. Agricultural Produce Market Committee (APMC) Model Act was implemented in Maharashtra and Gujarat which has given way to direct marketing and contract farming. Further, emphasis was also given on improving the irrigation potential and utilization in this region. However, almost 70 per cent of cultivated area still remains rainfed.

TABLE 2
Agricultural GDP Growth

	1980-1 to 1989-0	*1990-1 to 1999-0*	*2000-1 to 2010-1*
Maharashtra	3.83	3.84	4.84
Gujarat	-1.02	2.24	5.42
India	2.99	3.21	2.79

Source: Government of India 2013

The intra-regional and intra-state disparity and contradictions are quite pronounced in this region. For example, in Maharashtra, the suicide prone districts—Amravati, Yavatmal, Buldhana, Akola, Washim and Wardha have higher size of landholding as compared to state and national average (Kalamkar, 2010). It is important to note that in spite of this, crop cultivation is not economical in these areas. This is something that needs to be looked at more closely. However, efforts are underway to address this issue in the research and policy arena.

There is in general lack of emphasis on producing food for providing balanced food through agricultural research and interventions. Attention is needed to increase availability of nutritious food that caters to both macro and micro nutrient requirements. Biofortification of crops (achieved either through conventional plant breeding or through genetic engineering) have the potential to reduce micronutrient deficiencies and bring about health benefits (WHO, 2014). Appropriate location specific interventions for biofortification of crops especially the staples could contribute effectively towards alleviating malnutrition especially for the marginalized and vulnerable. However, further research and adequate policy support in this area is required to capitalize its benefits.

II b) Trends in area and productivity of major crops

The cropping pattern in the region has changed considerably. From the Table 3, it is apparent that there has been a consistent decline in the area under coarse cereals. The area under coarse cereals declined approximately by 17 per cent per decade since TE 1992-1993. On the other hand the area under sugarcane and cotton has increased considerably (Table 3). Thus overall there has been a shift away from food grain to cash crops in this region. The increase in area under sugarcane crop is cause of concern as it is a water intensive crop in a region which has only around 30 per cent area under irrigation.

At the same time, one can see that the average yield rates in the western region have increased across the crops, except

TABLE 3

Change in the Cropping Pattern in the Western Region

Crops	*Area under major crops ('000 hectares)*				*Change in cropped area (per cent change from previous period)*		
	TE 1982-83	*TE 1992-1993*	*TE 2002-2003*	*TE 2011-2012*	*TE 1992-1993*	*TE 2002-2003*	*TE 2011-2012*
Rice	2021.87 (6.65)*	2190.47 (6.74)	2209.97 (6.88)	2333.64 (6.59)	8.34	0.89	5.60
Wheat	1803.77 (5.94)	1362.67 4.19)	1272.47 (3.96)	2244.67 (6.34)	–24.45	–6.62	76.40
Coarse Cereals	11544.86 (37.99)	10821.30 (33.30)	8963.27 (27.91)	7366.65 (20.80)	-6.27	-17.17	-17.81
Pulses	3326.63 (10.95)	5931.73 (18.25)	4214.40 (13.12)	4431.64 (12.51)	78.31	-28.95	5.15
Oilseeds	4477.20 (14.73)	5390.20 (16.59)	5347.17 (16.65)	6663.99 (18.81)	20.39	-0.80	24.63
Cotton	4261.33 (14.02)	3777.77 (11.63)	4780.03 (14.88)	6540.33 (18.46)	-11.35	26.53	36.83
Sugarcane	331.53 (1.09)	543.50 (1.67)	773.87 (2.41)	1097.24 (3.10)	63.94	42.39	41.79
GCA	30387.9	32493.8	32116	35,422			

*Figures in parentheses indicate percentage share to gross cropped area in western region

Source: Ministry of Agriculture (2014)

for rice during the period 2005-11 (Table 4). This increase in yield is due to the extensive research that has been devoted towards increasing productivity.

TABLE 4
Trend Growth Rate of Yield of Major crops in Western Region (per cent)

Crop	*1980-84*	*1985-89*	*1990-94*	*1995-00*	*2000-04*	*2005-11*
Rice	-0.29	9.07	1.38	-6.93	4.36	-0.32
Wheat	0.86	6.99	5.57	-2.79	4.78	2.90
Coarse Cereals	-1.67	10.10	2.56	-1.16	1.62	4.72
Pulses	5.74	6.33	5.25	2.92	2.57	3.94
Oilseeds	-1.68	12.60	4.82	-1.17	8.20	2.95
Cotton	-0.31	4.58	9.60	-3.11	19.30	3.71
Sugarcane	0.03	0.16	-1.57	1.56	-4.53	2.43

Source: Ministry of Agriculture (2014)

II c) Consumption Pattern in Rural Areas

Recommended Daily Allowance (RDA) of cereals and millets for one consumer unit (sedentary man of having more than eighteen years of age) is 460 g/day (Indian Council for Medical Research, 2009). Table 5 shows that the consumption of cereals and millets has reduced over time in the rural areas (National Nutrition Monitoring Bureau, 1999; National Nutrition Monitoring Bureau, 2012). This coupled with the changing cropping pattern is a cause for concern since growing coarse cereals like millets is feasible in the western region where almost 70 per cent of the cropped area is rain-fed. In addition, millets are good source of micronutrients and can address problem of hidden hunger. In the year 2011-12, the consumption of cereals and millets was much below the RDA. However, there is overall improvement in the consumption of pulses and of fats and oils. In Gujarat the consumption seems to have increased beyond the recommended levels and may lead to a fresh set of problems in terms of nutrition and health.

Table 5
Consumption of Cereals and Millets, Pulses, Fats and Oils in Rural Areas

Year	*Cereals & Millets(g/cu/day)*				*Pulses(g/cu/day)*				*Fats & Oils(g/cu/day)*			
	1975-79	*1988-90*	*1996-97*	*2011-12*	*1975-79*	*1988-90*	*1996-97*	*2011-12*	*1975-79*	*1988-90*	*1996-97*	*2011-12*
Maharashtra	502	463	443	319	37	36	33	34	13	15	16	17
Gujarat	452	493	431	370	30	32	34	41	17	21	19	24
RDA	460	40	20									

Source: NNMB Report of Third Repeat Survey (2012), NNMB Report of Second Repeat Survey (1999)

Consumption of Green Leafy Vegetables

Diversification of agriculture in favour of fruits and vegetables is quite visible in this region (Table 6).In the context of micronutrients, the consumption of fruits and vegetables are important for their high quantity and quality of diverse vitamin and mineral content. The consumption pattern as revealed by NNMB surveys show that while consumption of green leafy vegetables has drastically increased, it is still much below the RDA in Maharashtra and Gujarat. The consumption of other vegetables has reduced since 1996-97. In the year 2011-12 consumption of other vegetables was much below the RDA in both the states. However, per capita production of vegetables in this region is sufficient to meet the requirements of the population (Table 8). One of the major reasons for consumption not matching with the need and supply might be the affordability of fruits and vegetables. The prices of fruits and vegetables have soared immensely in the recent years. The irony is that there are very high post-harvest losses, in case of fruits and vegetables, usually in the range of twenty per cent to thirty per cent. The fruits and vegetables are more susceptible to such losses due to their perishability and require special need in handling and transporting. While various initiatives by the government through the National Horticulture Mission have borne fruit, much is left to be done.

TABLE 6
Area and Productivity of Fruits and Vegetables in the Western Region

Area ('000 hectares)					
	1991-92	*2001-02*	*2010-11*	*2011-12*	*2012-13*
Fruits	351.9	742.9	1897.9	1924.8	1941.7
Vegetables	363.4	640.4	1133.4	1115.3	1087.6
Yield (tonne/hectare)					
	1991-92	*2001-02*	*2010-11*	*2011-12*	*2012-13*
Fruits	53.33	45.4	34	42	35.6
Vegetables	46.9	49.9	30.5	34.3	36.5

Source: Government of India (2014a)

TABLE 7
Consumption of Green Leafy and Other Vegetables

Year	Green Leafy Vegetables (g/cu/day)				Other Vegetables (g/cu/day)			
	1975-79	1988-90	1996-97	2011-12	1975-79	1988-90	1996-97	2011-12
Maharashtra	15	13	9	16	50	55	52	34
Gujarat	8	4	7	10	58	60	53	41
RDA	40	60						

Source: NNMB Report of Third Repeat Survey (2012), NNMB Report of Second Repeat Survey (1999)

TABLE 8
Per Capita Production of Fruits and Vegetables
(2011-12) (gm/capita/day)

	Fruits	*Vegetables*
Goa	290.59	146.89
Gujarat	340.99	455.56
Maharashtra	237.71	198.01
Daman and Diu	0.00	0.00
Western Region	271.82	282.13
India	173.01	353.90

Source: Government of India (2014c)

III. Linking Agriculture and Nutrition

It is being recognized that agricultural initiatives alone cannot solve the under-nutrition problem, but it has potential to influence poverty reduction through appropriate policies, innovative technologies and improved marketing systems (Gillespie, Harris & Kadiyala, 2012). The availability and access to diverse foods, thereby, impacting dietary diversity and nutrition can be achieved through seven different pathways viz., " *i) agriculture as a source of food ii) agriculture as a source of income iii) link between agricultural policy and food prices- supply and demand factors affecting prices of various marketed food and non-*

food crops iv) income derived from agriculture and how it is actually spent – degree to which nonfood expenditure is allocated to nutrition relevant activities v) women's socioeconomic status and say in intra household decision making vi) women's ability to manage the care, feeding, and health of young children vii) women's own nutritional status", as identified by Gillespie et al., 2012.

These pathways depend on the existing agricultural system, inequalities, taste and preferences and government initiatives towards nutrition improvements and get modified according to the prevailing situation.

The significance of many of these pathways are yet to be explained to understand the linkages between agriculture and nutrition, such as (a) linkages between diversification of agricultural produce and diversification of diet leading to improvement in nutrition outcome (b) proportion of agricultural income being spent on diet at farmer level (c) way income earned from non-food crops are spent on nutritious diet etc. A good and comprehensive data is required to establish such linkages.

It is being observed that studies that focus on nutritional outcome generally concentrate on consumption of calories, micro and macro nutrients and anthropometric measures. While agricultural studies emphasize on increasing productivity and profitability. There is lack of data that combines information on both, making it difficult to analyse variations in nutritional status across regions and social groups with respect to different agricultural situations. Therefore, there is need to systematically collect the data which can establish the linkage between agriculture and nutrition.

In light of the above discussions it is required to have a concrete plan for improving the food security of the people in this region. The large intra-regional and intra-state disparities require a standard "nutrition-considerate farming system model", which can be modified to cater location-specific need. The Farming System for Nutrition (FSN) model suggested by Das, Bhavani & Swaminathan (2014), could be one possible option. This model has been developed to identify location specific inclusive models to address the nutritional need of farm and non-farm families based on their resource endowments and surrounding environment.

While the above model provides a means of collecting location specific data for monitoring and assessment purposes, it would be useful to build an evidence base in order to inform policy through deeper analysis of pathways from agriculture to nutrition and their relative effectiveness. An integrated dataset with new sets of indicator relevant to understand the linkages between agriculture and nutrition would help in this regard. An initiative 'SPANDAN' (System of Promoting Appropriate National Dynamism for Agriculture and Nutrition) by Bill and Melinda Gates Foundation is a step towards this direction.

IV. Conclusion

Western India has witnessed very high economic growth, and agriculture continues to play an important role here. Ironically, undernourishment cases also continue to be very high. If the agricultural priorities are set right and food security given its due in the policy area, agriculture sector has the potential to tackle under-nutrition through its direct and indirect linkages. Therefore, policies that seek to tackle food security through agriculture are the need of the hour.

Agricultural research in this region hitherto largely continues to focus on increasing productivity and profitability of the system. The research needs to be expanded in scope to understand the linkages between agriculture and nutrition and increase availability of nutritious food catering to both macro and micro nutrient requirements. However, there is lack of data that combines information on both agriculture and nutrition, making it difficult to analyze variations in nutritional status across regions and social groups with respect to different agricultural situations. Therefore, there is need to systematically collect the data which can establish the linkage between agriculture and nutrition.

Farming technologies and produce need to be aligned with the constraint that almost 70 per cent of the cultivated area is rain-fed. Efforts are required for increasing production of millets, better marketing of high value crops and reducing postharvest losses. Concrete efforts in bio-fortification of crops, is important in the battle to tackle under-nutrition. The large intra-regional disparities require a "nutrition-considerate farming system model", which can be modified to cater location-specific need. It is important to undertake nutrition awareness programmes, and introduce monitoring systems for assessing their impact. The understanding of what works and what does not, needs to be understood and formalized according to local requirements, to combat under-nutrition.

References

Das, P.K., Bhavani, R.V. and Swaminathan, M.S. (2014), "A Farming System Model to Leverage Agriculture for Nutritional Outcomes", *Agricultural Research*, 3(3):193-203.

Deaton, A., Dreze J. (2009), "Food and Nutrition in India: Facts and Interpretations." *Economic and Political Weekly*, 44 (7): 42-65.

Dev, S.M. & Pandey, V.L. (2013), "Performance and Key Policy Issues of Indian Agriculture." In S.M. Dev (Ed.), *India Development Report 2012-2013* (pp. 79-92). New Delhi: Oxford University Press.

Food and Agriculture Organization, (2013), "The State of Food and Agriculture: Food Systems for Better Nutrition." *FAO*, Rome.

Gillespie, S., Harris J., Kadiyala S. (2012), "The Agriculture-Nutrition Disconnect in India, What Do We Know?" *IFPRI Discussion Paper 01187*, June 2012.

Gillespie, S., Kadiyala S. (2011), "Exploring the Agriculture-Nutrition Disconnect in India." *Leveraging Agriculture for Improving Nutrition and Health, 2020* Conference Brief 20.

Government of Maharashtra (2014), Economic Survey of Maharashtra, 2013-14, Directorate of Economics and Statistics, Planning Department, Government of Maharashtra, India. Available at https://www.maharashtra.gov.in/PDF/EcoSurvey_2013_Eng.pdf Accessed on 15 October 2014.

Government of India, (2009), National Family Health Survey (NFHS-3) 2005–06. New Delhi: Ministry of Health and Family Welfare. Retrieved from http://www. measuredhs.com/pubs/pdf/FRIND3/00FrontMatter00.pdf. Accessed 28 Sept 2014 Accessed 15 July 2014.

Government of India, (2011), *India Human Development Report 2011.* Institute of Applied Manpower Research, New Delhi: Planning Commission,

Government of India, (2013), *Economic Survey 2012–13.* New Delhi: Ministry of Finance. Retrieved from http://indiabudget.nic.in/budget2013-2014/es2012-13/echap-01.pdf. Accessed 11 July 2014.

Government of India, (2014a), *State-wise GSDP at Factor by Industry of Origin (at 2004-05 Prices): 2004-05 to 2013-14 (P).* Data Tables, CSO, Planning Commission, New Delhi.

Government of India, (2014b). Indian Horticulture Database 2013, *National Horticulture Board*. Retrieved from nhb.gov.in/area-pro/Indian per cent20Horticulture per cent202013.pdf accessed on 1st Nov2014.

Government of India, (2014c), *Hand Book on Horticulture Statistics 2014.* Ministry of Agriculture, Government of India. Available at http://agricoop.nic.in/imagedefault/whatsnew/handbook2014.pdf Accessed on 21st November 2014.

Kalamkar, S.S. (2010), *Patterns and Determinants of Agricultural Growth in Maharashtra*. Ministry of Agriculture, Government of India, New Delhi. Retrieved from http://www.academia. edu/1279603/Patterns_and_Determinants_ of_Agricultural_Growth_in_Maharashtra Accessed on 12 August 2014.

Masset E., Haddad, Corneliu, Isaza-Castro L. A. J. (2011), *A Systematic Review of Agricultural Interventions That Aim to Improve Nutritional Status of Children*. EPPI-Centre, Social Science Research Unit, Institute of Education, University of London, London.

Menon P., Deolalikar A., Bhaskar, A. (2009), *India State Hunger Index: Comparisons of Hunger Across States*. Washington, D.C., Bonn, and Riverside: International Food Policy Research Institute, Welthungerhilfe, UC Riverside.

Menon, P. & Aguayo, V. (2011), "The 1000 Day Window of Opportunity for Improving Child Nutrition in India: Insights from National-Level Data." *India Health Beat*, *5*(3), 1-4.

Ministry of Agriculture (2014), Agricultural Statistics at a Glance 2012. Directorate of Economics and Statistics, Department of Agriculture and Cooperation, Government of India. Retrieved from http://eands.dacnet.nic.in/latest_2006.htm Accessed on 19th August 2014.

National Horticulture Mission (2014), Available at http://nhm.dacnet.nic.in/feedback/AllIndiaReports.aspx Accessed on 3rd September 2014.

National Nutrition Monitoring Bureau (NNMB) (1999), Report of second repeat survey-rural (1996-1997), NNMB Technical Report no. 18, National Institute of Nutrition, Indian Council of Medical Research, Hyderabad.

National Nutrition Monitoring Bureau (NNMB) (2012), Diet and Nutritional Status of Rural Population, Prevalence of Hypertension and Diabetes among Adults and Infant &Young Child Feeding Practices, Report of third repeat survey-rural, NNMB Technical Report no. 26., National Institute of Nutrition, Indian Council of Medical Research, Hyderabad.

WHO (2014), Biofortification of staple crops. Available at http://www.who.int/elena/titles/biofortification/en/, accessed on 12th September 2014.

21

Social Exclusion Research

Ramesh Dandge

In this paper an attempt has been made to examine the nature of social exclusion, discrimination and their consequences on socio-economic condition of marginalized communities in India. A brief review of research projects conducted and seminars, workshops etc organized by Centre for the Study of Social Exclusion and Inclusive Policy, Shivaji University, Kolhapur has been discussed and some recommendations for reducing the process of social exclusion and discrimination are given.

1) Conceptual Understanding of Social Exclusion, Discrimination

At outset let us discuss the nature and forms of social exclusion, discrimination their consequential impact of socio-economic condition of marginalized communities in India. Social exclusion is a multi dimensional concept, hence it needs to be understood through various perspectives. Social exclusion is the denial of equal opportunities imposed by certain groups of society on the others, which ultimately lead to the inability of an individual to participate in the basic social, political, economic functioning of society. The process of social exclusion is being operated in various forms such as 1) the denial of ownership, access and control over natural resources and access to capital. 2) The denial of opportunities for health care, education, housing, public amenities and other basic needs. 3) the denial of the rights to participate in social, economic, political and cultural life and denial of interaction with the society.4) the denial of human rights, human dignity and constitutional rights. It is a process of segregating group of people/ communities from the social, political, economic, cultural, educational and religious domains of societal life. Consequently people/ communities get excluded from livelihood opportunities, employment, earning assets, housing, minimum consumption required for survival. The process of social exclusion and discrimination results in economic deprivation of the marginalized communities in term of high magnitude of poverty, unemployment, low standard of living and social deprivation in term of low educational status, lack of access of housing, medical facilities and other social amenities.

In India, social exclusion revolves around the social inter-relation and institutions that exclude, discriminate, isolate and deprive some groups on the basis of group identities like caste, race gender etc. Historically in India the caste system has regulated the social and economic life of people which is based on the division of people into social groups or castes, in which the civil, culture and economic life of people are predetermined or ascribed by birth and made hereditary which in turn, put restriction on change and mobility. Thus, social exclusion has historical roots which led to a stratification of society resulted in socio-economic inequalities in society. Among marginalized communitiesdalits are most disadvantaged groups because due to notion of untouchability and low social strata. The practice of social exclusion and discrimination operates in economic, social, religious, political spheres etc.

(i) *Economic Sphere:* It is practiced in land market, labour market, input market and product market. In rural area, land has been significant asset as main source of income to the majority of households and determines socio-economic status and credit worthiness of households. Hence the nature of distribution of land resources among the cultivating households determines the pattern of distribution of income, wealth and social status. In India, the distribution of land and caste system are closely linked with each other. Higher Castes enjoy special right and privilege over the ownership of land resources. While dalits are placed at the bottom of social hierarchy are deprived from such rights through the process of social exclusion and discrimination.

Moreover dalits also suffer from discrimination in the land lease market. They don't get land for cultivation on lease even if they are ready to pay higher rent. Moreover they are discriminated in sale and purchase of land both for agricultural use and residential purpose. Dalits are not allowed to purchase land from higher caste or higher castes. People are reluctant to sell their lands to the dalits, even if dalits are ready pay more than market price for the land. They also face discriminatory treatment in access of common land resources ie. grazing land and also in purchase of land for residential purpose in high caste localities. Moreover the discrimination in labour markets against marginalized communities is practiced. It refers to the situation of unequal treatment given to the workers possessing same skills and efficiency but belonging to different race, caste, gender in hiring labour and wage payment. It reveals the preferences in hiring labour, wage employment to one group over other with identical capacities. Dalits workers having equal capability, efficiency and skills are excluded from labour market and those who are engaged in labour markets are subjected to the practice of discrimination either in terms of promotion, wage payment of working condition. Thus employment opportunities are denied in labour market particularly in unorganized and private sectors on the ground of the caste and notion of untouchability even though they are found to be equally competent and efficient. Moreover there is compulsory and forced inclusion of dalits in low graded and unskilled labour markets. In India it is observed that labour markets are separated on the basis of caste and social hierarchy, not on the basis of labour efficiency criteria. Higher castes people are mainly engaged in skilled labour market. While dalit workers are mainly concentrated in unskilled and unorganized labour market. Moreover dalit households who are engaged as self employed households in various economic enterprises in urban areas have to face caste discrimination in various types of markets such as credit market, input market and product market etc. They don't get adequate credit, inputs in proper time and in adequate quantity because financial institutions and other inputs supplying agencies are controlled by higher castes. Even in the product market Dalit entrepreneurs have to face discrimination in selling their products, even they keep good quality of products for marketing, due to notion of untouchability. Generally higher castes consumers don't purchase goods from dalit sellers which ultimately adversely affect growth prospect of business of such dalit entrepreneurs. Therefore their participation in industrial sector as self-employed/entrepreneurs is found to be low.

(ii) *Social sphere*: Dalits face social exclusion and discrimination in access for social infrastructure like, education, housing, healthetc provided by government public institutions or private institutions. In civil and cultural spheres, social exclusion occurs in the public services like entry into temple, public distribution scheme and common property resources. In the political sphere, dalits/tribes face discrimination in the use political rights and in participation in the decision making process. The cumulative impact of such social exclusion and discrimination has been resulted to socio-economic deprivations of Dalits and created significant inequality between Dalits and non-dalits.

2) Major Areas of Social Exclusion Research

Social exclusion research is a major component of social science research. As it is related tovarious problems of the society which are multi-dimensional in nature. Major areas of social exclusion research are (i) Social issues : social behavior, social custom, social relation, caste system, social exclusion and discrimination across social groupsetc (ii) Religious attitude of the society toward social exclusion and discrimination (iii) availability of social amenities such as education, housing, health, drinking water sanitationetc across social groups (iv) poverty, unemployment among social groups, magnitude of economic inequality, growth, land maket, labour market, capital and product market discrimination across social groups (v), illiteracy, HDI, birth and death rate, mortality rate etc among various societies (vi) Environmental issues, pollution and other related issues of the various societies (vii) availability and accessibility of natural resources like land,water etc to marginalized communities and other societies (viii) human settlements of various communities and their social interaction etc. Social exclusion research is considered as inter-disciplinary, multidisciplinary and multi-dimensional research which is complicated in nature because main objective of such research is to examine modus operandi . of social discrimination and exclusion across various disciplines among groups of society based on religion/gender/caste etc and their consequential impact on socio-economic condition of discriminated communities. In fact, to examine the nature and process mechanism of social discrimination among various groups of different communities is very complicated because itis influenced by social phenomena, social behavior, social custom, psychological attitude of the people which is out of the control. Therefore it is difficult to derive any uniform conclusion and approach due to complex social factors and these differ from place to place, religion to religion,society to society and even person to person. Therefore it is not possible to measure perfect relationship among the variables relating to social exclusion and discrimination due the influence of social factors. Moreover subjectivity on the part of researcher is serious problem. Moreover collecting information from respondents is serious issue because it is affected by psychological behavior of respondents. Moreover there is always considerable heterogeneity of the groups to be experimented, hence it is difficult and complicated to examine various social issues relating to social exclusion and discrimination.

3) Present Trends in Social Exclusion Research

Trends in social exclusion research have been changing over time. Earlier conceptual research was used to formulate/ develop social theories relating to social exclusion and discrimination. It was mainly concerned with generalization, formation of theories, gathering knowledge for knowledge sake While conceptual research was related to abstract ideas, or theory It was used by philosophers, thinkers to develop new concepts or to re-interprete existing ones. Moreover descriptive research, qualitative research were used to study social problems. The main purpose of descriptive research was to describe facts as they exits at present. Researcher could report what has happened or what is happening. Now empirical research/applied research, analytical research are being used to investigate social problems, nature of various forms of social discrimination, the extent of social exclusion and other related issues and their impact on socio-economic condition of marginalized communities more scientifically. What extent, magnitude social discrimination has been practiced in the society and how far communities have been affected adversely. Recentlythere has been improvement in research methodology and technique of data processing. This, besides, action oriented research, policy oriented research, evaluative research are also being used to study social problems relating to social exclusion and discrimination.

4) Social Exclusion Research Projects and Academic activities of the Centre

Against background of social exclusion and discrimination Centre for the Study of Social Exclusion and inclusive Policy (CSSEIP)), Shivaji University, Kolhapur has organized eighteen seminars, workshops, and also conducted fifteen research projects during 2007-2014. (i) International Seminar on Social Exclusion and Inclusive Policies in South Asia March 17-19 2008 (ii) National Seminar on Gender-based Discrimination in India, March 3-4, 2009 (iii) Workshop on Social Exclusion and Discrimination of Marginalized Communities in India, Feb 17-18 2009 (iv) Workshop on De-notified and Nomadic Tribes, Dec 15-16 2009 (v) National Seminar on "Accounting the Social Sector Development" Feb 1-2. 2010 (vii) National Seminar on "Socio-Economic Status of Muslims in India" Jan 15-16. 2010. (viii) Workshop on Impact of Globalization on Nature of Social Exclusion and Discrimination in Modern India, Feb. 16-17 2010 (ix) Workshop on Role of NGOin Socio-economic Upliftment of Marginalized Communities, Nov 20, 2010 (x) Workshop on Atrocities on Dalits in India, Jan 4-5, 2011 (xi) Workshop on "Role of NGOs in Socio- Economic Upliftment of Marginalized Communities", March 12-13, 2013. (xii) Workshop on "Research Methodology in the area of Social Exclusion and Discrimination", August 30-31 2013 (xiii) Workshop on "Women Participation in Panchayat Raj Institution" Aug. 13. 2013 (xiv) workshop on "DT/NT communities and Jat-panchyat" Sept. 13. 2013 (xv) National Seminar on "Socio-Economic Status of Minority Communities in India" November 21 22, 2013 (xvi) National seminar on "Environmental Issues and Social Exclusion" Feb. 11 122014 (xvii) National seminar on Media and social exclusion (xviii) "National seminar on "Phule, Shahu and Ambedkar Thought and Their inclusive strategies" January 30-31, 2015.

Moreover Research projects are also carried out by the centre. These are (i) "Social Exclusion of de-notified tribes: Kanjar Bhat, Makadwala Community in Kolhapur city" (ii) Socio-Economic Culture of Waaghya and Murali Community in Pali and Jejuri villages (iii) "Socio-Economic Study of Vadar community in Kolhapur City" (iv) "Socio-economic Condition of Matang Community in Solapur district" (v) Poverty and Environment with reference to Slum Areas in Kolhapur City" (vi) "Impact of Water Pollution on Socio-economic condition of Fishermen communities and Their livelihood (vii) Man and Wild-life Conflicts in Western Ghats (viii) Discrimination and Displacement with Reference to Urmodi Dam (ix) Faculty Recruitment under Policy of Reservation as Tool of Social Inclusion in Colleges in Kolhapur city (x) Gender Discrimination in Unorganized Sector in Kolhapur (xi) Socio-Economic Status of SC and ST post-Graduate Students (xii) Role of Government in Women Empowerment (xiii) The Perspective of Youth towards Inter-Caste Marriage System (xiv) Social Profile of the Students admitted to Post Graduate Courses in Shivaji University, Kolhapur (xv) The Participation of Marginalized communities in the Panchayati Raj Institution in Panhala Taluka, Kolhapur District."

5) Major Observations

It was observed from seminars/workshops and research projects that process of racial/caste/gender based discrimination and social exclusion have been active in the society. Due to prevalence of caste system Dalits, women, DT/NT, minority communities have been suffering at varying magnitudes with respect to social discrimination and exclusion. Among these groups dalits are most sufferers due to notion of untouchability, Women have been victimized due to caste and gender,therefore their participation in panchayat raj institution was quite low. There has been caste based distribution of land among the various castes, Land which is major source of income in rural areas has been controlled by mostly upper caste communities. and marginalized communities particularly dalits have been deprived from possessing such productive resources. Moreover labour market discrimination in unorganized sector is serious issue.In unorganized sector caste/ gender based discrimination was observed which respect over hiring the labours, assignment of work, difference in salary of male and female, treatment to workers. Due to gender based discrimination female faced feeling of insecurity at the work place. Poverty, unemployment and caste system are highly correlated with each other. Marginalized communities have been suffering from higher magnitude of poverty, unemployment and overall economic backwardness. With respect to social amenities like primary education, public health services, drinking water, PDS, the condition of these communities is not much satisfactory, It was also observed that new economic policy did not much create positive impact on the socio-economic upliftment of these communities. In fact traditional occupation of these communities have been adversely affected due to availability of substitute goods at cheaper rates in market. Upper caste members havinghad political linkages had greater influence on decision making process in Gram Panchayat. It was observed that the level of participation of excluded groups in the Gram sabha was extremely low due to timing of meeting and working place and were politically isolated from the other higher castes because they were not informed about the activities of Gram Panchayat. Negative feeling, illiteracy and lack of awareness among excluded groups also caused low participation in the meeting. of Gram-panchayat and decision making process. It was observed that lower caste students were interested in inter-caste marriage, while open caste students were reluctant toward inter-caste marriage. It was found that the level of education has least impact on the perspectives towards Inter-caste marriage. Because, the majority of the students were greatly influenced by culture, religion and their parents pressure. It was found that culture, customs, norms, education were major factors influencing on the perspectives of youths relating to inter-caste marriage at varying magnitudes.

6) Recommendations and Future Direction

Lack of access to land and other productive assets, low level of employment, lower involvement in business activities of marginalized communities particularly Dalits, caused by the process of social exclusion and discrimination all put together ultimately resulted in higher magnitude of economic backwardness of these communities both in rural as well as urban areas. Hence it is required to implement an inclusive policies at wider scale for reducing the level of social exclusion and thereby improving the socio-economic condition of these communities. Reservation policy in employment market for these communities and groups that have suffered social, educational, and economic exclusion associated with caste, ethnicity, gender, and religious identities has been implemented. However it has benefitted to the small section of the marginalized communities. Hence the policy of social and economic empowerment is essentially directed towards improving ownership of capital assets such as agricultural land and business along with the educational levels and skills of discriminated groups is required to implement at wider scale. As it has been reality that economic deprivation through economic exclusion has been mainly concentrated in landless labourers, small farmers and workers in unorganized sector hence broad basedsocio-economic inclusive policies are required for their sustainable and overall development. Against this background, there is a need to rethink about reorganization of existing agrarian structure in which re-llocation of land resources be made on the basis of the relative share of social groups (SC, ST etc) in total population and the relative socio-economic backwardness of the each caste because in rural areas land is major source of income. This strategy would be useful in breaking up monopoly of higher castes over the ownership of land resources. Moreover cultivable land, government land be transferred to these communities oral ternatively village cooperative farming at village level with active involvement of farmers across the various social groups be thought of because the existing farming system has been proved as ineffective in promoting agricultural growth.

More over professional training is needed to the discriminated groups/communities who are engaged in self-employment activities. On the line of joint stock company big business enterprises through skill improvement programme for these communities can be developed with adequate support from government and other funding agencies. Moreover workers belonging to these communities where they are subjected to economic exclusion, discrimination in hiring labour and wage payment and working condition the existing labour policy be implemented rigorously. An effort should be that employment opportunities should be made available at global level to the workers of these marginalized communities. Keeping in view the nature of social exclusion and discrimination and their adverse consequences on socio-economic condition on discriminated communities; more and more emphasis should be made on social exclusion research at wider scale. Each dimension of social exclusion discrimination should be examined empirically and more scientifically without any subjective bias on the part of investigator in years to come.

References

Ambedkar, B.R. (1979), "Caste in India" in Vasant Moon (ed), *Dr. Babasaheb Ambedkar: Writing and Speeches,* Vol. I Government of Maharashtra.

Becker, Gory (1957), *The Economics of Discrimination University of Chicago,* Chicago.

Deshpande, Satish and Yogesh Yadav (2006), "Regarding Affirmative Action-Caste and Benefits in Higher Education," *Economic and Political Weekly,* Vol. 7.

Nancharaiah, G. (1988), *Land and Caste,* Himalaya Publishing House, Delhi.

Shrinivas, M.N. (1996), *Caste and its Modern Avatar,* Vikin Publication, New Delhi.

Singh, R.K. (1986), *Alienation Among Scheduled Caste,* Manas Publication, Delhi.

Shah, Ghanshyam (2006), *Untouchability in Rural India,* Sage Publication, New Delhi.

Thorat, S.K., Narender Kumar edited (2008), *B.R. Ambedkar Perspectives on Social Exclusion and Inclusive Policies,* Oxford University Press.

Thorat, S.K., Katherine, S. Newman (2010), *Blocked by Caste Economic Discrimination in India,* Oxford University Press.

Thorat, S.K. (2002), *Oppression and Denial: Dalit Discrimination in 1990, EPW,* Feb

Index

Above Poverty Line (APL), 47
action research, 123
agricultural research, 394, 404
anthropological research, 26
anthropologist, 25, 26, 204, 209
anthropology, 25, 26, 203, 209, 211
    development 209
attribution, 63

behavioural school of thought, 24
Below Poverty Line (BPL), 47
Body Mass Index (BMI), 47, 48, 371, 376, 379

capability approach to development, 369
Ccaste, 9, 363
    hierarchy, 44, 357
casteism, 30, 249
classification, 64
common sense, 51
community need based research, 31
Constitution of India, 8
construct validity, 196
critical theory, 181
cultural heterogeneity, 44, 357

Dalit, 35, 299, 300, 304, 319
    entrepreneurs, 55, 411
    intellectual collective, 304
    knowledge-subject, 33
    movement, 39, 321
    scholars, 299, 301
    scholarship, 300, 301, 303
    studies, 32, 38, 318
    workers, 55, 410, 411
diaspora, 35, 308
disability, 31, 272, 276, 278
    advocacy, 276
discrimination, 54, 266
dividing practices, 291

economic inequality, 8
educational research, 18, 121, 122, 125, 132
educational technology, 128, 129
entrepreneurial capabilities, 91

epistemology, 118
evaluative research, 127

fact, 179
Farming System for Nutrition (FSN) model, 50, 403
feminist studies, 29, 236
formative research, 89

gender, 254, 255
    studies, 29, 234, 235, 238
grounded theory, 9

gealth, 248, 276
hegemony, 51
higher education, 20

Ideological state Apparatus (ISA), 51
inclusion, 271
Indian Council for Social Science Research (ICSSR), 9, 10, 16, 19, 67, 68, 112, 136
Indian psychology, 30
Inter-rater reliability, 197
Interdisciplinarity, 11, 12, 58, 61, 62
Interdisciplinary research, 5, 63
Intersectionality, 208

knowledge, 7

liquid education, 142, 143
liquid modernity, 140
liquidity, 142

malnutrition, 46, 369
Marxism, 22, 182
measurement, 195
medical model, 278, 280
methodological monism, 111
methodological sanskritization, 16, 112
migration, 44, 356, 359
model, 198, 199

need, 255
Neo-Buddhist, 320
nutrition, 46, 369, 393

objectification, 292
ontology, 118

parallel-forms reliability, 197
persons with disabilities, 260
policy relevant research, 127
political economy, 23
political philosophy, 185
political science, 23, 184
political sociology, 23
political theory, 24, 188
positive psychology, 30, 252
poverty, 46, 370, 373
prediction, 6
psychological research, 29
psychologist, 248

qualitative methodology, 84
qualitative research, 8
quantitative analysis, 194
quantitative method, 194

recommended daily allowance (RDA), 399
reference group, 319
    theory, 39
reification, 179
relating, 63
relative sectoral product per

worker (RSPW), 333
reliability, 196
religious plurality, 44, 357
repressive state apparatus (RSA), 51
research, 102, 137
ethics, 119
management, 124
manager, 124
methodology, 16, 110, 112
reservation, 9
role theory, 227

Scheduled Tribe 370
scholarship, 137
science, 175, 180, 181
scientific attitude, 258
scientific classification, 291
scientific inquiry, 102
scientific knowledge, 178, 185
scientific perspectivism, 185
selective nationalism, 189
social exclusion, 54, 55, 408, 409
social exclusion research, 412, 413
social inequality, 8
Social justice, 8, 9, 262
counselling, 262
enquiry, 8
Social model, 278, 281
Social research, 5
Social researcher, 6, 7, 10
social science research, 5, 6, 9, 11, 20, 65, 138
Social science researcher, 9
social science, 7, 20,
social scientific knowledge, 5, 6
social scientist, 3, 4, 5, 7, 20, 137
social stratification, 44
social work practice, 102
social work research, 13, 14, 15, 78, 97, 100, 101, 103, 104, 105
social work researcher, 96, 105
social work, 13, 76, 101
sociology of education, 129
stratified, 44
subjectification, 292
symbolism, 210

Tribal Health 374
Tribal population 379
Tribal poverty 383
Tribe, 368
children 373

Unemployment blues, 263
Unhappy crisis, 21

validity, 196
Varna, 249

women, 253, 254
studies, 27, 218, 221, 222, 223, 224, 225, 237, 238
studies sociologist, 28, 224
World Social Science Report, 11, 59

youth, 263, 264
development, 264